MW00637627

Monographs in Visual Communication

David F. Rogers
Editor

Roy Hall

Illumination and Color in Computer Generated Imagery

With 116 Illustrations, 17 in Color

Springer-Verlag
New York Berlin Heidelberg
London Paris Tokyo

Roy Hall
Wavefront Technologies
Santa Barbara, CA 93103
USA

Editor

David F. Rogers
Aerospace Engineering Department
United States Naval Academy
Annapolis, MD 21402
USA

Library of Congress Cataloging-in-Publication Data
Hall, Roy.
Illumination and color in computer generated imagery.
(Monographs in visual computing)
Bibliography: p.
Includes index.
1. Color computer graphics. I. Title. II. Series.
T385.H327 1988 006.6 88-20102

Printed on acid-free paper

Camera-ready copy provided by the author.
Printed and bound by Quinn-Woodbine, Inc., Woodbine, New Jersey.
Printed in the United States of America.

9 8 7 6 5 4 3 2 1

ISBN 0-387-96774-5 Springer-Verlag New York Berlin Heidelberg
ISBN 3-540-96774-5 Springer-Verlag Berlin Heidelberg New York

Foreword

In a very broad sense the historical development of computer graphics can be considered in three phases, each a giant step down the road towards "realistic" computer generated images. The first, during the late 1960's and early 1970's, can perhaps be characterized as the "wire frame" era. Basically pictures were composed of lines. Considerable emphasis was placed on "real time" interactive manipulation of the model. As models became more complex and as raster technology developed, eliminating the hidden lines or hidden surfaces from the image became critical for visual understanding. This requirement resulted in the second phase of computer graphics, the "hidden surface" era, that developed during the 1970's and early 1980's. The names associated with hidden surface algorithms read like a who's who of computer graphics. The culmination of the hidden surface era and the beginning of the current and third era in computer graphics, the "rendering" era, was Turner Whitted's incorporation of a *global* illumination model into the ray tracing algorithm. Now the goal was not just to generate an image, but to generate a realistic appearing image.

Roy Hall's book is about generating realistic images. Many of the early attempts at illumination models adopted ad hoc or heuristic models. Basically, if the results looked good or better than previous results, then a new illumination model was born. Realistic, in the sense of physically correct, images cannot be generated with these models. To generate realistic images it is necessary to return to the fundamental physics governing the interaction of light with materials and its perception by the human eye-brain combination. Originally educated as an engineer, Roy's physics and mathematics background uniquely qualifies him to both conduct original research in this area and to place all the previous work, including the early ad hoc models, into the context of a general illumination model. His wide experience in successfully implementing commercial renderers uniquely qualifies him to organize and discuss the practical implications of illumination models.

Today an engineer or scientist must communicate verbally, graphically, mathematically and computationally. The clear concise verbal explanations, profusely illustrated and mathematically well grounded, confirm Roy's skills in these areas. The comparative illustrations of the various illumination models are particularly informative. Perhaps more important, for both students and the practicing professional, are the algorithms presented in the book. These algorithms provide the necessary mechanism required to understand the many details of each of the models. They also serve as a standard basis for the development of future models.

In a sense, Roy Hall's book is a result of frustration on my part. While writing *Procedural Elements for Computer Graphics*, it became obvious that a more fundamental basis for the many existing illumination models was required. It was also obvious that the effort was beyond both the scope of *Procedural Elements* and the patience of my long suffering publisher. Shortly after finishing *Procedural Elements*, Rae Earnshaw of the University of Leeds invited me to be Co-chairman of a Summer Institute on the State-of-the-Art in Computer Graphics to be held at Stirling University, in Scotland, during the Summer of 1986. Roy Hall was invited to present a paper on illumination models with the comment that there was a need to unify the existing work. Roy had the same idea. The invitation was propitious. The resulting paper was impressive. Roy was prevailed upon to consider it the basis of a monograph on the subject. With the cooperation and enthusiasm of Springer-Verlag, the current volume is the result. It is worth all of Roy's more than considerable efforts that went into its creation. The book will undoubtedly become a standard reference on illumination models.

Roy is to be congratulated on producing a volume of fundamental and lasting value to computer graphics.

David F. Rogers
Annapolis, Maryland
May 1988

Preface

The creation of this book spans an academic period intent on simulating reality followed by a period producing special effects where the intent was anything but reality. In both cases, the vehicle of expression was the imagery created using computers, but the needs and goals were entirely different.

When Dave Rogers approached me about writing this book, it sounded like a logical conclusion to much of the work I had done. The next eighteen months made me painfully aware of the magnitude of the problem of correctly treating illumination. After his first review of the draft I realized how much was still unclear. As I was finishing, Dave asked me whether I had learned anything. All I could say was that I learned how little I really knew, have clarified many relationships in my own thinking as I filled in the gaps, and have generated a long list of ideas for research.

Rendering techniques receive a great deal of attention in the computer graphics literature, however, it is often difficult to collect the background and historical information required for a full understanding of these techniques. This text is an attempt to collect and collate the background information required for a full understanding. This information is gathered from physics, optics, visual perception, colorimetry, display technology, current practice, and the experience of writing several rendering systems. I have attempted to sort out the details relevant to computer generated imagery and to present them in a coherent fashion.

Two years ago I published an article which outlined the parallel development of illumination models and rendering techniques. This paragraph was included in the conclusion:

> *"Current analytical models are limited to diffuse environments. The advances traced in this characterization of illumination models and shading techniques point to continued emphasis on greater realism supported by more powerful computing equipment. It is clear that the analytical models will play a prominent part in directing the research effort towards even greater realism in computer generated imagery."*

I am pleased to observe that the research that has been presented between then and now has far exceeded my expectations. The next several years promise the migration of these efforts into products that will be widely available to the public. I hope this text helps provide a better understanding of these products. While I think this text reflects timely information for the near future, I also look forward to the advances that will make it obsolete.

While writing a book sometimes seems like a singular effort, it is the continued support and encouragement of many that make it possible. I would like to express my gratitude to people who have helped along the way: foremost to my family for their support, encouragement, and patience through my seemly continuous life crises; to Don Greenberg for introducing me to computer graphics, for supporting my early research at the Program of Computer Graphics at Cornell, and for continued friendship and advice; to T. Magruder, G. Kratina, and W. Bird for helping me learn to see the forest for the trees; to Dave Rogers and Gerhard Rossbach for support in starting and finishing this project; to Gary Meyer for introducing me to the concepts of colorimetry, whose work I borrowed from heavily for chapters 3 and 5, and for review of Chapter 5; to Joseph Kane, currently Chairman of the SMPTE monitor calibration committee, for many discussions about how NTSC really works, information about the current activities of SMPTE, and for review of Chapter 5; to John Wallace and Michael Cohen for review of Chapter 4; to Jon Barber for pointing out sources of numerical failure in early implementations of the color clipping algorithm; to Holliday Alger, Jon Pittman, Dave Immel, and Dave Rogers for exhaustive editorial and/or technical review of the entire manuscript; and to my colleagues at Wavefront Technologies, Inc. for support and encouragement throughout this project.

Special thanks to David Yost for introducing me to the software "underground" that is producing the software tools required to support a project like this, and for advice on production methodologies. This book was written in *troff* using the Grand editor (from Grand Software, Inc.). The *troff* source was processed into *device independent troff (ditroff)* using *profficient*™ (from prototype/inc.). Previewing and layout was done on a SUN 3/160 using suntroff (from Malcolm Slaney). The *ditroff* was processed into PostScript® using **devps**™ (from Pipeline Associates, Inc.), which was in turn processed on a Linotronic typesetter to create camera ready page proofs. Figures were generated to Interleaf™ format and Interleaf™ was used to add captions and other text. The book left my hands in the form of a tape to the typesetter, and final figures and slides to Springer-Verlag for stripping into the text.

Roy Hall
May 1988

Contents

Illumination and Color in Computer Generated Imagery

1

Introduction

"A picture is an intermediate something between a thought and a thing."
- Samuel Taylor Coleridge

Realism is often a primary goal in the creation of computer generated imagery. A key element in realism is displaying the correct colors for the objects in an image. Color is described in Webster's (Guralnik 1978) as *"the sensation resulting from stimulation of the retina of the eye by light waves of certain lengths"*. This implies a human perceptual color component, the *sensation produced*; and a physical color component, the *light waves of certain lengths*.

Realistic color representation in computer graphics requires quantifying light and materials, developing rules that describe their interaction (illumination models), and presenting the results through some display medium so that the correct perceptions are created. Both color determination and color display are based upon an understanding of the nature of light and the perception of color. Physics and optics describe the nature of light. Colorimetry provides the required background for exploring the color reproduction process.

Satisfying the above requirements entails solving a series of problems. A total solution arises only if all the problems are adequately addressed. Illumination models are often discussed in the computer graphics literature in a theoretical sense, however, when put into practice the models are greatly compromised by the limitations of shading technique, of image display, and of the knowledge of physical properties required to apply the model. The interrelationships of perception, physics, rendering techniques, and display techniques coupled with the current state of the art make it nearly impossible to make significant new advances by addressing only one of these topics in isolation. If this text establishes an awareness of the total context in which we are attempting to solve appearance related problems in computer graphics, then it has served its purpose.

Realism is a vague term when applied to computer graphics and is discussed in its various meanings throughout this text. Realism can mean anything from the rigorous simulation of the physical phenomena of light bouncing through an environment to the illusion of realism created by empirical approximations. In the first case, we are attempting to mimic the workings of reality. In the second case, we are representing an impression. Thus, realism takes on a meaning that is modulated by the context in which it is considered.

1.1 Intent and Overview

This text is intended to be a practical reference for the computer graphics professional. To accomplish this goal, the presentation provides both theoretical background and an examination of current practice. This, in combination with coding examples in the appendices, allows the reader to develop a comprehensive understanding of techniques and to reproduce the results described.

The rapid progress and sweeping changes in computer graphics and computational hardware will render current practice obsolete in short order. To prepare the reader for this, the historical context of current practice, the theoretical background for light and color, and a discussion of techniques that have received attention in the academic research environment are presented. This casts the current practice as a step in a continuum of development in the field of computer graphics and provides the tools for the reader to make the next steps along this development path.

Much of this text is based upon the experience of implementing several commercial image generation systems. This experience has highlighted the problems in bringing theory and research into rigorous application. Original references are used wherever possible to highlight the evolution of current practice. This text attempts to highlight the problems that have been uncovered in the implementation of these techniques by practitioners in the field.

Understanding natural illumination processes provides the basis for controlling the image generation process and a solid foundation for experimentation. Chapter 2 discusses the physical processes of illumination and the events that occur to direct light to the eye. Chapter 3 concentrates on the perception of color. Chapters 4 and 5 apply the theoretical foundation laid out in Chapters 2 and 3 to address the practical issues of computing and displaying imagery. Chapter 4 looks at the development of illumination models in computer graphics and Chapter 5 at image display issues. The remainder of this chapter provides a broad overview of these issues.

1.2 The Process of Creating Images

Generating images with computers allows us to communicate and extend our understanding of the world. Computer generated imagery provides access to information that would otherwise escape our perception.

- We can "see" things that don't currently exist because they are only in design or visualization stages.
- We can "see" things that cannot otherwise be observed because they are outside the realm of our visual perception.

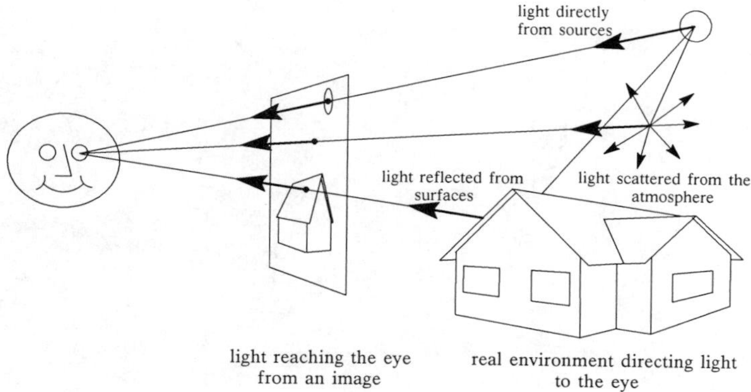

Figure 1.1: Viewing an environment or an image.

- We can "see" things that could not exist. That is, we can create data and display concepts that are inconsistent with a three dimensional reality.
- We can "see" abstract concepts or concepts for which the true visual reality is confusing.

Improving the quality of these images enhances the information content. However, evaluation of quality is often subjective. That is, improvements in quality are measured by the increase in realism or the improvement in communication of an idea, neither of which is easily quantified.

The problem we attempt to solve in creating computer generated imagery is most easily described in a real-world context. Consider viewing an environment, Figure 1.1. Viewing an image is similar to viewing an environment in the sense that light of some color is reaching the eye from each direction within the field of view. In viewing an environment, light comes to the eye through the processes of reflection, refraction, and scattering, as well as directly from light sources. In viewing an image, this light is radiating from a video display or projection screen, or is reflected from a printed surface. In simulating realism we are attempting to match the viewer's perception of the real environment by reproducing the correct color and intensity of light from every point on the image.

In photography the camera replaces the viewer and records a projection of the environment on film. The film is an image plane and the intensity and color of the light from the environment is focused (projected) onto the image plane by the camera lens and recorded by the film. The film is processed into a display media such as a photographic print or a slide. Viewing the display media results in a mental reconstruction of the environment that was photographed.

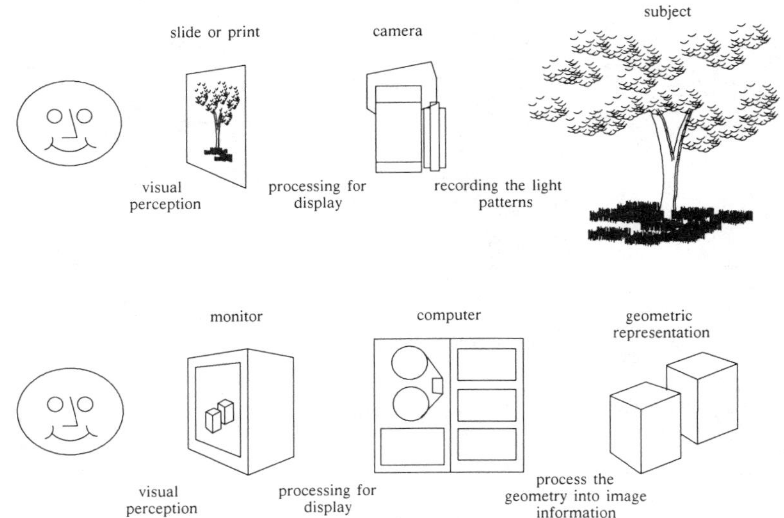

Figure 1.2: Analogy between the photographic process and computer image generation.

The process of creating an image is analogous to this photographic example. The real environment is replaced by a mathematical description of the environment. This description is processed by computer to determine the position, visibility, and color of objects on an image plane thus creating an image file. The image file is, in turn, processed for display and the display viewed, Figure 1.2.

Processing a geometric description of a scene into a shaded image can be separated into three major functions:

- Determining placement and visibility of objects on the image plane.
- Determining the appearance of objects, i.e., color, texture, shading.
- Providing the most accurate display of the image.

The image plane is a fictitious plane within the cone of vision and perpendicular to the field of view. The environment is projected onto this image plane to create an image. The geometry of the cone of vision and the image plane must be preserved in viewing images to prevent distortion. Specifically, the ratio of the width of the image plane to the distance from the image plane to the eye should be the same as the ratio of the image width to the image viewing distance. This can be thought of in terms of a wide angle photograph. A wide angle photograph looks distorted because it typically fills only a small portion of the field of view when we look at it. If we hold the picture close enough to our eye that it

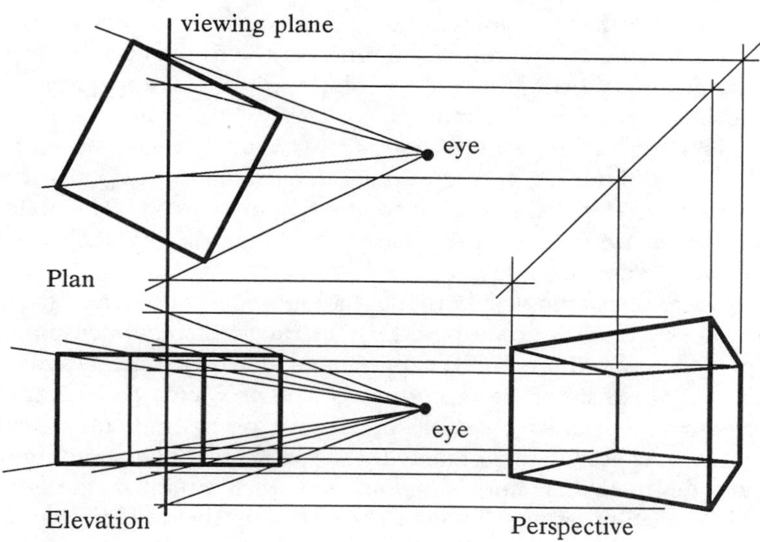

Figure 1.3: Perspective projection in drawing

fills the same field of view that was photographed, then the distortion is minimized.[1]

A number of well established techniques can be used for determining placement and visibility of objects (Sutherland, et al. 1974). Each of these methods projects objects in the environment onto the image plane. Perspective projection has been used in art and architecture long before the advent of computer graphics to project events in the environment onto an image plane, Figure 1.3. These techniques have been formalized into the perspective transformation which is detailed in (Foley and Van Dam 1984, 267-318) (Newman and Sproull 1979, 339-342, 355-366) (Rogers and Adams 1976, 59-78) and is not repeated here. An alternate projection technique is ray tracing (Whitted 1980) (Rogers 1985, 363-383) (Foley and Van Dam 1984, 585-588). The major difference in these techniques is that perspective transformation projects the environment onto the image plane through a nonlinear transformation, while ray tracing projects points on the image plane out into the environment.

The visibility problem associated with projection onto the image plane was once regarded as one of the major problems to be solved in computer graphics, but the wide variety of algorithms and increasingly faster and more powerful hardware have reduced this consideration.

Now that we have the power to perform visibility calculations for complex environments, the issues of correct color, texture, and shading

[1] There are distortions due to focusing the image through a lens that are not removed by correct placement of the image.

move to the forefront of image generation concerns. Users expect the quality of shading and texture to be consistent with the visual complexity of the geometry being rendered. Color and textural appearance have been addressed empirically until quite recently, primarily because of the subjective nature of realism. While it is easy to demonstrate that perspective projection and visible surface determination are correct, it is very difficult to verify that color and shading are correct. This makes it difficult to quantify the improvements in image quality that are produced through new techniques.

Significant limitations in both the photographic process and the computer imagery process are imposed by the image display medium. Display processes are limited in dynamic range, linearity, repeatability, and the color range that can be reproduced. The problem of verification of correctness is amplified by these limitations of color display devices. While it is not possible to eliminate these problems, understanding them can provide an insight into compensations that minimize the adverse effects of these limitations. Image display has received little attention in the graphics literature, thus, the discussion of image display is primarily from personal experience and discussions with other practitioners.

1.3 Representation or Simulation of Reality

Two opposing schools of image synthesis technique prevail:

- Rigorously simulating natural illumination processes.
- Projecting the illusion of realism.

While these sound similar on the surface, the underlying assumptions are vastly different.

Simulating real processes dictates accurately modeling immutable rules of physics and geometry that rigidly govern the technique. In general, the greater the rigor in the simulation, the less flexible the outcome of the image synthesis process. It is the correct representation and modeling of physical processes that is of primary importance, not the control of the imaging medium. Rigorous simulation is inevitably confronted with the question: *How do we tolerate the need for effect - the need to create imagery that is outside the visual reality of the physical world in order to convey a message?* Many applications require imagery that is beyond the realm of realistic image synthesis, but demand realistic elements.

Projecting the illusion of realism simply means that elements of realism are generated only to the degree necessary to convey the idea or impression. This is similar to the work of the magician who presents enough perceptual clues to make the illusion seem real. The impressionist period in art also demonstrates approach to communicating ideas. A discussion of the cognitive process of interpreting visual information is beyond the scope of this discussion.

Michael Mills (1985) provides an examination of computer realism in the context of art history. Appropriately he asks, "*Is there a better - or at least more sophisticated - way of conceiving the task of depiction in computer graphics than as a contest with reality, a quest to 'fool' the perceptual system via imitation of the real world?*" While this question cannot be answered here, the relationship between theory and practice is discussed in detail. Successful use of computer graphics as a communication tool comes from understanding the process of modeling reality and extracting from it the elements that best convey the essence of an idea.

2

The Illumination Process

"It is important that we can understand the true physical behavior so when we make approximations we recognize the consequences."
- Donald P. Greenberg (1988)

The elements of the illumination process that are useful in computer generated imagery are highly dependent upon the rendering technique that is used. The advancement of image generation techniques is characterized by alternating leaps in illumination models and in rendering technique. Rendering techniques are just now approaching the level of sophistication that requires an accurate energy representation of the illumination of surfaces. The information presented in this chapter will aid in the formulation of new illumination models to meet this challenge.

2.1 Light and Materials

There are two illumination phenomena of major importance in generating imagery. The first is the interaction of light with the boundaries between materials. The second is the scattering and absorption of light as it passes through a material.

Boundaries between materials are the surfaces which make up an environment. The visually interesting boundaries can be characterized as boundaries between two dielectric (electrically nonconducting, or insulating) materials such as air and glass, or between a nonconducting material and a conducting material such as air and copper. Boundaries between two conducting materials are not visually interesting because conducting materials are opaque and the boundary is never seen.[1] Light striking a boundary is either reflected or transmitted. For opaque materials, absorption occurs after light has passed through the boundary, Figure 2.1.

If the boundary is very smooth the reflected and transmitted light are scattered very little. An optically smooth surface struck by a thin beam of light both reflects and transmits a thin beam of light. If the surface is very rough the light is scattered in all directions. At boundaries between dielectric materials most of the light is transmitted. At the boundary with a conductor (metal) most of the light is reflected. As the

[1] We often see the edge of boundaries between metals in jewelry and other metal products. However, what we observe is not light interactions between the metals, but the change in light interaction between air and the different metals where they abut.

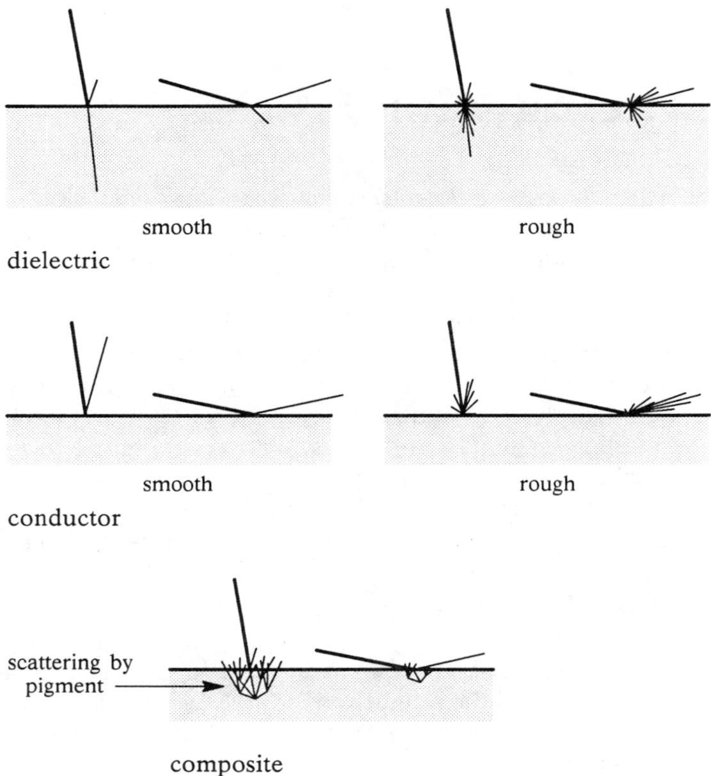

Figure 2.1: Generalized behavior at a boundary.

incident angle approaches grazing, i.e., is nearly parallel with the surface, almost all of the light is reflected, Figure 2.1. Dielectrics are generally transparent and conductors are opaque.

The transparent nature of dielectrics is often a source of confusion because many dielectrics appear opaque upon first examination. Consider sand as an example. Sand is typically thought of as an opaque powder, however, pure quartz (silicon) crystals are very transparent. Sand is primarily silicon. The opaque appearance is partially from conductive impurities in the silica, and primarily from the perception of sand in terms of the aggregate behavior of many small particles. Another example of this is a shattered pane of safety glass. The aggregate behavior provides an opaque appearance, but each fragment is equally as transparent as the original glass pane. The illumination relationships for light incident on a single fragment are identical to the relationships for the entire pane.

When light travels through a material, a fraction of the light is scattered and another fraction is absorbed. An example is fog, in which the water droplets in the air scatter light so that objects are obscured in a short distance, and illumination seems to come from all directions. Another example is the atmosphere which scatters the blue component of light (short wavelengths) much more than the red component of light (long wavelengths). The sky appears blue from the scattered light while the sun appears yellow or red. Some materials such as photographic filters absorb parts of the spectrum as light passes through the material.

An important form of scattering occurs in composite materials such as plastic or paint. A pigment is suspended in a dielectric material such as the paint vehicle or vinyl substrate. There is boundary reflection and transmission with the suspending material. There is also scattering of the light by the pigment and some of the scattered light is transmitted back through the boundary.

There are a wide range of other effects such as fluorescence, phosphorescence, and diffusion that have been left essentially untouched by computer graphics. These are also left untouched by this text as they fall outside the realm of typical imagery that is created using computer graphics. These effects, when required, are generally added using a variety of image post-processing tricks.

A basic principle necessary to describe and understand the movement of light through an environment is that energy is conserved during interactions with material boundaries. Specifically, all the energy that reaches a boundary is either reflected or transmitted at the boundary. The sum of the reflected energy and transmitted energy is equal to the incident energy.

Maintaining wavelength or *spectrally* dependent information throughout the visible range is required for accurate modeling of color. The visible range of light is generally agreed to be within the wavelengths 380nm to 770nm. While the visible spectrum is normally used for image generation, the principles and procedures described are not limited to the visible spectrum and can be extended into the ultaviolet or infrared regions.

This chapter provides an overview of the theoretical background for understanding the illumination process as applied to computer graphics. A basic overview useful to all readers is presented at the beginning of each section. The detailed information later in each section is most meaningful when reviewed in the context of the illumination models presented in Chapter 4. Section 2.2.1, *Vector Notation,* is critical to the implementation of illumination models described in Chapter 4.

2.2 Background Optics and Physics

This section provides a background for understanding the illumination process. Terminology and conventions are defined followed by an examination of the optical and physical mechanisms of surface illumination, and finally, a comprehensive model for surface illumination is presented. Illumination models used in commercial image generation systems are largely empirical in nature and ignore much of the theory which is presented here. Understanding the illumination process helps the practitioner control appearance with predictable results. Additionally, the theoretical foundation is increasingly emphasized in recent research advances.

Table I.1 in Appendix I, *Terminology*, provides a summary of the terminology used herein. The terminology used to describe light propagation and illumination models varies from reference to reference within the optics, physics, and computer graphics literature. Throughout this text, all referenced information is cast into a uniform terminology for consistency and clarity. Where applicable, functional dependencies are indicated in the table.

2.2.1 Vector Notation

All vectors are normalized vectors that are directed away from the surface (boundary) being considered. They are represented as boldfaced letters. **N** is the surface normal, **V** is the view vector (surface to viewer), **L** is a light vector (surface to light), **R** is a reflection vector and is subscripted indicating to which vector it is referenced, **H** is the vector bisector of an **L** and **V** vector pair, and **T** is a transmission vector and is subscripted to indicate which vector generates this transmission, Figure 2.2.

It is convenient to attach a coordinate system to the boundary between two materials to provide a context for examination. Any model that correctly describes the events that occur at this boundary is independent of the coordinate system. A spherical coordinate system is used for convenience in this text. The origin of this coordinate system is the point on the boundary being considered. The primary axis is defined by the normal to the boundary with the positive direction to the "outside" of the boundary. In computer graphics the outside of the boundary always the side the view ray is incident on. The secondary axis lies in the plane of the incident light and the primary axis and is tangent to the surface. The direction of any vector can be described by its angular deviation from the normal, θ, and the angle ϕ between the plane containing the primary and secondary axes and the plane containing the vector and the surface normal. Note that $\phi = 0$ for the light vector.

This convention is sufficient for a directionally isotropic surface, however, as pointed out by Kajiya (1985), many surfaces are not iso-

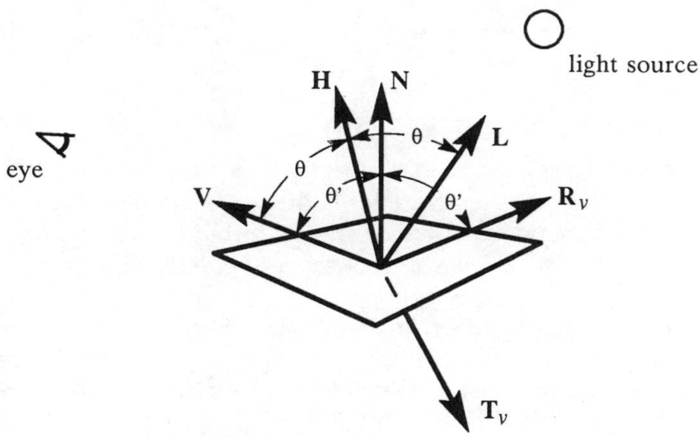

Figure 2.2: Vector notation for illumination models.

tropic. These surfaces are described by attaching the frame of reference to the surface using the surface normal and a tangent vector in the direction of the *grain* of the surface. In this case, the light vector generally has a nonzero angle ϕ.

Geometric description and rendering typically use a global Cartesian coordinate system that must be related to the local spherical coordinate system of the illuminated surface. The vectors previously described are normally expressed in terms of the unit basis vectors i, j, and k which are parallel to the X, Y, and Z axes of the Cartesian coordinate system. The vectors are described by triplets which are multipliers of the basis vectors.[2] For example, the **N** vector is also expressed by the triplet $[\mathbf{N}_i\ \mathbf{N}_j\ \mathbf{N}_k]$.

Many expressions describing illumination involve the use of the trigonometric functions of θ. This simplifies the transformation between the global and local coordinate systems because the trigonometric functions are easily expressed in terms of the global coordinate system representation of the vectors. The previously described unit vector notation is convenient for calculation. Consider the incident angle θ for light incident from the **L** direction. The trigonometric functions are:

$$\cos\theta = (\mathbf{N}\bullet\mathbf{L}) = \mathbf{N}_i\mathbf{L}_i + \mathbf{N}_j\mathbf{L}_j + \mathbf{N}_k\mathbf{L}_k \tag{2.1a}$$

$$\sin\theta = \sqrt{1.0 - \cos^2\theta} = \sqrt{1.0 - (\mathbf{N}\bullet\mathbf{L})^2} \tag{2.1b}$$

$$\tan\theta = \frac{\sin\theta}{\cos\theta} = \frac{\sqrt{1.0 - (\mathbf{N}\bullet\mathbf{L})^2}}{(\mathbf{N}\bullet\mathbf{L})} \tag{2.1c}$$

[2] It is assumed the reader is familiar with vector geometry. The author has found Barnett and Fujii (1963) to be a good introductory text on the subject.

$$\cot\theta = \frac{\cos\theta}{\sin\theta} = \frac{(\mathbf{N} \bullet \mathbf{L})}{\sqrt{1.0 - (\mathbf{N} \bullet \mathbf{L})^2}} \tag{2.1d}$$

2.2.2 The Wave Nature of Light

Several models are used to describe the behavior of light. The model most relevant to computer graphics is the wave model. Light is a transverse electromagnetic wave which travels through a vacuum at roughly $3.0{\times}10^8$ m/s. The wavelength, λ, of the wave determines the color that we perceive.

The electrical properties of a material affect the way light passes through the material. The differences in material properties on either side of a material interface determine the character of reflection and refraction at that interface.

A detailed exploration of the wave model is required for the derivation of optical properties. Fortunately this is not required for use of the optical properties in computer graphics. The adventurous reader can find the wave model described in detail in Hecht and Zajac (1987), Ditchburn (1976), and Jenkins and White (1976).

In a transverse electromagnetic wave there is an oscillating electric field perpendicular to the direction of wave propagation. A magnetic field mutually exists with any electrical field. The magnetic field is mutually perpendicular to both the direction of the wave propagation and the electric field, Figure 2.3.

The energy in the wave is proportional to the square of the amplitude of the wave. Thus, if the interactions between the wave and the environment are described in terms of their effects on the amplitude of the wave, the resulting energy relationships are easily obtained.

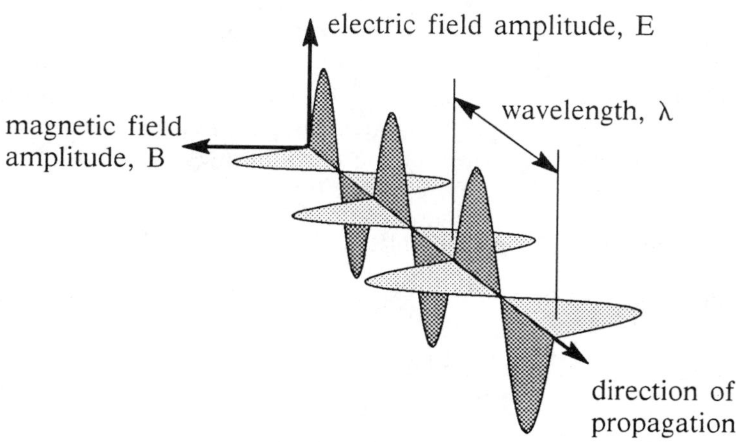

Figure 2.3: Light as a transverse electromagnetic wave.

The directional nature of the electric and magnetic fields explains the phenomena of polarization. Polarized light is filtered so the electrical fields have a parallel orientation.

The electrical properties of a material have the greatest effect on the passage of light through the material. The magnetic field of the wave affects the electrons in materials. The freedom of the electron to respond to this disturbance controls the optical properties.

A dielectric is largely unaffected by the passage of light through the material. Dielectrics have electrons which are in very stable orbits and are essentially oblivious to the passage of light.[3] As a result, the light is largely unaffected by the dielectric in its passage. The major effect is a decrease in the speed of the electromagnetic wave. The index of refraction of a material, n, is the ratio of the speed of light in a vacuum to the speed through the material.[4] The index of refraction is always greater than 1.

Conductors contain free electrons, that is, electrons that are free to move through the material. The magnetic field of a light wave causes the electrons to oscillate. The oscillations match the frequency of the light wave. These oscillations, in turn, generate electric and magnetic fields that reradiate (reflect) the light wave.

In a conductor there are still forces that resist the movement of electrons. This results in the resistance of metals to the passage of electrical current. The resistance damps (slows) the motion of the electrons, thus absorbing energy in the form of heat. As a result of this damping, the reflected energy is less than the incident energy. The absorption index is a measure of the light absorption properties of a material.

2.2.3 Illuminating Hemisphere and Solid Angle

Figure 2.4 describes the concept of an illuminating hemisphere. The illuminating hemisphere is a notational convenience for describing the illumination *events* above or below a surface. These events, such as light sources or other reflecting surfaces, are projected onto this hemisphere. Typically a projection hemisphere of radius 1 is used for computational convenience.

A solid angle, ω, describes amount of the illuminating hemisphere that is covered by the projection of the illumination event onto the illuminating hemisphere. A differential solid angle is defined as a projected

---

[3] The mechanism of light propagation through a dielectric is rather complex and is not described here. The interested reader can find a detailed treatment in Hecht and Zajac (1987, 63-8).

[4] In computer graphics it is common to think of the index of refraction as relating to air rather than a vacuum since the speed in air is nearly the same as in a vacuum. The index of refraction for air is 1.000292 at standard temperature and pressure (Jenkins and White 1976).

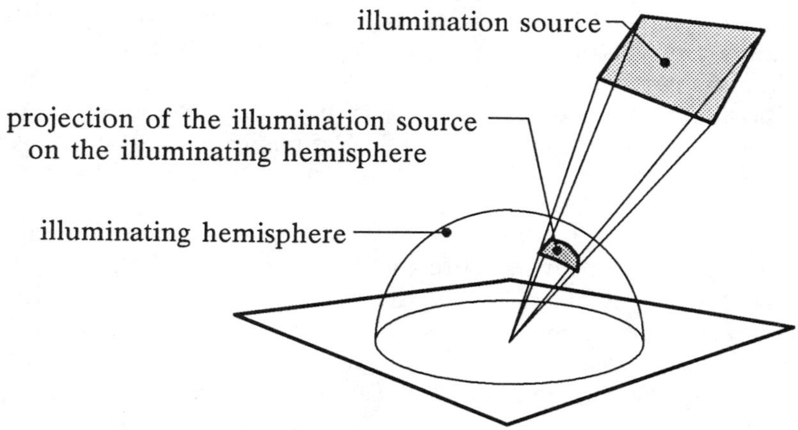

Figure 2.4: The illuminating hemisphere.

differential surface element on the hemisphere (projected from the illuminating event) divided by the square of the radius of the hemisphere. The solid angle of an illumination event is determined by integrating the differential solid angle over the bounds of the projection of the event.

Consider a circular source as seen from a surface, Figure 2.5. The solid angle of this source is determined by projecting it onto the illuminating hemisphere above the surface and integrating the area of the projection. The angle θ defines the projected outline of the source by: $\theta = \arctan(r_s / r_o)$. A differential area of the projection of the source onto the illuminating hemisphere (radius = 1) is expressed by: $dA = \sin\theta d\phi d\theta$. Integrating over the bounds of the projected area, the solid angle is expressed by:

$$\omega = \int^{2\pi} \int^{\arctan(r_s / r_o)} \sin\theta d\theta d\phi = 2\pi(1 - \cos(\arctan(r_s / r_o))) \tag{2.2}$$

If rigorously calculated, solid angles are computationally expensive. However, consider the case of $r_s \ll r_o$, that is, a very small solid angle. For this case the approximation $\theta = \arctan(r_s / r_o) \approx \sin(r_s / r_s) \approx r_s / r_o$ is valid. Thus, a small solid angle is approximated by:

$$\omega \approx \int^{2\pi} \int^{r_s / r_o} \theta d\theta d\phi = \frac{\pi r_s^2}{r_o^2} \tag{2.3}$$

Note that πr_s^2 is the area of the source (Figure 2.5) projected towards the illuminated surface, A_p.[5] Small solid angles are often approximated as

[5] Projected area refers to the area projected onto a plane that is perpendicular to a viewing direction. The projected area of a surface is found by multiplying the area of the surface by the dot product between the surface normal and the direction of view.

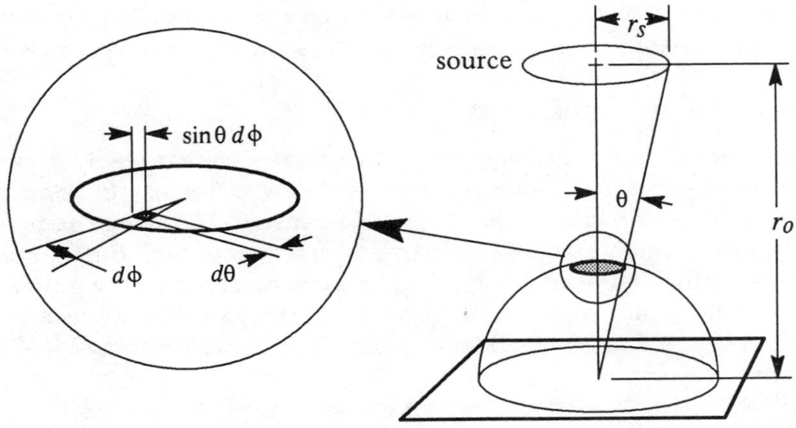

Figure 2.5: Projecting a circular source onto the illuminating hemisphere.

the projected area divided by the distance squared:

$$d\omega \approx dA_p / r_o^2 \tag{2.4}$$

The relative error of this approximation is given in Figure 2.6.

Integrating over the hemisphere means considering all events above the surface weighted by the solid angle of their projections onto the hemisphere. In simple terms, this means that the importance of an illuminating event, such as a light source, is a function both of the character of the event and the solid angle of the event. That is, the amount of energy received from the source depends both on the brightness of the source

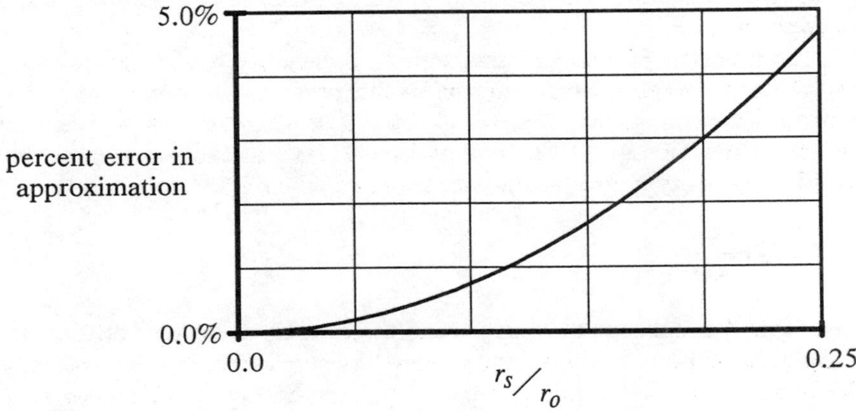

Figure 2.6: Error in the solid angle approximation.

and the solid angle of the source as seen by the viewer. For reference, the solid angle of a hemisphere is 2π and the solid angle of a sphere is 4π.

2.2.4 Intensity and Energy

Light intensity and light energy are often used interchangeably in non-technical discussions. However, they are very different. In common terms, what we describe as brightness is intensity. The energy received by a viewer or an illuminated surface is a function of both the intensity and the portion of the field of view (solid angle) covered by the source of the intensity. Some aspects of surface illumination are directly related to the intensity of the illuminating sources, others are a function of the energy that is received.

Energy flux, Φ, is energy per unit time. Energy density $|E^2|$ is the energy per unit time per unit area (recall that E is the magnitude of the electric field). Intensity, I, is defined as the energy flux per unit projected area of the source, A_{ps}, per solid angle, ω, through which the source radiates:

$$I = \frac{\Phi}{A_{ps}\omega} \tag{2.5}$$

To clarify this, consider a spherical light source of radius r_s radiating a total energy of Φ_s equally in all directions. The projected area of this source in any direction is πr_s^2. The solid angle through which the source radiates is 4π (the solid angle of a sphere). The intensity of the source in any direction, I_s, is then expressed by:

$$I_s = \frac{\Phi_s}{4\pi^2 r_s^2} \tag{2.6}$$

Note that the intensity of the source is independent of viewer distance from the source.

Consider the problem of determining the energy density at a surface illuminated by the source describe in the previous example. At a distance r_o from the source, the energy flux is passing through a sphere of radius r_o and area $4\pi r_o^2$. The energy density at a distance r_o is given by dividing the energy flux by the area through which it radiates:

$$|E^2| = \frac{\Phi_s}{4\pi r_o^2} \tag{2.7}$$

Note that this is based on considering the area of the sphere at distance r_o, and that for any point on that sphere, the surface normal is parallel to the direction the light energy is traveling from the source. To determine the energy flux for a surface oriented in another direction, the projected area must be considered. The dot product between the the surface normal, $\mathbf{N}_o$, and the vector towards the source is factored into the expression. The energy density is then given by:

$$|E_o^2| = |E^2|\,(\mathbf{N}_o \bullet \mathbf{L}) = \frac{\Phi_s(\mathbf{N}_o \bullet \mathbf{L})}{4\pi r_o^2} \tag{2.8}$$

The energy density is expressed in terms of the intensity of the source by combining Eqs.(2.6) and (2.8). The energy density is expressed in terms of the intensity of the source by:

$$|E_o^2| = \frac{I_s(\mathbf{N}_o \bullet \mathbf{L})\pi r_s^2}{r_o^2} = I_s(\mathbf{N}_o \bullet \mathbf{L})\omega_s \tag{2.9}$$

Note that $\pi r_s^2 / r_o^2$ is the approximation for the solid angle of the light source as viewed from the surface, ω_S. The energy flux varies inversely as the square of the distance between the source and the receiver.

These relationships between energy flux, energy density, and intensity illustrate several fundamental concepts implicitly used in computer graphics:

- To accurately portray an object projected onto an image plane, the intensity at the image plane image should be the same as that of the object (intensity is independent of distance).
- Intensity is proportional to energy, all other factors held constant. If the energy is doubled, then the intensity is doubled if all other factors are held constant.

These relationships can be applied to the general case of evaluating the energy reaching a surface patch from an illumination source, Figure 2.7. If the source and surface patches are sufficiently small compared to the

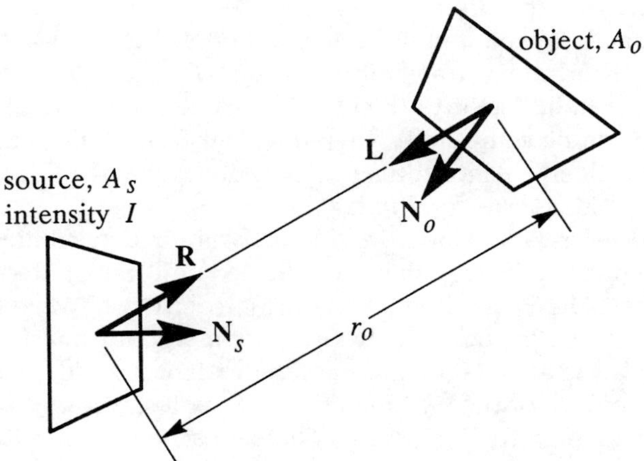

Figure 2.7: Calculating the energy flux from a source received at a surface.

distance, the solid angle approximation, Eq.(2.4), is appropriate. Integrating over the solid angle and projected area results in the expression for received energy:

$$\Phi = \frac{I\, A_s\, A_o\, (\mathbf{N}_s \bullet \mathbf{R})\, (\mathbf{N}_o \bullet \mathbf{L})}{r_o^2} \tag{2.10}$$

2.2.5 Reflection and Refraction

Reflection and refraction result when light waves encounter an interface between materials. The index of refraction and the absorption index are a measure of properties that determine the character of reflection and refraction at the interface. The law of reflection and Snell's law of refraction explain the directions of reflection and refraction using the wave theory of light. This explanation is found in any standard optics text (Hecht and Zajac 1979, 81-85) (Jenkins and White 1976, 11-20). To summarize, the law of reflection states that the reflected angle is equal to the incident angle:

$$\theta_r = \theta_i \tag{2.11}$$

Snell's law of refraction relates the angle of refraction to the angle of incidence through the indices of refraction for the two materials. It is given by:

$$n_t \sin\theta_t = n_i \sin\theta_i \tag{2.12}$$

The geometry of reflection and refraction is shown in Figure 2.8. Given a light vector, **L**, and a surface normal, **N**, the reflected vector, $\mathbf{R}_l$, and the transmitted vector, $\mathbf{T}_l$, are determined using the algorithms given in Appendix III.1, *Geometric Utilities*.

Additionally, given a light vector, **L**, and an arbitrary reflected vector, $\mathbf{R}_l$, or an arbitrary transmitted vector, $\mathbf{T}_l$, the surface normal required for the light vector to the be reflected or transmitted in the $\mathbf{R}_l$ or $\mathbf{T}_l$ direction can be computed. These ideal surface normals are called **H** and **H′** respectively. Algorithms for computing **H** and **H′** are also given in Appendix III.1, *Geometric Utilities*.

The Fresnel relationships provide a basis for determining the fractions of the incident energy that are reflected and transmitted at a material interface. The Fresnel equations are a solution to Maxwell's equations for electromagnetic wave behavior at a smooth interface between two materials. These relationships are dependent upon the indices of refraction, n_i and n_t, of the two materials, the polarization of the incident light, and the angle of incidence. The ratios of the amplitude of the reflected wave to the incident wave, r, for light polarized parallel and perpendicular to the plane of the **L** and **N** vectors at an interface between

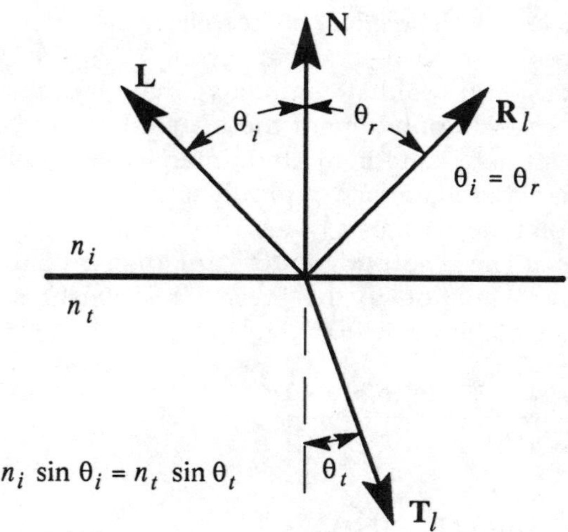

Figure 2.8: Geometry of reflection and refraction.

dielectric media are:[6]

$$r_{\parallel} = \frac{n_t(\mathbf{N}\bullet\mathbf{L}) + n_i(\mathbf{N}\bullet\mathbf{T})}{n_t(\mathbf{N}\bullet\mathbf{L}) - n_i(\mathbf{N}\bullet\mathbf{T})} \tag{2.13}$$

$$r_{\perp} = \frac{n_i(\mathbf{N}\bullet\mathbf{L}) + n_t(\mathbf{N}\bullet\mathbf{T})}{n_i(\mathbf{N}\bullet\mathbf{L}) - n_t(\mathbf{N}\bullet\mathbf{T})} \tag{2.14}$$

The energy in a wave is proportional to the square of the amplitude. The ratio of reflected energy to incident energy is expressed by the square of r, and is termed the Fresnel reflectance, F_r. For the purposes of image synthesis, it is convenient to assume light is always circularly polarized[7], and that interactions are characterized as the average of the perpendicular and parallel components of polarized light. Thus, the reflectance is expressed by:

$$F_r = \frac{1}{2}(r_{\parallel}^2 + r_{\perp}^2) = \frac{\Phi_r}{\Phi_i} \tag{2.15}$$

As a consequence of the law of conservation of energy the transmittance, F_t, is expressed as $F_t = 1.0 - F_r$.

When conductive materials are considered, the Fresnel relationships take on a more complex form. Conductive properties arise from the ex-

[6] These formulas may appear inconsistent with optics texts. However, recall that the **N** and **T** vectors are in opposite directions from the surface. Thus, $\cos\theta_t = (-\mathbf{N}\bullet\mathbf{T})$.

[7] Circularly polarized means there is no preferred or dominant orientation to the magnetic and electric field of the wave.

istence of free electrons. The effect of free electrons on the reflection of light is qualitatively discussed earlier in Section 2.2.2, *The Wave Nature of Light*. That discussion notes that conductive materials absorb light and are opaque. As a result, only one of the materials at a visible interface can be conductive (there is no light at an interface between two opaque materials) and the other material is typically air.

The absorption index, k/n, is a measure of the absorption characteristics of a conductor. The absorption index can range roughly from .001 to 70. A useful approximation to the Fresnel relationships that is valid when $n^2+k^2 \gg 1$ is (Ditchburn 1976):

$$r_{\parallel}^2 = \frac{(n_t^2+k_t^2)(\mathbf{N} \bullet \mathbf{L})^2 - 2n_t(\mathbf{N} \bullet \mathbf{L}) + 1}{(n_t^2+k_t^2)(\mathbf{N} \bullet \mathbf{L})^2 + 2n_t(\mathbf{N} \bullet \mathbf{L}) + 1} \tag{2.16}$$

$$r_{\perp}^2 = \frac{(n_t^2+k_t^2) - 2n_t(\mathbf{N} \bullet \mathbf{L}) + (\mathbf{N} \bullet \mathbf{L})^2}{(n_t^2+k_t^2) + 2n_t(\mathbf{N} \bullet \mathbf{L}) + (\mathbf{N} \bullet \mathbf{L})^2} \tag{2.17}$$

The derivation of the Fresnel equations is available in many texts, (Ditchburn 1976, 511-9, 535-43) (Hecht and Zajac 1987, 92-104) (Jenkins and White 1976, 523-43) and is not repeated here.

To aid in understanding of the Fresnel relationships, they are plotted for glass and copper in Figure 2.9. The high reflectance of copper is characteristic of conductors. The low reflectance of glass is characteristic of dielectrics. Note also that the energy curve for perpendicularly polarized light reflected from glass is equal to zero at an incident angle near 55°. This is because the amplitude of the wave changes sign at this point. The reflectance curves for conductors never reach zero as a result of the

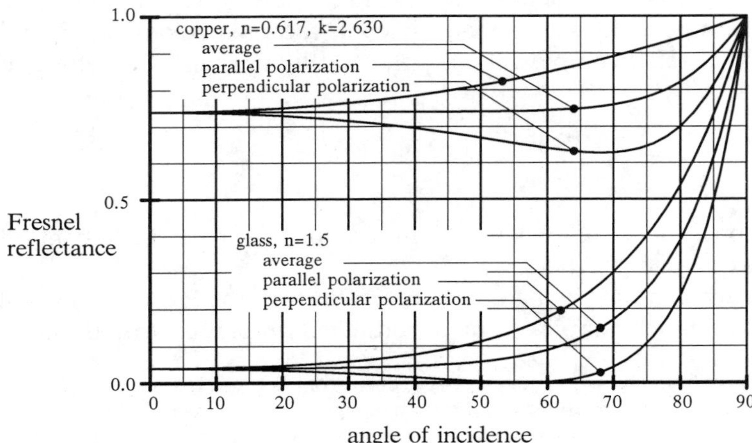

Figure 2.9: Fresnel reflectance for glass and copper.

nonzero value of k. Additionally, as the incident angle approaches grazing[8] all materials become 100% reflective.

An important principle demonstrated by the Fresnel equations is the law of reciprocity. The law of reciprocity states that the reflective and refractive relationships are independent of the direction of energy propagation. Specifically, this means that the reflectance, F_r, for light reaching a surface in the **L** direction and reflecting in the $\mathbf{R}_l$ direction is identical to that for light reaching the surface from the $\mathbf{R}_l$ direction and reflecting in the **L** direction. Similarly, the transmittance, F_t for light reaching the surface from the **L** direction and transmitting in the $\mathbf{T}_l$ direction is identical to that for light reaching the surface from the $\mathbf{T}_l$ direction and transmitting in the **L** direction.

The Fresnel equations provide a valuable insight into behavior of light at the boundary between layers. However, their usefulness is limited in computer graphics due to the need for complete material property specifications before these relationships can be applied. Complete data is seldom available.

The index of refraction and the absorption coefficient for some materials are found in reference literature. However, it is common to find disagreement in values because of different surface preparation and measuring techniques. It is also possible to locate spectral curves for many materials. The spectral nature of materials indicates the index of refraction and absorption index are wavelength dependent. A single value for the index of refraction and absorption index does not sufficiently characterize a material for computer graphics applications.

Glass is a notable exception to the general lack of information. We know from the common experience of observing a prism that different wavelengths of light travel through glass at different speeds, and are thus separated during refraction. Color separation results in an undesirable phenomena in lenses known as chromatic aberration. To characterize the wavelength dependence of the index of refraction to aid in eliminating chromatic aberration, measurements have been made for a wide variety of glasses. These measurements are commonly made using spectral lines at 434.0nm, 486.1nm, 589.2nm, and 656.3nm.[9] Information and tables for a variety of glasses are found in (Jenkins and White 1976, 18-20, appendix IV). In addition, information for a wide variety of other materials are found throughout that reference.

A methodology for approximating the Fresnel relationships for a materials when insufficient data is available was developed by Cook and

---

[8] The grazing angle is the point where incidence is parallel to the surface and perpendicular to the normal.

[9] These are the C,D,F, and G′ Fraunhofer lines. Fraunhofer was a pioneer in the observation and measurement of spectral phenomena. The Fraunhofer lines are prominent lines in the solar spectrum.

Torrance (1982). This method is detailed in Appendix III.5, *Fresnel Approximation*.

2.2.6 Geometry of a Surface

The previous sections have described terminology and relationships for smooth surfaces. However, most objects encountered in computer graphics do not have smooth surfaces. They are idealized as being composed of small planar surface patches called microfacets. The roughness of a surface is described by a function, $\zeta(x,y)$, that gives the height of the surface above or below the average surface at any position, (x,y), on the surface. The mean value of this roughness function, denoted by angular brackets $<>$, is the average surface, thus $<\zeta(x,y)> = 0$.

The root mean square height, σ, describes the average variation in height from the mean surface, and is related to the roughness function by:

$$\sigma = <\zeta^2(x,y)>^{1/2} = \left[\iint \zeta^2(x,y)dxdy\right]^{1/2} \tag{2.18}$$

The average distance between a local peak and a local valley in the surface is called the correlation distance, τ. The average slope of the surface, m, is used to characterize a surface, Figure 2.10. A simple approach to determining the average slope used by Beckmann (1963, 89) is to use the average height difference between peak and valley, 2σ, and the correlation distance, τ, to express the slope by:

$$m = \frac{2\sigma}{\tau} \tag{2.19}$$

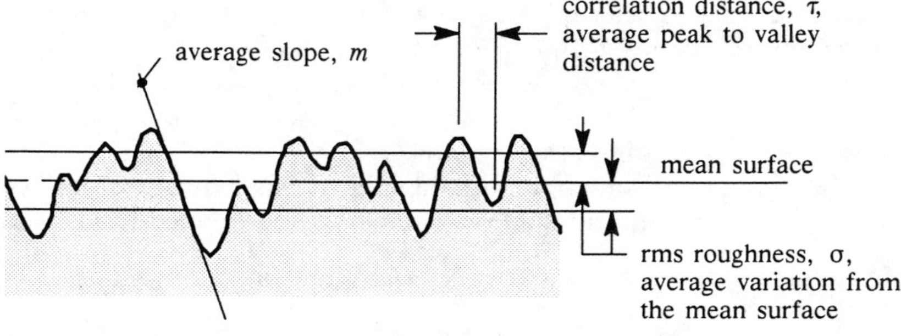

Figure 2.10: Geometry of surface roughness.

For a surface with random roughness, $\zeta(x,y)$, given by a Gaussian distribution a more rigorous approach presented in Bennett and Porteus (1961) gives m by:[10]

$$\overline{m} = \frac{\sigma\sqrt{2}}{\tau} \tag{2.20}$$

The question of which relationship of m, σ, and τ is correct is a question of context. The relationship used by Beckmann is primarily for notational convenience while the relationship by Bennett results from rigorous statistical analysis.

In an effort to give some physical meaning to the surface geometry described in this section, Table 2.1 describes the roughness parameters associated with some common surface finishes.[11]

σ (microinch)		material	finish
with grain	cross grain		
3	5	stainless	fine grind
3	9	aluminum	fine grind
15	28	stainless	coarse grind
22	55	aluminum	coarse grind
25	40	stainless	circular mill
15	40	aluminum	circular mill
30	45	stainless	side mill
30	80	aluminum	side mill

Table 2.1: Typical surface finishes

2.2.7 Geometric Attenuation

The surface geometry for rough surfaces also introduces conditions where parts of the surfaces shade or mask other parts of the surface, Figure 2.11. The geometric attenuation function, G, describes the fraction of the microfacets oriented to reflect light from the source to a viewer which are visible to both the light and the viewer (not self shaded by the

[10] The notation m and $\overline{m}$ is used to differentiate between the expressions for slope. The m given by Eq.(2.19) is used through most of the text and in the program examples in Appendix III. The $\overline{m}$ given by Eq.(2.20) is used for consistency with original sources.

[11] These values were obtained by having small blocks of stainless steel and aluminum machined with different tools. The finishes were measured with a profilometer® both with the grain and cross-grain over a distance of 0.030 inches. The profilometer physically drags a stylus over the surface to make the measurement. Bennett and Porteus (1961) demonstrated that profilometer readings are suspect for very smooth surfaces because the size of the surface irregularities is small compared to the size of the stylus.

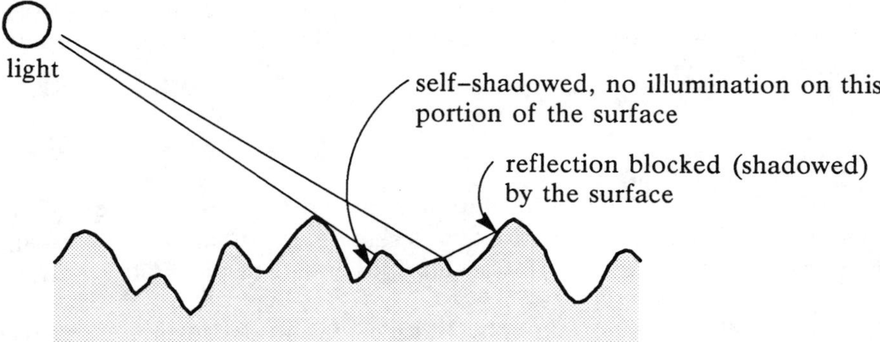

Figure 2.11: Self shading in rough surfaces.

surface). Torrance and Sparrow (1967)[12] investigated this phenomena and derived a formulation for G assuming:

- Each facet comprises one side of a symmetric V-groove cavity.
- The longitudinal axis of the cavity is parallel to the plane of the mean surface.
- The upper edges of the V-grooves are all in the same plane.
- The grooves do not have a preferred orientation, i.e., they are in all directions along the surface.

The resulting attenuation function is given by:

$$G = \min\left[1, \frac{2(\mathbf{N}\bullet\mathbf{H})(\mathbf{N}\bullet\mathbf{V})}{(\mathbf{V}\bullet\mathbf{H})}, \frac{2(\mathbf{N}\bullet\mathbf{H})(\mathbf{N}\bullet\mathbf{L})}{(\mathbf{V}\bullet\mathbf{H})}\right] \tag{2.21}$$

An alternate shadow function for random rough surfaces with Gaussian distributions of height was introduced by Sancer (1969).[13] It is given by:

$$G = \frac{1}{1 + C_i + C_r} \tag{2.22a}$$

$$C_i = \frac{\exp(-c_1)}{2\sqrt{\pi c_1}} - \frac{1}{2}\operatorname{erfc}(\sqrt{c_1})\,; \quad c_1 = \frac{(\mathbf{N}\bullet\mathbf{L})^2}{2\overline{m}^2(1 - (\mathbf{N}\bullet\mathbf{L})^2)} \tag{2.22b}$$

$$C_r = \frac{\exp(-c_2)}{2\sqrt{\pi c_2}} - \frac{1}{2}\operatorname{erfc}(\sqrt{c_2})\,; \quad c_2 = \frac{(\mathbf{N}\bullet\mathbf{V})^2}{2\overline{m}^2(1 - (\mathbf{N}\bullet\mathbf{V})^2)} \tag{2.22c}$$

---

[12] Geometric attenuation was first introduced into computer graphics literature by Blinn (1977).

[13] This formulation for geometric attenuation was first introduced into the computer graphics literature by Koestner (1986).

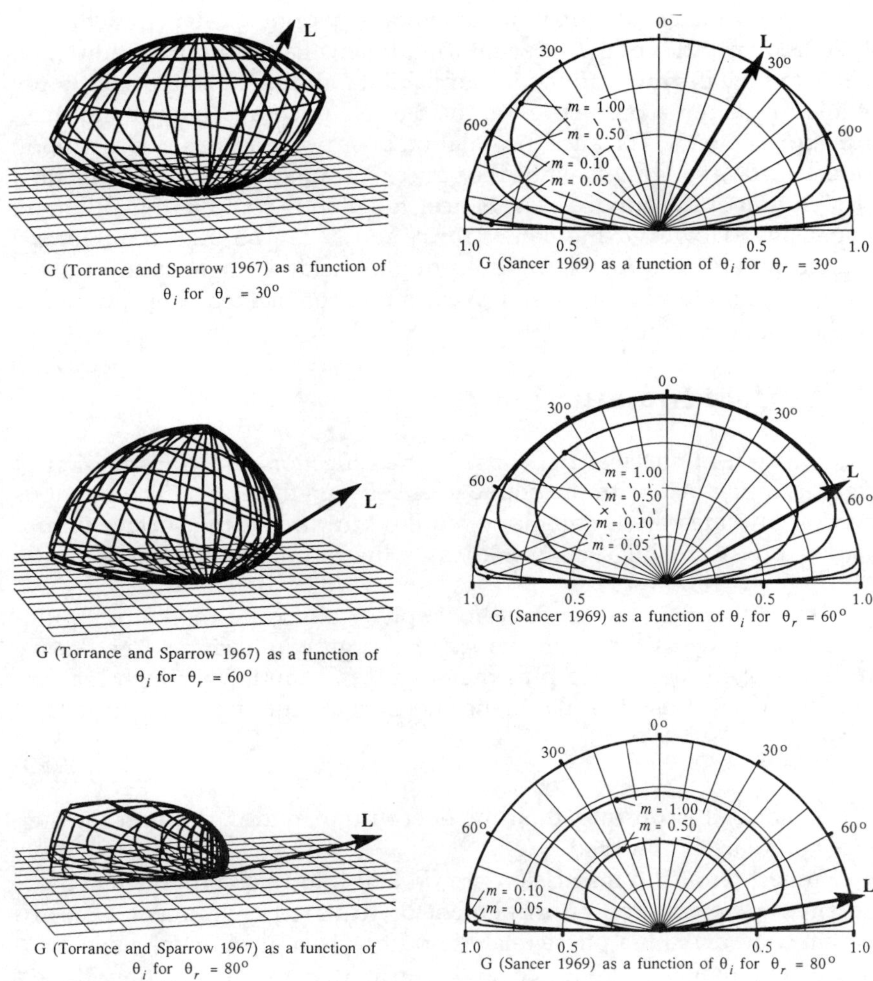

Figure 2.12: Geometric attenuation functions plotted.

The function presented by Torrance and Sparrow is independent of surface roughness, exhibits sharp discontinuities, and is asymmetric, centering around the mirror direction. These properties are a result of surface geometry defined by the assumptions. The function presented by Sancer considers a more generalized rough surface description and is both symmetric and continuous, Figure 2.12. In the Sancer formulation, increasing m either by decreasing the correlation distance, τ, or the rms height of the the surface irregularities, σ, causes the shading to begin at a smaller incident or reflecting angle as is intuitively expected. The Sancer function is symmetric about the normal and depends upon the elevation angles of incidence and reflection only.

The geometric attenuation function is seldom used in practice, so there is very little comparative information available. Illumination models using the Torrance function can exhibit banding at the discontinuity while this is not a problem with the Sancer function. In applying these functions note the Torrance formulation does not require any description of the surface roughness while the Sancer formulation requires a detailed description of the surface. The Sancer function is computationally more expensive. However, the values for c_i and c_r can be precomputed and loaded into a lookup table indexed by the incident angle. Since the expressions for c_i and c_r are identical except for the incident angle, only one lookup table is required.

2.3 Surface Illumination

Illumination of surfaces depends on the reflection and transmission of light as it interacts with the boundaries between materials. The previous section provides the terminology required to discuss the surface illumination process. This section addresses the illumination process in detail.[14]

A fundamental requirement for a physically valid model of an illuminated surface is the maintenance of energy equilibrium. The energy reflected from the surface plus the energy transmitted through the surface boundary must be equal to the energy that illuminates the surface.

$$\Phi_i = \Phi_r + \Phi_t \tag{2.23}$$

If the material is opaque, then the energy transmitted through the surface boundary is absorbed.

Reflection and transmission are broken into two components, a coherent component and an incoherent or scattered component. The coherent component is a phase related or diffraction phenomena. The incoherent component is reflected and transmitted in all directions based upon the geometry of the surface (the surface roughness description). Phase information is lost in the incoherent component.

2.3.1 Coherent Illumination

The coherent component of illumination is characterized by considering the behavior of a wave front that is incident upon a material boundary. An optically smooth boundary is one with infinitely small surface varia-

[14] The theoretical work most commonly applied to illumination for computer graphics is largely from research for radar applications. The illumination is analogous to the radar signal, and the illuminated surface to the terrain reflecting the radar signal. This theoretical basis treats reflection. A theoretical basis for considering transmission has not yet been related to computer graphics.

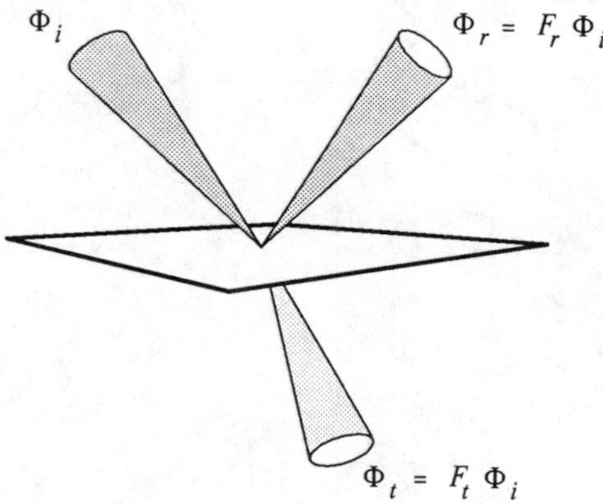

Figure 2.13: Coherent illumination for optically smooth surfaces.

tion compared to the wavelength of light. Optically smooth surfaces display coherent illumination only.

Incident light is reflected in the mirror direction and transmitted in the direction given by Snell's law.[15] The Fresnel relationships provide the coefficients, F_r and F_t that relate the reflected and transmitted energy to the incident energy, Figure 2.13. The resulting illumination expression is:

$$\Phi_i = F_r\Phi_i + F_t\Phi_i \; ; \qquad F_r + F_t = 1.0 \tag{2.24}$$

Using this relationship, the relative intensities of the reflected and transmitted light are determined. Consider light reaching a small surface patch, dA, through a small solid angle, $d\omega_i$, at an incident angle θ_i, Figure 2.13. The expressions relating energy to intensity for the incident, reflected, and transmitted light are:

$$\Phi_i = I_i dA \cos\theta_i d\omega_i \tag{2.25}$$

$$\Phi_r = F_r\Phi_i = I_r dA \cos\theta_r d\omega_r \tag{2.26}$$

$$\Phi_t = F_t\Phi_i = I_t dA \cos\theta_t d\omega_t \tag{2.27}$$

The law of reflection dictates that the geometry of the reflection is mir-

[15] For very small surfaces patches (diameter / wavelength <30) the coherent component is actual a multilobed diffraction pattern. Fortunately the surfaces found in computer graphics are large and the diffraction pattern collapses into single spikes in the mirror and Snell's law directions. It may be observed, however, that these diffraction patterns are evident at the edge of a large reflecting patch.

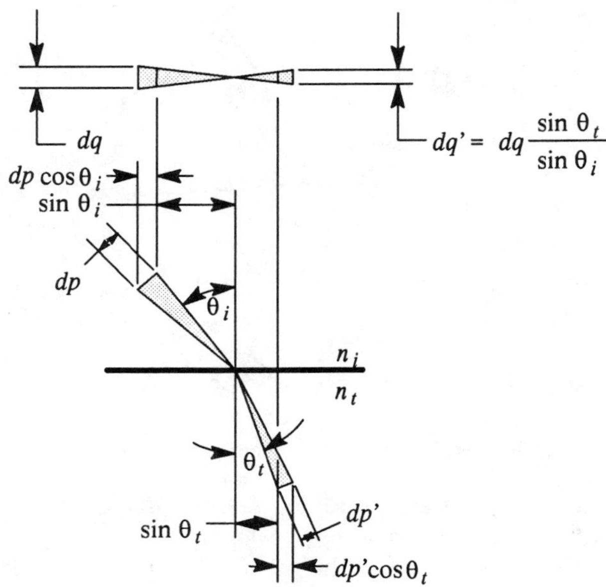

Figure 2.14: Geometry of coherent refraction.

rored about the surface normal, thus $\theta_r = \theta_i$ and $d\omega_r = d\omega_i$. Eqs.(2.25) and (2.26) are combined to relate reflected to incident intensity by:

$$I_r = F_r I_i \tag{2.28}$$

However, the geometry for the transmitted light is not so simple. Consider a small incident solid angle projected through an area $dpdq$ at a radius 1 from the surface. The incident solid angle is then $dpdq/1.0^2 = dpdq$. Consider the geometry of refraction described in Figure 2.14. We can relate dq to dq' using similar triangles. Substituting Snell's law, Eq.(2.12), this relationship becomes:

$$dq' = \frac{dq\sin\theta_t}{\sin\theta_i} = \frac{dq\frac{n_i}{n_t}\sin\theta_i}{dq\sin\theta_i} = \frac{n_i}{n_t}dq \tag{2.29}$$

Using Snell's law once again, dp' is related to dp as noted in Figure 2.14:

$$n_i(\sin\theta_i + dp\cos\theta_i) = n_t(\sin\theta_t + dp'\cos\theta_t) \tag{2.30}$$

Subtracting Eq.(2.12) gives:

$$dp' = \frac{n_i\cos\theta_i}{n_t\cos\theta_t}dp \tag{2.31}$$

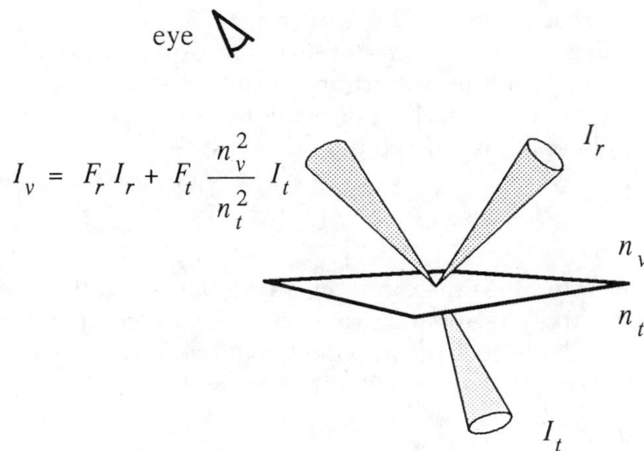

Figure 2.15: Coherent illumination.

Combining Eqs.(2.29) and (2.31), the transmitted solid angle is related to the incident solid angle by:

$$d\omega_t = dp'dq' = \frac{n_i \cos\theta_i}{n_t \cos\theta_t} dp \frac{n_i}{n_t} dq = \frac{n_i^2 \cos\theta_i}{n_t^2 \cos\theta_t} d\omega_i \tag{2.32}$$

Combining this with Eqs.(2.25) and (2.26), the transmitted intensity is related to the incident intensity by:[16]

$$I_t = F_t \frac{n_t^2}{n_i^2} I_i \tag{2.33}$$

Using reciprocity relationships, the intensity from a smooth surface towards a viewer is expressed in terms of the energy reaching the surface from the reflected and transmitted directions to the view vector, Figure 2.15, by:

$$I_v = F_r I_r + F_t \frac{n_v^2}{n_t^2} I_t \tag{2.34}$$

An optically smooth surface is an ideal that cannot really be achieved. A complete coherent illumination function is written by adding coherent attenuation terms for reflection and transmission, r_σ and t_σ, and similar geometric attenuation terms. The resulting model is given by:

$$I_v = r_\sigma G F_r I_r + t_\sigma G F_t \frac{n_v^2}{n_t^2} I_t \tag{2.35}$$

16 Hecht and Zajac (1987) show the factor to be n_t/n_i for a planar incident wave.

Bennett and Porteus (1961) and Beckmann (1963) examined the effects of surface roughness on the coherent reflection. Attenuation of the coherent reflection is a result of diffraction phenomena. These effects are dependent upon the wavelength, λ, of the light incident on the surface. An apparent roughness, g, is defined by:

$$g = \frac{4\pi^2\sigma^2}{\lambda^2}(\cos\theta_i + \cos\theta_r)^2 \tag{2.36}$$

σ/λ is the rms roughness measured in wavelengths and the $(\cos\theta_i+\cos\theta_r)$ factor indicates that the apparent roughness is a function of incident and reflected angle. Note that the apparent roughness is greatest at normal incidence. The coherent attenuation is given by:[17]

$$r_\sigma = \exp(-g) \tag{2.37}$$

The coherent attenuation accounts for destructive interference of the reflected waves. Consider waves reaching a rough surface with high spots that are $\lambda/4$ above the low spots. A wave normally incident has reflected components that are out of phase by $\lambda/2$ resulting in destructive interference. The energy lost to this attenuation function is accounted for by incoherent illumination mechanisms.

Figure 2.16 plots the ratio of the coherently reflected energy to the incident energy, Φ_r/Φ_i, as a function of surface properties and incident angle. As previously noted, this is also the ratio of reflected intensity to incident intensity, I_r/I_i, due to the mirrored geometry of reflection. The first plotted surface does not include the geometric attenuation. The remaining surfaces include the geometric attenuation for different rms slope values, m, for the surface. These surfaces are plotted for light with a wavelength of 580nm. The Fresnel relationships are ignored, that is, a Fresnel reflectance of 1 is assumed for the material at all wavelengths and incident angles.

At normal incidence the coherent attenuation drops to zero when the rms roughness reaches approx 150nm (approx 6 microinch). As the incident angle approaches grazing the coherent attenuation reaches 1 for any roughness, σ, because the apparent roughness drops to zero. Addition of the geometric attenuation provides a complete picture of the attenuation of coherent reflection due to roughness.

2.3.2 Incoherent Illumination

Incoherent illumination accounts for the majority of the surface illumination we observe. The incoherent reflection is, at best, difficult to understand and/or predict.

---

[17] The author is not aware of any similar development of the expression for t_σ.

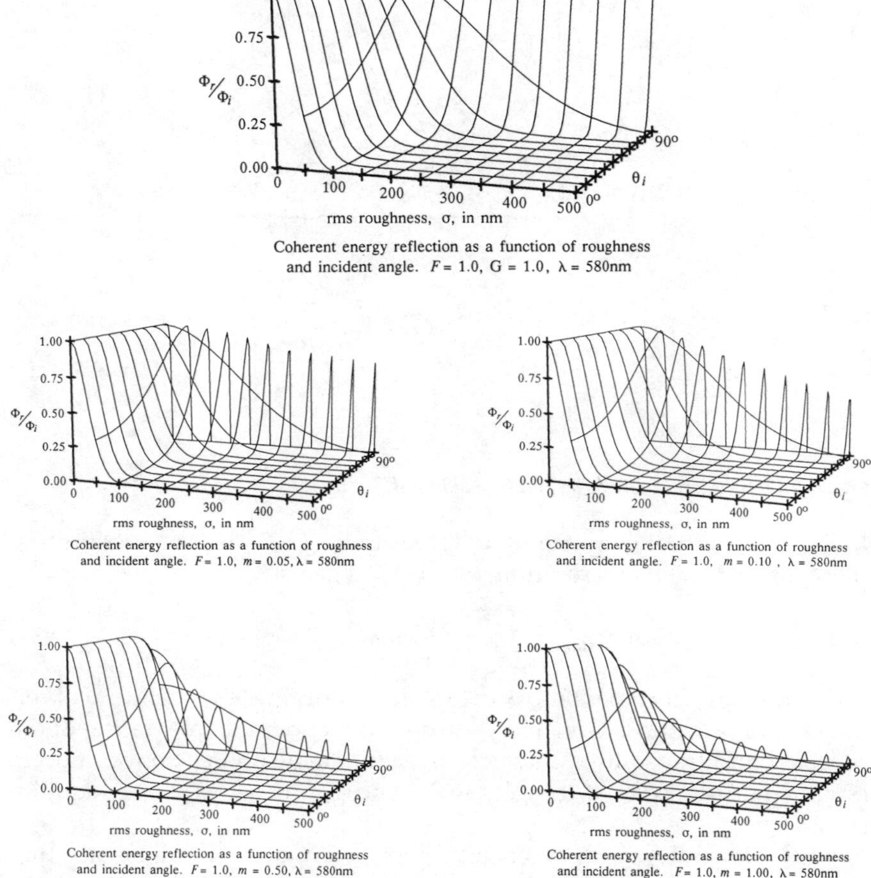

Figure 2.16: Coherent contribution to reflected energy ignoring Fresnel relationships.

Incident light is incoherently scattered in all directions from a rough surface, Figure 2.17. The light is reflected with some intensity $I_r(\theta,\phi)$ and transmitted with some intensity $I_t(\theta,\phi)$. The reflected and transmitted intensity functions are integrated to determine the reflected and transmitted energy. If illumination is incoherent only, then the energy equilibrium expression, Eq.(2.23), is given by:

$$\Phi_i = \int^{2\pi} I_r(\theta,\phi) A \cos\theta_r d\omega_{front} + \int^{2\pi} I_t(\theta,\phi) A \cos\theta_t d\omega_{back} \tag{2.38}$$

We define a bidirectional reflectance, R_{bd}, and bidirectional transmittance, T_{bd} that describe the ratio of the reflected or transmitted intensity to the incident energy density at the surface. The bidirectional factors are functions of the geometry of the **N**, **V**, and **L** vectors, of the surface roughness ζ, and of the wavelength λ. The reflected intensity is

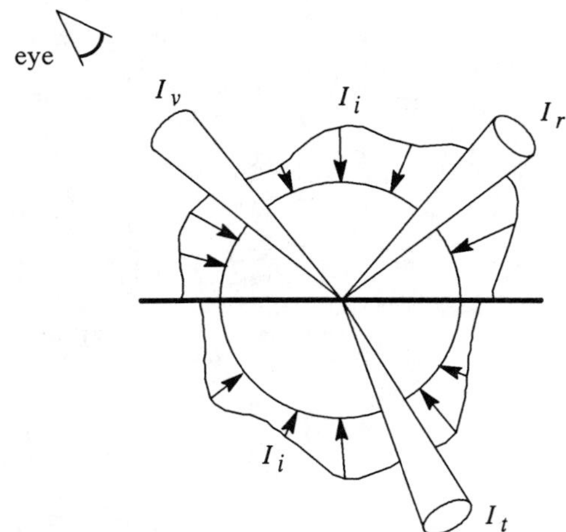

Figure 2.17: Incoherent reflection and transmission.

$I_r = R_{bd}\ |E_s^2|$ and the transmitted intensity is $I_t = T_{bd}\ |E_s^2|$. Substituting these into Eq.(2.38) and dividing by $(A\ |E_s|)$ gives:

$$1.0 = \int^{2\pi} R_{bd}\cos\theta_r d\omega_{front} + \int^{2\pi} T_{bd}\cos\theta_t d\omega_{back} \tag{2.39}$$

This equation becomes a basic tool for verifying the validity of bidirectional functions. Given any incident direction, the integration of the reflected and transmitted intensity over the hemispheres above and below the surface is equal to unity if R_{bd} and T_{bd} preserve energy equilibrium.

The bidirectional functions also allow computing the intensity that leaves a surface in a given direction as a result of the illumination incident on that surface. The integration of the incident intensity gives the incident energy. When factored by the bidirectional functions, this provides the intensity leaving the surface in any specified direction. The resulting expression for intensity leaving the surface is:

$$I_v = \int^{2\pi} I_i R_{bd}\cos\theta_i d\omega_{front} + \int^{2\pi} I_i T_{bd}\cos\theta_i d\omega_{back} \tag{2.40}$$

2.3.2.1 Incoherent Mechanism

The incoherent mechanism is best described by considering the surface to be a collection of small, flat facets (called microfacets), each reflecting light, Figure 2.18. Each microfacet is thought of as an optically smooth facet that can be characterized by coherent illumination. On a microscopic level each microfacet reflects light in the mirror direction to it's local normal. The Fresnel relationships provide the relationship between

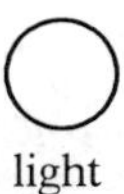

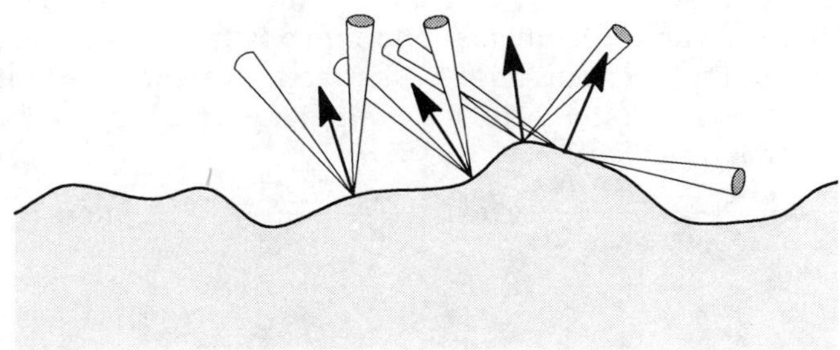

Figure 2.18: Incoherent scattering by rough surface microfacets.

the incident intensity and reflected intensity of the microfacet.

The surface is actually viewed from a macroscopic level. That is, the contributions from individual microfacets are blended, resulting in perception of the surface as an average of all of the microfacet interactions. Koestner (1986) points out that "*...since the visual system is only sensitive to a large number of individual waves passing through a region of space over a long period of time (compared to the period of the wave of visible light), the time averaged field is all that is needed to predict the reflected intensity.*" Stated another way, we perceive an average, aggregate behavior of the surface.

In addition to the Fresnel relationship, the self shadowing of the surface and the probability that mircofacets are correctly oriented for reflection or transmission in a given direction must be considered. Cook and Torrance (1982) present a bidirectional reflectance function expressed by:

$$R_{bd} = \frac{DGF_r}{\cos\theta_i \cos\theta_r} \tag{2.41}$$

G is the geometric attenuation function previously described. F_r is the Fresnel reflectance relative to the microfacet normal. The microfacet normal is the vector bisector of the incident and reflected directions (the **H** vector). D is a microfacet distribution function that describes the fraction of the surface for which microfacets are oriented so the normal is the vector bisector of the incident and reflected vectors (in the **H** direction). The microfacet distribution is a function of the surface roughness, ζ, and the angle, α, between the surface normal and the microfacet normal.

2.3.2.2 Microfacet Distribution

Beckmann (1963) and Bahar (1980) provide a detailed theoretical treatment of reflections of electromagnetic waves from random rough surfaces. These treatments relate the energy density of the incident field to the energy density of the reflected field at any viewpoint in space. The area of the reflecting surface is A and the distance from the surface to the viewpoint is r. These treatments ignore geometric attenuation, Fresnel effects, and multiple reflections at the surface. Koestner (1986) interprets these treatments in a form useful for computer graphics given by:

$$\frac{|E_r^2|}{|E_i^2|} = \frac{A}{r^2}\,\frac{1}{4\pi m^2\cos^4\alpha}\,g^2\exp\left[-\left(g+\frac{v_{xz}^2\tau^2}{4}\right)\right] \qquad g\ll 1 \qquad (2.42a)$$

$$\frac{|E_r^2|}{|E_i^2|} = \frac{A}{r^2}\,\frac{1}{4\pi m^2\cos^4\alpha}\,\sum_{i=1}^{\infty}\frac{g^{i+1}}{i!\,i}\exp\left[-\left(g+\frac{v_{xz}^2\tau^2}{4i}\right)\right] \qquad g\approx 1 \qquad (2.42b)$$

$$\frac{|E_r^2|}{|E_i^2|} = \frac{A}{r^2}\,\frac{1}{4\pi m^2\cos^4\alpha}\,\exp\left(\frac{\tan^2\alpha}{m^2}\right) \qquad g\gg 1 \qquad (2.42c)$$

where:

$$v_{xz}^2 = \frac{4\pi^2}{\lambda^2}\sin^2\theta_i - 2\sin\theta_i\sin\theta_r\cos\phi_r + \sin^2\theta_r \qquad (2.42d)$$

These relationships are useful only if $|E_r^2| / |E_i^2|$ can be related to R_{bd} in a meaningful way. The incident energy density is related to the energy density at the surface by the ratio of the projected area to the surface area, $\cos\theta_i$:

$$|E_s^2| = \frac{|E_i^2|}{\cos\theta_i} \qquad (2.43)$$

The reflected intensity from the surface, I_r, is related to the energy density at the viewpoint and the solid angle of the surface, ω_r, as seen from the viewpoint by:

$$I_r = \frac{|E_r^2|}{\omega_r} \qquad (2.44)$$

The approximation for the solid angle, Eq.(2.4), is used to rewrite this as:

$$I_r = \frac{|E_r^2|\,r^2}{A\cos\theta_r} \qquad (2.45)$$

The bidirectional reflectance, R_{bd} can now be expressed in terms of $|E_r^2| / |E_i^2|$ by:

$$R_{bd} = \frac{I_r}{|E_s^2|} = \frac{1}{\cos\theta_i \cos\theta_i} \frac{r^2}{A} |E_r^2| / |E_i^2| \tag{2.46}$$

Combining this with Eq.(2.41), the microfacet distribution is expressed by:

$$D = \frac{r^2}{A} |E_r^2| / |E_i^2| \tag{2.47}$$

The microfacet distribution function completes a full definition of the bidirectional reflection function in a form suitable for image generation. Once again there is a conspicuous lack of information for transmitted light. This is due to the orientation of research and verification towards reflective phenomena observed with radar and radio signals.

2.3.2.3 Computing Incoherent Illumination

Computation of incoherent illumination using the functions described in the previous section is not simple. Three relationships are provided for the microfacet distribution of the surface, Eq.(2.42). Both the mircofacet distribution and the geometric attenuation depend upon the roughness character of the surface. Additionally, the microfacet distribution and the Fresnel reflectance depend upon the wavelength. This section explores the application of the previous information to the problem of computing illumination.

Consider first, the microfacet distribution. The derivation of these functions by Beckmann (1963) uses the slope, roughness, and correlation distance (σ, m, and τ) relationship given in Eq.(2.19). Note that the mircofacet expression for very smooth surfaces ($g \ll 1$), Eq.(2.42a), is simply the first term of the series expression of Eq.(2.42b). The microfacet expression for rough surfaces ($g \gg 1$), Eq.(2.42c), was demonstrated to represent the convergence of the series expression of Eq.(2.42b). Notice also that the first two expressions include wavelength dependence which does not appear in the rough surface expression. The questions of application are:

- Which expression should be used?
- How are the transitions between expressions handled?
- How is the wavelength dependence handled?

Wavelength dependence is the easiest to accommodate. Review of the coherent and incoherent reflection show that as surface roughness increases, the coherent illumination is replaced by incoherent illumination. The inclusion of wavelength shifts the roughness at which the transition occurs. However, the net result (the energy sum of coherent and incoherent) is roughly the same. A suggested methodology is to compute the

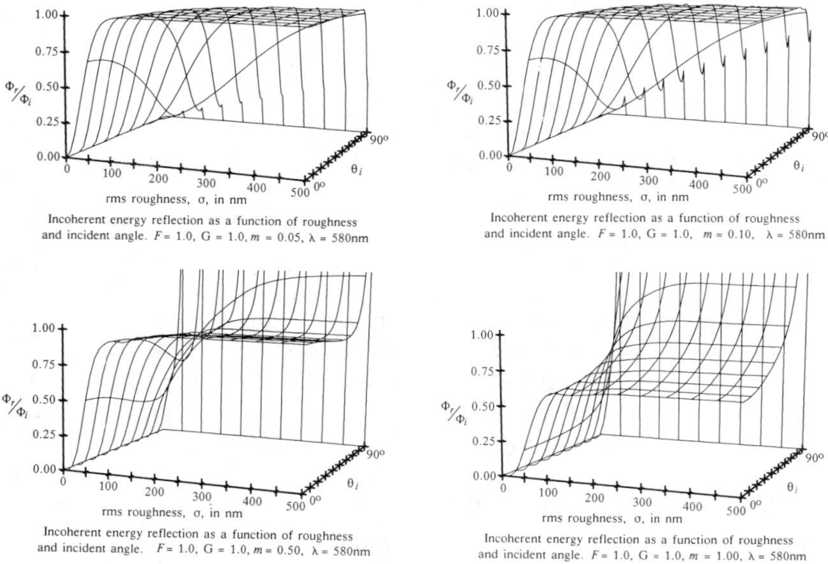

Figure 2.19: Incoherent contribution to reflected energy including microfacet distribution only (geometric attenuation and Fresnel effects are neglected).

coherent and incoherent functions for an average wavelength and apply the result to the entire spectrum.

Use of the series requires selecting a convergence criteria and summing terms until that criteria is met. Koestner (1986) suggests termination when the contribution of the next term in the series falls below 0.00001. He also suggests that the transition between the series expression, Eq.(2.42b), and the rough surface expression, Eq.(2.42c), be treated by defining a transition zone in which both expressions are evaluated and then interpolated. He suggests using the region $5<g<8$ for this transition. This implementation is demonstrated in Appendix III.4, *Microfacet Distributions*. Energy surfaces for incoherent reflection considering microfacet distribution only (neglecting geometric attenuation and Fresnel effects) are plotted in Figure .

The Fresnel term for the microfacets responsible for the reflection is calculated using the microfacet normal, **H**, and the incident direction **L**. The Fresnel term can be explicitly computed for each wavelength if sufficient material data is available, or approximations is used as demonstrated in Appendix III.5, *Fresnel Approximation*.

Two geometric attenuation functions were described in Section 2.2.7, *Geometric Attenuation*. The function described by Torrance and Sparrow has received the most attention in computer graphics and is the easier of the two to compute. However, the function described by Sancer is much better behaved and has been formulated based upon a Gaussian surface

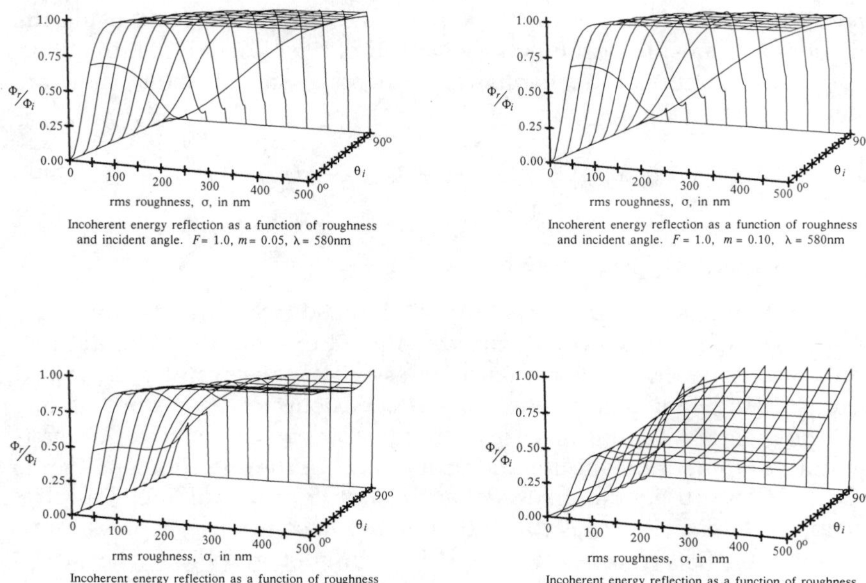

Incoherent energy reflection as a function of roughness and incident angle. $F = 1.0$, $m = 0.05$, $\lambda = 580$nm

Incoherent energy reflection as a function of roughness and incident angle. $F = 1.0$, $m = 0.10$, $\lambda = 580$nm

Incoherent energy reflection as a function of roughness and incident angle. $F = 1.0$, $m = 0.50$, $\lambda = 580$nm

Incoherent energy reflection as a function of roughness and incident angle. $F = 1.0$, $m = 1.00$, $\lambda = 580$nm

Figure 2.20: Incoherent contribution to reflected energy including microfacet distribution and geometric attenuation (Fresnel effects are neglected).

roughness. The geometric attenuation described by Sancer, Eq.(2.22), uses the slope, roughness, and correlation distance (σ, m, and τ) relationship given in Eq.(2.20). This geometric attenuation is cast in terms of the slope described for the distribution function by multiplying the c_1 and c_2 terms by 2.0. This implementation is demonstrated in Appendix III.3, *Geometric Attenuation*. Energy surfaces for incoherent reflection considering both microfacet distribution and geometric attenuation (neglecting Fresnel effects) are plotted in Figure 2.20.

2.3.2.4 Ideal Diffuse Illumination

Ideal diffuse reflection or transmission results in a reflected or transmitted intensity that is constant over the illuminated hemisphere. This is a common approximation for very rough surfaces. It is also a convenient mechanism to use to account for illumination effects that result from multiple reflection and/or transmission at a surface.

Diffuse reflectance is often referred to as directional hemispherical reflectance, R_{dh} or R_d. Directional hemispherical denotes illumination from some direction resulting in uniform reflected intensity over the illuminated hemisphere. The directional hemispherical reflectance and transmittance are constants. This means that the reflected intensity is independent of the direction of the incident energy. A better understanding of diffuse illumination results from considering an ideal diffuse surface. The energy equilibrium expression, Eq.(2.38), is applied using the directional hemispherical functions instead of the bidirectional functions. Since the directional hemispherical functions are constant, they are brought outside the integral:

$$1.0 = R_{dh}\int^{2\pi}\cos\theta_r d\omega_{front} + T_{dh}\int^{2\pi}\cos\theta_t d\omega_{back} = \pi(R_{dh}+T_{dh}) \tag{2.48}$$

2.3.3 Emissive Illumination

Emissivity refers to a surface acting as a light source. Surface emissivity is usually caused by elevated surface temperature and the resultant molecular activity. In a general sense, emissivity is the result of absorbed energy being radiated or emitted from the surface as visible light.[18] Computer graphics typically treats emitters as constant sources of energy independent of the illumination conditions of the environment. Some materials absorb light and subsequently emit light of a different spectral character. This behavior is currently ignored in computer graphics.

Lighting fixtures are often used in computer graphics. The model can treat a source as having a spectral character and a directional intensity distribution based upon the type of lighting fixture (Verbeck and Greenberg 1984). In recent work, area sources of illumination such as windows or fluorescent ceiling panels are used. These sources also have a spectral character and an associated directional distribution function. This description of a source is the emissivity, ε, and is implicitly a function of wavelength and direction.

2.3.4 A Generalized Illumination Expression

The generalized illumination model has several components. These are the coherent reflection and transmission, the bidirectional incoherent reflection and transmission, diffuse reflection and transmission, and the emissivity of the surface. These components are combined into a generalized illumination model of the form:

$$I_v = \varepsilon_v + r_\sigma G F_r I_r + t_\sigma G F_t \frac{n_v^2}{n_t^2} I_t \tag{2.49}$$

$$+\int^{2\pi} I_i R_{bd}\cos\theta_i d\omega_{front} + K_d R_d\int^{2\pi} I_i\cos\theta_i d\omega_{front}$$

$$+\int^{2\pi} I_i T_{bd}\cos\theta_i d\omega_{back} + K_d T_d\int^{2\pi} I_i\cos\theta_i d\omega_{back}$$

[18] Emissivity refers to energy leaving the surface at any wavelength. However, in computer graphics we are typically concerned only with energy in the visible spectrum.

As described earlier, in computer graphics it is traditionally assumed that the emissivity is a function that is independent of the illumination incident on the surface. It is common to completely ignore reflection and refraction for emissive surfaces.

The generalized illumination expression must meet energy equilibrium constraints if it is a valid model of surface behavior. The Fresnel relationships determine the distribution of the incident energy between the reflected energy and transmitted energy. Assuming a Fresnel reflectance of 1 allows examination of the generalized illumination expression for a surface reflecting all energy. Assuming a Fresnel reflectance of 0 allows examination of the generalized illumination expression for a surface transmitting all energy. The generalized expression for evaluating the satisfaction of energy equilibrium is:

$$1.0 = r_\sigma G F_r + t_\sigma G F_t \frac{n_v^2}{n_t^2} \tag{2.50}$$

$$+ \int^{2\pi} R_{bd} \cos\theta_r d\omega_{front} + K_d R_d \int^{2\pi} \cos\theta_r d\omega_{front}$$

$$+ \int^{2\pi} T_{bd} \cos\theta_t d\omega_{back} + K_d T_d \int^{2\pi} \cos\theta_t d\omega_{back}$$

Consider a surface that reflects all of the incident energy. The magnitudes of the coherent roughness attenuation and of bidirectional incoherent are fixed by the geometry of the surface finish and by the wavelength of the illumination. Any energy unaccounted for by these is attributed to diffuse reflection.

The numerical integration of the incoherent functions suggested by rigorous theoretical analysis demonstrates that all the incident energy is not accounted for. This is particularly true when geometric attenuation is included. Geometric attenuation is a measure of self shading. If the reflected ray is blocked by the geometry of the surface, then multiple reflections have occurred. The theoretical solutions ignore multiple reflections, so another mechanism must account for this.

The reflected energy surfaces for coherent and incoherent illumination, Figures 2.16 and 2.20, are summed to create a surface that describes the energy accounted for by these mechanisms, Figure 2.21. The disparity between the sum of the coherent and incoherent energy and energy equilibrium can be attributed to ideal diffuse reflection. The diffuse energy surfaces that provide equilibrium are given in Figure 2.22.

The surface represents the value of the diffuse coefficient K_d that is required to meet energy equilibrium requirements. There are several important observations to be made:

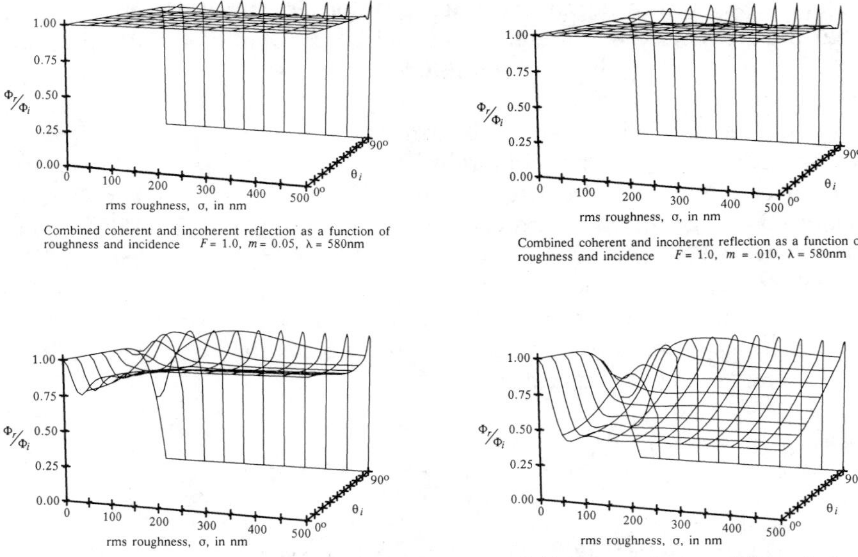

Figure 2.21: Summed reflected coherent and incoherent energy contribution.

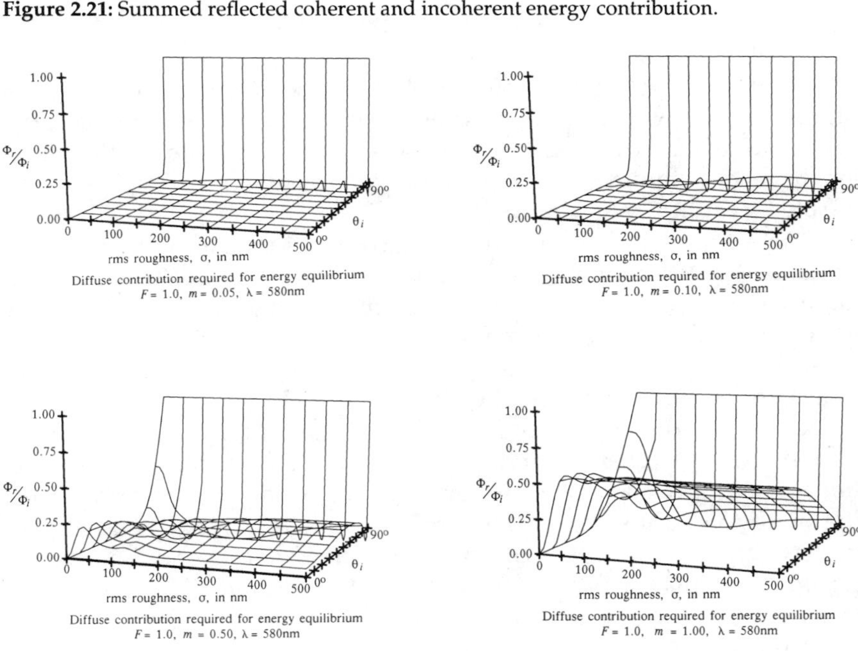

Figure 2.22: Diffuse energy surfaces for energy equilibrium.

- The theoretical model for incoherent scattering breaks down as the rms slope of the roughness function increases and the incident angle approaches grazing. The theoretical model predicts greater reflected energy than incident energy.
- For a given set of surface roughness parameters m, τ, and σ, the magnitude of the diffuse coefficient required for energy equilibrium is not constant.
- To produce energy equilibrium with the coherent and directional incoherent reflection functions, a negative diffuse coefficient is sometimes required.

The characterization of the behavior of light at a surface boundary is not simple. This chapter has collected and presented various components that help predict the behavior. Additional work in characterizing transmissive behavior is sorely needed. It is also apparent that there are irregularities near grazing incidence which require additional attention.

3

Perceptual Response

"Our goal in realistic image synthesis is to generate an image that evokes from the visual perception system a response that is indistinguishable from that evoked by the original environment."
- Hall and Greenberg (1983b)

The visual system detects, assimilates, and interprets information about our surroundings. The perceptual mechanisms are very complex. The detection apparatus is the eye, which selectively detects different *colors* of light. Two eyes placed at different locations provide two geometries interpretation, thus allowing the visual system to interpret depth relationships. Image processing in the mechanism enhances edges, motion, color patterns, and spatial textures.

Image generation and presentation provides an alternate to the rich stimulation provided by the world that surrounds us. Current image presentation techniques can only reproduce a small subset of the stimuli that are available in real environments. If we are to attempt realistic representation in imagery, it is necessary to relate the perceptual processing of visual information to the image display technology.

This chapter discusses color perception and its relationship to both color computation and color reproduction. Computer graphics has tacitly assumed that the RGB color space of a monitor is the appropriate space for color definition and for color computation. It is demonstrated here that the RGB color space suffers from a lack of standard definition and is different between monitors or between different calibration of the same monitor. It is also demonstrated that the RGB color space is not meaningful as a computational space and suggests alternates that produce more meaningful results. A separate chapter has been devoted to practical application of this information for display.

3.1 Describing Color

Color is qualitatively described using the terms hue, saturation (also referred to as chroma), and value (also referred to as brightness or intensity). These terms characterize a natural color organizing tendency. A natural first ordering is to group like colors such as "red", "blue", and "yellow". This ordering by hue, that is, it associates the color with a position in the spectrum.

Within each hue colors are then ordered by brightness and saturation. The brightness is the range from black to white. At a given bright-

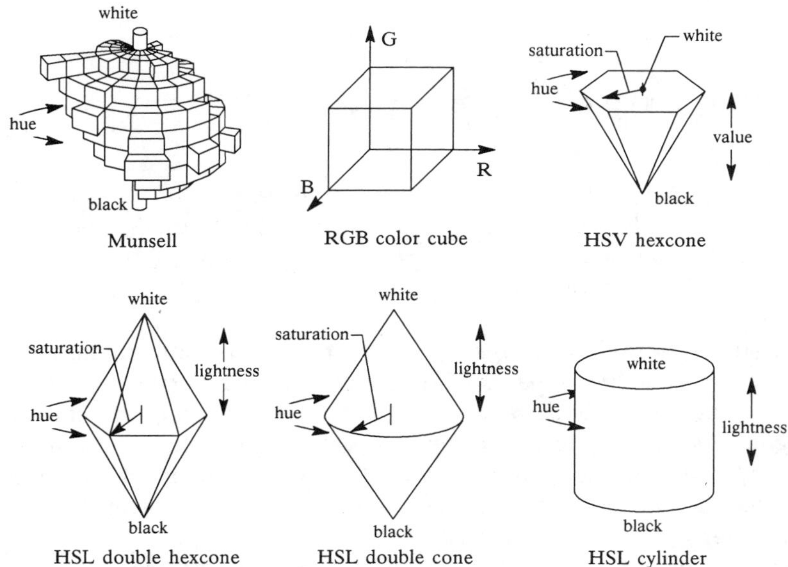

Figure 3.1: A summary of color representations.

ness, the color ranges from neutral to a very pure color. The very pure color is called a saturated color while the neutral color is desaturated. This ordering schema is described by Meyer (1983.) A rigorous definition of color description terminology is found in (Hunt 1977,1978).

The Munsell color system conceptualizes this classification scheme using a neutral value axis from black to white, with saturation represented by the distance from the neutral axis, and hue as the radial position, Figure 3.1.

A variety of conceptual color representations common in computer graphics are related to the red, green, and blue color primaries of video display monitors. Some of the more common representations shown in Figure 3.1 are:

RGB color cube
: This represents the red, green, and blue monitor primaries as orthogonal axis. The colors that are displayable on a monitor are within the cube from (0,0,0) to (1,1,1). The neutral axis is a line from the black point to the white point.

HSV hexcone
: The HSV (hue, saturation, and value) hexcone uses a neutral axis from black to white. At the white point is a hexagon with vertices representing the colors at the vertices of the color cube. This representation was proposed by Smith (1978).

HSL double hexcone

The HSL (hue, saturation, and lightness) double hexcone is a similar representation to the HSV hexcone with the exception that the full colors are represented with a value of 0.5 instead of being equal in value to white. This representation is detailed in (Rogers 1985).

HSL double cone

The HSL double cone presented by Joblove and Greenberg (1978) is very similar to the double hexcone model, except that the cross section is circular.

HSL cylinder

The HSL cylinder, also presented by Joblove and Greenberg (1978), expands the base and top of the double cone into a black and white circles respectively.

These color representations used in computer graphics are closely tied to the color reproduction device or to artistic color selection. The color cube is a "natural" coordinate system in the sense that the three color components are mapped into an orthogonal coordinate system in the same fashion as 3 dimensional geometry. The other representations are intended for ease of color selection. Colors are quickly selected by picking the hue from a section through the color space perpendicular to the neutral axis, and then picking the saturation and intensity from a slice though the solid parallel to the neutral axis and at the selected hue. None of these representations are terribly useful for realistic image synthesis.

3.2 Colorimetry

Colorimetry is a perceptual science; that is, it studies and attempts to quantify how the human visual system perceives color. This study of perception has resulted in an empirically and statistically derived system of standards that can be applied to computer graphics with desirable and predictable results.

The human visual system responds to a very limited portion of the electromagnetic spectrum. When we discuss light, we are generally referring to electromagnetic radiation from 380nm to 770nm. The observed color of light is a result of the mix of intensities at different wavelengths that make up the light that reaches our eyes.

Imagine an experimental setup where a test light can shine on one half of a viewer's field and a set of control lights shine on the other half, Figure 3.2. The control lights are sources at 1nm wavelength increments throughout the visible spectrum with an intensity control for each source. When a test light is shown on half the field, the viewer matches the color of the test field by adjusting the intensities of the control lights illuminating the other half of the field. This is an idealization of the

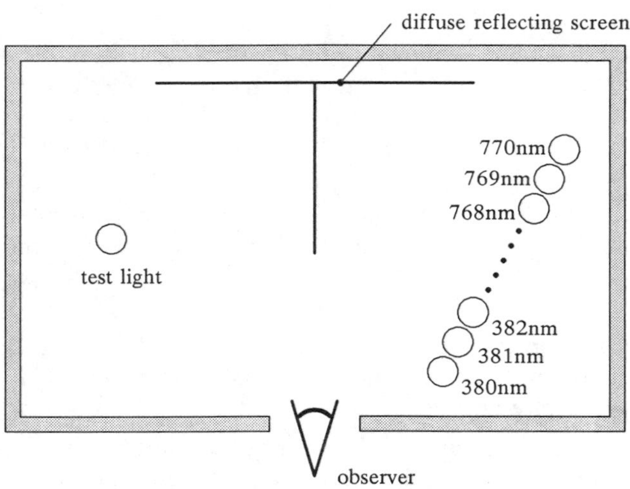

Figure 3.2: Color matching with control sources at 1nm increments.

types of color matching experiments that were performed in colorimetry research.

For most colors, there are limitless different combinations of control source intensities that provide a match. This leads to speculation that the visual system does not have a receptor for each wavelength. Studies of the eye observe three types of color receptors called cones. By selectively exciting the types of cones it is possible to produce any color sensation. With three correctly selected control lights in the short, medium, and long wavelength range most test colors can be matched. Cornsweet (1970) presents a detailed discussion of these physiological aspects of color perception.

Matching a test color with some combination of intensities of three control lights is useful if the required intensities can be predicted given the spectral curve of the test color. The graph of intensity as a function of wavelength is the spectral curve for the test color. The test color sensation is a summation of sensations produced by the intensity of the test color at every wavelength in the visible range. If the same summation of visual sensation is produced by some combination of the control light intensities, there is an observed color match. Note that it is the matching of sensations that is the concern, not attempting to match the spectral curves.

Suppose the intensity of each control light required to match any wavelength is known. The color sensation produced by a mix of wavelengths can be matched by summing the control light intensities required to match each of the individual wavelengths. The *matching curves* for a set of control lights are plots of the intensities of the control lights required to match any wavelength as a function of wavelength. Predicting

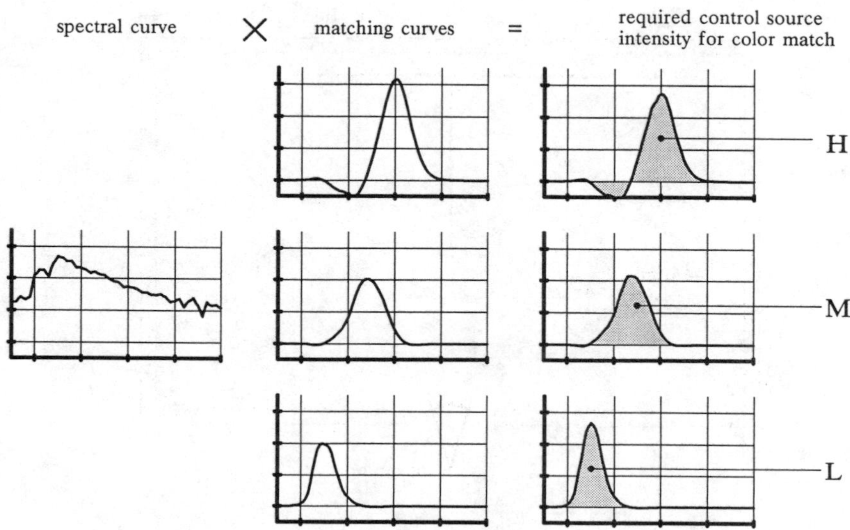

Figure 3.3: Schematic for determining control light intensities given the test color spectral curve and the matching functions

the intensities of the three control colors required to match a test color is a matter of multiplying the spectral curve of the test color by the matching curves and then integrating the three resulting curves, Figure 3.3.

The matching curves are determined experimentally.[1] Three control lights are chosen. The only constraint is that no control source can be matched by some combination of the other two. Consider the use of control lights at 445nm, 535nm, and 630nm.[2] Pure spectral lines are matched to generate the matching curves. The only lines that can be matched exactly are those of the control lights. The observer can match the hue of the other spectral lines, but not the saturation. The test lights can be matched in hue by a combination of two of the control lights, but the observer needs to subtract some of the third control light color in order to match saturation. Obviously, color cannot be subtracted from the control side, however, adding some of the third control color to the test side will produce the same result. The color matching experiment is now configured with control lights on both the control side and the test light side as shown in Figure 3.4. The results of this experiment are shown in Figure 3.5.

---

[1] This discussion is intended only to familiarize the reader with concepts used later in the chapter. It should be considered no more than a brief overview. Refer to Judd and Wyszecki (1975) for a detailed discussion of the color matching experiment.

[2] These values are arbitrarily selected to be in the low, medium, and high wavelength regions of the visible range. They are not selected to represent the results of a specific matching experiment, they were selected to demonstrate the principle.

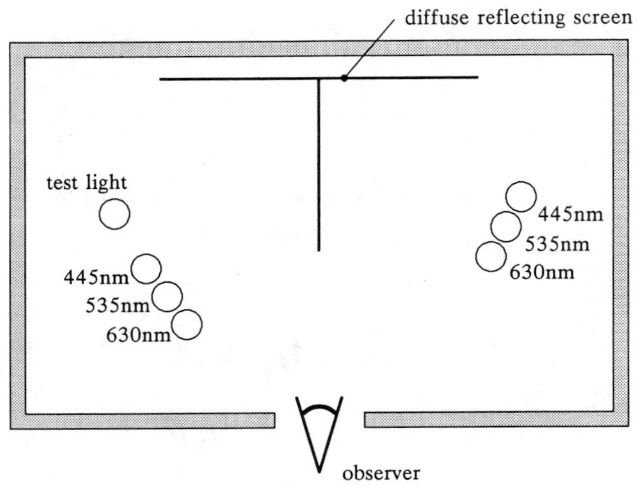

Figure 3.4: Color matching with 3 control sources.

A chromaticity diagram is a commonly used representation created by a 2-D projection of the 3-space plot of these values. Each orthogonal axis represents one of the control sources, L (low wavelength, blue), M (medium wavelength, green), and H (high wavelength, red). For each wavelength the vector LMH is plotted and extended until it intersects the plane $L + M + H = 1$. The coordinates of this intersection, LMH′ are found by dividing each of L, M, and H by the sum $L + M + H$, Figure 3.6. The curve defined by the intersection points of the vectors and the plane is then projected into 2D by looking down the –L axis, Figure 3.7.

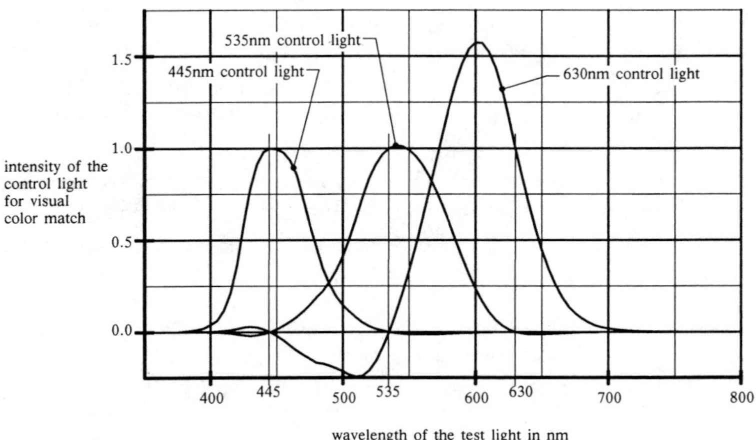

Figure 3.5: Graph of the matching curves for 445nm, 535nm, and 630nm control sources.

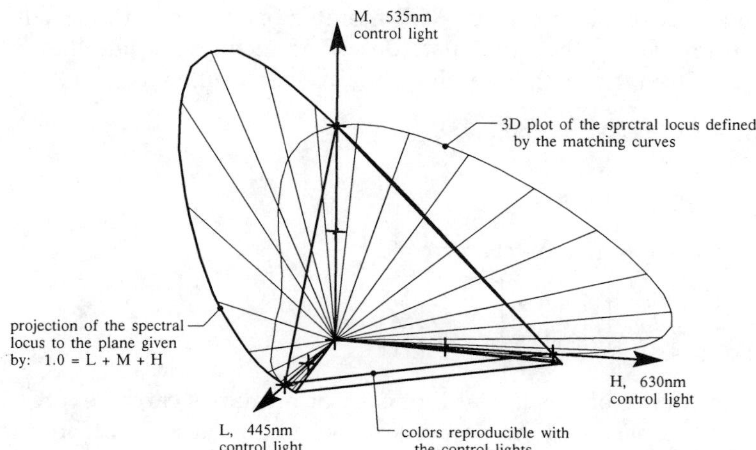

Figure 3.6: Projection of the chromaticity diagram.

The triangle created by intersections of the three axis and the plane describes all of the colors that can be reproduced by the three primaries. The intensity of the color is not represented in this projection. The curve describes the pure spectral colors. All of the visible colors are represented by the interior of the curve. The chromaticity of a color is its position on this plot. The chromaticity describes hue and saturation.

Fortunately, these experiments have already been performed and it is possible to apply the results to any set of primaries used for color re-

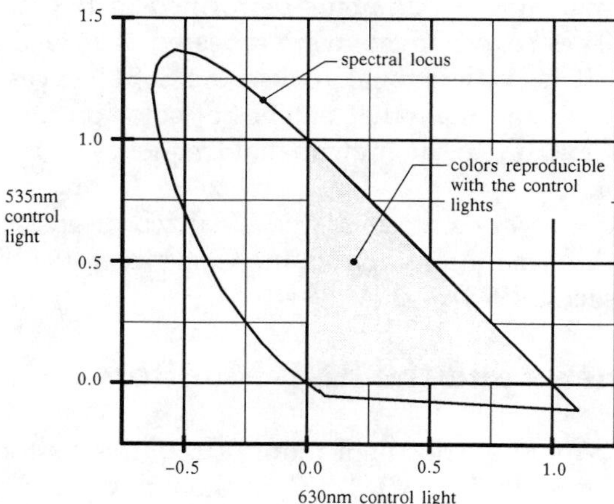

Figure 3.7: Chromaticity diagram for 445nm, 535nm, and 630nm control sources.

production. Consider a set of RGB monitor primaries with known spectral curves. Using the previously described technique, the intensities of LHM required to match each phosphor are determined as:

$$\begin{aligned} R &= aL + bM + cH \\ G &= dL + eM + fH \\ B &= gL + hM + iH \end{aligned}$$

Which are written in matrix form as:

$$\begin{bmatrix} R \\ G \\ B \end{bmatrix} = \begin{bmatrix} a & b & c \\ d & e & f \\ g & h & i \end{bmatrix} \begin{bmatrix} L \\ M \\ H \end{bmatrix} = \begin{bmatrix} & & \\ & T & \\ & & \end{bmatrix} \begin{bmatrix} L \\ M \\ H \end{bmatrix} \tag{3.1}$$

The significance of this is that if one set of primaries can be expressed in terms of another, then the transformations $[T]$ into the first from the second, and $[T]^{-1}$ out of the first to the second, are easily defined. Specifically, if the chromaticities of a monitor are known relative to some standard, then the transformations to and from the standard can be determined. In addition, if the chromaticities of a second color monitor are known, then the transformation between monitors are easily determined.

The CIE (Commission Internationale d'Eclairage) set up a standard hypothetical primary set, XYZ, that results in all visible colors being in the positive octant, in the integration of matching functions being equal, and in the Y function matching the intensity sensitivity function (luminous efficiency function). Figures 3.8 and 3.9 display the CIEXYZ matching curves and the CIEXYZ chromaticity diagram. The implication of equal area matching functions is that a flat spectral curve (equal intensity at all wavelengths) is represented by equal XYZ values. The values for the CIEXYZ tristimulus matching functions are found in (Judd and Wyszecki 1975) and are included in Appendix III.7, *Color Transformations*.

The color matching experiments performed in 1931 used a 2 degree field of view. These experiments were repeated in 1964 with a 10 degree field of view. It is conventional to use the 1931 curves for computer graphics under the rationale that patches of color on the screen cover a small field of view due to the high spatial frequency of most realistic imagery.

This has been a very simplified and idealized discussion of colorimetry. In-depth information is found in (Cornsweet 1970), (Hunt 1975), (Judd and Wyszecki 1975) and (Meyer 1983).

3.3 Colorimetry and the RGB Monitor

Proper display of a color on a monitor requires first knowing either the spectral curve or the CIEXYZ chromaticity of the color to be displayed. Additionally, the transformation from CIEXYZ to the RGB primaries of the monitor must be known. The spectral curve of the color

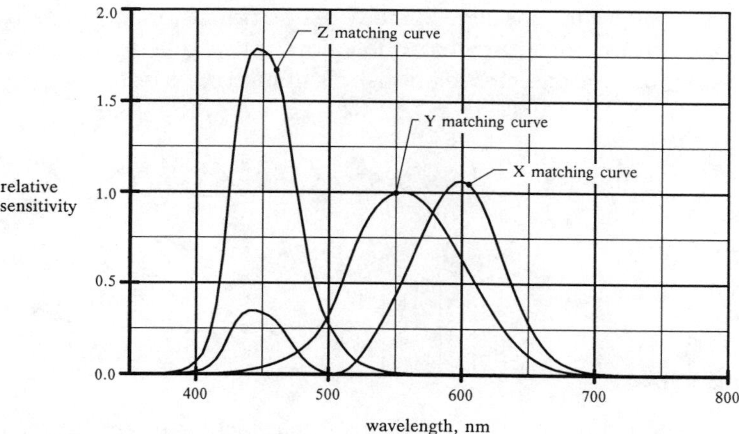

Figure 3.8: CIEXYZ matching curves.

is sampled into CIEXYZ by multiplying the curve by the CIEXYZ tristimulus matching functions and integrating the resulting curves. The CIEXYZ color is then transformed into the RGB values for display.

Alternately, the CIEXYZ matching functions are transformed into the monitor color space. These curves are then used to sample the spectral curve directly into RGB values for display.

The CIEXYZ to RGB matrix is generated using chromaticity data for the monitor phosphors. This can usually be obtained from the monitor manufacturer, otherwise, the chromaticities can be measured using an

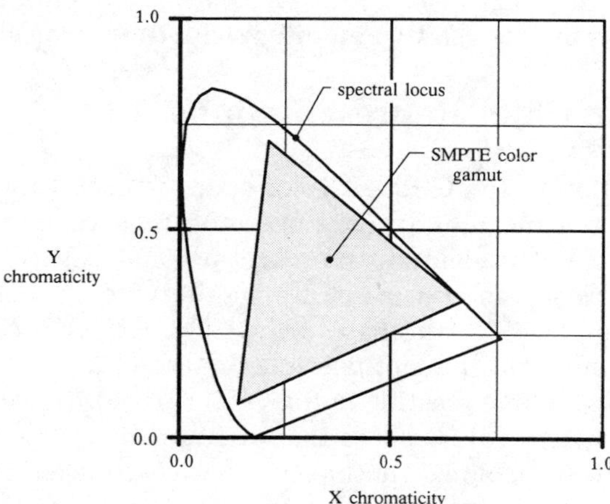

Figure 3.9: CIEXYZ chromaticity diagram.

incident light chromaticity meter. The transformation matrix is generated from the monitor phosphors and the white point by expressing the chromaticity relationships in matrix form:

red phosphor:	r_x	r_y	$r_z{=}1{-}r_x{-}r_y$
green phosphor:	g_x	g_y	$g_z{=}1{-}g_x{-}g_y$
blue phosphor:	w_x	w_y	$b_z{=}1{-}b_x{-}b_y$
white point:	w_x	w_y	$w_z{=}1{-}w_x{-}w_y$

$$\begin{bmatrix} X \\ Y \\ Z \end{bmatrix} = \begin{bmatrix} S_r(r_x) & S_g(g_x) & S_b(b_x) \\ S_r(r_y) & S_g(g_y) & S_b(b_y) \\ S_r(r_z) & S_g(g_z) & S_b(b_z) \end{bmatrix} \begin{bmatrix} R \\ G \\ B \end{bmatrix} \tag{3.2}$$

In this relationship, S_r, S_g, and S_b are scale factors for red, green, and blue, that set the correct white point for the transformation. Select RGB and XYZ values corresponding to the white point and then solve for S_r, S_g, and S_b. The transformations are typically normalized so that Y for the white point is 1. The RGB white point is (1,1,1); and the XYZ white point is $(w_x/w_y, 1, w_z/w_y)$. Refer to Appendix III.7, *Color Transformations*, for details of generating this matrix for a set of monitor primaries.

The transformations between RGB and CIEXYZ matrices are also required to generate the transformation between RGB monitors with different primary chromaticities and/or different white points. The transformation for image data from RGB for the first monitor to R′G′B′ for the second monitor is expressed as:

$$\begin{bmatrix} \text{R'G'B'} \\ \text{to} \\ \text{XYZ} \end{bmatrix}^{-1} \begin{bmatrix} \text{RGB} \\ \text{to} \\ \text{XYZ} \end{bmatrix} \begin{bmatrix} R \\ G \\ B \end{bmatrix} = \begin{bmatrix} R' \\ G' \\ B' \end{bmatrix} \tag{3.3}$$

Refer to Appendix III.7, *Color Transformations*, for details of generating this transformation between two monitors with dissimilar phosphors.

3.4 Alternate Color Representations

Color specification in the CIEXYZ color space is useful for color reproduction, but is not meaningful for evaluating relative changes in color. Often times it is not possible to represent a color exactly. A means of evaluating the closeness of a match by an alternate color is required to aid in selecting the best alternate color. The CIEXYZ color space is perceptually nonlinear. It is not possible to predict the perceptual closeness of colors by relative position in the CIEXYZ color space.

There are several color spaces that attempt to represent colors in a perceptually linear fashion. These color spaces are used for color comparison. Each of these is a triaxial color space in which the perceptual distance between colors is proportional to the geometric distance between colors. The transformations into these spaces are nonlinear. Judd and Wyszecki (1975) provide a detailed historical development of uniform color scales.

Two uniform color spaces are reviewed here. The first is $L^*a^*b^*$ which is based upon a third order approximation of the Munsell notation system. The second is $L^*u^*v^*$ which is evolved from the CIE 1964($U^*V^*W^*$). The CIE 1964($U^*V^*W^*$) was an attempt to create a standard uniform color space. The transformation from XYZ to $L^*a^*b^*$ is given by:

$$L^* = 25\left(\frac{100Y}{Y_o}\right)^{1/3} - 16\,; \qquad (1 \le Y \le 100) \tag{3.4}$$

$$a^* = 500\left[\left(\frac{X}{X_o}\right)^{1/3} - \left(\frac{Y}{Y_o}\right)^{1/3}\right]$$

$$b^* = 200\left[\left(\frac{Y}{Y_o}\right)^{1/3} - \left(\frac{Z}{Z_o}\right)^{1/3}\right]$$

The transformation from XYZ to $L^*u^*v^*$ is given by:

$$L^* = 25\left(\frac{100Y}{Y_o}\right)^{1/3} - 16\,; \qquad (1 \le Y \le 100) \tag{3.5}$$

$$u^* = 13L^*(u' - u'_o)$$

$$v^* = 13L^*(v' - v'_o)$$

where

$$u' = \frac{4X}{X+15Y+3Z} \qquad v' = \frac{9Y}{X+15Y+3Z}$$

$$u'_o = \frac{4X_o}{X_o+15Y_o+3Z_o} \qquad v'_o = \frac{9Y_o}{X_o+15Y_o+3Z_o}$$

$X_oY_oZ_o$ define the color of the nominally white color, or the white point of the monitor. These transformations are detailed in Appendix III.7, *Color Transformations.* Figure 3.10 shows the RGB color cube transformed into both the $L^*a^*b^*$ and $L^*u^*v^*$ color spaces. The RGB color cube used is based upon the NTSC standards described in Section 5.1.1, *Color Correction for Display*.

3.5 Color Spaces for Color Computation

The common practice of computing colors using RGB values leads to gross errors when complex illumination models are used. There has

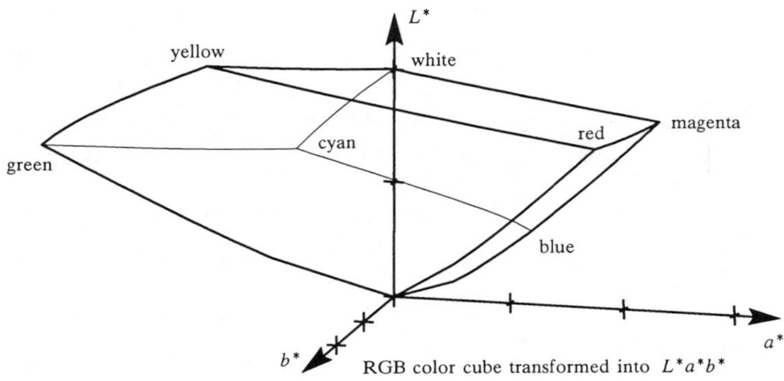

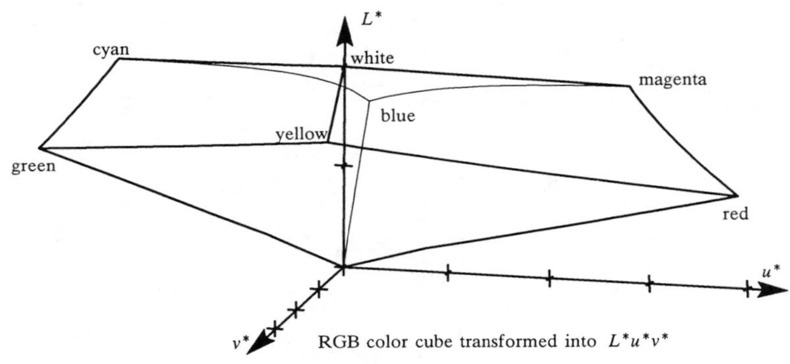

Figure 3.10: RGB color cube mapped into $L^*a^*b^*$ and $L^*u^*v^*$.

been a great deal of attention given to illumination models and color reproduction in computer graphics. Accurate illumination models and color calibrated equipment will not produce realistic images unless accurate material and light source data is supplied to the illumination model, and the computation method does not distort this data. This section establishes the source of the computational errors introduced by RGB computations and explores techniques to reduce the error.

3.5.1 Color Computation in RGB

Illumination models are generally expressed without specific reference to the wavelength of the light used. The implicit assumption is that the calculation is repeated for every wavelength. The general interpretation is repetition of the color calculation using red, green, and blue color values for materials and lights.

Several potential causes for error in computing colors using RGB values can be identified:

- Information is lost when the spectral curves are sampled and represented by only 3 values.
- The RGB sampling functions are not selected on the basis of sampling theory, but determined by perceptual criteria. The perceptual criteria consider color reproduction, not color computation requirements.
- The RGB sampling functions are specific to the RGB primaries used. Computations in different RGB color spaces may not produce the same result (after color space compensation).

The RGB color space is an obvious choice for color computation. Colors are often selected using a palette displayed on an RGB monitor. The user simply selects the colors for materials and lights based on an aesthetic judgement instead of using measured material and light source spectral curves. As a result, materials and lights are often expressed in terms of the RGB of the monitor used for selection.

Current trends towards realism emphasize the use of measured material and light source properties. The concerns of computation in RGB are demonstrated by a trivial example. Consider light reflected from a perfect mirror. The reflectance curve for the mirror has a value of 1 at every wavelength. If this curve is sampled using the CIEXYZ tristimulus matching functions[3] the resulting XYZ values are (106.85,106.86,106.93).[4] Transforming this to RGB based upon a monitor matching NTSC standards, the RGB value is (119.85,102.15,98.01). Clearly, RGB values of (1,1,1) are required for the material to behave as a perfect mirror in RGB computations.

Scaling can be incorporated in the sampling without effecting the sampled chromaticity. For example, the CIEXYZ curves can be scaled by normalizing the area under the Y curve. This results in an XYZ value of (1,1,1) and an RGB value of (1.12,0.96,0.92). Clearly, this is still not an identity material for RGB color computation.

Suggested solutions to this dilemma include using the CIEXYZ space for computation; shifting the white point of the monitor so the mirror spectral curve is sampled to an RGB of (1,1,1); and, normalization of the RGB sampling functions to have equal area (which shifts the chromaticity of the sampled value). The basis of the problem is performing wavelength based computations after colors have been translated out of the wavelength domain into a perceptual domain.

---

[3] As noted earlier, curves for the 1931 standard colorimetric observer are used. These curves are for a 2 degree field of view.

[4] The CIEXYZ primaries were established so that the area under the matching functions is identical. This slight variation can be attributed to error in function interpolation and numerical integration.

3.5.2 Spectral Sampling Approaches

Alternate color computation methods recommend computation based on the spectral curves prior to the transformation into a perceptual space (Hall 1983a,1983b,1987)[5] (Meyer 1988). These methods effectively low pass filter and/or point sample each spectral curve to generate a set of sample values for computation. After computations are complete, a spectral curve is reconstructed from the computed point samples. The resulting reconstructed curve is then sampled into CIEXYZ or RGB for storage and display. The key element is the completion of color computations prior to sampling into the perceptual color space for display.

Hall suggested box sampling and reconstruction functions. The number and position of these samples was determined by a brute force search. A number of material and light source curves were selected and an interactive search performed adjusting the sample locations until the error is minimized.[6] The difference in the $L^*u^*v^*$ uniform color space between the original curve and the sampled then reconstructed curve was used as the error metric. This was an ad hoc attempt to begin addressing the problem, and to establish the methodology for separating perceptual sampling from the color computation. It was never suggested, however, that this approach was a good solution.

The details of this technique are clarified by considering the sampling and reconstruction functions shown in Figure 3.11. The boundaries of the sampling functions are denoted as $\lambda_{n,s}$ and $\lambda_{n,e}$ for the start and end of the sample n. The functions used do not overlap nor are there any unsampled regions between sample functions. Each sample function has an area of 1. The reconstruction functions share the same bounds as the sampling functions and have a height of 1. The only exception is the first and last reconstruction function which continue with a value of 1 beyond the limits of the visible spectrum. Flat spectral curves, such as a perfect mirror, are sampled and reconstructed exactly by these functions.

The need for this type of approach was demonstrated in images of a simple test environment consisting of two blocks of a filter material on a white base, Figure 3.12. The two filter materials have very sharp cutoff frequencies. The spectral curve of the light that passes through the first filter is found by multiplying the spectral curve of the light by the spectral curve of the filter. This is then multiplied by the spectral curve of the second filter to determine the color where the filters overlap. Note that

[5] This work was instigated by a series of lengthy debates with Meyer about the proper methodology for color computation and the need to defer perceptual considerations until display.

[6] The search technique started with equally spaced samples in the visible range. The sample locations were iteratively shifted to reduce perceptual error until a local minimum was found. While it seemed like a good idea at the time, I would not suggest this approach as an optimum solution.

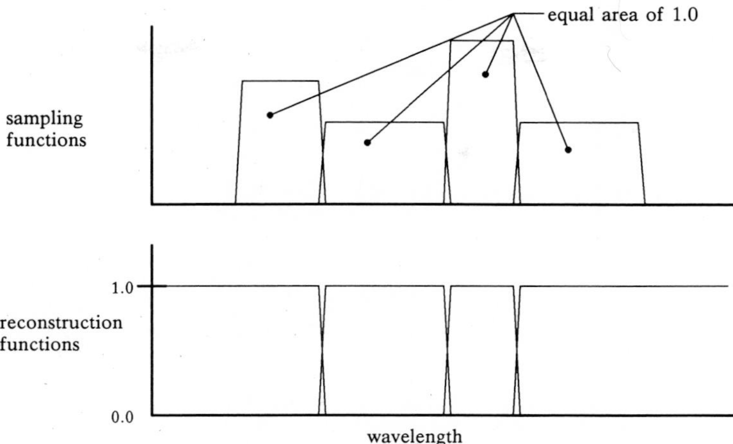

Figure 3.11: Box sampling and reconstruction Functions for 4 spectral samples.

there are no overlapping nonzero values in the curves of the two filter materials. Thus, the overlap area should be black. Figure 3.13 shows the results of computation performed in the RGB color space, in the CIEXYZ color space, using 9 sample points, and at 1nm increments. The 1nm increment image is correct (within the limits of the illumination model). Note the incorrect colors in images computed in RGB and CIEXYZ.

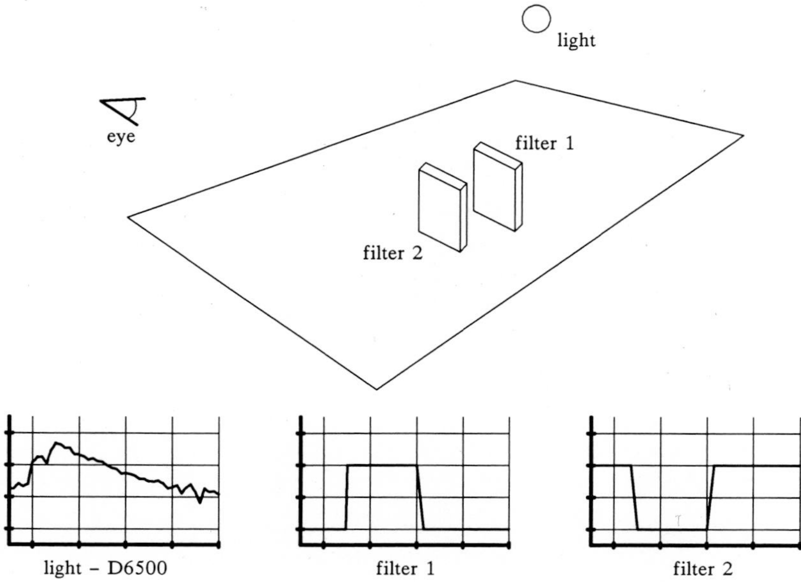

Figure 3.12: Environment to test color computation techniques.

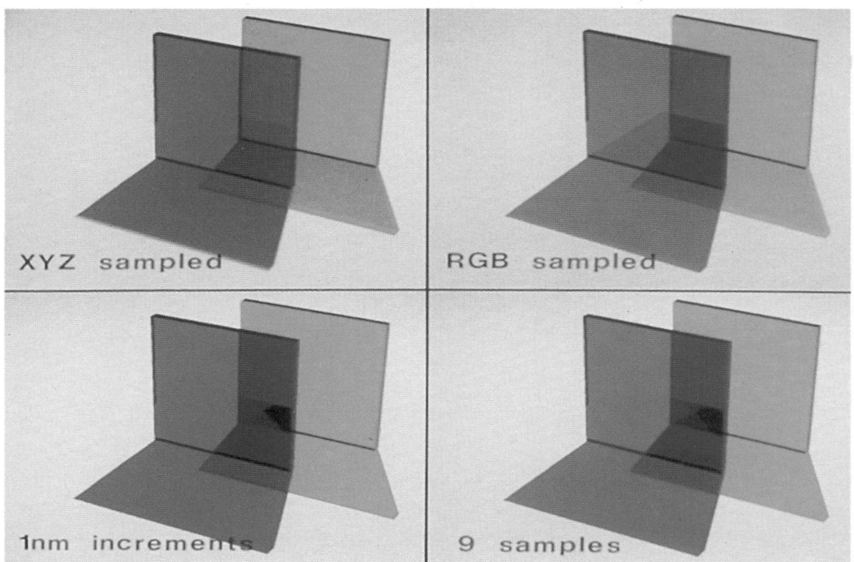

Figure 3.13: Comparative image showing the results of color computation techniques.

Meyer (1988) presents a technique that takes advantage of the observation that most spectral curves can be approximated by low order polynomials, coupled with an specially defined color space and Gaussian quadrature, to determine the appropriate sampling. In this technique point samples are used at selected wavelengths. The Gaussian quadrature techniques numerically integrate the low order polynomials that pass through the computed sample points resulting in the color coordinates of the reconstructed spectral curve.

Ultimately the color space representation is determined by multiplying the spectral curve by sampling functions and then integrating the resulting curve. Gaussian quadrature techniques perform the integration of a curve over some by sampling the curve at prescribed locations and applying some weighting function to the sampled value. For example, with 3 sample points at the correct locations within an interval the exact integral of any 3rd degree polynomial that passes through those points is computed.

Meyer examines the sensitivity of the visual system and derives a set of color axes that *"pass through the regions where the tristimulus values are most likely to occur"*. He calls this coordinate system the AC_1C_2 space. The AC_1C_2 space is related to CIEXYZ by:

$$\begin{bmatrix} A \\ C_1 \\ C_2 \end{bmatrix} = \begin{bmatrix} -0.0177 & 1.0090 & 0.0073 \\ -1.5370 & 1.0821 & 0.3209 \\ 0.1946 & -0.2045 & 0.5264 \end{bmatrix} \begin{bmatrix} X \\ Y \\ Z \end{bmatrix} \tag{3.6}$$

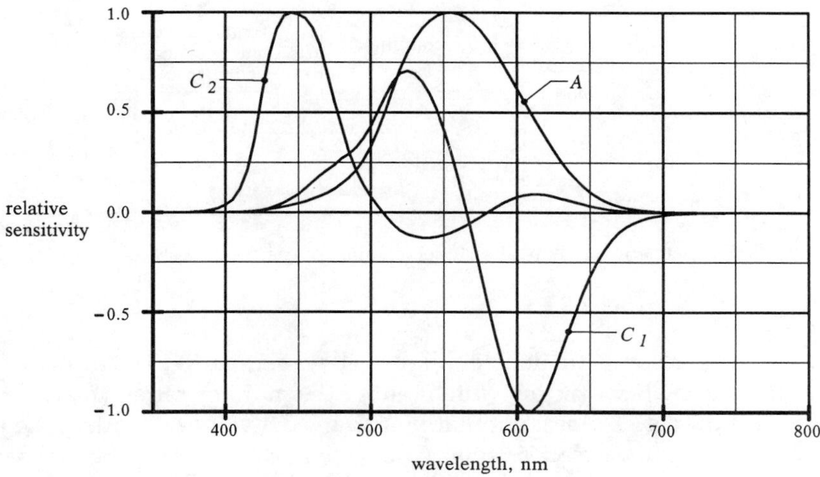

Figure 3.14: Sampling curves for AC_1C_2 space.

Meyer examined a number of different samplings to determine an optimum Gaussian quadrature of AC_1C_2 for the purpose of image synthesis. The number of samples used ranged from 4 to 29 and integration orders from 1 to 10. After evaluation of the results he determined that a 4 sample approach that combined Gauss points from a 6 point sampling provided good results for image generation. The sampling curves for the AC_1C_2 space are given in Figure 3.14. A subjective comparison study of generated images of a Macbeth ColorChecker™ chart and real Macbeth ColorChecker™ chart was performed to confirm that this technique resulted in a better color match than other techniques.

This approach to color computation may sound complicated, however, its use is very straightforward, Figure 3.15. A sampling subroutine reduces each spectral curve to a number of sample values. The illumination model computations are repeated for the number of samples instead of the typical RGB repetition. The spectral curve for the computed color is reconstructed and the reconstructed curve is sampled into RGB or CIEXYZ for display or storage; or, the samples are transformed directly to the RGB or CIEXYZ color space for image display and/or storage. The implementation of this procedure is detailed in Appendix III.8, *Spectral Sampling*.

3.5.3 Sources of Confusion

The use of color descriptions other than RGB are often very confusing to users. The source of the confusion is readily apparent. Consider the case where colors are selected by RGB value as opposed to spectral curve. It is natural to think of an RGB material color of (1,1,1) as a perfect reflector. The reflected light from this material is naturally expected to

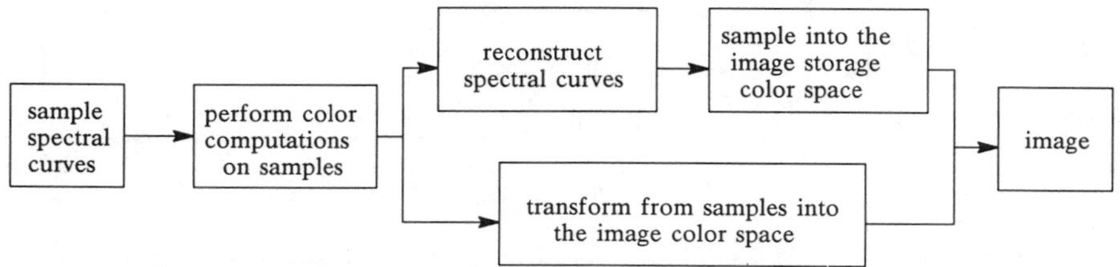

Figure 3.15: Schematic describing the implementation of spectral sampling.

be the same color as the incident light. However, an RGB color of (1,1,1) has the chromaticity of the white point of the monitor rather than that of a perfect mirror. Color computation using RGB values produces the expected, though incorrect results. Conversely, the use of a spectral sampling will produce more correct results, but they are not what is expected.

Chromatic Adaptation adds to the confusion. In the context of computer graphics this means that a user sitting in front of a monitor will adjust his/her perception of white to be consistent with the monitor. While white may be markedly different between two monitors, the user will still think of the RGB color of (1,1,1) as white.

The confusion can be traced to the method of color specification. When users are specifying all colors in terms of RGB, then RGB color computation may be most appropriate. When the intent is faithful color rendition of real lights and materials, then spectral curves and spectral sampling techniques must be used. The option to mix both spectral curves and RGB for source and material specification should be avoided because of the confusion that results. If mixing spectral curves and RGB values is an option, then the users must be educated about the computational techniques used.

4

Illumination Models

"Unfortunately, the price of increased realism is a huge increase in computation costs"
- Turner Whitted (1982)

The application of research in physics and optics to computer graphics constitutes an evolution governed by the current visible surface algorithms, by what is considered computationally reasonable, and by the level of realism that is acceptable. The illumination models used in practice differ greatly from the theoretical treatment of Chapter 2. The illumination models used fall into three general classifications: empirical, transitional, and analytical. The shading techniques that evolved with these models fall into three corresponding classifications: incremental, ray tracing, and radiosity methods, Table 4.1. In addition, a hybrid classification has recently emerged that combines the radiosity and ray tracing approaches.

Early illumination models were empirical in nature. They were evaluated after the geometry was transformed into the perspective space (screen space) used for visible surface computation. The same incremental techniques used to exploit scanline coherence in visible surface determination were also applied to the illumination computations. These models and application techniques were an adjunct development to scanline visible surface algorithms (Bouknight 1970), (Warnock 1969), (Gouraud 1971), and (Phong 1975).

Transitional models use prior work in physics and optics to improve the earlier empirical models. Texture mapping (Catmull 1975) and (Blinn and Newell 1976), reflection mapping (Blinn and Newell 1976), and recursive ray tracing (Whitted 1980) demonstrate an increasing concern for color, shading, and visual detail in imagery supported by the increasing computational power of the hardware. These illumination models require the use of the Euclidean geometry (object space geometry) prior to perspective transformation so that reflections, refractions, and shadows are geometrically correct. Initially ray tracing was restricted to very smooth reflective surfaces. Cone tracing and distributed ray tracing attempt to extend the ray tracing methodology to include diffuse environments (Cook, et al. 1984), (Amanatides 1984), and (Kajiya 1986).

Rendering Technique	Reference	Shading and Illumination Additions	Figure
Perspective (screen space) geometry: scanline techniques, incremental updating empirical illumination	(Bouknight 1970)	Constant color across polygons	4.29
	(Warnock 1969) (Romney 1970)	Distance attenuation, primitive highlights	
	(Gouraud 1971)	Color interpolation across polygons	4.30
	(Newell, et al. 1972)	Pseudo transparency	
	(Phong 1975) (Duff 1979) (Bishop and Weimer 1986)	Normal interpolation across polygons, refined highlights	4.31
Euclidean (object space) Geometry: ray tracing, empirical and theoretical illumination models	(Catmull 1975) (Blinn and Newell 1976)	Texture mapping, reflection mapping	4.32
	(Blinn 1977)	Incoherent reflection	
	(Kay and Greenberg 1979)	Distance attenuation and refraction in transparent materials	
	(Whitted 1980)	Recursive coherent reflection, refraction	4.33
	(Hall and Greenberg 1983b)	Incoherent transmission	4.34
	(Cook, et al. 1984) (Amanatides 1984)	Distributed sampling and area sampling	
	(Kajiya 1985)	Anisotropic illumination	
	(Kajiya 1986)	Energy equilibrium in distributed ray tracing	
Energy Equilibrium: radiosity, and energy equilibrium models	(Cook and Torrance 1982)	Spectral character of highlights, energy formulation	
	(Goral, et al. 1984)	Diffuse energy equilibrium	
	(Cohen and Greenberg 1985a) (Nishita and Nakamae 1985) (Cohen, et al. 1986)	Complex diffuse environments including shadows	4.35
	(Immel and Greenberg 1986a)	Specular highlights in radiosity solutions	4.36
	(Max 1986) (Rushmeier and Torrance 1987) (Nishita and Nakamae 1987)	Atmospheric effects	
Hybrid	(Wallace, et al. 1987)	Radiosity diffuse, ray traced specular	4.37

Table 4.1: Classification of Shading Technique and Illumination Models.

Analytical approaches make the illumination model the driving force for the application of energy equilibrium techniques to computer imagery (Cook and Torrance 1982), (Goral, et al. 1984), (Cohen and Greenberg 1985a), and (Nishita and Nakamae 1985). In addition to maintaining true geometry, the movement of light energy through the environment must be modeled to provide the information required to evaluate the illumination model. Initially radiosity techniques were restricted to ideally diffuse reflective surfaces. The introduction of specular effects soon followed (Immel, et al. 1986a).

The hybrid rendering technique integrates the radiosity and ray tracing techniques to handle diffuse and specular effects respectively (Wallace, et al. 1987). Each technique is used to model the illumination components for which it is best suited. Translucency and refraction are also included in the hybrid model.

These four classifications describe a shift in research from solving the hidden surface problem, to creating realistic appearance, to simulating the behavior that creates the appearance.

4.1 Shading and Illumination Basics

The generalized illumination expression, Eq.(2.49), is the implicit basis for all models used to approximate surface colors. The shading technique determines how this model is applied. Evaluating the integrals in this expression to determine the intensity reflected or transmitted from a point on a surface towards the viewer or towards any other surface requires a knowledge of the intensity reaching that surface from the illuminating hemispheres above and below that surface. This means that intensity from all other surface elements and from the light sources in the environment must be considered. Many of these relationships are trivial because the elements are obscured by other elements in the environment, thus eliminating them from consideration. However, even the simplest environment remains a challenge if this expression is to be rigorously applied.

The philosophy of applying the illumination model must be examined to gain a full appreciation of the shading techniques used. One school of thought starts at the eye and considers the surfaces that are visible. For the visible surface at each pixel, the question is asked: *What information is required to evaluate the color for this surface?* The information required dictates what other surfaces must be considered, and the question is asked again for these surfaces. This process continues recursively until some criteria for not requesting additional information is satisfied. An example of this approach is ray tracing.

The second school of thought starts at the light sources and traces the light energy as it moves through an environment. Every surface is reviewed relative to the light sources and light emitters in the environ-

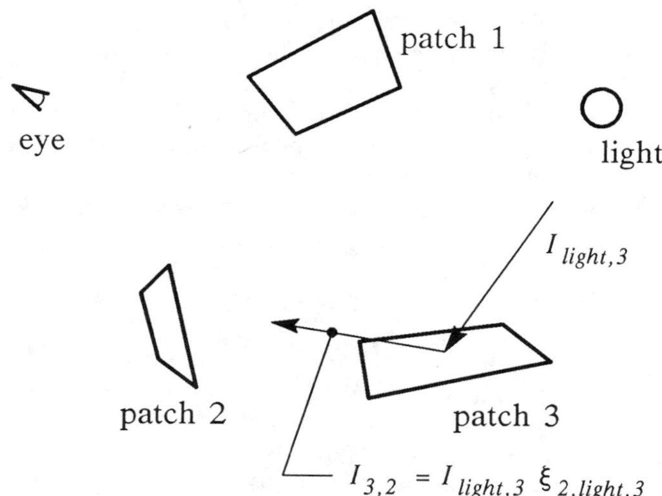

Figure 4.1: A simple environment for rendering.

ment, and the question is asked: *How is this light reflected or transmitted by this surface.* Every illuminated surface then becomes a light emitter. Every surface is reviewed again, and the process continues recursively until equilibrium is reached. An example of this approach is radiosity.

The first method prepares a *view dependent* map of light moving through the environment from selected surfaces to the eye. A new map is created for every new viewer position. The second method prepares a *view independent* map of the light moving through the environment from the light sources to all surfaces. This map is used to render the environment for any viewer position.

Consider rendering a simple environment consisting of a light source and several surface elements (patches) suspended in space, Figure 4.1. Suppose that for each patch in the environment we can generate a coefficient which relates the intensity reflected or transmitted to a target patch to the intensity received from a source patch, $\xi_{target,source,active}$. We will use the notation $I_{source,destination}$ to denote the intensity from a source to a destination.

The size and surface character of the patches used in calculating the ξ coefficients constrain the utility of ξ. For ideally diffuse surfaces any incoming energy is reflected equally in all directions. The entire hemisphere over the surface contributes to the intensity of the surface. Thus ξ is meaningful for relatively large patches due to the omnidirectional nature of the interaction.

Perfectly smooth surfaces reflect and refract very directionally. Therefore, the patches considered degenerate to a point sampling and ξ relates intensity leaving a point in a single direction from a point in the mirror direction or the refracted direction. Thus, many very small patches are required to model the interactions accurately.

4.1.1 Starting from the Eye

Shading techniques that begin the illumination calculation at the eye are an obvious solution for computer graphics. Visibility calculations are made from a viewpoint and the surfaces which must be shaded are identified by the visibility calculation. This approach is typified in both the incremental and ray tracing shading techniques.

The illumination expression is applied to the visible surface at any pixel. Consider the simple environment of Figure 4.1. If a point on patch 3 is visible, the illumination expression (illumination model) is applied. The first question is: *What information is required to evaluate the model at that point?*.

The earliest rendering techniques assume ideally diffuse surfaces illuminated by light sources only. The light sources are queried for information and the illumination model is evaluated. The remainder of the environment is assumed to be filled with *ambient* light of equal intensity throughout the environment. This technique works very well for isolated objects floating in space and illuminated by the sun.

Later illumination models allow for smooth surfaces with highlights. Still, only primary light sources are considered. The highlights are always the color of the light source. These models resulted in a period of "plastic" looking images due to the white highlights. The directional nature of the illumination means that global information is less important in evaluating the illumination model.

The logical extension of the technique is to ask what intensity reaches the visible surface from the reflected direction, and to factor that into the illumination model. A technique called *reflection mapping* was first used to determine the intensity from any direction (Blinn and Newell 1976). This technique uses a projection of the environment about the reflective object. The intensity from the mirror direction is determined by a simple lookup into the projected environment, Figure 4.2. A problem with this technique is that all rays reflected in the same direction reflect the same point on the map regardless of the starting position of the ray. Thus, planar mirrors tend to reflect a single color. Reflection mapping works best for curved, isolated objects when the reflected environment is distant from the object.

Ray tracing eliminates the geometric distortions of reflection mapping by performing visible determination for the reflected ray. This preserves geometric relationships. The surface seen by the reflected ray requires evaluation of the illumination model. If this surface is reflective then information from the mirror direction is required. This process continues recursively to some maximum depth or until some cutoff threshold is reached. The ray tracing methodology is extended for transparent

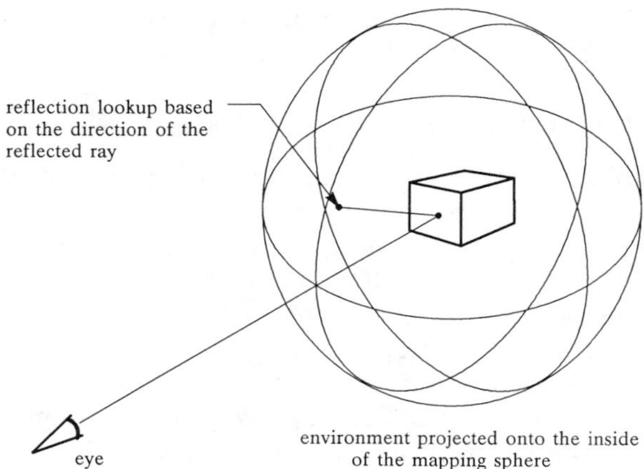

Figure 4.2: The reflection mapping process.

objects by asking what is received from the refracted direction and factoring this into the illumination model.

Reviewing this methodology in terms of the generalized illumination expression, Eq.(2.49), we see that if the surface is optically smooth the incoherent terms drop out. The ray tracing solution then fits ideally. No evaluation of integrals is required and point sampling provides all required information. This methodology led to a "glass sphere" period in computer generated imagery where highly reflective objects floating in space were the subject of most imagery and spheres were a popular geometric object due to the ease of ray intersection calculations.

Ray tracing was originally limited to simple environments because of the computation required to solve the ray/object intersection problem,

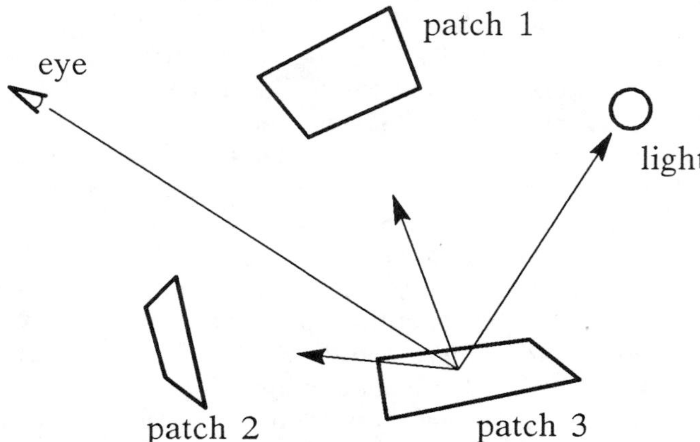

Figure 4.3: First approximation starting from the eye.

and to highly reflective environments because of the limitations of the illumination model. Advancements in sorting algorithms and computing speed made ray tracing computationally tractable for more complex environments. Addressing diffuse environments is a more serious problem.

Consider once again the simple environment of Figure 4.1 as a diffuse environment. When patch 3 is visible the color is calculated using the illumination model. To provide adequate information for the illumination model, the contributions from all other surfaces in the environment must be known. Thus, the first approximation is expressed by:

$$I_{eye,3} = \xi_{eye,light,3} I_{light,3} + \xi_{eye,1,3} I_{1,3} + \xi_{eye,2,3} I_{2,3} \tag{4.1}$$

The intensity of the source is the only known quantity for the first approximation, thus $I_{1,3}$ and $I_{2,3}$ are assumed to be either 0 or some global ambient value. This first approximation accounts for light from the source and a global ambient approximation only, Figure 4.3. This is the statement of the original models for computer graphics.
In the second approximation $I_{1,3}$ and $I_{2,3}$ are expanded:

$$I_{1,3} = \xi_{3,light,1} I_{light,1} + \xi_{3,light,2} I_{light,2} + \xi_{3,2,1} I_{2,1} + \xi_{3,3,1} I_{3,1} \tag{4.2}$$

$$I_{2,3} = \xi_{3,light,2} I_{light,2} + \xi_{3,light,2} I_{light,2} + \xi_{3,1,2} I_{1,2} + \xi_{3,3,2} I_{3,2} \tag{4.3}$$

Using an approximation for the global ambient of zero and substituting Eqs. 4.2 and 4.3 into 4.1 gives a second approximation of:

$$I_{eye,3} = \xi_{eye,light,3} I_{light,3} + \xi_{eye,1,3} \xi_{3,light,1} I_{light,1} + \xi_{eye,2,3} \xi_{3,light,2} I_{light,2} \tag{4.4}$$

This second approximation considers single and double reflection of light before it reaches the eye, Figure 4.4.

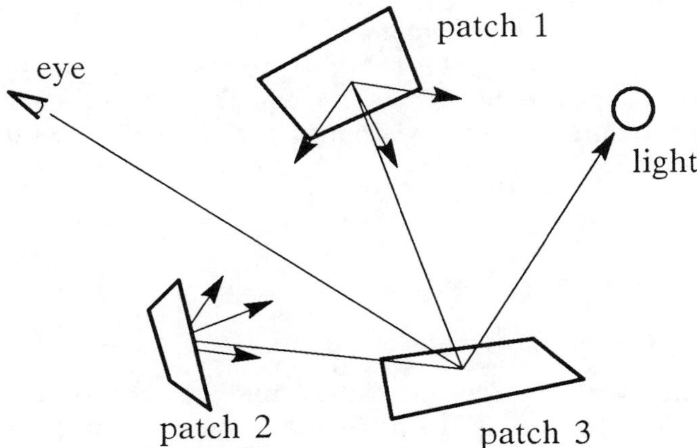

Figure 4.4: Second approximation starting from the eye.

It is readily apparent that if the environment is complex the calculations for a single pixel become overwhelming. Additionally, many calculations are repeated for the next pixel. Note that there are n^3 of the ξ coefficients required, where n is the number of patches.

The next step in ray tracing came with the careful selection of a bundle of rays used for representative sampling of the environment instead of attempting to model all of the relationships. Cone tracing and distributed ray tracing were two methods for selectively sampling environments. The distributed ray tracing approach had several other side benefits including motion blur, depth of field, and fuzzy shadows (Cook, et al. 1984).

Rendering techniques that start exclusively at the eye reached a peak with the work of Kajiya (1986) where 40 rays per pixel were used to sample the environment. The reflection and refraction of each ray through the environment was carefully controlled and a single reflection or refraction ray spawned at each intersection.

4.1.2 Starting from the Light

Shading techniques that begin illumination calculations at the light are not an obvious solution for the generation of imagery. Calculations are performed for surfaces that are not seen, which seems very wasteful. However, if diffuse surfaces are to be correctly rendered, the complexity of solutions that start from the eye becomes overwhelming. In addition, if several images of the same environment are to be made, the illumination calculations starting from the light need only be made once.

An ideal diffuse environment greatly simplifies the computations. The intensity leaving any surface is independent of direction for ideal diffuse surfaces. Thus the ξ term becomes $\xi_{source,active}$ relating the intensity radiated in any direction from the active patch to the intensity received from the source. This requires n^2 coefficients, where n is the number of patches in the environment.

The diffuse environment is solved by recursively asking what is the intensity of the patches in the environment. Examining the simple environment of Figure 4.1, the environment is characterized by these relationships:

$$I_1 = \xi_{light,1} I_{light} + \xi_{2,1} I_2 + \xi_{3,1} I_3 \tag{4.5a}$$

$$I_2 = \xi_{light,2} I_{light} + \xi_{1,2} I_1 + \xi_{3,2} I_3 \tag{4.5b}$$

$$I_3 = \xi_{light,3} I_{light} + \xi_{1,3} I_1 + \xi_{2,3} I_2 \tag{4.5c}$$

The first iteration provides illumination from the light source only, Figure 4.5. The intensities of the patches are zero at the beginning of the first iteration. The second iteration includes the first bounce of light from the surfaces, Figure 4.6. The total energy leaving a surface is al-

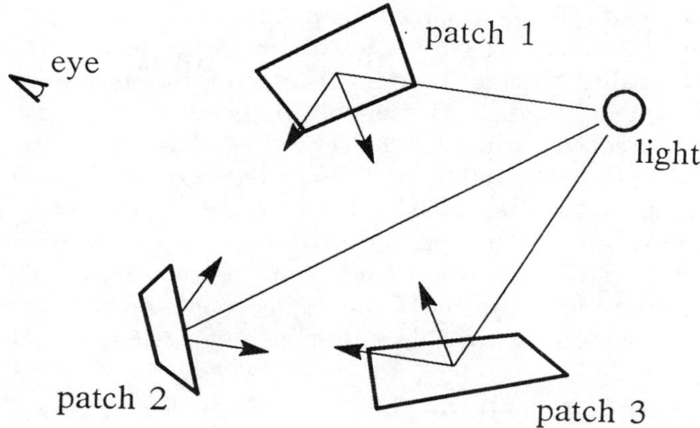

Figure 4.5: First approximation starting from the light.

ways less than the energy incident on the surface. Rapid convergence is guaranteed due to this physical restriction on the validity of the ξ coefficients.

The equation set for the ideal diffuse case is solved iteratively, or, it is solved directly since there are an equal number of equations and unknowns. Standard numerical techniques, such as Gaussian elimination, Gauss-Jordan iteration, and Gauss-Seidel iteration, are available for solution of the equation set. It can readily be seen that for simple diffuse environments with few patches the technique of starting from the eye is not computationally prohibitive.

This technique, known as radiosity, is routinely used in radiation and heat transfer computation. It was only recently introduced into computer graphics by Goral, et al. (1984).

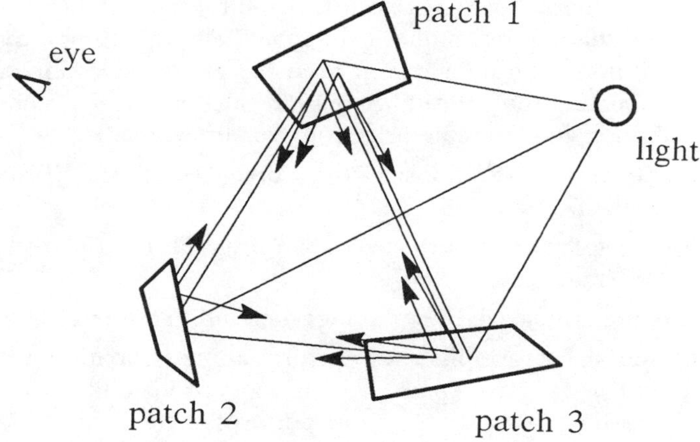

Figure 4.6: Second approximation starting from the light.

For a non-diffuse environment both the coefficients, ξ, and the intensities are directional. This adds great complexity to the equation set. The directionality of the reflected intensity terms means there are now n^2 equations with n^3 coefficients to be solved. In addition, the use of smaller patches is required with more reflective materials.

The most complete rendering technique that starts exclusively at the light source was demonstrated by Immel (1986a,1986b). Methods were introduced to simplify the characterization of the interrelationships between the patches in the environment, and simplify the resulting equation set in an attempt to make the inclusion of specular illumination effects computationally tractable within the radiosity framework.

4.1.3 Combined Techniques

Combined techniques integrate the respective advantages of view dependent and view independent methods to handle environments containing both diffuse and specular surfaces in a consistent fashion. Combined techniques were introduced with the work of Wallace, et al. (1987). The exploration of combined techniques is just beginning. The results are very impressive. Combined techniques are a fertile area for future research.

4.2 Incremental Shading, Empirical Models

Many of the early visible surface techniques processed events in scanline order and used incremental updating of information both across a single scanline, and when moving from one scanline to the next (Sutherland, et al. 1974). The illumination models originally implemented with scanline rendering systems used incremental updating techniques and coherence information similarly to their use for visibility computation. The key point of these shading techniques is incrementally updating a minimum amount of illumination information from the previous scanline or pixel instead of repeating the entire illumination calculation. The concerns in image generation cited in references from that time are:

- Real-time display (Watkins 1970), (Phong 1975), and (Bishop and Weimer 1986).
- Realistic display of smooth curved surfaces (Phong 1975) and (Bishop and Weimer 1986).
- Minimizing artifacts of digital image generation (Phong 1975).

The visible surface algorithms used perform an initial mapping from object space into perspective space. All subsequent visibility calculations, and often shading calculations, were performed in perspective space. The perspective transformation is a nonlinear transformation, thus, the geometry of perspective space is distorted relative to the object space geometry. This perspective distortion simplified visibility calculation, but had adverse effects for shading.

The task of determining visibility was paramount and little computation time was devoted to image shading. This led to shading assumptions that reduce the complexity of the illumination geometry such as a single light source at infinite distance (sometimes in the direction of the eye), and the eye at infinite distance (the actual position used for perspective calculation is ignored).

The illumination models are presented here in their original form with a discussion of commonly used extensions that increase the versatility of the model. Simple extensions provide general models that are commonly used in practice.

The illumination models used for scanline applications are subsets of an illumination model of the form:

$$I(\lambda) = f(d) \times (\text{ambient} + \text{diffuse} + \text{specular})$$

$$I(\lambda) = f(d) \times \left[K_a(\lambda) I_a(\lambda) + K_d(\lambda) \sum_{n=1}^{ls} (\mathbf{N} \bullet \mathbf{L}_n) I_n(\lambda) + K_s \sum_{n=1}^{ls} f(\mathbf{V}, \mathbf{L}_n, \mathbf{N}, \zeta) I_n(\lambda) \right] \tag{4.6}$$

This is an approximation of the incoherent reflection term of Eq.(2.49). The incoherent reflection is broken into three components: ambient, diffuse, and specular. The ambient and diffuse components are taken from ideal Lambertian diffuse surfaces. The reflected intensity for these components is equal in all directions. The specular term is a directional term where $f(\mathbf{V}, \mathbf{L}_n, \mathbf{N}, \zeta)$ is a directional reflection function. This produces highlights which are related to the geometry, **V**, **L**, **N**, and the surface roughness function, ζ. In this expression, $f(d)$ is an attenuation as a function of the distance, d, between the viewer and the illuminated surface.

The shading techniques are view dependent and the model requires specific illumination information from the light sources only. The light sources are considered to be the only significant form of illumination requiring special calculation. All other global illumination information is lumped into the global ambient illumination, $I_a(\lambda)$ which is a nondirectional constant light level existing within the environment.

4.2.1 Diffuse Illumination

The model described by Bouknight (1970) is representative of the first illumination models. This model uses the ambient and Lambertian diffuse terms only, no distance attenuation, and one light source which is placed at infinite distance in the direction of the eye. The ambient intensity and light source intensity are implied in the formulation. The model was originally used for grayscale images only. The model is given by:

$$I = K_a + K_d(\mathbf{N} \bullet \mathbf{L}); \qquad (K_a + K_d) < 1.0 \tag{4.7}$$

Note that $\mathbf{L} = [0\ 0\ 1]$ when the light is at an infinite distance in the direction of the eye. The illumination expression then reduces to:

$$I = K_a + K_d \mathbf{N}_k \tag{4.8}$$

The normal used is the normal in object space. The model is evaluated once per polygon and the visible area of the polygon is filled with the color. During the scanning, pixel color changes if visibility changes, otherwise the current pixel is the same color as the last pixel. This model is easily extended to account for color (wavelength) of both light source and material, light sources placed anywhere in the environment, and multiple light sources as:

$$I(\lambda) = K_a(\lambda) I_a(\lambda) + K_d(\lambda) \sum_{n=1}^{ls} (\mathbf{N} \bullet \mathbf{L}_n) I_n(\lambda) \tag{4.9}$$

Note that explicit ambient intensity and light source intensity terms are added (these are implied in the original expression of the model). Light source vectors are constant for lights at an infinite distance, but must be recalculated for each polygon for every light that is within the environment. Since there is only one calculation per polygon, an average polygon point, such as the centroid, is used to determine the light vector. If multiple light sources are used, K_a, K_d, and the light source intensities I_n must be carefully chosen to keep the computed polygon intensity within the displayable range. If it is possible for calculated intensities to go beyond the displayable range, provisions must be made for color clipping or compression (see Section 5.1.3, *Color Clipping and Compressing for Display*).

Ideal diffuse shading from a point source exhibits Mach banding[1] at the transition between the ambient area and the combined ambient and diffuse area, Figure 4.7. This is due to a sharp discontinuity between the constant color of the ambient area and the rapidly changing diffuse shading near the transition. The transition occurs when the slope of $(\mathbf{N} \bullet \mathbf{L})$ is maximum. This discontinuity can be eliminated by using an exponent on the dot product which is slightly larger than 1. In reality, the finite size of the light sources combined with diffraction phenomena blend the diffuse area into the ambient area and eliminate the sharp discontinuity.

---

[1] Mach banding is a perceptual phenomena noted by E. Mach in the 1860's. Mach bands are caused when the first derivative (rate of change) of intensity across a scene is discontinuous. The perceptual mechanism of the eye enhances the discontinuity by making it appear lighter or darker than the surroundings.

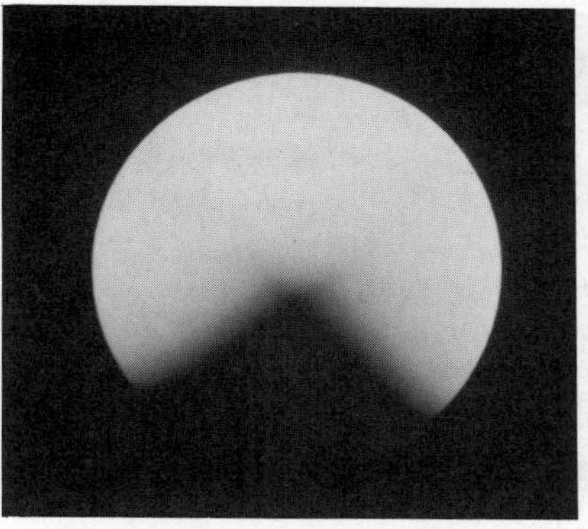
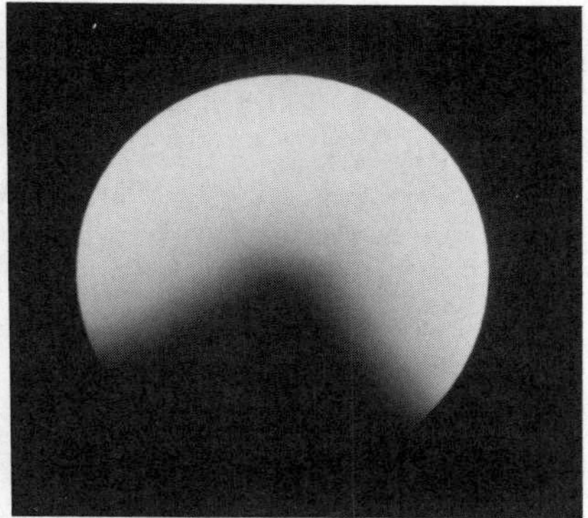

Figure 4.7: Mach banding in diffuse shading. Computed with no exponent on the left and an exponent of 1.5 on the right

4.2.2 Atmospheric Attenuation

It was quickly noted that diffuse models evaluated only once per polygon result in overlapping parallel polygons being indistinguishable from each other because they are shaded identically (in the case of infinite distance viewpoint and light sources). Atmospheric attenuation functions were introduced as a solution to this problem. Early attenuation functions were documented in the computer graphics literature. The functions that are found in current practice are largely undocumented and the roots of these formulations are not clear.

A $1/d$ attenuation function is presented by Warnock (1969)[2], and a $(1/d)^x$ attenuation function is presented by Romney (1969, 132-138)[3].

In these functions d is a measure of distance from the eye. Warnock's function was intended to account for attenuation due to fog or haze. Romney's attenuation function was intended to account for the inverse square law for energy from a point source.

Romney reviews several alternatives for the power x and concludes that for a point source at the eye, theory dictates using x=2. However, his empirical experience led to the use of x=4 for the best appearance. In

[2] This is often incorrectly referenced to:

Warnock, John E. (1968) "A Hidden Surface Algorithm for Halftone Picture Representation," Department of Computer Science, University of Utah, Salt Lake City, Technical Report TR4-5.

which discusses the hidden surface algorithm only and does not elaborate on the shading method. The shading method is described in his dissertation only.

[3] This is often incorrectly referenced to:

Romney, G. W. (1970) "Computer Assisted Assembly and Rendering of Solids," Department of Computer Science, University of Utah, Salt Lake City, Technical Report TR4-20.

The origin of this incorrect reference is mysterious. The University of Utah does not acknowledge any record of this document.

general application, the function describes both an attenuation of the source intensity before it reaches the surface and an atmospheric attenuation of the light from the surface to the eye.

A form that is commonly used in commercial image generation systems fades the object intensity, $I_o(\lambda)$, into a fog color, $I_f(\lambda)$. The fog color, start fade distance, s, and end fade distance, e, are specified for this function. The start fade distance is the distance at which fading begins, and the end fade distance is the distance at which the environment fades completely into the fog color. The general form is:

$$I(\lambda) = \begin{cases} I_o(\lambda) & \text{if } d \le s \\ \dfrac{(e-d)}{(e-s)} I_o(\lambda) + \dfrac{(d-s)}{(e-s)} I_f(\lambda) & \text{if } s < d < e \\ I_f(\lambda) & \text{if } d \le e \end{cases} \tag{4.10}$$

Note that this is a linear attenuation function as opposed to the inverse distance functions originally suggested. The justification is that the inverse functions were based upon theoretical treatments while the models are being applied using shading techniques that cannot capture the information required for theoretically based models. In addition, subjectively good image appearance is obtained with this function. Modifying the start, s, and end, e, values allows the user to empirically tune the attenuation for effect.

Recent work by Max (1986), Rushmeier and Torrance (1987), and Nishita and Nakamae (1987) provides a detailed treatment of atmospheric phenomena. The emphasis in this work is on modeling the actual behavior that creates the phenomena. The results are quite impressive. These techniques are outside the scope this text. The reader is encouraged to consult these references for more detail.

4.2.3 Specular Highlights

We note that shiny objects in our environment have highlights, and that the highlights are reflections of light sources or other bright objects in the environment. Empirically, we can imagine modeling this with a function that has a maximum in the mirror direction from the light sources and falls off rapidly as the direction deviates from the mirror direction.

Romney (1969) suggests that a cosine raised to a power will create the appearance of highlights. In the environments he rendered, the light source is at the eye position. Thus, when a surface is normal to the view vector, the mirror direction is directly back to the viewer. Deviation from this position shifts the mirror direction away from the view vector. The expression that Romney found produced the best imagery was $(\mathbf{N} \bullet \mathbf{L})^2 / r_o^4$, where r_o is the distance from the surface to the eye. He also describes methods for adjusting the appearance of the image by adjusting the cosine power and the distance power.

Phong (1975) formalizes a more general model using ambient, diffuse, and specular terms in combination. The $f(\mathbf{V}, \mathbf{L}_n, \mathbf{N}, \zeta)$ term of Eq.(4.7) is replaced by a directional reflectance function $(\mathbf{V} \bullet \mathbf{R}_l)^{Ns}$ where Ns is a measure of surface roughness. Note that in the Phong model K_s is not a wavelength dependent function, thus the highlights are always white. In the original implementation, the eye and the light source are considered to be at infinite distance so that the **V** and **L** vectors are constant. The law of reciprocity is used to write an alternate form of the specular term $(\mathbf{R}_v \bullet \mathbf{L})^{Ns}$. The illumination model used is:

$$I(\lambda) = K_a(\lambda) + K_d(\lambda)(\mathbf{N} \bullet \mathbf{L}) + K_s(\mathbf{R}_v \bullet \mathbf{L})^{Ns} \tag{4.11}$$

The vector $\mathbf{R}_v$ is easier to compute than $\mathbf{R}_l$ because the **V** vector has two zero components, that is, $\mathbf{V} = [0\ 0\ 1]$ before the perspective transformation when the eye is at infinite distance. The expression for the reflected vector, $\mathbf{R}_v = 2\mathbf{N}(\mathbf{N} \bullet \mathbf{V}) - \mathbf{V}$, developed in Appendix III.1, *Geometric Utilities*, reduces to:

$$\mathbf{R}_v = [\mathbf{R}_{vi}\ \ \mathbf{R}_{vj}\ \ \mathbf{R}_{vk}] \tag{4.12a}$$

$$\mathbf{R}_{vi} = 2\mathbf{N}_k\mathbf{N}_i \tag{4.12b}$$

$$\mathbf{R}_{vj} = 2\mathbf{N}_k\mathbf{N}_j \tag{4.12c}$$

$$\mathbf{R}_{vk} = 2\mathbf{N}_k\mathbf{N}_k - 1 \tag{4.12d}$$

An alternate form of the specular reflection function proposed by Blinn (1977), uses the vector bisector, **H**, between **V** and **L**, instead of the reflection vector, $\mathbf{R}_v$.[4] The rationale is that **H** represents the surface normal producing mirror reflection from the light to the eye. The reflection function describes the probability that microfacets of the surface are oriented in a particular direction. Thus, the normal of the surface and the normal for the microfacets in question are required to evaluate the reflection function.[5] Whitted (1982) points out that this formulation can result in considerable computational efficiency. If the light source and

[4] This adaptation is typically cited as the Phong illumination model. The functions are actually quite different. The Phong function maintains the same shape with respect to the reflected direction regardless of the angle of incidence. The Blinn function maintains the same profile relative to the reflected direction, but gets narrower as the angle of incidence approaches grazing. The functions are identical when the incident light is coincident with the normal, with the exception that a higher specular exponent, *Ns*, is required for the Blinn function to produce the same result.

[5] Blinn presents this in conjunction with several other functions for evaluating surface distributions that are based on the **H** vector (described later in this Chapter). The theoretical basis for this was developed throughout Chapter 2.

eye are at infinite distance, then the **H** vector need only be computed once for the entire scene.

This model is easily extended to account for the color (wavelength) of both light source and material and for multiple light sources placed anywhere in the environment as:

$$I(\lambda) = K_a(\lambda)I_a(\lambda) + K_d(\lambda)\sum_{n=1}^{ls}(\mathbf{N}\bullet\mathbf{L}_n)I_n(\lambda) + K_s\sum_{n=1}^{ls}(\mathbf{N}\bullet\mathbf{H}_n)^{Ns}I_n(\lambda) \tag{4.13}$$

The lighting parameters K_a, K_d, K_s, and Ns are empirically determined. The selection of K_a, K_d, K_s, and Ns to produce images that "look good" is a black art. Since the model is empirical, there is no clear connection between these parameters and any properties that can be easily measured. There is no substitute for experience in selecting values that will produce imagery that looks good. A discussion of value selection is presented in Appendix II, *Controlling Illumination*.

4.2.4 Geometric Smoothing

Scanline algorithms generally use polygonal data and represent curved surfaces as a collection of approximating polygons. The result is faceted appearance. Gouraud (1971) presented a method for creating the appearance of a curved surface by interpolating color across the polygons. The curved surface normal is used instead of the approximating polygon normal to compute the color at each vertex. The color is then interpolated across the polygons using incremental updating as the image is scanned. The illumination model does not change but the method of application results in better visual quality with minimal added computation expense.

The process of incremental parameter updating is diagramed in Figure 4.8. The parameter to be updated is evaluated at the vertices of each polygon and loaded into the edge database along with the rate of change per scanline. When an edge becomes active, the start value of the parameter is used as the value at the edge. For each subsequent scanline in which the edge is active, the parameter is updated by adding the rate of change per scanline. When the scanline is processed, a visible span for the polygon is created. A start pixel for the span is determined and the parameter value at the start pixel is computed. Additionally, the rate of change of the parameter per pixel is determined. When the span becomes active, the parameter start value is used. For each pixel during which the span is active, the current parameter value is incremented by the rate of change per pixel.

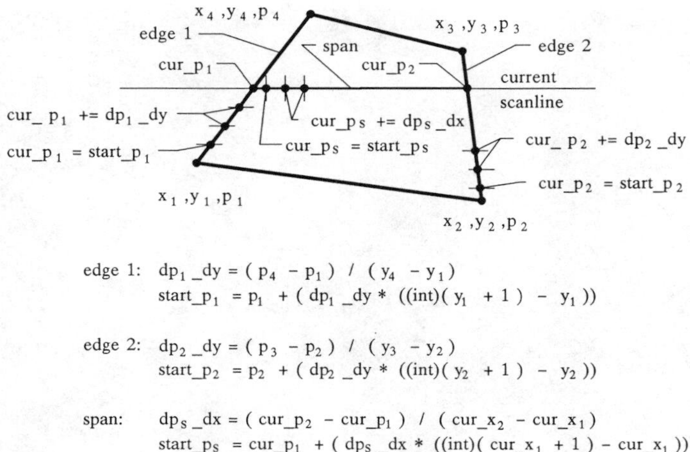

Figure 4.8: Incremental parameter updating.

A variety of problems have been noted in this approach including:

- Pronounced Mach banding at polygon boundaries due to discontinuities in the first derivative of intensity, Figure 4.9, (Phong 1975). The rate of change is constant across a polygon, but usually does not match the rate of change in adjacent polygons.
- Shading is not invariant with scanline orientation, Figure 4.10, (Duff 1979). This causes "shimmering" or "crawling" of highlights when objects are in motion.
- If illumination models with highlights are used the highlights are easily misplaced or completely omitted, Figure 4.11 (Phong 1975). This effect is exaggerated with animation, again causing "shimmering" and "crawling".

Phong (1975) presented a shading technique that interpolates surface normals instead of color across the face of polygons. This technique geometrically smooths the surface. The normals match at polygon boundaries, however, there can still be discontinuities in the rate of change of the normal, therefore, Mach banding may still be present, but it is generally reduced. This technique also assures that highlights appear on polygons that should have highlights.

Phong shading does not solve the problem of variation in shading with scanline orientation. In practice, if problems are apparent during animation, polygons are subdivided so they cover a smaller screen area. In the limit, as the polygons approach pixel size, the normals converge to the geometrically correct values. Thus, the screen orientation problem can be circumvented.

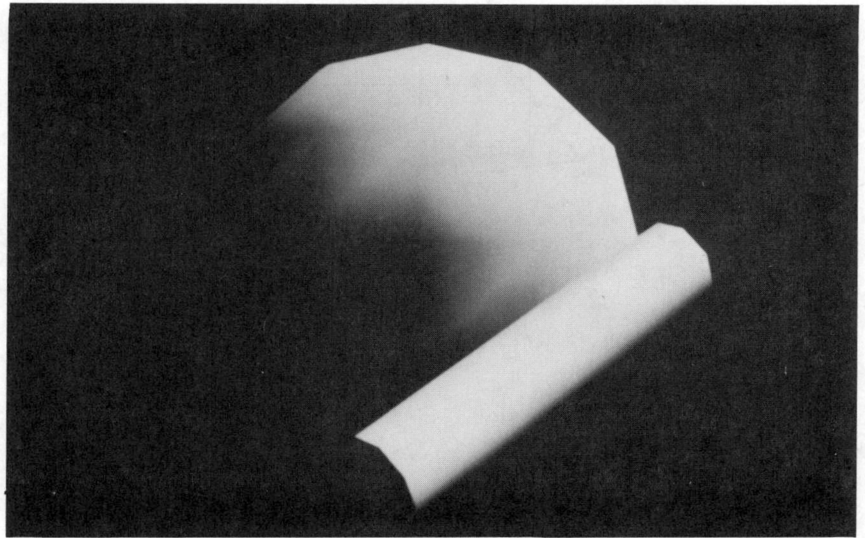

Figure 4.9: Example of Mach banding in Gouraud shading.

Duff (1979) and Bishop and Weimer (1986) discuss more efficient methods of applying the Phong shading technique by embedding the normal interpolation into the evaluation of the illumination model. Duff solves the resulting expression using forward differences techniques. Bishop uses a Taylor's series approximation. While these provide a more efficient application of geometric shading they still fail to address the problem of variation as a function of scanline orientation.

The position of the surface as well as the orientation must be interpolated for every pixel when extensions of the illumination models are used that allow light sources within the environment. Due to the non-

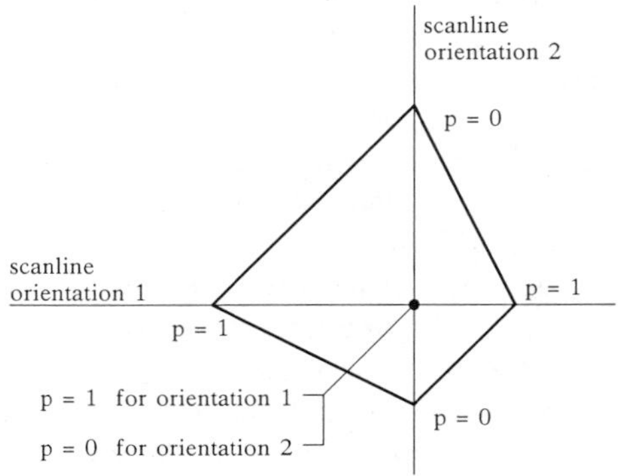

Figure 4.10: Variation as a function of scanline orientation.

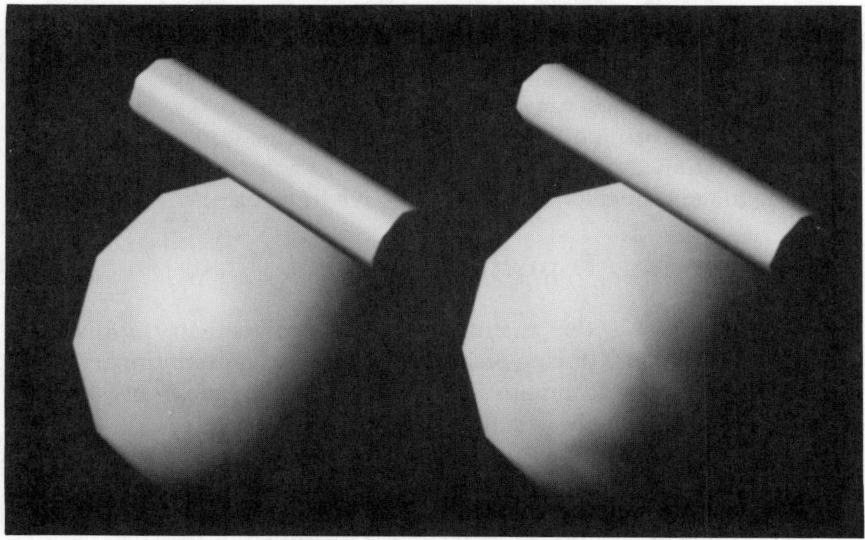

Figure 4.11: Example of missing highlight in Gouraud shading.

linearity of the perspective transformation unacceptable results often occur when these interpolations are performed in perspective space. Examination of a rendered environment consisting of a triangulated square tipped away from the viewer and illuminated by a local source demonstrates the problem, Figure 4.12. Distortion of position in the interpola-

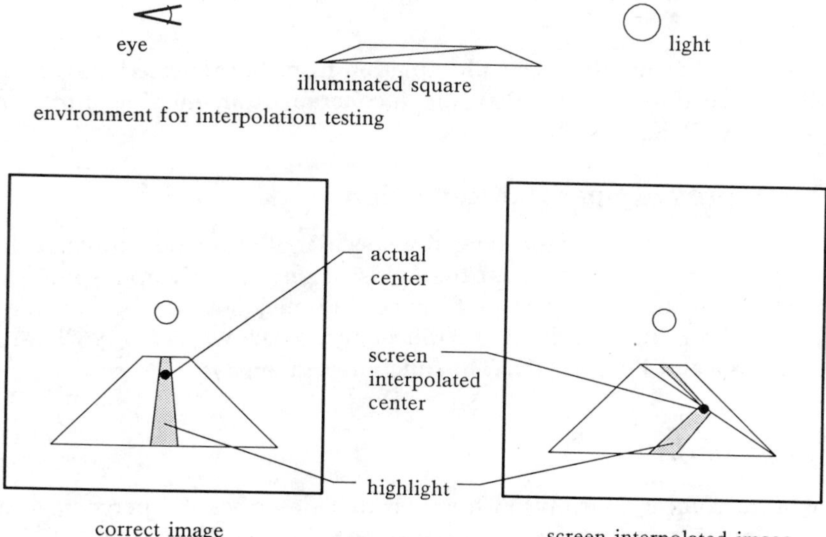

Figure 4.12: Distortion from perspective transform non-linearity.

tion can cause bizarre effects. Again, these are minimized by fine subdivision of the polygons. However, this does not address the root of the problem.

Ray tracing, as described in the next section, performs all illumination calculations using object space geometry. This eliminates the problems of variation due to orientation by removing the anomalies introduced by the non-linearity of the perspective transform.

4.3 Ray Tracing, Transitional Models

Rendering techniques that maintain object space geometry information can be grouped as ray tracing techniques. The key computational consideration of ray tracing techniques is that geometric information as well as color information must be calculated for each pixel.

The illumination models used for ray tracing applications are subsets of an illumination model of the form:

$$I(\lambda) = \text{ambient} + \text{diffuse} + \text{specular} + \text{transmitted}$$

$$I(\lambda) = K_a(\lambda)I_a(\lambda) + K_d(\lambda)\sum_{n=1}^{ls}(\mathbf{N}\bullet\mathbf{L}_n)I_n(\lambda) \tag{4.14}$$

$$+ K_s(\lambda)\left[I_r(\lambda) + \sum_{n=1}^{ls} f_r(\mathbf{V},\mathbf{L}_n,\mathbf{N},\zeta)I_n(\lambda)\right]$$

$$+ K_t(\lambda)\left[I_t(\lambda) + \sum_{n=1}^{ls} f_t(\mathbf{V},\mathbf{L}_n,\mathbf{N},\zeta)I_n(\lambda)\right]$$

The I_r and I_t terms represent illumination from the reflected and transmitted directions. Note that an incoherent transmission function, $f_t(\mathbf{V}, \mathbf{L}_n, \mathbf{N}, \zeta)$, has also been added.

4.3.1 Improved Specular Reflection

Blinn (1977) explored improving the specular illumination function by incorporating knowledge from the fields of physics and optics into the model. Blinn suggests alternate forms of the specular reflection function $f_r()$, based on the work of Torrance and Sparrow (1966,1967), and Trowbridge and Reitz (1967). The function is given by:

$$f_r() = \frac{\mathrm{DG}F_r}{(\mathbf{N}\bullet\mathbf{V})} \tag{4.15}$$

D is a microfacet distribution function that describes the percentage of surface microfacets whose normal is oriented in the **H** direction. G is a geometric attenuation function that accounts for surface self-shading. F_r is the Fresnel reflectance of the microfacets oriented in the **H** direction.

The Fresnel reflectance was discussed in detail in Section 2.2.5, *Reflection and Refraction*. Blinn used the formulation for dielectrics and did not consider the wavelength dependence of the Fresnel reflectance. The material was considered to have a single index of refraction. The Fresnel approximation method presented by Cook and Torrance (1982) introduces the wavelength dependency. This approximation method is detailed in Appendix III.5, *Fresnel Approximation*.

The geometric attenuation function is also detailed in Section 2.2.7, *Geometric Attenuation*. Blinn used the function described by Torrance and Sparrow (1967) for geometric attenuation. Torrance and Sparrow compare theoretical predictions to experimentally measured reflections. The agreement between prediction and measurement is impressive. They attribute the factor $G/(\mathbf{N}\bullet\mathbf{V})$ to be the cause of observed peaks in specular reflection that are at an angle greater than the mirror direction.

The geometric attenuation function described by Sancer (1969) is much different than the function developed by Torrance and Sparrow. It eliminates the discontinuities of the Torrance and Sparrow function and can, therefore, be expected to eliminate any Mach banding effects that might occur with the Torrance and Sparrow function. More surface information is required for evaluation of the Sancer attenuation function than for the Torrance and Sparrow formulation. To the author's knowledge, no commercial systems currently use the $G/(\mathbf{N}\bullet\mathbf{V})$ term in illumination models.

Blinn presents three possible microfacet distribution functions. The first is a revised Phong function given by:

$$D = (\mathbf{N}\bullet\mathbf{H})^{Ns} \tag{4.16}$$

The second roughness function, based upon the a Gaussian distribution used by Torrance and Sparrow (1967), is given by:

$$D = \exp(-(C_1 \arccos(\mathbf{N}\bullet\mathbf{H}))^2) \tag{4.17}$$

A third function, based upon the work of Trowbridge and Reitz (1967), is given by:

$$D = \left[\frac{C_2^2}{(\mathbf{N}\bullet\mathbf{H})^2\,(C_2^2 - 1) + 1}\right]^2 \tag{4.18}$$

Blinn notes that each of the functions has a peak value of 1 when $\mathbf{H} = \mathbf{N}$. The constants Ns, C_1, and C_2 effect the shape, or rate of fall off for the distribution function. The shapes of the three functions are similar. Blinn suggests that the three functions can be compared by selecting Ns, C_1, and C_2 so that the functions fall to a value of $1/2$ at the same angular deviation of **H** from **N**. He calls this angle β and relates *Ns*, C_1, and C_2 to β by:[6]

$$Ns = -\frac{\ln(2)}{\ln(\cos\beta)} \tag{4.19a}$$

$$C_1 = \frac{\sqrt{\ln(2)}}{\beta} \tag{4.19b}$$

$$C_2 = \left(\frac{\cos^2\beta - 1}{\cos^2\beta - \sqrt{2}}\right)^{\frac{1}{2}} \tag{4.19c}$$

The distribution functions are plotted in Figure 4.13.

Note the similarity in the distribution functions. The Blinn power cosine function is prevalent in commercial application. The similarity in shape suggests that any of the functions would produce visually equivalent imagery. To the author's knowledge, no definitive comparative study has been performed with these distribution functions. Thus, it is not possible to present any information about the realism and computation time compromises between these roughness functions.

Figure 4.14 describes the relationship between β and *Ns* for the Phong distribution, *Ns* for the Blinn distribution, C_1, C_2, and *m* for the Beckmann function used by Cook and Torrance (1983) (described later in this chapter).

4.3.2 Macroscopic Surface Properties

Catmull (1975) and Blinn and Newell (1976) describe mapping parameter textures such as roughness, color, and normal perturbation onto surfaces prior to performing the color computation. This provides greater visual detail and complexity for a subjectively more realistic appearance. Textures are used to change surface properties on a macroscopic level, that is, a level where the changes do not affect the application of the illumination model.

In the general form, the *texture* is a 1, 2, or 3 dimensional array of data describing a parameter. The mapping relates a location on the object to a location in the texture array. After the visible point of a surface is determined, the texture coordinates are computed. The texture coordinates are used to lookup the parameter value in the texture. The surface geometry and material properties are then altered based upon the texture parameter before the illumination model is applied. The illumination model is not altered when used with textured surfaces.

---

[6] The Phong specular function is compared by using $Ns = -\ln(2)/\ln(\cos(2\beta))$.

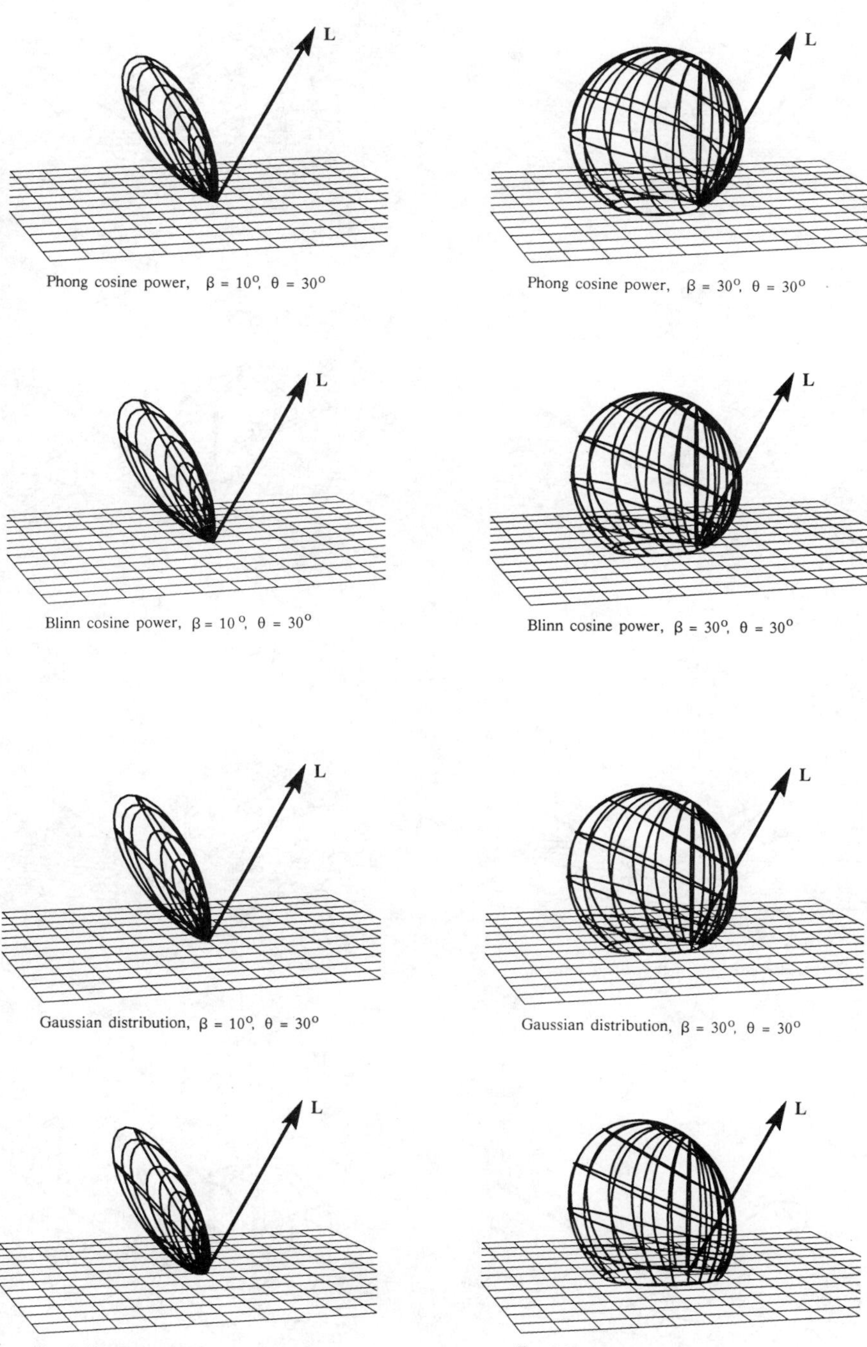

Figure 4.13a: Comparison of distribution functions used by Blinn.

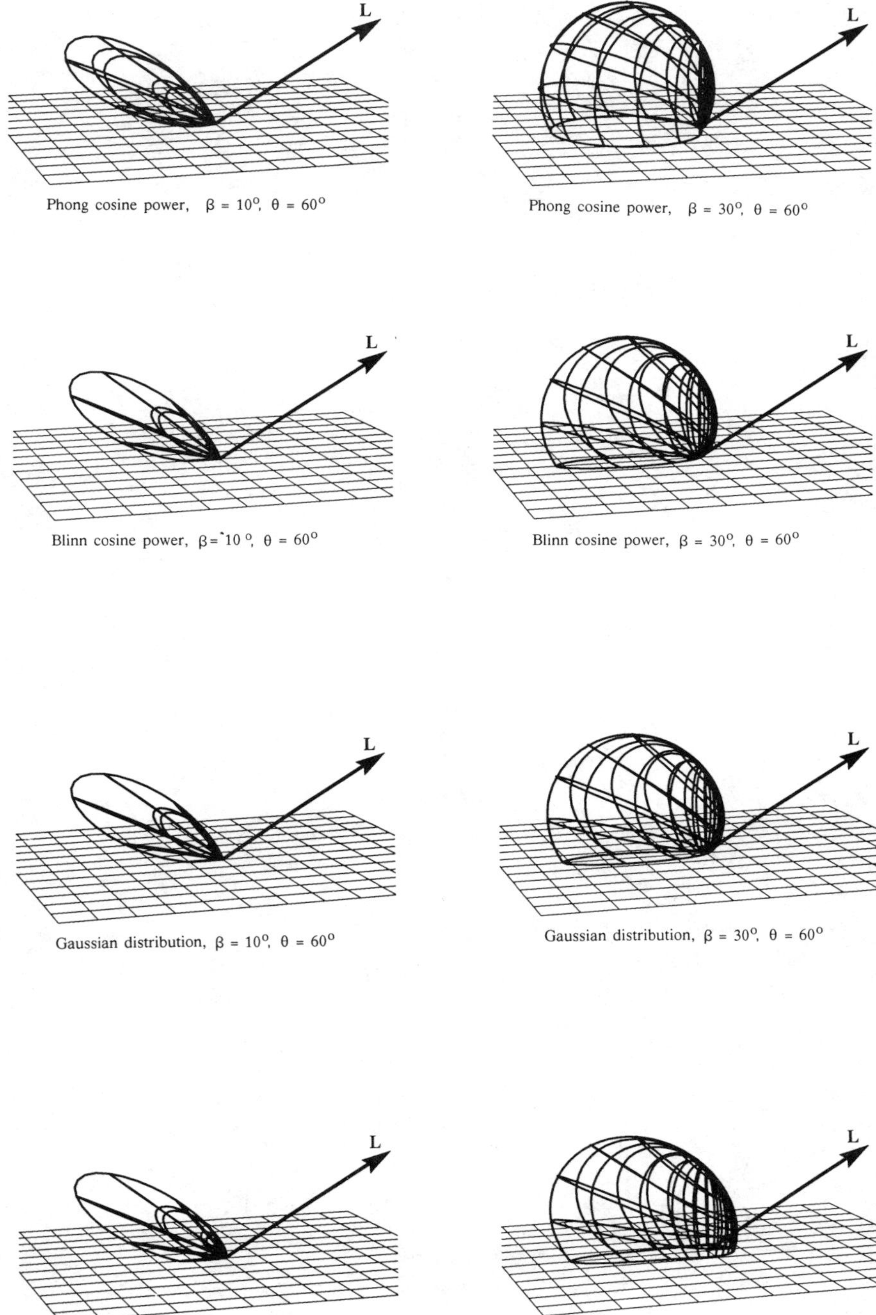

Figure 4.13b: Comparison of distribution functions used by Blinn.

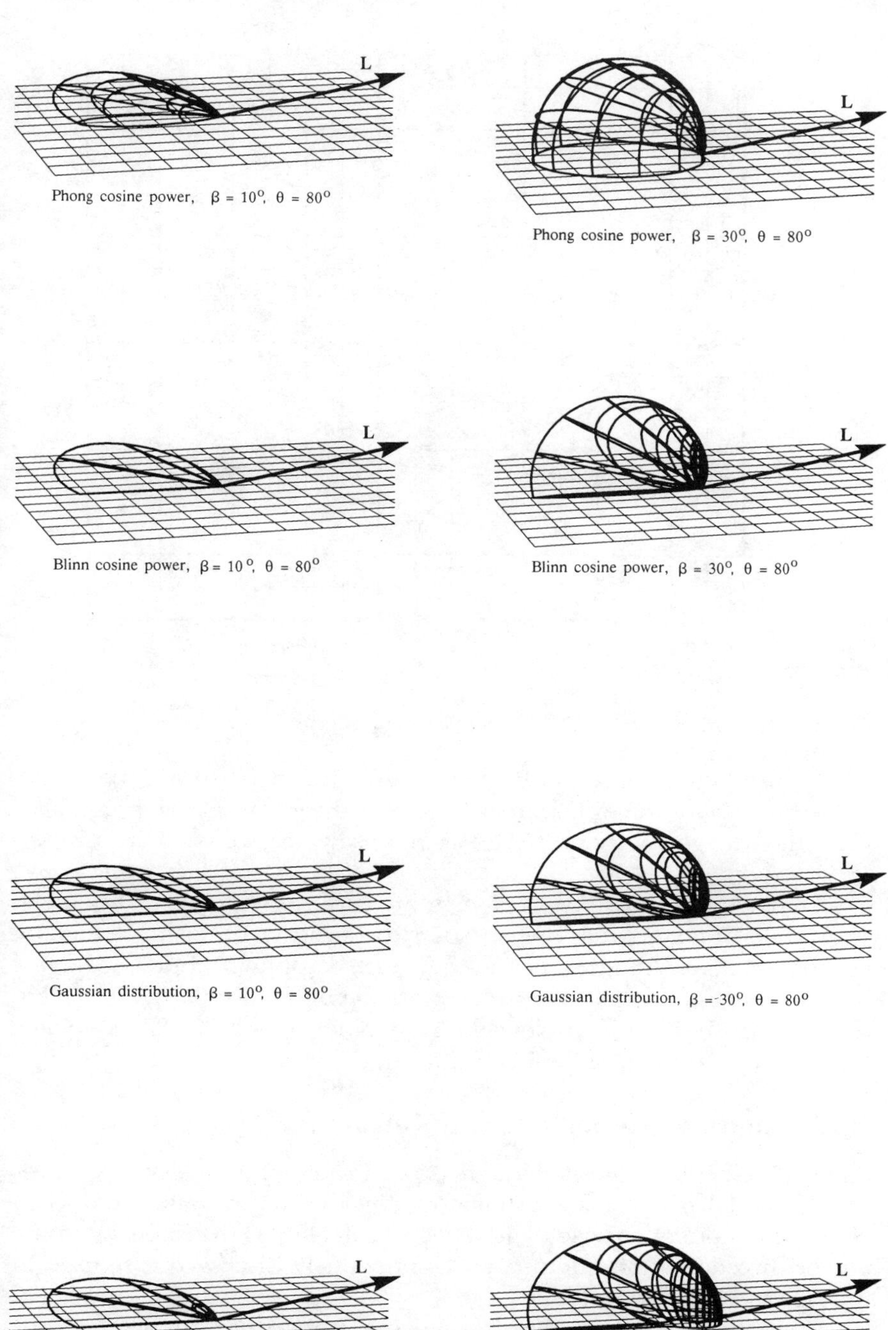

Figure 4.13c: Comparison of distribution functions used by Blinn.

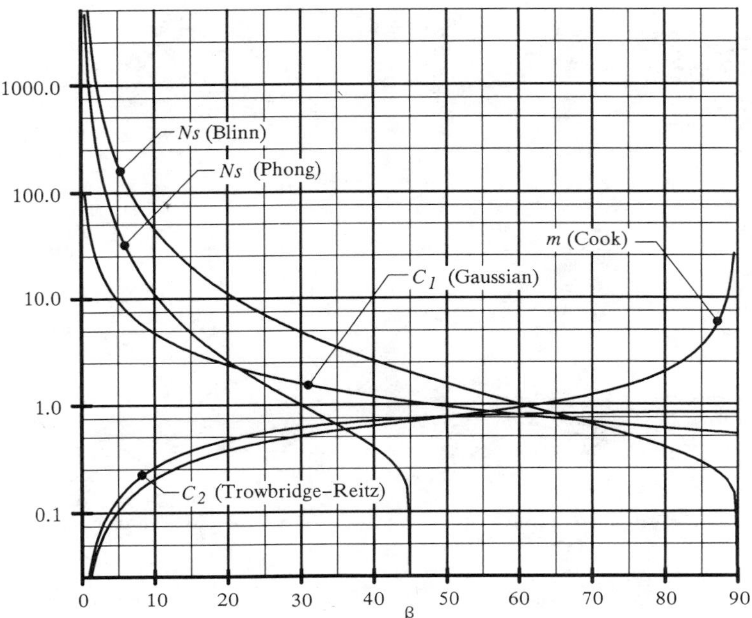

Figure 4.14: Phong *Ns*, Blinn *Ns*, C_1, C_2, and m as a function of β.

Texture coordinates are typically interpolated across polygons. Thus, the application of texture is subject to the same anomalies as shading if the true geometry of surfaces is not used (see Section 4.2.4, *Geometric Smoothing*).

The methodologies for implementing texture mapping vary widely. The details of texture mapping are outside the scope of this book and are not treated here. An introduction to texture mapping is found in Rogers (1985). There are many sources for more detailed information including Catmull (1975), Blinn and Newell (1976), Norton, et al. (1982), Williams (1983), Crow (1984), and Perlin (1985).

4.3.3 Recursive Reflection and Refraction

Blinn (1976,1978), suggests that reflections from highly reflective surfaces can be modeled using a specular function that has a value of 1 when $\mathbf{H} = \mathbf{N}$, and zero otherwise. The reflected intensity is the intensity in the mirror direction. Reflection maps, as previously discussed, are used to provide the reflected intensity.

Whitted (1980) formalized a general procedure to account for reflection and refraction when he introduced recursive ray tracing to computer graphics. At each visible surface, the lights are queried, and the environment is queried for information from the mirror and refraction directions. A visible surface determination is performed to identify the surfaces seen in the reflected and refracted direction. Evaluation of the illumination model to determine the intensities from these surfaces again asks what is seen in the mirror and refracted directions. This technique captures repeated reflections and refractions for greater realism. Additionally, the path from each light source to the object is checked for blockage by shadowing objects. The remarkable realism of this method results primarily from the recursive shading technique. Changes in the illumination model to accommodate this technique are minimal. The resultant illumination model is an extension to the generalized Phong model to include terms for light incident from the mirror reflection and the Snell refraction direction:

$$I(\lambda) = K_a(\lambda)I_a(\lambda) + K_d(\lambda)\sum_{n=1}^{ls}(\mathbf{N}\bullet\mathbf{L}_n)I_n(\lambda) + K_s\left[I_r(\lambda) + \sum_{n=1}^{ls}(\mathbf{N}\bullet\mathbf{H}_n)^{Ns}I_n(\lambda)\right] + K_tI_t(\lambda) \quad (4.20)$$

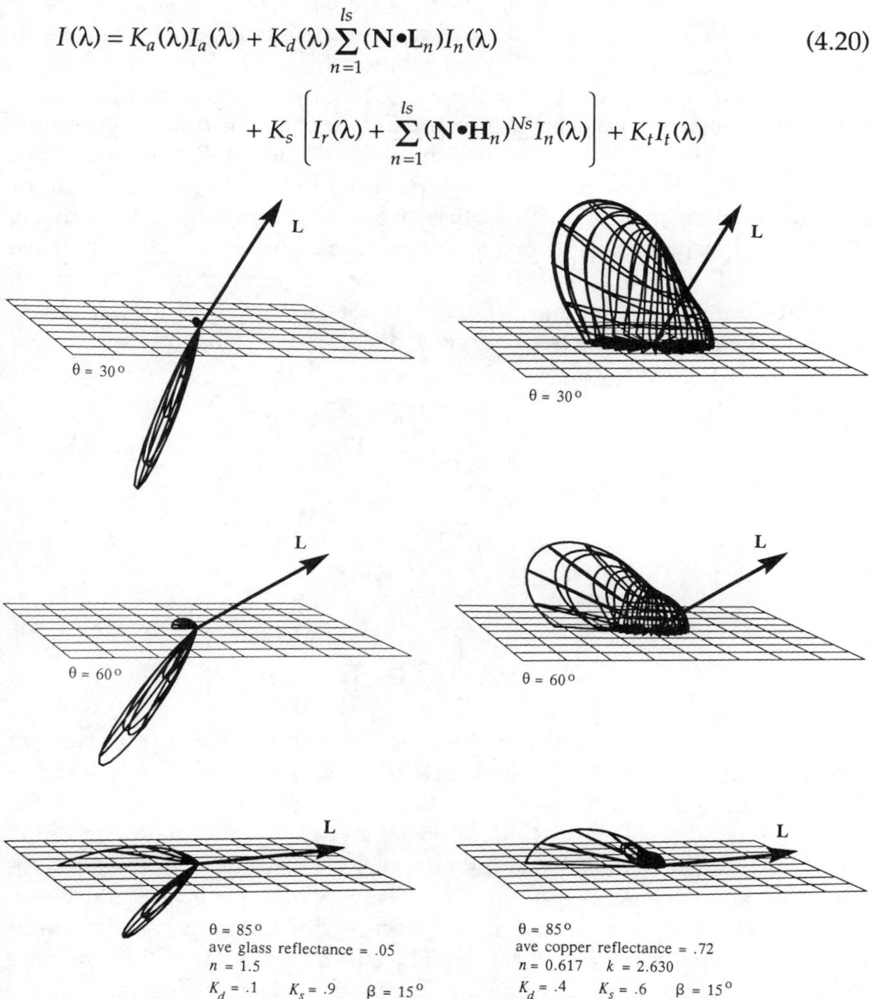

Figure 4.15: The Hall illumination model for glass and copper surfaces.

The criteria for stopping the recursive casting of rays described by Whitted was a maximum limit on the number of reflections and/or refractions per viewing ray. Only reflective objects require mirror direction information, and only transparent objects require information from the refracted direction. The maximum depth was set empirically before beginning computation of the image.

Kay and Greenberg (1979) address attenuation of light passing through a material while traveling between intersections, extending the coherent reflection and refraction terms to $K_s I_r A_t^d$ and $K_t I_t A_t^d$ respectively. The A_r and A_t factors are the attenuation per unit length of travel and d is the distance that I_r or I_t has traveled from the previous intersection. The result is better representation of transparent objects.

Hall and Greenberg (1983b) add a term for incoherent transmission and relates K_s and K_t to the Fresnel relationships. The incoherent transmission term provides better representation of light sources seen through transparent objects. The cosine power specular function presented by Blinn (1977) is used in this model and adapted for incoherent transmission. The Fresnel relationships provide better representation of reflections from metals and of glints from near grazing light sources. The Fresnel approximation presented by Cook and Torrance (1982), see Appendix III.5, *Fresnel Approximation,* is used to account for wavelength and incident angle dependencies of the reflection and transmission terms. This model collects previously disjointed work into a single expression of the form:

$$I(\lambda) = \text{ambient} + \text{diffuse} + \text{specular} + \text{transmitted}$$

$$I(\lambda) = K_a M(\lambda) I_a + K_d M(\lambda) \sum_{n=1}^{ls} (\mathbf{N} \bullet \mathbf{L}_n) I_n(\lambda) \tag{4.21}$$
$$+ K_s \left[F_r I_r(\lambda) A_r^d + \sum_{n=1}^{ls} (\mathbf{N} \bullet \mathbf{H}_n)^{Ns} F_r I_n(\lambda) \right]$$
$$+ K_s \left[F_t I_t(\lambda) A_t^d + \sum_{n=1}^{ls} (\mathbf{N} \bullet \mathbf{H}'_n)^{Ns} F_t I_n(\lambda) \right]$$

The wavelength dependency of the specular reflection and transmission terms is embodied in the Fresnel factors, F_r and F_t. Cook's approximation technique allows these to be estimated from the spectral curve for the material.

Note that the material spectral curves, $M(\lambda)$, are used in the ambient and diffuse terms as well as in the Fresnel terms. The material curve used for ambient and diffuse is not necessarily the same as the curve used for the specular Fresnel terms. The curve for the Fresnel terms may be for a substrate material like glass or vinyl, and the diffuse and ambient curve may be for a suspended pigment. Figure 4.15 demonstrates the Hall illumination model for glass and copper surfaces.

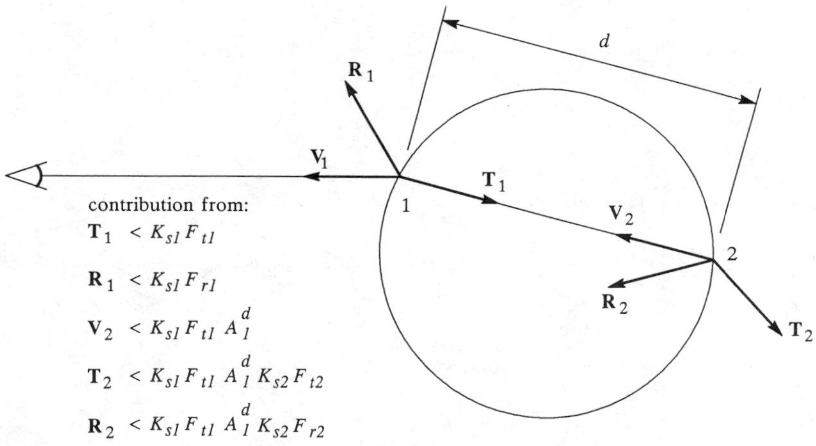

Figure 4.16: Dynamic reflection/refraction depth adjustment.

Hall also introduced the use of dynamic reflection and refraction depth adjustment. A minimum contribution threshold is established which is usually less than one color resolution step in the image file. The maximum contribution that is made by the first reflection is $K_s F_r$, and for the first refraction $K_s F_t$. For the next reflection, the A_r^d attenuation and the $K_s F_r$ is factored in. This repeats until the maximum contribution falls below the threshold. Note that this assumes all of the calculations are made in a normalized environment where the intensity does not exceed 1, Figure 4.16.

A single value for the index of refraction of a material is considered when computing the Snell refraction direction. This means that chromatic aberrations and prismatic effects are not captured.

The transitional models and ray tracing techniques described attempt to model actual behavior of light but are still constrained by lack of information. In addition to the primary sources, contributions from the reflected and transmitted directions are considered, but this is still a very limited description of the illumination incident on the surface. The methods work well for very smooth reflective surfaces, however, the results are disappointing when the techniques are used for semi-gloss surfaces. Shadows are very hard edged, and reflections are very crisp. In general, ray traced images have a very sharp "graphic" appearance and lack the subtlety of reality.

4.3.4 Distributed Ray Tracing

Cook, et al., (1984) uses a method of pseudorandom perturbation of many of the vectors in the model to provide greater global information

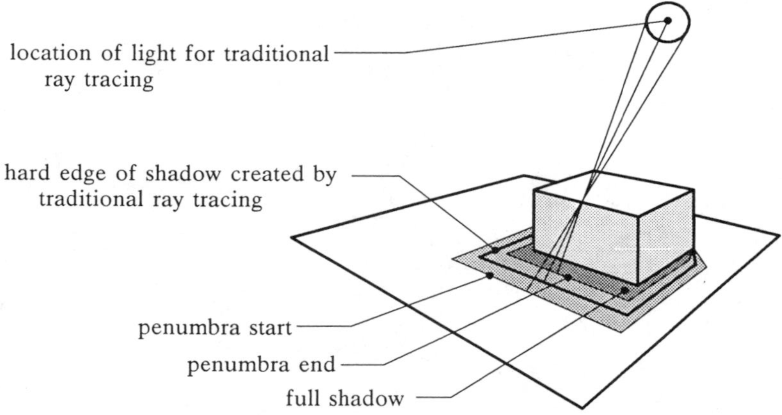

Figure 4.17: Traditional vs. correct shadowing in ray tracing.

for the final evaluation of color. Amanatides (1984) traces cones into the environment for greater global information. These approaches begin a transition toward energy equilibrium rendering techniques. The distribution of point samples or the area sampling of traced cones attempts to quantify what is happening in the global illuminating hemisphere.

The distributed ray tracing technique is the most easily generalized to a wide range of object types, and to complex environments. The paradigm for distributed ray tracing is simple, and the actual implementation is straightforward, but, not completely obvious. Distributed ray tracing provides a method for modeling diffuse and translucent surfaces, soft shadows, motion blur, and depth of field.

Ray tracing traditionally uses a single ray for every information query. The eye position, light position, object position, and geometry for reflection and refraction are rigidly fixed for an image. Greater global information is obtained by using bundles of rays for each query. For example, a bundle of rays could be cast toward a light source for shadow testing, or a bundle of rays could be cast for information from the reflected direction.

Shadows cast from a non-point light source provide an insight into the technique. Consider the casting of a shadow, Figure 4.17. Traditional ray tracing uses a single ray to the light source for shadow testing and illumination calculations. The result is shadows with hard edges and no penumbras.

Verbeck and Greenberg (1984) suggest modeling distributed sources as a collection of point centers for the light. Suppose 4 point centers were used for the light. A bundle of 4 rays would be used for shadow testing, one for each light center. A schematic of this is shown in Figure 4.18.

There are two drawbacks to the "bundle of rays to fixed light centers" solution. The first is that the use of fixed locations for the light cen-

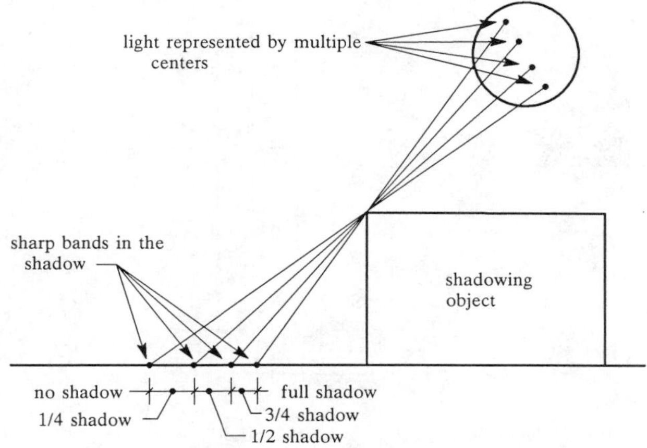

Figure 4.18: Schematic for shadow testing with a bundle of rays.

ters results in banding in the shadow as noted in Figure 4.18. The second is the increased computation time for the additional rays.

The first drawback is a result of attempting to represent an area event with a fixed set of samples. This produces aliasing as though the illumination is from 4 point sources. A solution mentioned by Verbeck is to use a large number of sub-lights. This solution converges to an acceptable image when there are sufficient sub-lights to reduce the bands to sub-pixel size. However, it is undesirable due to the additional computation required. An alternate solution is the use of a random light center generator. For each query, the generator randomly picks a position on the light for sampling. This solution produces unacceptable noise in the image. A third solution is a combination of the two, selecting several light centers and using a randomizing function that perturbs the center within the area it represents. This is known as jitter sampling. The magnitude of the randomizing provides a trade-off between banding and noise. Cook (1986) presents a detailed discussion of this approach from both a practical and theoretical level.

The second drawback is that a bundle of rays is used for each sampling. It can easily be seen that if a bundle of rays is projected for reflection that many new branches are added to the ray tree resulting a tremendous work being done to gather the information that provides the smallest impact on the color of a pixel. Cook, et al., (1984) suggests that since it is common to use more than one ray per pixel to provide anti-aliasing, the bundle of rays associated with each query could be distributed over the samples for the pixel. He uses a fixed sampling rate of 16 rays per pixel and distributes the ray bundles so there is one ray per query per pixel. For example, 16 light centers are used. One light center is assigned to each pixel ray. A randomizing perturbation is applied to the centers to eliminate banding.

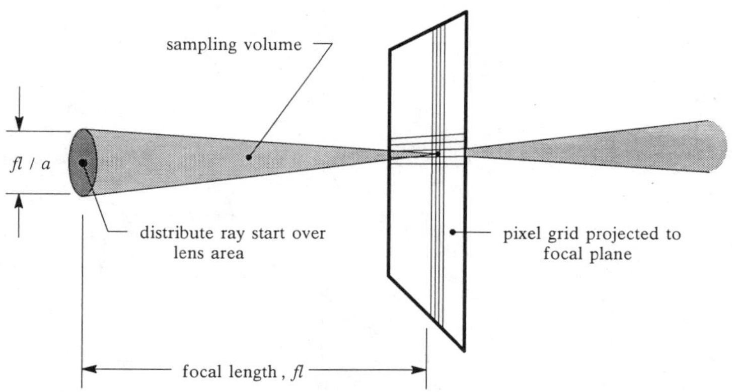

Figure 4.19: Schematic describing modeling depth of field.

Diffuse and translucent materials are modeled by distributing a bundle of rays in the reflected and refracted directions. Cook, et al., (1984) notes that the distribution should be weighted based upon the microfacet distribution function of the illumination model. The distribution is made by dividing the distribution function into cone-shaped volumes with an equal integral over the volume. The ray location is the center of the volume and a randomizing function is added to prevent aliasing (Cook 1986).

Motion blur is accomplished by distributing the rays for a pixel over the time duration of the frame. Transformation of the objects to the position represented by each time sample is required. This provides motion blur of objects, shadows, and reflections.

Depth of field is easily implemented by projecting the pixel sample grid (usually the hither plane) out to the focal distance, and distributing the ray start position (eye position) over the area of the lens. The diameter of the lens is *fl*/*a* where *fl* is the focal length and *a* is the aperture. This is schematically described in Figure 4.19.

Cook (1986) notes that antialiasing is improved by perturbing the sample point locations on the pixel sample grid. This is another feature that works well with distributed ray tracing.

The primary difficulty in implementing distributed ray tracing is selecting the locations of the rays that are distributed. A fixed distribution results in aliasing in the form of banding in the image. Introducing too much randomization results in unacceptable noise in the image which manifests as grainy appearance. Kajiya (1986) explored the methodology for distributing rays in great detail. Additional discussion of ray distribution is found in (Lee, et al. 1985) and (Dippé and Wolb 1985).

Distributed ray tracing produces very inspiring imagery. Unfortunately, there is a high cost associated with the extra rays per pixel required to provide a good sampling of diffuse effects. Although more information is available in distributed ray tracing, the issue of energy equilibrium in the rendered environment is not fully addressed.

4.4 Radiosity, Analytical Models

The energy equilibrium illumination models are subsets of the general illumination expression of Eq.(2.49). The development of these models has been limited by the inability of the existing rendering techniques to provide sufficient information for evaluation of the model. Research in the area of improved energy equilibrium illumination models is forcing the development of new rendering techniques.

The illumination models and techniques presented in this section are still limited to research applications. The computational and data storage demands render these techniques impractical for commercial applications. However, as the performance cost of hardware continues to fall, we can expect variations of these techniques to become common practice.

4.4.1 An Energy Equilibrium Illumination Model

Cook and Torrance (1982) propose an energy formulation for the illumination model. This model uses the energy instead of intensity that reaches the illuminated surfaces from the light sources. As with previous models, the illumination is divided into ambient, diffuse, and specular contributions. The resulting model is:

$$I(\lambda) = K_a(\lambda)I_a + K_d R_d(\lambda) \sum_{n=1}^{ls} I_n(\lambda)(\mathbf{N} \bullet \mathbf{L}_n)d\omega_n + K_s \sum_{n=1}^{ls} R_{bd}(\lambda) I_n(\lambda)(\mathbf{N} \bullet \mathbf{L}_n)d\omega_n \tag{4.22}$$

The diffuse reflectance, R_d relates the reflected intensity in any direction to the energy flux per unit area incident on the surface. Typically, $R_d(\lambda) = M(\lambda)/\pi$, where $M(\lambda)$ is the measured material spectral curve for the diffuse component of the material. As a result of the law of reciprocity, $K_a(\lambda) = M(\lambda)$ for consistency between the diffuse and ambient reflection. K_s plus K_d equals one in the original formulation. The bidirectional reflectance function, R_{bd} relates the reflected intensity in a specified direction to the energy flux per unit area incident from a given direction. The bidirectional reflection function is a combination of a Fresnel term, a roughness function, a geometric attenuation function, and some additional factors to satisfy energy equilibrium as introduced in Section 2.3.2.1, *Incoherent Illumination*. Briefly reviewing, this is given by:

$$R_{bd} = \frac{DGF_r}{(\mathbf{N}\bullet\mathbf{L}_n)(\mathbf{N}\bullet\mathbf{V})} \tag{4.23}$$

The microfacet distribution function used by Cook is adapted from the work of Beckmann (1963):[7]

$$D = \frac{1}{4\pi m^2(\mathbf{N}\bullet\mathbf{H}_n)^4}\exp\left[\frac{(\mathbf{N}\bullet\mathbf{H}_n)^2 - 1}{(\mathbf{N}\bullet\mathbf{H}_n)^2 m^2}\right] \tag{4.24}$$

Note that this is the rough surface function described in Section 2.3.2.1, *Incoherent Illumination*. The shape of the Beckmann distribution function is similar to those discussed by Blinn (Eqs.(4.16), (4.17), (4.18)) for small values of m ($m < 0.6$ or $\beta < 40^{\circ}$), Figure 4.20. Cook suggests that the advantage of this function is that it *"gives the absolute value without introducing arbitrary constants"*. The value of m is related to the β used by Blinn for distribution function comparison by:

$$m^2 = -\frac{\tan^2\beta}{\ln((\cos^4\beta)/2)} \tag{4.25}$$

The Fresnel term accounts for wavelength dependency of the highlight. Cook presents an approximate method for determining the Fresnel reflectance which is detailed in Appendix III.5, *Fresnel Approximation*. This approximation has been adopted for illumination models used for ray tracing. The geometric attenuation function, G, used by Cook was that presented by Torrance and Sparrow (1967). However, the function proposed by Sancer (1969) can also be used.

A theoretically valid model stands up to scrutiny for energy equilibrium. If the Fresnel reflectance is set to 1, then all energy is reflected. If the ambient illumination is zero, then energy reaches the surface from light sources only. Since the distribution function can be used without the introduction of arbitrary constants, K_s is set to 1. The energy equilibrium expression for incoherent illumination given by Eq.(2.39) can be used to examine this model. Figure 4.21 plots the integration of the bidirectional reflectance using including the microfacet distribution only ($G = 1$, $F_r = 1$), and including both microfacet distribution and geometric attenuation ($F_r = 1$).

---

[7] The factor of 4 in the denominator of D was missing in the formulation originally presented by Cook (1981,1982, l)illumination model This omission was discovered during numerical integration of the function over the illuminated hemisphere, and confirmed by Koestner (1986).

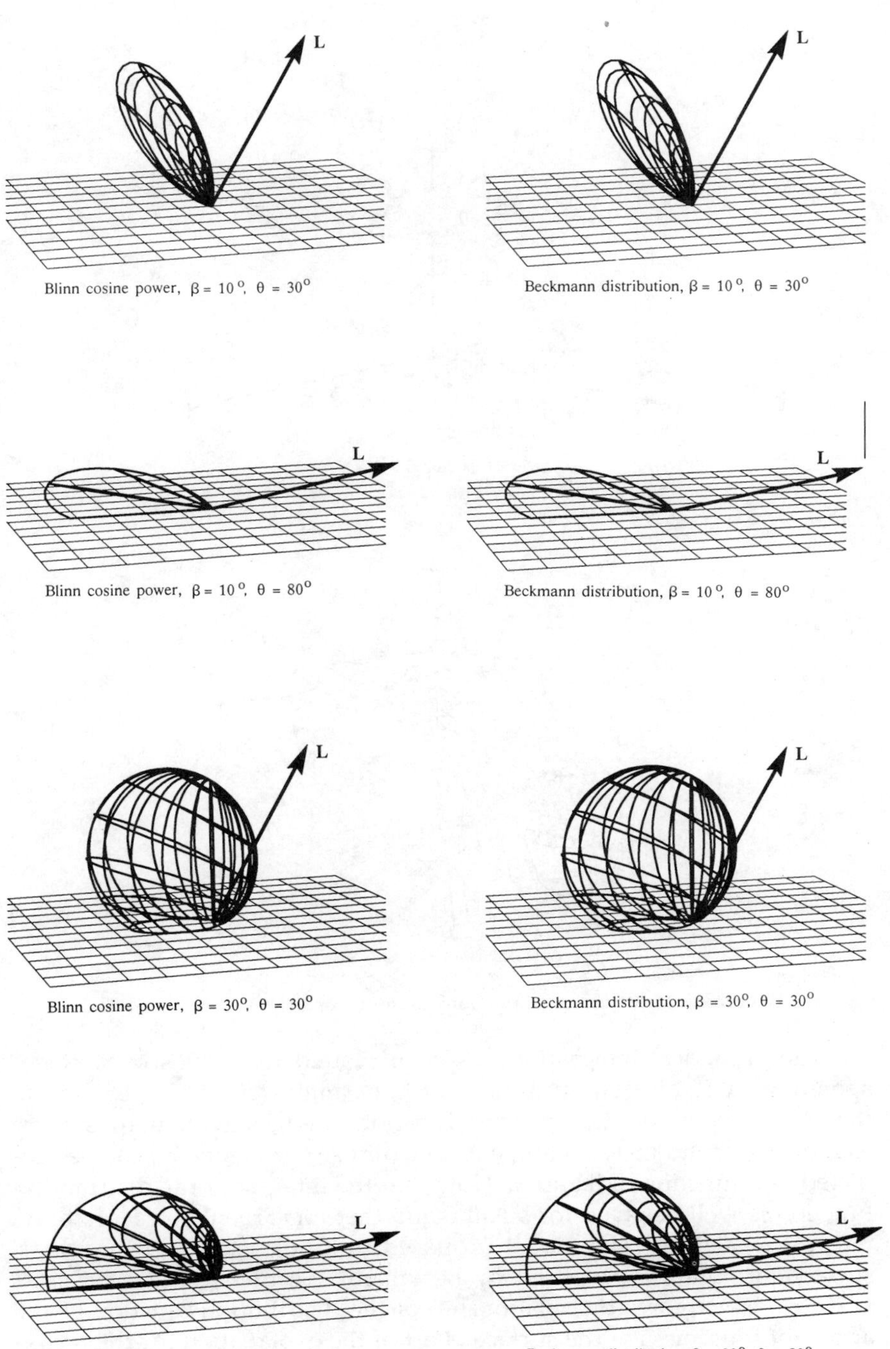

Figure 4.20: Blinn cosine power and Beckmann microfacet distribution functions.

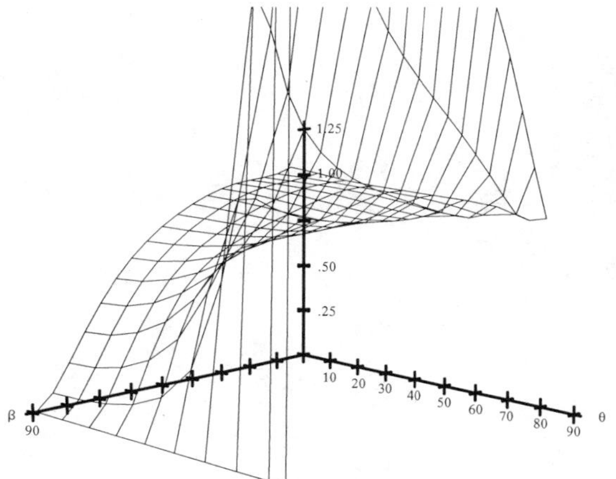

Energy surface for the bidirectional reflectance, G=1.0, $F_r = 1.0$

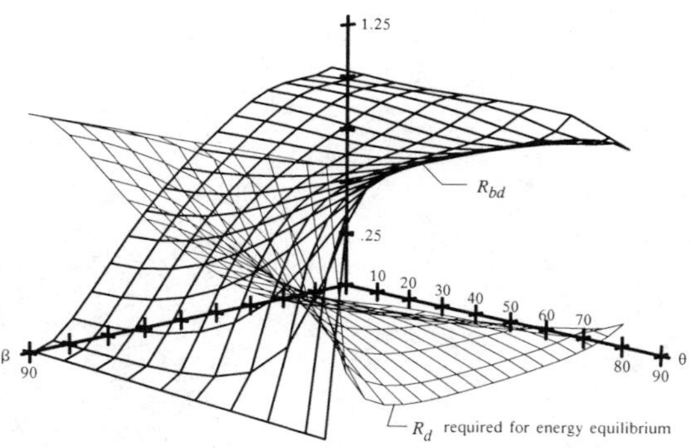

Energy surface for the bidirectional reflectance including G, $F_r = 1.0$

Figure 4.21: Numerical integration of the Cook illumination model.

The numerical integration has been plotted for values of *m* corresponding to $5^{\circ} < \beta < 90^{\circ}$ and incident light angles of $0^{\circ} < \beta < 85^{\circ}$. Note that the integral of the specular function changes with both surface roughness, β, and incident angle θ. The diffuse coefficient, K_d can be predicted as a function of β and θ. Note that the integral of the distribution function is well behaved for small θ and that for large θ and large β the integral exceeds 1. The model proposed by Cook uses only the rough surface formulation proposed by Beckmann. Section 2.3.2.2, *Microfacet Distribution*, explores the relationship of the distribution function to the apparent roughness of the surface. Part of the explanation for the breakdown is that the apparent roughness of the surface decreases as θ approaches grazing. A different distribution function is required for low apparent roughness.

4.4.2 Radiosity for Diffuse Environments

Goral, et al., (1984) adapts radiosity techniques used in thermal engineering to model the movement of light energy through an environment. This technique assumes all surfaces are rough and the materials are opaque reducing the complete expression of Eq.(2.49) to the incoherent reflection and emissivity terms only. Additional simplification is achieved by assuming the surfaces are ideal diffuse (Lambertian) reflectors and emitters. The illumination model used is:

$$I(\lambda) = \varepsilon(\lambda) + R_d(\lambda)\int^{2\pi} I_{\mathrm{L}}(\lambda)(\mathbf{N}\bullet\mathbf{L})d\omega \tag{4.26}$$

R_d is the diffuse or directional hemispherical reflectance as described in Section 2.3.2.4, *Ideal Diffuse Illumination*. Typically, $R_d(\lambda) = M(\lambda)/\pi$.

Evaluation of the illumination model for a specific patch, n, in the environment is approximated by summing contributions from all patches in the environment:

$$I_n(\lambda) = \varepsilon_n(\lambda) + R_{d,n}(\lambda)\sum_{m=1}^{p} I_m(\lambda)\mathrm{F}_{m,n} \tag{4.27}$$

The form factor, $\mathrm{F}_{m,n}$, is introduced as a notational convenience. It is a factor that relates the energy density incident on patch n from patch m to the intensity reflected from patch m. Specifically:

$$\Phi_{m,n}/A_n = |\mathrm{E}^2_{m,n}| = I_m\mathrm{F}_{m,n} \tag{4.28}$$

Substituting the energy relationship of Section 2.2.4, *Intensity and Energy*, Eq.(2.9) and the solid angle expression of Section 2.2.3, *Illuminating Hemisphere and Solid Angle*, Eq.(2.4) the form factor is given by:

$$\mathrm{F}_{m,n} = \frac{1}{A_n}\int^{A_n}\int^{A_m}\frac{\cos\theta_n\cos\theta_m dA_m dA_n}{r^2_{m,n}} \tag{4.29}$$

Figure 4.22 describes the form factor. The computation of form factors is described in detail by Goral and is not repeated here.[8] Explicit form factor calculation has been replaced by numerical approximations in practice.

The form factor is a function of geometry only. Once the form factors have been computed for an environment, they remain valid provided the geometry does not change. Patch reflectances and emissivities can be changed without requiring recomputation of the form factors.

---

[8] This discussion is presented in terms of intensity for consistency throughout this chapter. The original presentation of radiosity was expressed in terms of energy flux per unit area. Energy formulation results in an additional factor of π in the denominator of the form factor.

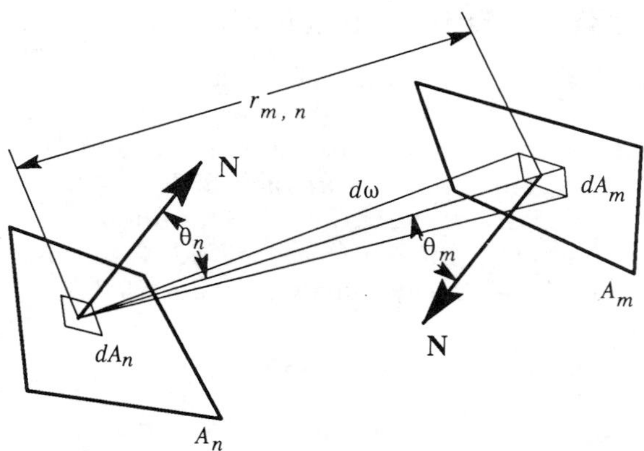

Figure 4.22: The form factor for radiosity (adapted from Goral 1984).

Consider once again the very simple environment of Figure 4.1. The light is generalized as patch 4. This patch has a nonzero emissivity. In this example the patches are suspended in space. There is no ambient light except that generated by reflection from the patches. An additional restriction is that none of the patches are shaded from each other by other patches.

The technique for applying this illumination model is similar in concept to that discussed in Section 4.1.2, *Starting from the Light*.

Note that I, ε, and R_d are wavelength dependent quantities. The functional dependence on wavelength, λ is omitted for clarity in the presentation of the technique. The equation set that describes this simple environment is:

$$I_1 = \varepsilon_1 + R_{d1} I_1 \mathrm{F}_{1,1} + R_{d1} I_2 \mathrm{F}_{2,1} + R_{d1} I_3 \mathrm{F}_{3,1} + R_{d1} I_4 \mathrm{F}_{4,1} \tag{4.30a}$$

$$I_2 = \varepsilon_2 + R_{d2} I_1 \mathrm{F}_{1,2} + R_{d2} I_2 \mathrm{F}_{2,2} + R_{d2} I_3 \mathrm{F}_{3,2} + R_{d2} I_4 \mathrm{F}_{4,2} \tag{4.30b}$$

$$I_3 = \varepsilon_3 + R_{d3} I_1 \mathrm{F}_{1,3} + R_{d3} I_2 \mathrm{F}_{2,3} + R_{d3} I_3 \mathrm{F}_{3,3} + R_{d3} I_4 \mathrm{F}_{4,3} \tag{4.30c}$$

$$I_4 = \varepsilon_4 + R_{d4} I_1 \mathrm{F}_{1,4} + R_{d4} I_2 \mathrm{F}_{2,4} + R_{d4} I_3 \mathrm{F}_{3,4} + R_{d4} I_4 \mathrm{F}_{4,4} \tag{4.30d}$$

This equation set is rewritten in a generalized matrix form for an n patch environment as:

$$\begin{bmatrix} 1-R_{d1}\mathrm{F}_{1,1} & -R_{d1}\mathrm{F}_{2,1} & \cdots & -R_{d1}\mathrm{F}_{n,1} \\ -R_{d2}\mathrm{F}_{1,2} & 1-R_{d2}\mathrm{F}_{2,2} & \cdots & -R_{d2}\mathrm{F}_{n,2} \\ \cdot & \cdot & & \cdot \\ \cdot & \cdot & & \cdot \\ -R_{dn}\mathrm{F}_{1,n} & -R_{dn}\mathrm{F}_{2,n} & \cdots & 1-R_{dn}\mathrm{F}_{n,n} \end{bmatrix} \begin{bmatrix} I_1 \\ I_2 \\ \cdot \\ \cdot \\ I_n \end{bmatrix} = \begin{bmatrix} \varepsilon_1 \\ \varepsilon_2 \\ \cdot \\ \cdot \\ \varepsilon_n \end{bmatrix} \tag{4.31}$$

Goral uses Gaussian elimination with partial pivoting to solve the equation set. Note that there is a set of equations for every color sample used. The form factors are the same for each color sample equation set, but R_d, ε, and I are different.

The radiosity technique computes the intensity (color) of each polygon independent of processing for display. A Gouraud shading algorithm was then used to render images with the vertex colors determined by averaging the colors of adjacent patches on a surface. Goral's work in conjunction with that of Meyer, et al., (1986a) is particularly noteworthy because it includes the creation of a real control environment for comparative study and measurement. The real environment and the image were displayed side-by-side through cameras in a very controlled fashion. It was reported that when observers were asked to select which display was the computer generated image, they *"did no better than they would have simply by guessing"* (Meyer, et al. 1986a).

Cohen, et al., (1985a,1985b,1986), developed an extension to the radiosity method that provides a general methodology for approximating form factors and accounting for shadowing within the environment. This extension allows the rendering of more complex environments using radiosity techniques.

Cohen observes that any two patches that have the same projection on the illuminating hemisphere have the same form factor. He proposes projecting the environment onto the illuminating hemisphere over a given patch by performing visible surface calculations from that patch. Each sample point in the visible surface projection represents some solid angle, and a corresponding form factor, ΔF_q. The form factor for a particular patch is approximated by summing the form factors of the sample points, s, covered by the patch:

$$F_{mn} = \sum_{q=1}^{s} \Delta F_q \tag{4.32}$$

Visible surface projection onto a hemisphere is difficult, and Cohen suggests the use of a *hemi-cube*, or half of a cube for the projection of visible surfaces, Figure 4.23.

A hemi-cube is positioned at the center of each patch. A visible surface computation is made for each surface of the cube using any visible surface algorithm.[9] Note that only the patch identifier for the visible surface is required. No shading calculations are performed at this time. The sampling frequency of the hemi-cube is fixed for the environment. Cohen suggests a resolution of 50x50 to 100x100. The algorithm for generating form factors is detailed in Appendix IV.1, *Hemi-cube Form Factors*.

---

[9] The only requirement for the visible surface algorithm is that it be able to identify the visible surface for any pixel. The selection of the type of visible surface algorithm used is not critical because no color computations are performed at this step.

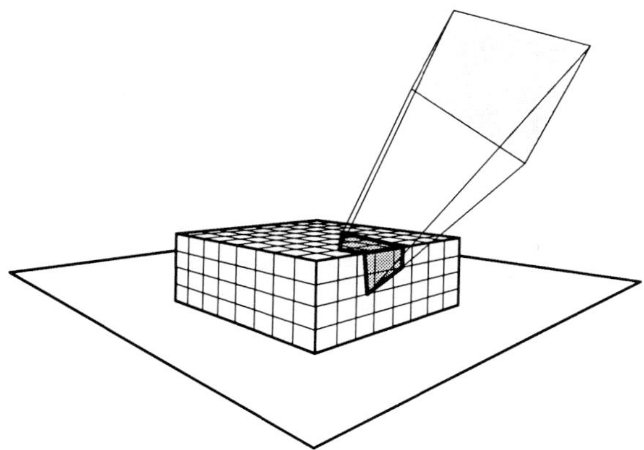

Figure 4.23: A hemi-cube for form factor evaluation (adapted from Cohen 1985a).

The matrix describing the energy movement through the environment, Eq.(4.31), is used without change. Cohen notes that the physical limits on form factors and reflectance assure that the matrix is strictly diagonal dominant. Therefore, solution can be obtained using iterative techniques such as Gauss-Siedel iteration and quick convergence is guaranteed.[10]

The rendering technique is similar to that used by Goral with two significant exceptions:

- The scheme to determine vertex colors is to average the color of surrounding patches for vertices that are on the interior of a surface, and to extrapolate colors to the edge vertices. The extrapolation assumes that the color at the center of the distance from the edge vertex to the adjacent interior vertex is the average color of the surrounding patches, Figure 4.24.
- The color interpolation for each patch is performed in object space rather than screen space. As noted earlier in this chapter, screen space interpolation introduces anomalies due to the nonlinear perspective transformation. Interpolation in object space eliminates these anomalies.

Additional description of radiosity techniques is found in Greenberg, et al., (1986) which provides a good overview of the technique, Cohen, et al., (1986) which discusses techniques for subdividing the surfaces in the environment for efficient processing, and Baum, et al., (1986) which discusses extensions for efficient processing of dynamic environments for multiple frame animation.

---

[10] Iterative techniques are much less computationally intense than Gaussian elimination (as used by Goral) if quick convergence is assured.

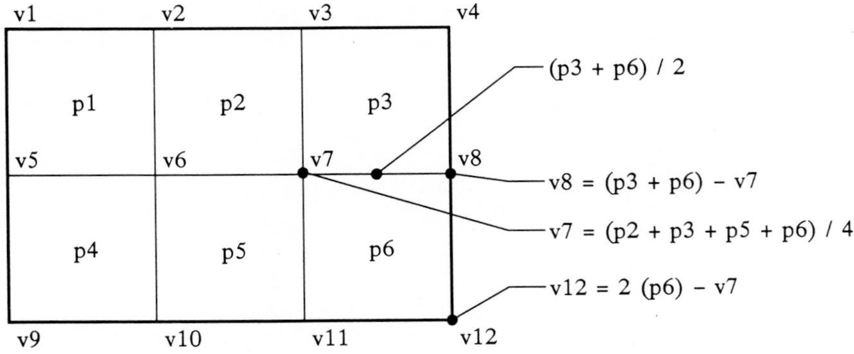

Figure 4.24: Resolving patch colors to vertex colors.

4.4.3 Radiosity for Specular Environments

Immel (1986a,1986b) presents an extension to the radiosity technique that demonstrates that it is possible to include specular or directional effects in the radiosity solution for illumination of an environment. He is quick to point out that the computation and data storage demands place this technique beyond the current limits of practicality.

The emphasis in this work was in the extension of the radiosity technique, and not in the illumination model. Illumination models that are candidates for this technique must be valid energy equilibrium models. The illumination model was selected for ease of implementation. Immel uses a variation of the Phong model with factors to insure energy equilibrium.

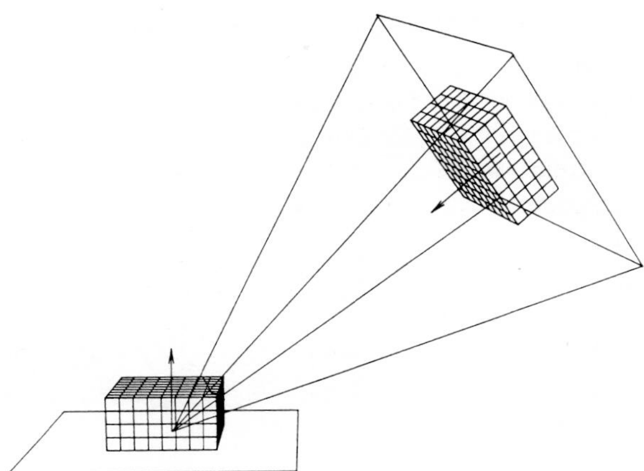

Figure 4.25: Local orientation of the hemi-cube (Immel 1986b).

Consider using a directional illumination model with the hemi-cube of Figure 4.23. A non-directional illumination model results in a solution with a single intensity per patch (per color sample). A directional illumination model results in a solution with an intensity for each sample direction of the hemi-cube. For a hemi-cube with a resolution of 50 there are 50×50×3=7500 sample points. The illumination solution contains 7500 intensities per patch (per color sample). This requires tremendous data storage for even a very simple environment.

A non-directional illumination model requires a single coefficient to relate the incoming energy to the reflected intensity. A directional illumination model requires that for each input direction there is a coefficient to relate the energy from that direction to the intensity reflected in each output direction. There would be 7500×7500=56,250,000 coefficients required to describe the interactions for a single patch. The matrix that describes the relationships between patches grows from an $n \times n$ matrix to an $n \times 7500 \times n \times 7500$ matrix!

The technique used by Immel computes much of the information on-the-fly and uses a generalization to the hemi-cube to facilitate determining the relationships between patches. The hemi-cube used by Cohen is locally oriented to the patch, Figure 4.25. The directional relationship between two hemi-cubes is not easily defined. Specifically, it is not simple to determine which outgoing direction of the source hemi-cube illuminates a particular incoming direction of the target hemi-cube.

Immel uses a globally oriented cube for each patch, Figure 4.26. An incoming direction for a target cube is illuminated by the inverse direction from the source cube. Clever indexing of the cube allows determining the sample point representing the outgoing direction as a simple index calculation from the sample point representing the incoming direction, as detailed in Immel and Greenberg (1986a).

The solution technique keeps a visibility buffer and an outgoing intensity buffer for each global cube. The visibility buffer describes which patch is visible in each cell of the global cube. The outgoing intensity buffer is set to zero for non-emissive patches and is loaded with the emitted intensity for emissive surfaces. Each patch is solved in turn by cycling through the cells in the cube and applying the illumination model to reflect the incoming intensity for the cell into the cells of the outgoing intensity buffer. This process of solving for all the patches in the environment continues until some convergence criteria is met. This algorithm is detailed in Appendix IV.2, *Specular Radiosity*.

The results of this work, Figure 4.36, demonstrate the subtle reflection of the yellow cube on the partially reflective floor. Artifacts become visible when the surfaces are mirror-like. The use of point locations around which global cubes are centered results in aliasing when environment features change rapidly. This condition occurs on the reflected edges of both objects and pools of light reflected from surfaces.

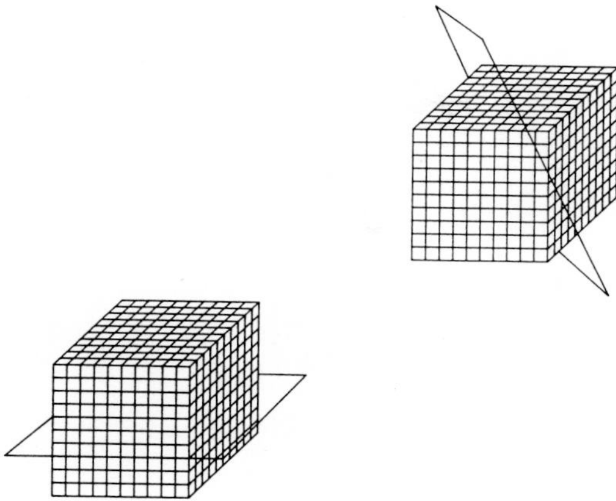

Figure 4.26: The globally oriented illumination cube (Immel 1986b).

While this is not a technique used in practice, it provides an example of rigorous application of an illumination model with energy conservation techniques to solve for the illumination of non-diffuse environments. In combination with distributed ray tracing, this sets the stage for hybrid solution techniques.

4.5 Hybrid Techniques

Wallace, et al., (1987) presents a methodology for implementing a hybrid technique. The hybrid technique combines ray tracing and radiosity techniques using each to greatest advantage.[11]

The illumination process is divided into two parts, a diffuse part and a specular part. The observed intensity is a sum of the emissivity, diffuse intensity, and specular intensity:

$$I = \varepsilon_v + I_{diffuse} + I_{specular} \tag{4.33}$$

where

$$I_{diffuse} = K_d R_d \int^{2\pi} I_i(\mathbf{N} \bullet \mathbf{L}_i)\, d\omega \tag{4.34a}$$

$$I_{specular} = K_s \int^{2\pi} R_{bd} I_i(\mathbf{N} \bullet \mathbf{L}_i)\, d\omega \tag{4.34b}$$

The reflected diffuse and specular components depend upon intensity incident from all directions. Since incident intensity is reflected intensity from other surfaces, I_i contains both diffuse and specular components.

[11] The hybrid technique presented by Wallace was based on a theoretical foundation laid by Rushmeier (1986).

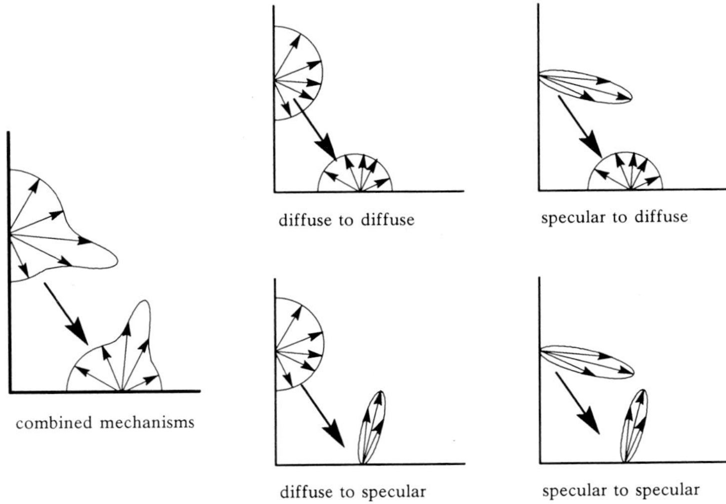

Figure 4.27: The four "mechanisms" of illumination (adapted from Wallace 1987).

This interdependence of diffuse and specular illumination does not allow for the simple summation of a diffuse radiosity solution with ray traced reflections.

Wallace identifies four *mechanisms* of illumination. He notes that the incident illumination is a combination of a diffuse and a specular component. Each of these results in both a diffuse and a specular reflection. Thus, the reflected color is a summation of a diffuse incident to diffuse reflected component, a diffuse incident to specular reflected component, a specular incident to diffuse reflected component, and a specular incident to specular reflected component, Figure 4.27.

The hybrid method uses two passes for illumination calculation. The first is a view independent pass, similar to the diffuse radiosity computation, which computes the diffuse illumination of the scene. The second is a view dependent pass, similar to distributed ray tracing, which uses the first pass to provide global illumination information and selective sampling to provide the specular components.

4.5.1 View Independent Illumination

The view independent pass solves for the diffuse illumination component, Eq.(4.34a). As noted earlier, determining the reflected diffuse intensity depends upon incident intensity from other surfaces. This incident intensity from other surfaces contains both diffuse and specular components. Thus, the view independent pass must include all four illumination mechanisms.

The diffuse to diffuse transfer is handled by the diffuse technique previously discussed in Section 4.4.2, *Radiosity for Diffuse Environments*.

The specular effects are included only to the extent that they influence the diffuse illumination. The technique used to account for specular illumination extends the utility of the form factor.

Recall that the form factor is a geometric term that describes the fraction of reflected energy from one patch that reaches another. Diffuse radiosity assumes energy is reflected in an ideal diffuse fashion, that is, equal intensity in all directions. The hybrid technique uses two components for the form factor, a diffuse to diffuse component and a specular to diffuse component, Figure 4.27.

Suppose patch A is illuminated by patch B through a sample point on the hemi-cube. The form factor for the sample point on the hemi-cube, when multiplied by the intensity incoming through that sample point, $I_{B,A}$, gives the energy flux per unit area reaching patch A through that sample point. The incoming intensity is made up of a diffuse component, $I_{B(diffuse)}$, and a specular component, $I_{B,A(specular)}$. Note that the diffuse component is non-directional, and that the specular component is directional. The diffuse component is accounted for by the form factor from patch B to A. The specular component is accounted for by determining which patches contribute to the specular intensity, $I_{B,A(specular)}$, and assigning them a form factor weighted by the specular reflectivity or transmissivity of patch B, Figure 4.28. The generation of form factors in this fashion is detailed in Appendix IV.3, *Hybrid Form Factors*.

Wallace simplified the process of determining the specular contribution to the form factor by assuming optically smooth specular surfaces during form factor calculation. This results in coherent reflection only. There is then only one direction that contributes to the specular reflection. In addition, it is not necessary to perform area integration to

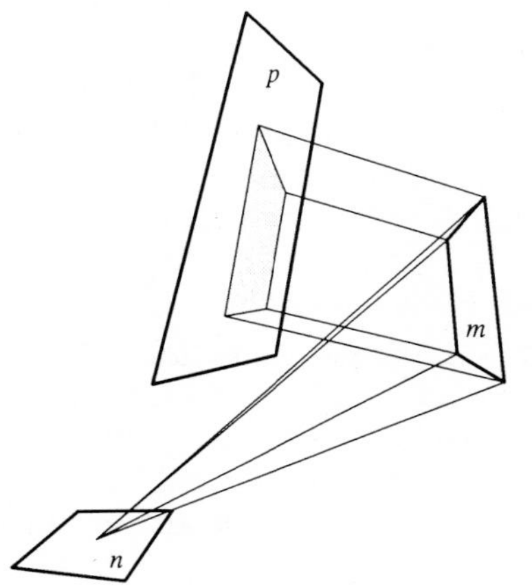

$F_{n,m}$ relates the energy incident on n from m to the diffuse intensity of m

$F_{n,p} = K_s F_{n,m}$ relates the energy incident on n from p via specular reflection through m to the diffuse intensity of p

Figure 4.28: Combined diffuse and specular form factor.

determine incident energy. The incident intensity and coherently reflected intensity are simply related by a reflectivity factor (Section 2.2.5, *Reflection and Refraction*).

In addition, Wallace extended the hemi-cube concept to include transparent materials by using another hemi-cube to describe illumination from the transmitted direction. This extension results in the capability to represent varying degrees of translucency in transparent materials.

The diffuse illumination is computed by solving the resultant equation set, Eq.(4.31). The solution method used is that previously described for diffuse radiosity. Note that the equation set is the same size for the hybrid diffuse solution as for the solution of earlier ideal diffuse radiosity techniques. The additional work is imbedded in the computation of the form factors.

4.5.2 View Dependent Illumination

The actual generation of an image occurs in the view dependent step. Ray tracing is used to solve for the specular illumination component, Eq.(4.34b). This is summed with the previously described diffuse illumination to provide a complete solution to the illumination equation, Eq. (4.33).

The ray traced solution must account for both diffuse to specular and specular to specular illumination mechanisms. The specular component, $I_{specular}$, in Eq.(4.34b), depends upon incident intensities from the entire illuminating hemisphere. The technique used by Wallace is similar ray tracing with bundles of rays.

For each sample point on the image plane, the visible surface is determined, the diffuse illumination component is computed, the specular illumination component is computed, and finally, the diffuse and specular components are summed to generate the sample point color.

The diffuse illumination component is determined using standard radiosity techniques. These were described earlier in Section 4.4.2, *Radiosity for Diffuse Environments*. If the surface is not reflective, then only the diffuse illumination component needs is evaluated.

If the surface is reflective, then the specular illumination component of the illumination model is evaluated. A sampling frustum in the mirror direction from the view ray provides the incident intensity information required to evaluate the specular illumination model. Visibility is computed at low resolution in the sampling frustum. For every point in the sampling frustum this algorithm for computing the combined diffuse and specular illumination is recursively applied. Light sources receive no special consideration as in previously described ray tracing techniques.

The selection of the sampling frustum is dependent upon the illumination model. The sampling frustum is centered in the mirror direction and the view angle is dependent upon the spread of the specular function. A Gaussian distribution centered on the mirror direction was used for the specular reflection (Wallace 1988). The function centered on the reflection direction provides symmetry about the reflected. This results in a sample frustum with an aspect ratio of 1 and without a preferred orientation. All other specular functions (with the exception of the Phong function) discussed in this chapter would require an aspect ratio dependent on incident angle, which would, in turn, result in a preferred orientation.

A logical next step is the adaptation of the distributed ray tracing methodology to the solution for the specular (view dependent) component of the image. This would minimize ray tracing computations by reducing the number of rays traced to capture the specular illumination component.

4.6 Visual Comparison

Representative images of the illumination models and rendering techniques described in this text are presented here in Figures 4.29 through 4.37 for comparison. Many of the differences are subtle and are far more apparent on an RGB monitor than after photographing and printing.

Figure 4.29: Constant color for all polygons using the Bouknight illumination model. Note the faceted appearance.

Figure 4.30: Gouraud color interpolation across polygons using the Bouknight illumination model. Note the interpolation anomalies along the shadow edge.

Figure 4.31: Phong normal interpolation used with the Phong illumination model. Note the addition of specular highlights and the plastic appearance.

Figure 4.32: Ray tracing with the Blinn cosine power specular function and reflection mapping. Note the global horizon reflection but the lack of local reflection information.

Figure 4.33: Recursive ray tracing with the Whitted illumination model. Note the addition of shadows and local reflection and refraction.

Figure 4.34: Distributed ray tracing using the Hall illumination model. The light sources only are distributed. Note the spectral character of the reflection and the reflections at the edges of the crystal ball as a result of the Fresnel relationships. Also note the soft shadows.

Figure 4.35: Radiosity techniques with hemi-cube extensions for shadow inclusion using a diffuse illumination model. Note the color bleeding and subtle shading and shadowing (Courtesy C. Goral, Program of Computer Graphics, Cornell University).

Figure 4.36: Reflective environment rendered with radiosity (Courtesy D. Immel, Program of Computer Graphics, Cornell University).

Figure 4.37: Hybrid techniques with a modified Phong illumination model (Courtesy J. Wallace, Program of Computer Graphics, Cornell University).

4.7 Summary

The approximations and idealizations made in early illumination models are well justified. Empirical techniques were employed to generate something that looked realistic within the constraints of rendering technique and available hardware. The measure of realism was very subjective, and expectations were not terribly high. In contrast to black and white, nearly anything in a gray scale is more realistic. The same is true in the transition to color and to specular highlights.

Increased sophistication of the graphics user demands an increase in the sophistication of graphics imagery. The result is increased attention to the processes that result in shading and color.

The processes became more demanding of the rendering algorithm to provide sufficient information for evaluation. Current research is focused on rendering techniques that simulate the movement of light through an environment. The needs for energy equilibrium and complete global illumination information are clearly recognized. However, the current work is using primitive illumination models for the illumination calculations.

The subjectively incredible realism of the results suggests that the technique has again surpassed the sophistication of the viewer. It also suggests that energy equilibrium and complete global illumination information are more important in creating the illusion of reality than correct microfacet distribution functions or geometric attenuation. Another possibility is that it reflects a collective shift in attitude as the popularity of the crisp, polished imagery of traditional ray tracing has given way to blurred reflections and soft shadows. Regardless, we can expect to see attention shift to the integration of the new rendering techniques with sophisticated illumination models to create rendering tools of unsurpassed versatility.

Use of any of the illumination models demands that the context of the rendering technique is matched by the model. Attempting to use an energy equilibrium model in the context of a simple scanline renderer with no reflection or refraction produces dismal results. Conversely, attempting to use a model that does not preserve energy equilibrium produces unpredictable results with radiosity techniques.

Effort has been made to represent the cited works as accurately as possible. The true evolution of technique is not nearly as straightforward as presented in this discussion. As with any evolution there are many digressions from what appears to be the primary path.

5

Image Display

"All it takes is for the rendered image to look right."
- James Blinn (1985)

The display process begins with image information describing the color and intensity at any point on a image plane and is completed by an observer perceiving the resultant displayed image. The steps in getting from the image information to the observed perception involve transforming the image data so it can be displayed within the limitations of the display device. Traditionally, part of the transformation occurs within the rendering step before image files are written and the remainder of the transformation occurs when the image file is mapped into a specific display device.

This discussion is aimed towards video image display. However, many of the principles apply to all types of image display media. The primary difference is the additive color reproduction used for video as opposed to the subtractive color reproduction used in slides and print. In general, the additive reproduction media are far more predictable and controllable than the subtractive media.

The Society of Motion Picture and Television Engineers (SMPTE), the National Television System Committee (NTSC), and the Electronic Industry Association (EIA) have established equipment standards and standard practices for the broadcast video industry.[1] Many of these standards are directly applicable to computer graphics. However, many graphics applications use monitors operating at higher resolution, with different interlace standards, and with significantly different phosphors than those used for broadcast receivers. Thus, these recommendations must be considered in the context of the equipment being used.

This chapter reviews all aspects of the display process. The first sections address proper equipment configuration and setup. The final sections address the process of transforming the image data into the proper information to be stored in the image file and the final transformation from the image file to the display device. There is little published reference material in the computer graphics literature addressing many of these issues. Thus, this chapter is largely a collection of information from personal experience and discussions with other computer graphics professionals.

---

[1] Referenced standards can be ordered directly from SMPTE or EIA.

A familiarity with basic video display technology and display devices is assumed in this chapter. Recommended background references are Blinn 1979, Rogers 1986, and Conrac 1980.

5.1 Image File Considerations

There are two aspects of correcting image data for display. The first is mapping image colors into the color space of the monitor used for display. The second is correcting for intensity non-linearity or gamma of the monitor. Both correct color space mapping and correct gamma correction are required for proper appearance of an image.

Image files are an intermediate step between image computation and display. An issue that must be addressed is the form of the data stored in the image file. The correction process can happen prior to image storage or during the image display process. Traditionally image correction is deferred until as late as possible in the display process.

Current practice in most applications is to ignore color correction since colors are traditionally selected as RGB values using the same monitor that is used for image display. Images are commonly computed in floating point using a normalized RGB color space in which values of 0 to 1 represent the final image.[2] Frame buffers used for high quality graphics display are commonly 24-bit deep, 8-bits each in red, green, and blue. An additional 8-bit channel of pixel coverage information called a matte or alpha channel is also commonly kept with the image. Computed 0 to 1 image values are mapped into 0-255 in each of red, green, and blue for image storage.[3] Any image values above 1 are clamped to 1 or the pixel color is scaled prior to being saved in the image file. Image color computations generate intensity values on a linear scale. These are typically saved in the image file as linear values and the color lookup tables in the frame buffer are used for gamma correction.

Image resolutions commonly range from 512x486 for NTSC video (640x486 is also commonly used) to 1024x1280 for film applications.

---

[2] This is an observation based on personal experience and from discussions with professionals representing the entertainment animation field (Robert Abel and Associates, Digital Productions, Vertigo Computer Imagery, and Wavefront Technologies, Inc.), however, this is generalization. Integer image computation enjoyed some popularity prior to the wide availability of fast floating point processors (Pacific Data Images, circa 1983, and Cubicomp) and is popular in some special purpose hardware (PIXAR image computer).

[3] This is also a generality. It is becoming recognized that the de facto standard of 255 color levels in each of red, green, and blue, on a typical RGB monitor does not provide sufficient color resolution to prevent visible banding (observations from personal experience and from discussions with entertainment production professionals). Higher color resolution frame buffers are available but are not yet in common use.

Image display with less than 24-bit per pixel forces objectionable degradation in image quality. While display of this type is outside the scope of this text, many of the concepts presented in this section are applicable to less demanding image applications.

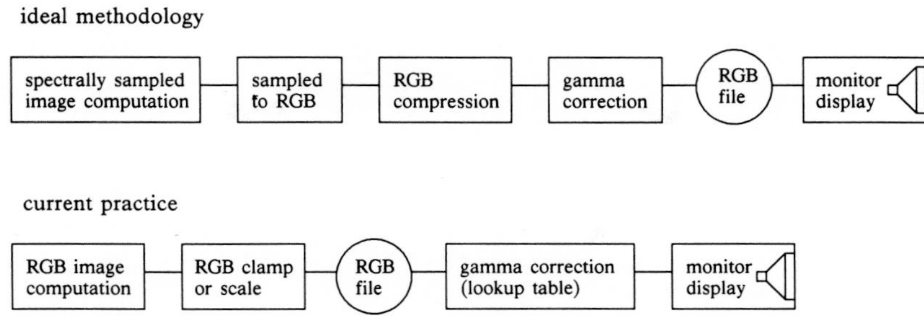

Figure 5.1: Methodology for image storage and display.

Higher resolutions can be expected to become more common in the future. Without data compression, a typical NTSC video image is about 3/4 megabytes of data at 24-bit per pixel (1 megabyte with a matte channel). If the image were stored as floating point values it would be approximately 3 megabytes of data. Data storage requirements generally dictate the use of encoded 24-bit per pixel image file. Data encoding schemes work well for pixel data and can produce a 50-85% reduction in image file size.[4]

To present the best possible image, it is necessary to perform color correction, color clipping, and gamma correction prior to the creation of the image file. It will become evident in the next sections that color transformation, correction for monitor gamma, and clipping out of range color values are very important issues in displaying high quality images with the correct appearance. The 24-bit per pixel image file format results in saving very limited color information for the image. Any corrections performed on the image file result in further degradation of the image information and should be avoided. The ideal methodology for image computation, storage, and display is contrasted with current practice in Figure 5.1.

5.1.1 Color Correction for Display

Color correction for display entails mapping the image from the color space used for color computation to the color space used for image display. Chapter 3 explored color computation requirements and suggested a number of suitable approaches. Chapter 3 also explored the limita-

[4] This reduction as accomplished using a run length encoding scheme similar to that described by Wallace (1981). There are a variety of data encoding schemes that can be applied to image data. Selection of an appropriate method requires analyzing compression, speed, and ease of data exchange considerations for the data compression schemes required.

tions of the three primary additive color reproduction system used for video display. Color correction resolves the differences between the computation color space and the display color space.

Color correction also applies to mapping an image into a different color space than that for which it was created. This situation arises when there are a variety of different monitors with different primary phosphors at a site. An image must look the same no matter which monitor and frame buffer combination is used for viewing. In a video application, the image must look the same during design as it does after video recording.

The first step in color correction is determining to which color space the image file should be corrected, and making sure information that defines this color space is included in the image file. RGB values are meaningful as an absolute specification of color only if the chromaticity of the RGB primaries and the white point are defined. If there is only one monitor at a site the images should be corrected to that monitor.

The image should be stored in the color space that is most critical to the end use of the image. An image can always be transformed to a different color space, however, the image is degraded with every transformation.[5]

Proper setup of the monitor establishes a D_{6500}[6] white point (SMPTE 1977). For video applications, the NTSC primaries are the basis for the transformation from the Y_tIQ of the NTSC composite video signal.[7] The transformation in the decoding circuitry of the monitor should have the correction from the RGB_{NTSC} primaries to the primaries of the monitor. The D_{6500} white point is used instead of the NTSC recommended illuminant C because the white point for the monitor is set independent of the

[5] Image degradation results both from the quantification and round-off errors due to the low color resolution of images as well as from the clipping of colors outside the displayable gamut of the target color space.

[6] The D_{6500} designation refers to a standard illuminant with a chromaticity of 0.313,0.329. The spectral curve for D_{6500} as well as the spectral curves for a variety of other standard illuminants can be found in Judd and Wyszecki (1975).

[7] For video applications SMPTE RP-145 (SMPTE 1987) suggests the chromaticities for professional television monitor phosphors of:

	x	y
red	0.630	0.340
green	0.310	0.595
blue	0.155	0.070

The monitor has circuitry to correct to the monitor phosphors assuming the signal is intended for the RGB_{NTSC} primaries. Therefore, correction to the SMPTE primaries is not appropriate for images generated for NTSC.

A	B	C	D	E	F
G	H	I	J	K	L
M	N	O	P	Q	R
S	T	U	V	W	X

The XYZ values are normalized for XYZ to RGB transformation using a transformation normalized to Y=1.0 for white

color	X	Y	Z
A. dark skin	0.092	0.081	0.058
B. light skin	0.411	0.376	0.303
C. blue sky	0.183	0.186	0.373
D. foliage	0.094	0.117	0.067
E. blue flower	0.269	0.244	0.503
F. bluish green	0.350	0.460	0.531
G. orange	0.386	0.311	0.066
H. purplish blue	0.123	0.102	0.359
I. moderate red	0.284	0.192	0.151
J. purple	0.059	0.040	0.102
K. yellow green	0.368	0.474	0.127
L. orange yellow	0.497	0.460	0.094
M. blue	0.050	0.035	0.183
N. green	0.149	0.234	0.106
O. red	0.176	0.102	0.048
P. yellow	0.614	0.644	0.112
Q. magenta	0.300	0.192	0.332
R. cyan	0.149	0.192	0.421
S. white	0.981	1.000	1.184
T. neutral 8	0.632	0.644	0.763
U. neutral 6.5	0.374	0.381	0.451
V. neutral 5	0.189	0.192	0.227
W. neutral 3.5	0.067	0.068	0.080
X. black	0.000	0.000	0.000

Figure 5.2: Macbeth ColorChecker™ Chart.

correction for the chromaticities of the primaries. Thus, the appropriate color space for video applications is:

	x	y
red	0.670	0.330
green	0.210	0.710
blue	0.140	0.080
white	0.313	0.329

The chromaticities of the phosphors should be available from the monitor manufacturer. In the absence of chromaticity data, the chromaticities can be measured using chromaticity meters or spectral analyzers. Some color analyzers (described later in Section 5.4, *Monitor Alignment and Calibration*) are equipped to measure chromaticities. A spectral analyzer provides the best information, but is very expensive and is generally not available to computer graphics users. The lower cost meters are generally repeatable and relatively correct, however, the absolute reading is subject to error. The measurements are generally adequate for generating the transformation between monitors but may introduce error in transforming from an absolute color space such as CIEXYZ.

The Macbeth ColorChecker™ Chart provides a useful visual reference for both gray scale and a range of colors that are considered representative for photography. This pattern is useful in determining whether the CIEXYZ to RGB transformation matrix is correct for a monitor, and in checking the RGB to RGB correction for two different monitors. A printed reference chart is available from most photographic supply stores. This test pattern is described in Figure 5.2. The CIEXYZ colors of the chart have been normalized for transformation into the RGB color space of the monitor. The normalization used is scaling the Y of the Macbeth colors so the dark neutral patch is black on the monitor and the brightest neutral patch is white. A technical description of the chart is found in McCamy, et al., (1976).

Image files must contain the color space primaries as part of the header information. Without this information, the correct absolute colors for the image are unknown and color correction for different monitors is not possible. Section 3.3, *Color Spaces for Color Computation*, developed the idea of computing images in a normalized sample space and of generating the transformation matrices to go from this sample space into CIEXYZ or into RGB. Section 3.3, *Colorimetry and the RGB Monitor*, developed the RGB to RGB transformations. All of these color space transformations must be available to assure that the image data can be correctly stored and displayed.

5.1.2 Gamma Correction for Display

Color computations are based on linear intensity values. For example, an RGB color of (0.5,0.5,0.5) has half the intensity of an RGB color of (1,1,1). Traditionally, images produced for computer graphics are written into files of linear intensity byte data with one byte for each of red, green, and blue at every pixel. Thus, a pixel value of (127,127,127) has half the intensity of a pixel value of (255,255,255).

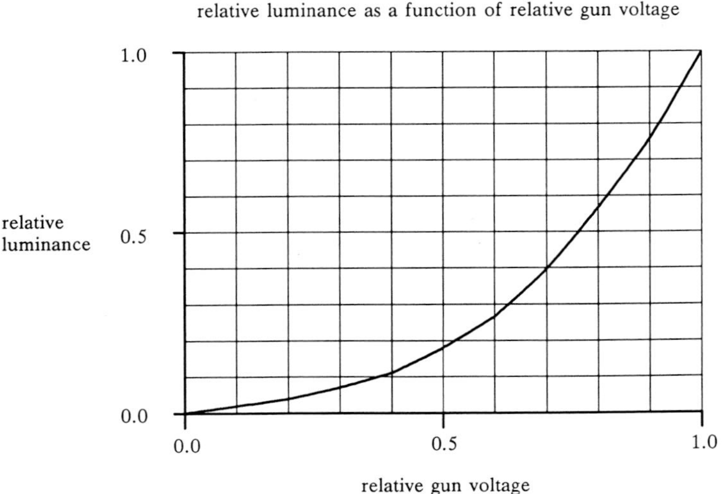

Figure 5.3: Typical monitor response curve.

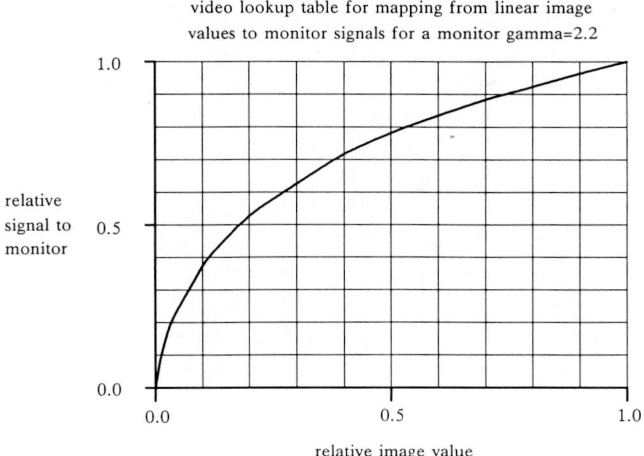

Figure 5.4: Typical video lookup correction curve.

Unfortunately, the response of typical video color monitors and of the human visual system is nonlinear and the storage of images in a linear format results in effective intensity quantization at a much lower resolution than the available 256 resolution per color. When a linear image is loaded into the frame buffer, a video lookup table (color map) is also loaded to correct for the non-linearity of the monitor. A typical monitor luminance curve is shown in Figure 5.3. The corresponding video lookup table values to correct for monitor nonlinearity are plotted in Figure 5.4.

The monitor correction function is an exponential function of the form:

$$\text{lookup value} = \text{intensity}^{1.0\,/\,\gamma} \tag{5.1}$$

Gamma (γ) represents the nonlinearity of the monitor. Monitors normally have a gamma value that is in the range 2.0 to 3.0. A gamma of 1 represents a linear device. A gamma of 2.2 is the NTSC signal standard.

Using an incorrect gamma value results in incorrect image contrast and chromaticity shifts. A gamma that is too large results in intensities being mapped brighter than is correct. A gamma that is too small results in intensities being mapped less intense than is correct. The black and white intensities are always correctly mapped. Incorrect gamma either increases or decreases the intensity of the mid-range of the image. Consider a color of (0,127,255). If the gamma is too high, the green component will be too intense resulting in a color shift towards green. If the gamma is too low, the green value is too low resulting in a shift towards blue. The red and blue intensities are not effected by an incorrect gamma because they represent normalized values of 0 and 1.

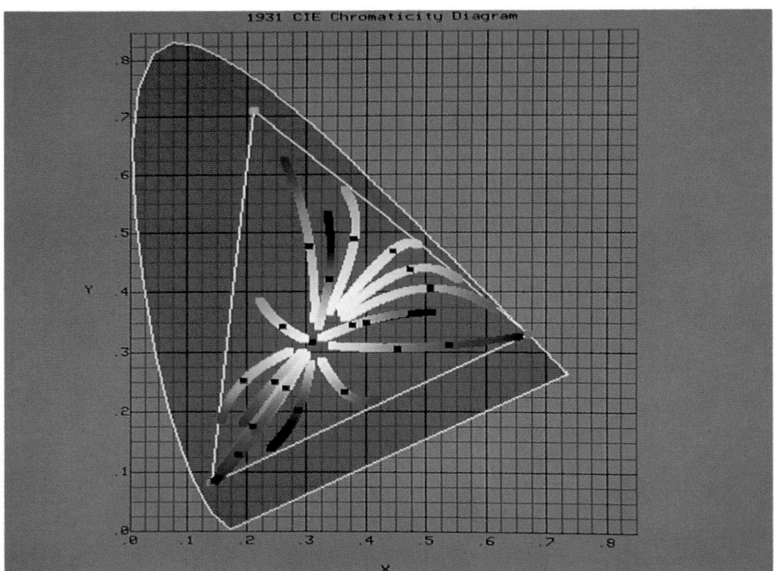

Figure 5.5: Shift of chromaticity of Macbeth ColorChecker™ colors as a function of gamma.

Figure 5.5 shows the chromaticity and contrast migration of the colors from the Macbeth ColorChecker™ chart. If the gamma is too high, the contrast is decreased and the colors are desaturated. If the gamma is too low, the contrast is increased and the colors migrate toward the primaries. The black point in each color trace is at the correct chromaticity of the color.

The gamma for the monitor is established by displaying a small field at different frame buffer values and measuring the intensity. An exponential curve is then fit through these points. A least squares fit provides the gamma value. It is necessary to normalize all the intensity readings before attempting to fit the curve. A problem with this technique is measurement errors at very low intensities unless a very sensitive intensity meter is used. Some trial and error may be required to determine the low intensity value to use for normalization prior to curve fitting.

In addition to establishing the correct monitor gamma, the decision to gamma correct images before storage or at the time of display is critical in image appearance. Perceived linear brightness is logarithmic with respect to actual intensity and is similar to the monitor response curve, Figure 5.6.[8] Thus, the typical monitor response provides roughly linear response in terms of perceived intensity.

[8] Steps in intensity are perceived as equal when $\Delta I/I$ is equal between the steps. The curve of Figure 5.6 was generated using a near 0 intensity black. Since the black intensity for the monitor is visually calibrated and dependent upon the viewing environment the initial slope of the curve may change.

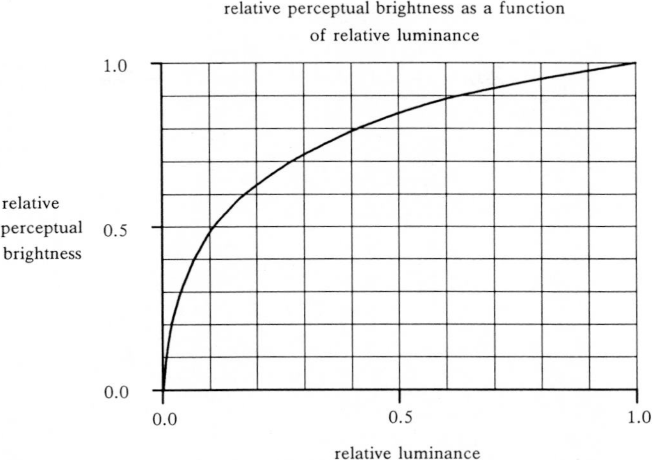

Figure 5.6: Perceived brightness as a function of intensity.

The values loaded into the video lookup table for correction of a typical monitor with a gamma of 2.2 are given in Table 5.1. The result of displaying an image through video lookup tables is that the lower 10% of the intensity values in the image file are stretched into the lower 35% of the display resolution range. Another way to look at this is that an increment of 1 in the image file is mapped into a much larger increment for display. Thus, the available resolution of the display system in the low intensity range, where the visual system is most sensitive, is not being used. For example, using Table 5.1 the image value 3 is mapped into 33 and the image value 4 is mapped into 38. The displayable steps between 33 and 38 are never used. The observable result is that images tend to be banded in the low intensity regions due to intensity quantizing to a lower resolution than the available resolution of the display device. Note also that the high intensity range maps several image values into the same display value. Thus, information in the image file is being ignored.

The gamma function can be applied to the computed color values from the illumination model before they are converted to byte values for storage. The result is an image that can be displayed with linear video lookup tables thus taking advantage of the full intensity resolution of the display device.[9]

[9] Blinn (1979) noted the desirability of storing image or frame buffer intensities using a logarithmic scale corresponding to the perception of equal intensity steps. This technique is preferable if the 8-bit values can be mapped into 10-bit or 12-bit values by the video lookup tables in the frame buffer so that resolution quantizing is minimized during video lookup. If the video lookup tables are 8-bit out, then the full resolution of the frame buffer is used only if a linear map is loaded into the lookup tables.

image value	table value	image value	table value	image value	table value	image value	table value
0	0	16	72	.	.	240	248
1	20	17	74	.	.	241	248
2	28	18	76	.	.	242	249
3	33	19	78	.	.	243	249
4	38	20	80	.	.	244	249
5	42	21	81	.	.	245	250
6	46	22	83	.	.	246	250
7	49	23	85	231	243	247	251
8	52	24	87	232	244	248	251
9	55	25	88	233	244	249	252
10	58	26	90	234	245	250	252
11	61	.	.	235	245	251	253
12	63	.	.	236	246	252	253
13	65	.	.	237	246	253	254
14	68	.	.	238	247	254	254
15	70	.	.	239	247	255	255

Table 5.1: Excerpt from correction table for 2.2 monitor gamma.

Figure 5.7 displays visual evidence of the banding that results from the use of video lookup tables to correct for monitor nonlinearity. Limitations in the printing reproduction process mask the banding problem in the 8-bit resolution images. To assure that the nature of the banding problem is evident, the image is also shown at 6-bit resolution in each of red, green, and blue.

In addition to the intensity banding, color banding can also be observed. This results from the surface color being non-neutral and the in-

Figure 5.7: Visual comparison of correction for monitor nonlinearity.

tensity steps in red, green, and blue occurring at different locations on the image. Each step in intensity of one of the primaries only results in a shift in chromaticity towards that primary. The color banding is also reduced by gamma correcting the image prior to storage.

While most frame buffers use 8-bits per primary per pixel, it should be noted that the visual system can discern the steps at 10-bits per primary per pixel in a very gradual low intensity gradation.[10] Fortunately the majority of imagery being produced is of sufficient complexity that large fields of this nature seldom appear. Thus, 8-bits per primary per pixel is generally sufficient for most applications.

5.1.3 Color Clipping and Compressing for Display

Monitors can display only a small subset of the perceptible colors. Image data must be clipped or compressed to lie entirely within this subset for display. This operation is essentially unmentioned in the computer graphics literature.

The monitor gamut of displayable colors is limited both by the chromaticities of the primaries of the monitor by the minimum and maximum intensities that can be displayed. As shown in the chromaticity diagram of Figure 3.9, the displayable colors represent a subset of the visible colors. The color gamut can be represented as a cube drawn on the RGB axis system. Any color can be plotted in this axis system, and any color outside the cube is not displayable. The colors that are not displayable fall into two categories:

- Colors which have chromaticities outside the displayable range,
- Colors which have displayable chromaticities but exceed the displayable intensity.

The first category results negative values for RGB when the color is transformed into the monitor color space. The second results in normalized RGB values greater than 1. Any undisplayable color must be clipped or compressed into the displayable color space. The method of clipping or compressing should create a minimal perceptual distortion of the color and should not create any noticeable clipping anomalies in the image such as Mach banding of color shifts.

The first category has been largely ignored in computer graphics. Traditionally, colors are computed in RGB, and spectral curves are not used to determine the RGB colors used in computation. Thus, the RGB colors selected do not have negative components and the results of the computations do not generate negative components. By virtue of the traditional process the first case has not appeared until spectral curves were

[10] This is a personal observation using 10-bit display hardware. The visibility of the step is dependent on the size of the constant intensity field on either side of the step. This suggests the step appears because of perceptual edge enhancement.

used to determine color values. One approach is to clamp negative color values to 0. However, Cook (1981) suggests this case is best handled by maintaining hue or dominant wavelength and desaturating the color (white is added) until it is within the displayable range.

There are several possible methods of handling the second case. One solution scales the entire image until there are no intensities too high for display. An alternate solution maintains the chromaticity and scales the intensity of the offending color. A third solution maintains the dominant hue and intensity of the color and desaturates the color. And a fourth solution clamps any color component exceeding 1 to 1.

All of these methods are used in practice. Each method has compromises in speed, ease of implementation, and resulting appearance. Any clipping method results in a color shift between the correct color and the color that is actually displayed. This shift can be in hue, saturation, and/or value.

Scaling the entire image is analogous to closing the aperture in photography. The contrast ratio of film is generally much lower than that of the phenomena being photographed. The aperture is typically adjusted so the intensities of the subject matter of interest fall within the nearly linearly sensitivity region of the film, thus providing the greatest contrast. Intensities outside of this range fall into low contrast ratio regions above and below the linear region (Hunt 1975).

The contrast range of the display is very small compared to the phenomena being modeled. Simple scaling often lowers the contrast ratio and compresses the most important image information in the low intensity range of the image, producing completely unacceptable results.

Consider a color gradient that starts at some low intensity value of a displayable color and extends to a high intensity value outside the displayable gamut, but with the same chromaticity. Figure 5.8 shows such a gradient mapped into the displayable RGB color cube. The selective scaling solution clips the gradient at the point where it emerges from the cube regardless of the magnitude beyond this point. This is implemented by simply scaling the color value so the maximum component is reduced to 1. This solution maintains hue and saturation, but modifies the chromaticity. Mach banding is often observed where the clipping starts in a gradation because there is a sharp discontinuity in the first derivative of intensity.

The solution that maintains intensity and hue, but modifies saturation produces a clipping path that goes from the intersection of the gradient and the color cube towards the white point. Ambiguities in the implementation of this clipping technique are the interpretations of *maintaining intensity* and of *maintaining dominant hue.* An analytical approach to maintaining intensity would maintain the Y value of the color since the Y tristimulus matching function matches the color luminous efficiency function (Judd and Wyszecki 1975). An alternate intuitive in-

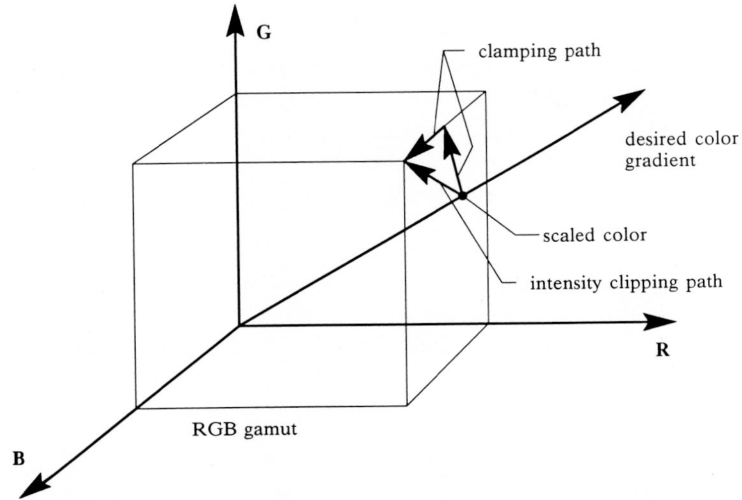

Figure 5.8: Examples of clipping paths for color gradients.

terpretation is that a plane perpendicular to the neutral axis is an equal intensity plane. Selecting the best white point for the direction of desaturation is largely a perceptual issue. Our perception of white is context dependent. Thus, the best white point is arguably related to the viewing environment, the monitor white point, and the image content. For ease of implementation, the neutral axis of monitor gamut is used. This method still exhibits a sharp discontinuity in the first derivative of the intensity if and when the clipping path reaches the white point.

Clamping can result in a shift in any combination of hue, saturation, and value depending upon the orientation of the gradient. For example, clamping a normalized RGB of (2,1,0) to (1,1,0) produces a color shift from orange to yellow.

Figure 5.8 describes the clipping paths for a number of gradients using the different clipping methods. The results of implementation of these clipping techniques is visually demonstrated in Figure 5.9. In this image bands of represent gradients that pass through the displayable gamut of the monitor. A clipping gamut that is a subset of the displayable gamut was defined. This allows the display of a correct color band with the clipping examples. Both categories of the clipping problem are demonstrated. For each gradient, bands are displayed as follows:

- The first band is a control strip displaying the correct color.
- The second band is clipped to maintain intensity and dominant hue. Planes perpendicular to the neutral axis are considered equal intensity and colors are shifted towards the neutral axis.

Figure 5.9: Visual comparison of color clipping techniques.

- The third band maintains hue and saturation by scaling the color. Negative color value are clamped to 0.
- The forth band clamps negative values to 0 and values greater than 1 to 1.

Figure 5.10 examines the perceptual deviation in the displayed color from the desired color for the different clipping techniques. The control color and clipped color are transformed into the $L^*a^*b^*$ perceptual space and the color difference is computed and plotted. Generally the clamping and scaling methods provide the closest match when minimum $L^*a^*b^*$ distance is used as a metric. However, these also clearly exhibit objectionable banding when clipping begins. The methods that maintain intensity appear more continuous, but do not necessarily produce a good color match.

It is not clear which clipping method will produce the best results. Appendix III.9, *RGB Color Clipping* provides the source for all of the clipping algorithms (used in the generation of Figure 5.8). This is an area fertile for future research.

5.1.4 Image Dither and Patterning

The 8-bit per primary color resolution most common in current display hardware is not sufficient to eliminate Mach banding in color critical imagery. Dither and patterning are two techniques that can be used to address this problem. Traditionally these techniques have been applied to

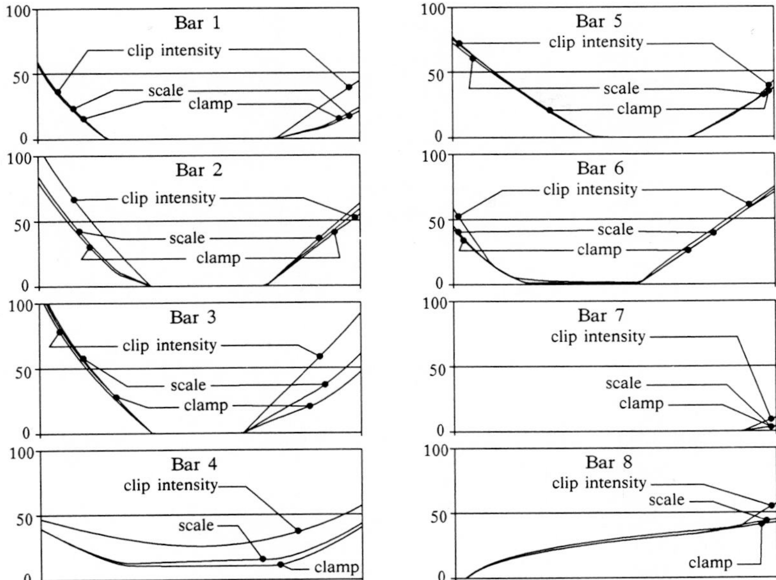

Figure 5.10: Perceptual color deviation for various clipping techniques.

low color resolution displays to provide an apparent increase in the color resolution. A general discussion of these techniques can be found in Foley and Van Dam 1984, 596-602, or Rogers 1985, 102-108.

Patterning sacrifices spatial resolution to increase color resolution. Pixels are grouped into cells of 2x2 pixels, 2x3 pixels, 3x3 pixels, etc. The average image color over the area covered by the cell is then approximated by turning on some number of pixels in the cell. Consider a simple black and white 1-bit display. If we display the image as a grid of cells covering 4 pixels each, then 5 intensity levels can be displayed by selectively turning on 0, 1, 2, 3, or 4 pixels within the cells, Figure 5.11. The index of the pattern that is displayed for the cell is determined by multiplying the average pixel value by the number of intensity steps in the pattern.[11] The decision on which cell pattern to display is made by adding the desired pixel values within the cell and multiplying by a number slightly less than 1.5 to get the index of the cell pattern. A greater number of effective intensity levels can be displayed if a larger cell size is selected.

In the context of 8-bits per primary, a 2x2 pixel cell allows for 1021 intensity levels instead of the usual 256. However, the spatial resolution is effectively reduced by 1/2 if the image is patterned.

---

11 The multiplier is actually the number of intensity steps less some small delta to prevent computing an invalid index if the image intensity is 1 for all of the pixels.

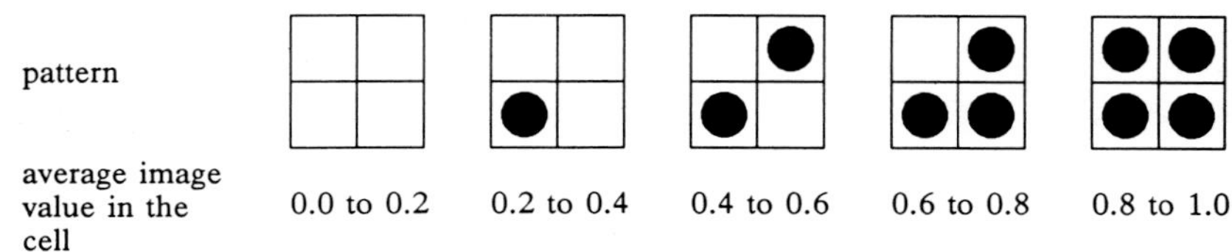

Figure 5.11: 1-bit halftone patterns using a 4 pixel cell.

Image dither introduces randomness into the traditional round-down of image color values. The intent is to produce the same apparent intermediate intensity values as with patterning without introducing the reduction in spatial resolution.

Two methods of introducing this randomness are used in dithering. The first method carries error in the display of a single pixel to the surrounding pixels. The second method introduces a random error to all pixel values prior to round-off for display.

The first technique was presented by Floyd and Steinberg (1975) and uses an algorithm that distributes the error for display of a given pixel to the pixels to the right and below that pixel. This method assumes sequential computation of the image starting at the upper left corner. For the present pixel the error term is the difference between the computed pixel value and the value actually stored in the file. This error is distributed by adding 3/8 of the error to the computed pixel value to the right, 3/8 of the error to the pixel below, and 1/4 of the error to the pixel to the lower right.

The second technique adds a random number to each computed image value before determining the value to be stored in the image file. Consider a gradual gradation normalized for 24 bit RGB display that has a value for one of the color components that ranges from 5.5 at the left edge of the screen and 7.5 at the right edge. Display without dither results in solid fields of 5, 6, and 7. Ideally the left edge of the screen would have an equal number of pixels with values of 5 and 6 and the right edge an equal number of pixels with values of 7 and 8 to give average values of 5.5 and 7.5 respectively. By adding a random number between 0 and 1 to each of the color components before rounding to the display color this type of distribution is achieved. Adding a completely random number does not necessarily produce optimum results (Bayer 1973). The problems are that random numbers are expensive to generate and that an even distribution over a small quantity of samples is not assured. An uneven distribution can result in visible patterning in the image.

An alternate approach, known as ordered dither, builds a table of pseudorandom numbers that are evenly distributed. This assures an even distribution and eliminates the need to continuously generate random numbers. Typically the pseudorandom numbers are arranged in cells which are tiled over the image surface. The dither pattern for a 2x2 pixel cell (Limb 1969) is:

1/8	5/8
7/8	3/8

The dither pattern for a 4x4 pixel cell (Jarvis, et al. 1976) is:

1/32	17/32	5/32	21/32
25/32	9/32	29/32	13/32
7/32	23/32	3/32	19/32
31/32	15/32	27/32	11/32

The cell of dither values is added to the computed image values after normalization to the display resolution.

Knuth (1987) notes that the Floyd-Steinberg approach is a serial process and that any pixel value affects all the pixels to the lower right of that pixel in the image. He notes the appearance of "ghosts" in some images, and the author has noted the appearance of moire patterns with this algorithm. Knuth notes that ordered dither techniques localize the effects of any single pixel but can result in loss of spatial resolution. Knuth describes a technique called dot diffusion which is somewhat like the Floyd-Steinberg algorithm confined to small cells of the image. The pixels in a cell are ordered for consideration. The pixels are taken in order and for each pixel an output value is determined and the error is then distributed to the pixels surrounding the current pixel which have not yet been considered (have a higher number in the ordering scheme). The details of this scheme are rather complex and are not repeated here.

Figure 5.12 contrasts ordered dither techniques for a simple gradation of the type that causes problems in 24-bit high resolution imagery. The gradation is a 3-bit grey scale displayed at 3-bit per primary with a horizontal resolution of 256.[12] The first band is the grey scale with no dithering. The second band uses the Floyd-Steinberg algorithm. The third band is ordered dither using a 2x2 pixel cell. The fourth band is ordered dither using a 4x4 pixel cell. The uses Knuth's dot diffusion technique with a 4x4 pixel cell.

As noted earlier, the dither techniques were originally developed to increase the apparent color resolution of a display without sacrificing spatial resolution. In 24-bit imagery the problem is to remove apparent

[12] Low spatial and color resolution are used for clarity and so that the scale is larger than anomalies introduced in the printing process.

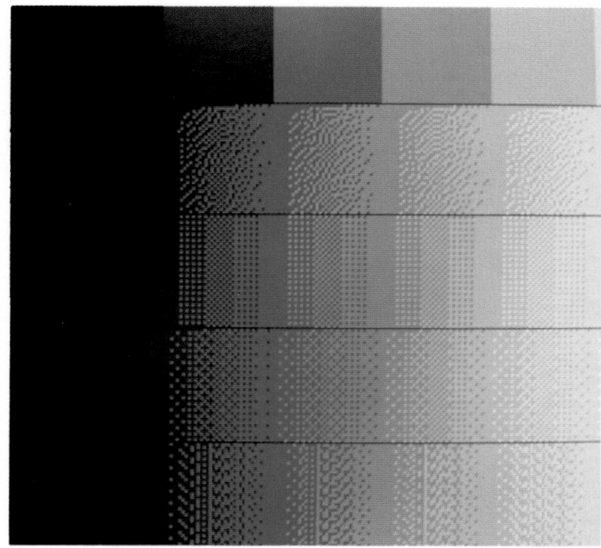

Figure 5.12: Comparison of dither techniques.

edges caused by very small changes in color which are a result of shading. Due to the high color resolution, adding dither does not introduce noticeable degradation of spatial resolution. Therefore, traditional ordered dither techniques produce acceptable results. In the author's experience a 2x2 dither cell introduces sufficient randomness to break up distinct boundaries between colors in gradual gradations. This reduces and usually eliminates Mach banding effects. In combination with gamma correction of the image prior to image storage this effectively eliminates banding for 24 bit images.[13] The dither is applied after image values are corrected to the gamma of, and normalized to the resolution of the image file or display device.

5.2 NTSC and RGB Video

A great deal of confusion often exists between what is meant by RGB and NTSC video signals. RGB video refers to separate signals for the red, green, and blue components of an image sent to a monitor. The signal standards vary depending on the type of monitor being used for display. NTSC normally refers to the composite video standard adopted by

[13] The response of users over time has lead the author to conclude that observations of this nature become "dated" very quickly. Users who were very happy with 24-bit undithered images three or four years ago are now very sensitive to the limitations of 24-bit color resolution. Image acceptability seems to be very subjective, and closely related to the experience or sophistication of the user.

the National Television System Committee (NTSC). The NTSC video signal encodes the red, green, blue, and timing information into a single signal.

Connecting an RGB signal source to an RGB monitor requires separate cables for the red, green, and blue signals. A synchronization (sync) signal tells the monitor where the frame starts within the incoming signal. The sync signal is often included in the green signal (internal sync). In high quality video work, a calibrated sync signal sent on a separate cable (external sync) is required.

Connecting an NTSC signal source to an NTSC monitor requires a single cable. The NTSC signal may be converted to an RGB signal using an NTSC decoder. An RGB signal may be converted to an NTSC signal using an NTSC encoder.

The NTSC encoding and decoding process uses an intermediate color representation called Y_tIQ.[14] The transformation from the NTSC prescribed color television primaries, RGB_{NTSC}, to Y_tIQ is given by:

$$\begin{bmatrix} Y_t \\ I \\ Q \end{bmatrix} = \begin{bmatrix} 0.299 & 0.587 & 0.144 \\ 0.596 & -0.275 & -0.321 \\ 0.212 & -0.528 & 0.311 \end{bmatrix} \begin{bmatrix} R \\ G \\ B \end{bmatrix} \tag{5.2}$$

The transformation from Y_tIQ to RGB_{NTSC} is given by the inverse of this matrix:

$$\begin{bmatrix} R \\ G \\ B \end{bmatrix} = \begin{bmatrix} 1.0000 & 0.9557 & 0.6199 \\ 1.0000 & -0.2716 & -0.6469 \\ 1.0000 & -1.1082 & 1.7051 \end{bmatrix} \begin{bmatrix} Y_t \\ I \\ Q \end{bmatrix} \tag{5.3}$$

The Y_tIQ signal is then encoded into a composite video signal. The Y_t signal has a bandwidth of 4.2 MHz. The I and Q color components are modulated on a 3.58 MHz signal 90 degrees apart. The result is superimposed on the Y_t signal. The details of this encoding process can be found in Conrac (1980). Implications of the encoding process are discussed later in Section 5.5, *NTSC Limitations*. A schematic of the encoding and decoding process is given in Figure 5.13.

Note that the decoding process in a video monitor includes decoding into the Y_tIQ and a final transformation into the $RGB_{monitor}$.[15] This final

[14] The Y_t notation in Y_tIQ is used to avoid confusion with the Y axis of the CIEXYZ color space.

[15] There is an intermediate representation between Y_tIQ and RGB called Y_t R-Y_t)(B-Y_t) that is used in some broadcast components and recording formats such as Betacam. The relationship between this and Y_tIQ is:

$$\begin{aligned} Y_t &= 0.299R + 0.587G + 0.114B \\ I &= 0.877(R-Y_t) \\ Q &= 0.493(B-Y_t) \end{aligned}$$

This representation is gaining in popularity because it maintains the information as three high bandwidth signals that are very easy to convert to Y_tIQ.

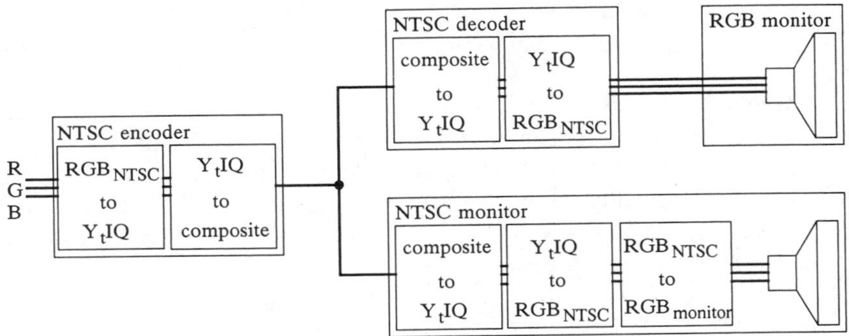

Figure 5.13: Schematic of the RGB to NTSC to RGB encoding and decoding.

transformation includes the transformation into RGB_{NTSC} and then a transformation into the primary space of the monitor phosphors.

The RGB signal standard that is timing compatible with the NTSC signal standard is the EIA RS-170 signal standard. This means analog processing only is required in the NTSC encoder. Other RGB signal standards require a great deal of processing to convert to an NTSC compatible signal.

5.3 Video Setup for Image Display

The key element in configuring a system for video display is getting the correct signal from the frame buffer to the monitor. Complicated display configurations using multiple frame buffers, multiple monitors, NTSC encoder, sync generator, and recording equipment, require careful attention to the image signals that are passing through the system. This section is an overview intended to alert you to the issues involved. There is no substitute for the experience of a qualified video technician when equipment is being specified and installed.

The simplest image display setup is a computer with integrated frame buffer and display as is found in many of the workstations currently available. The user has very little control of this equipment configuration. The next step is the component system with the frame buffer and monitor being separate devices. The simple case of a single frame buffer and monitor requires very little attention in terms of additional equipment. All the required setup can be accomplished through monitor calibration as described in the next section.

Consider a setup with two frame buffers, several RGB monitors connected through video switchers, and NTSC video recording station as pictured in Figure 5.14. In an ideal world a single image could be loaded into either frame buffer, displayed on either monitor in either RGB mode or NTSC mode, and the image would look the same. Unfortunately, we are not in an ideal world and additional equipment is required to

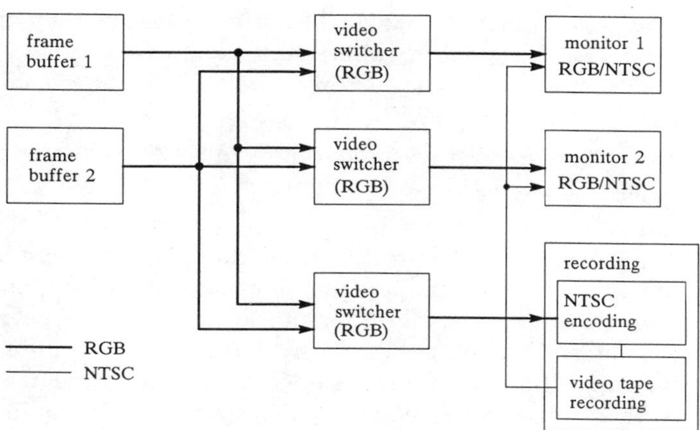

Figure 5.14: Schematic of a hypothetical video setup.

achieve this ideal. In reviewing Figure 5.14 we can identify several problem areas:

- Monitors and NTSC equipment are subject to electronic drift with changes in temperature. It is important that equipment be in a temperature stable environment and at operating temperature before alignment or color critical observation. The time required for temperature stabilization depends upon the environmental control system and the equipment configuration. It is common practice to keep video equipment running at all times to minimize temperature changes and subsequent drift.
- The video outputs from the frame buffers may not be matched. Small differences in electronics within equipment, even by the same manufacturer, result in mismatched signals. A white field may not produce the same red, green, and blue output signals on a single frame buffer or between multiple frame buffers. This results in a different appearance of a single image on a single monitor depending upon the frame buffer used.
- The monitors may not be the same. There are minor differences both in electronics and in picture tubes even within a single model line. The chromaticity of picture tube phosphors varies unless they are from the same manufacturing run. Often the intensity and subsequently the chromaticity of a constant color field varies across the face of a monitor. This makes it extremely difficult to get a good match between monitors.
- When equipment is reconnected to different frame buffers or the recording station the signal load changes. This results in signal variation depending on the equipment configuration.

- The input signals must be matched for different frame buffers before the encoder can be properly calibrated to produce the correct output for a given input signal level (this is related to the second point above).
- There are differences between the content of the NTSC signal and the RGB signal. In many cases an exact match is not possible.

In reviewing this list, we see the first point is related to the temperature stability of the environment. Great care should be taken to assure a stable environment. The third point is monitor related and independent of the input signal. Compensation for monitor mismatch is discussed earlier in this chapter. The last point is a function of the definition of the NTSC standard. While this cannot be altered there are some image considerations that minimize the effects of this problem. This is discussed later in Section 5.3, *NTSC Limitations*. The remainder of the list is a function of getting the correct signal to all of the equipment.

Matching the output levels of the frame buffers and eliminating problems due to different loading as equipment is reconfigured can be accomplished through the use of video distribution amplifiers (VDAs). The VDA isolates the signal source and the respective loads to minimize the effects of adding new loads. The isolation of outputs means that a single output line can have anything from a short circuit to an open circuit without affecting the other output signals from the VDA. One VDA is required for each signal distributed through the system. Additionally, VDAs typically have low level (black signal) and gain (white level) adjustments. This allows mismatched signals to be matched for distribution. For example, mismatched red, green, and blue signals from a single frame buffer or several frame buffers can be matched for the same black and white levels during distribution.

There should be a video distribution amplifier on each of the RGB lines and the levels should be identical for the VDA output for all lines when a black field is loaded into the frame buffer and when a white field is loaded into the frame buffer. An oscilloscope or waveform monitor is used to measure these signals. Output levels are matched to the expected input levels of monitors, encoder, etc. Some frame buffers do have adjustments for output levels. This may eliminate the need for video distribution amplifiers in simple installations.

Uniformity of signal distribution is the key to correct VDA use. Signals should not bypass the VDA. All equipment should be connected to the signal source through the VDA (if there is one for the signal). If multiple VDAs are required their inputs should be connected using loop through, not by connecting the output of one to the input of the other. Outputs of the VDA should be evenly loaded. Refer to Figure 5.15 for examples.

Video equipment is commonly supplied with loop through connectors. This means there is a signal in and a signal out connector. This al-

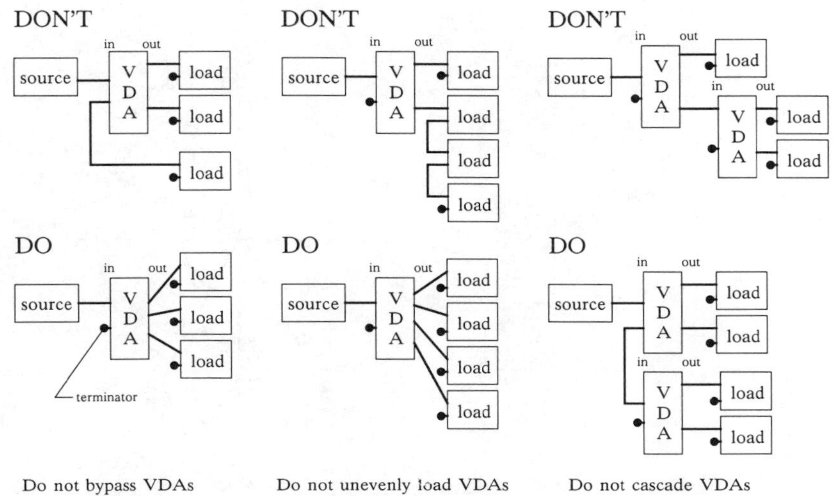

Figure 5.15: Video Distribution Amplifier Usage.

lows several pieces of equipment to be strung together. The last piece of equipment must *terminate* the line. Some equipment has a switch to terminate the line. If equipment is not supplied with termination switches, then a terminator must be used on the signal out connectors. All unused signal out connections must be terminated (except for VDA outputs).

A calibrated sync signal is required for broadcast quality work. The sync signal is produced by a sync generator and provides a reference timing signal tuned to NTSC specifications. All equipment must be able to lock onto this sync signal. External sync, as found on monitors, locks equipment to run at the same rate as the sync signal. Genlock locks equipment to run at the same rate as the sync signal and also provides time shifting (sometimes called phase shifting) so the signals can be made coincident.

Genlock is critical for frame buffers. Consider the connection of a frame buffer, sync generator, and NTSC encoder. If the lines from the sync generator to the frame buffer and from the frame buffer to the encoder are long compared to the line from the sync generator to the encoder, then the RGB signal to the frame buffer may be behind the sync signal. The signals are out of phase. The manifestation is that the picture will appear horizontally shifted from correct centering on the screen. Phase adjustment of the frame buffer is required to assure that the sync signal and RGB signals are in phase when they reach the encoder. Some frame buffers claim to have genlock but lack the phase adjustment.

The vectorscope and waveform monitor are used to monitor NTSC signals and for calibration of NTSC equipment. Any quality NTSC

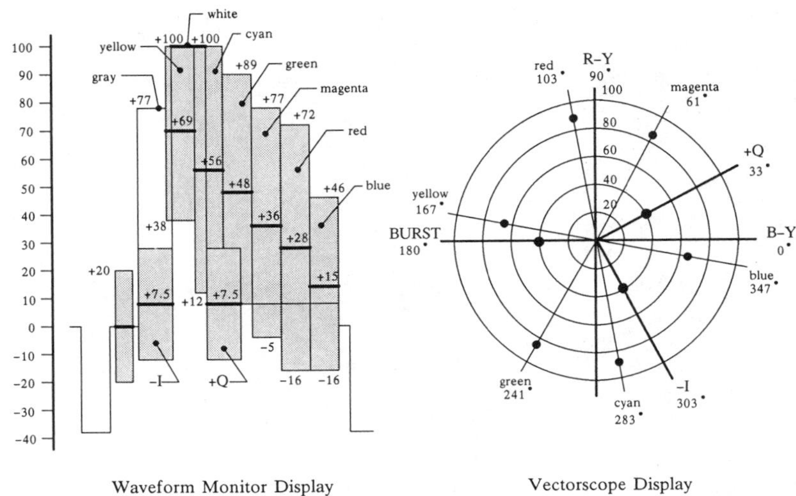

Figure 5.16: EIA Encoded Color Bar Signal (adapted from EIA RS-189-A).

encoder has a built in color bar test pattern matching EIA Standard RS-189-A, *Encoded Color Bar Signal* (EIA 1976). Setting the encoder to this test pattern allows adjusting the encoder output for the correct output signal, Figure 5.16.

In addition to adjusting the NTSC encoder for correct output signal with internal test patterns, the encoder input gains must be set to produce the correct output given a test pattern input signal. The color test bar pattern is loaded into the frame buffer and the RGB input gains adjusted so the output is correct. Note the -I and +Q bars of the EIA color bar signal cannot be exactly reproduced in the frame buffer because of the limitations of the encoding process. To overcome this, luminance, Y_t, can be added to the I and Q signals. This change results in a modified waveform monitor display, but maintains the vectorscope display for the standard pattern.

Figure 5.17 describes the frame buffer color bar test pattern. This should be loaded with linear lookup tables in the frame buffer. Since the RGB to Y_tIQ transformation is based on the NTSC standard primaries and assumes the monitor has these primaries, there is no need for correction to the monitor primaries when loading this test pattern.

Note that the NTSC black occurs at +7.5 IRE. This is called setup, and was introduced in 1953 to accommodate color broadcast.[16] The RGB black signal is at zero. Thus, when toggling an RGB/NTSC monitor be-

[16] It has been proposed that the +7.5 IRE setup be eliminated because of the problems it creates in component systems.

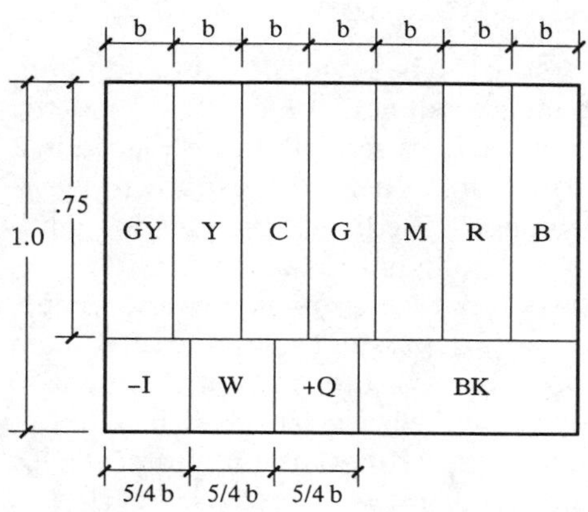

color		r	g	b
GY	gray	191	191	191
Y	yellow	191	191	0
C	cyan	0	191	191
G	green	0	191	0
M	magenta	191	0	191
R	red	191	0	0
B	blue	0	0	191
–I*		0	76	127
W	white	255	255	255
+Q*		75	0	139
BK	black	0	0	0

* –I signal centers at +29 IRE and +Q signal centers at +21 IRE on the waveform monitor display

Figure 5.17: EIA color bar test pattern for a frame buffer (adapted from EIA RS-189-A).

tween NTSC and RGB the image will never look the same. You cannot critically preview imagery intended for NTSC using RGB imagery.

The complete schematic for the video system is given in Figure 5.18. As previously stated, this section has been an overview discussing the considerations in configuring video equipment. There is no substitute for a qualified video technician in determining the correct equipment configuration for a specific installation. Reference texts devoted to video reproduction technology are Conrac 1980, Benson 1986.

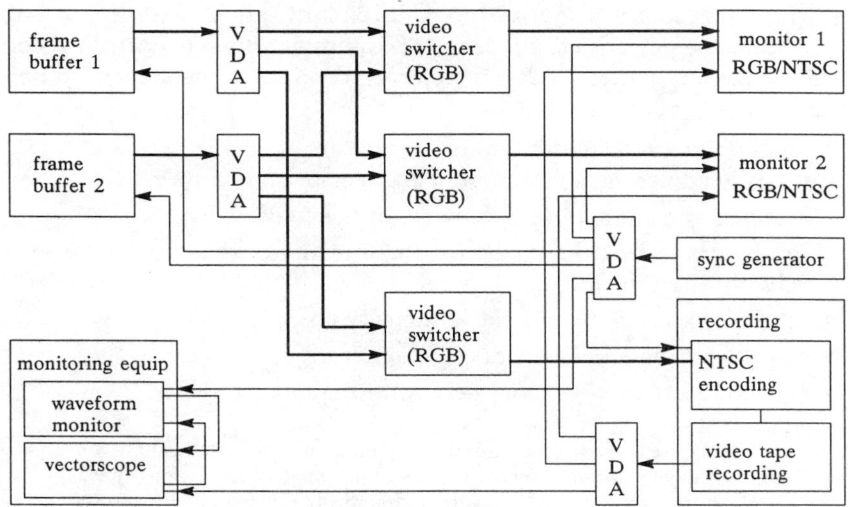

Figure 5.18: Schematic for a completely configured video system.

5.4 Monitor Alignment and Calibration

Regardless of the care taken in modeling the behavior of light and maintaining the spectral information, an image will not look correct unless the monitor on which it is displayed is correctly calibrated and is placed in a reasonable viewing environment. There are two distinct aspects of viewing that affect the perception of the image. The first is the viewing environment. The background viewing environment greatly affects the perception of colors in the image. The second is the display of the image. The appearance of the displayed image is dependent upon the care taken in correcting the image to the characteristics of the monitor. The image must be explicitly corrected to the monitor characteristics if it is to appear the same when displayed on several different monitors. Color transformation of an image for different displays is discussed earlier in Section 5.1.1, *Color Correction for Display*.

The monitor calibration process is described in detail in the SMPTE recommended procedure RP71-1977, *Setting Chromaticity and Luminance of White for Color Television Monitors Using Shadow-Mask Picture Tubes* (SMPTE 1977). Many of the adjustments in this procedure are visual, that is, they are based on the visual perception of color and/or intensity difference or sameness. The SMPTE recommended practice bulletin recognizes perception to be closely linked to the viewing environment and includes an appendix discussing the effect of the viewing environment. A neutral viewing environment with lighting character near D_{6500} and a light level not to exceed 3 foot candles is recommended. Visual adjustments must be made under the same conditions which will be used for viewing images. It is also noted that since many adjustments are visual, they should be performed by a single individual who has normal vision to minimize any variation due to color perception.[17] The steps in monitor alignment are:

- Prepare for color calibration.
- Visually adjust the white point using a color comparator.
- Establish the white point reference for the color analyzer.
- Set the gray scale, that is, adjust the tracking of the neutral chromaticity through the intensity range.
- Set the proper white and black intensity levels.
- Adjust chroma and hue for NTSC monitors.
- Recalibrate using the color analyzer at regular intervals.

---

17 The SMPTE recommendations are currently under revision as a result of human factors studies of viewing environments in video editing studios. The proposed change recommends a textured neutral gray (D_{6500}) background illuminated either from the top or bottom (creating a brightness gradation across the surface) with a maximum brightness not exceeding 10% of the monitor peak white (Kane 1987).

The SMPTE calibration procedure is discussed relative to NTSC video standards. Because many graphics applications are not using NTSC video the discussion in this text is targeted toward RGB applications using frame buffers to generate the required test patterns.

Proper instrumentation is vital to monitor calibration and recalibration. A partial listing of equipment suppliers is provided in Appendix V, *Equipment Sources*. The initial calibration is largely through visual comparison and is rather time consuming. Recalibration can be very quick and efficient if the proper instrumentation is available and if the monitor adjustments are easily accessible.

The instrument required for setting the correct white color is the split field visual color comparator. The color comparator displays a reference white on one half the field of view and the monitor screen on the other half. The monitor is adjusted until a visual match of the two fields is obtained.

The instrument for adjusting tracking and providing a recalibration reference is the color analyzer. The color analyzer measures the RGB balance of the monitor once the reference white has been set. The color analyzer is used to check the monitor at any intensity level to assure correctness of the neutral color. In addition, once the reference setting has been input into the color analyzer it can be used for resetting the monitor to the same reference white at a later date, or for quickly calibrating a number of monitors of the same type. Use of the color analyzer rather than the comparator for recalibration removes perceptual variations from the recalibration process, assures the repeatability of recalibration, and makes recalibration a very rapid procedure.

The following test patterns are required for monitor calibration:

Centered gray field or window pattern

The centered gray field should be a box large enough to cover the measuring head of the color analyzer, but no larger, on a black background. It must be possible to specify the color of the field. The reason for limiting the size of the field is due to monitor power supply limitations. The power supply is generally sized for the display of typical images with some additional reserve power margin. A full screen white field is an extreme image and often demands more power than is available. This results in a lower intensity display than the white that would appear in typical imagery. Restricting the size of the field assures that displayed colors are representative of their appearance as part of an image. In addition, restricting the size helps assure the measuring head of the color analyzer is repeatably positioned on the screen during recalibration.

PLUGE pattern

The PLUGE pattern is normally generated by video test equipment. It consists of three bars, a central black bar surrounded by a bar that

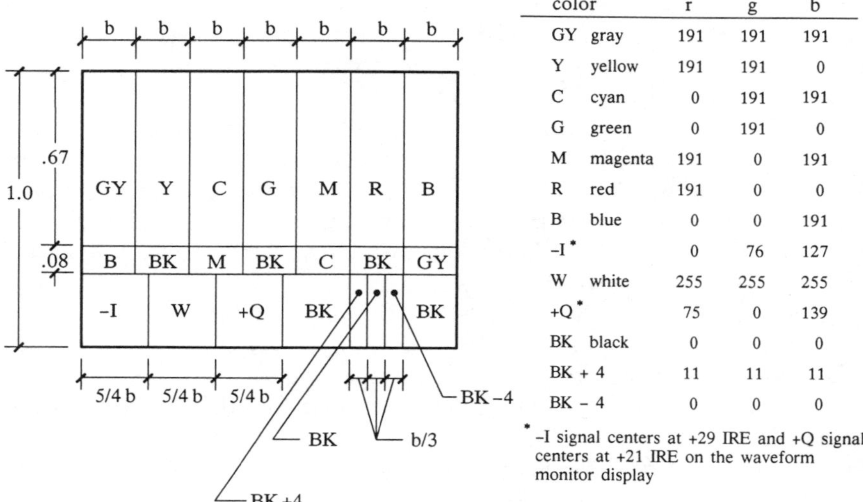

color		r	g	b
GY	gray	191	191	191
Y	yellow	191	191	0
C	cyan	0	191	191
G	green	0	191	0
M	magenta	191	0	191
R	red	191	0	0
B	blue	0	0	191
–I *		0	76	127
W	white	255	255	255
+Q *		75	0	139
BK	black	0	0	0
BK + 4		11	11	11
BK – 4		0	0	0

* –I signal centers at +29 IRE and +Q signal centers at +21 IRE on the waveform monitor display

Figure 5.19: SMPTE Color bar test pattern for the frame buffer (adapted from SMPTE ECR1-1978).

is 4% of the full signal range greater than black and a bar that is 4% of the full signal range less than black. For frame buffer display, the less than black bar cannot be generated and must be omitted. The SMPTE color bars, Figure 5.19, provide a PLUGE pattern (SMPTE 1978).

Split color bars

Split color bars are used for adjusting chroma and hue of NTSC monitors. Chroma and hue controls adjust decoding the composite signal into the separate Y_tIQ signals which are then transformed to the RGB signals which drive the guns of the picture tube. The SMPTE color bars (SMPTE 1978), Figure 5.19, also provide the split color bar pattern.

This alignment procedure is a compilation and summary of information from SMPTE RP71-1977, notes from Kane (1987), and personal experience:

1. Preparation:

The electronics of the monitor and the test signal source must be stable at the time of calibration. As noted earlier, stabilization is very important in minimizing drift. A minimum warm-up time of 30 minutes in a stable environment is required for monitors. It is standard practice to leave the monitor running at all times (Refer to manufacturers recommendations for operating environment and warm-up). The monitor should be in its operating position in its operating environment. During warm-up, a low level video signal such as a black field should be displayed. Avoid high intensity patterns such as color bars as these may burn the screen phosphors if left on for a prolonged time. It should be noted that some monitors require a sync signal to be present at all times. Monitor convergence, linearity, centering and picture size should be adjusted before beginning color calibration.

2. Set the white point:

Set the white point for the monitor. The exact procedure depends upon the capabilities of the color comparator and color analyzer, and upon the adjustment controls of the monitor. A variety of procedures have been discussed in standards literature. The exact methodology appropriate for a given installation requires some trial-and-error testing.

The idea is that a neutral signal, i.e., equal RGB, should have the same chromaticity through the intensity range of the monitor and that chromaticity should match a reference standard. A high quality monitor has adjustments for low intensity brightness (bias), gain (drive), and tracking (linearity) of the RGB guns. The low intensity adjustments set the neutral chromaticity in the near black region of operation. The gain sets the neutral chromaticity at high intensity. The tracking adjusts linearity so all guns are tracking evenly through the intensity range to maintain the correct neutral chromaticity. Some monitors have adjustments for red and blue only. The implicit assumption is that green is properly tuned at manufacture and remains that way.

When selecting monitors for an installation, calibration needs must be carefully considered. Appearance critical monitors that are used for image evaluation should have a full complement of calibration controls which are accessible from the front of the monitor. It is highly undesirable to move the monitor or to remove the monitor housing to perform calibration.

The split-field visual comparator is used with a centered white field to set the chromaticity of the white point. If a color analyzer is not available then a visual comparator with both high and low level references is required. Some comparators are fitted with a neutral wedge filter allowing for visual tracking of the neutral chromaticity through the intensity range of the monitor.

Visually match the intensity of the white field to the comparator using the contrast control then adjust the gun gains to match the color of the white field to the color comparator.[18] If a color analyzer is available, this white setting is used to establish a reference white for the color analyzer. The color analyzer is then used for the remaining

---

[18] The NTSC specification describes a neutral signal as representing the chromaticity of standard illuminant C. However, SMPTE RP37-1969 (reaffirmed 1982) recommends D_{6500} as the reference white. D_{6500} is most often used in practice (SMPTE 1969).

Figure 5.20: Video color analyzer (Courtesy Philips Test & Measuring Instruments, Inc).

adjustments. If a color analyzer is not available, the remaining adjustments must be made using the color comparator.

If a color analyzer is available, it must be "taught" this reference white. The color analyzer has red, green, and blue sensors. The process of "teaching" the color analyzer the reference color is by setting the calibrated white RGB levels as the reference. This cannot be done by the manufacturer of the color analyzer because the sensors respond differently to different phosphors. For this reason, a color analyzer has several memories allowing storage of several references. A stored reference should be used for each type of monitor at an installation. The phosphors between monitors of the same type are usually sufficiently similar so that a single memory setting can be used for calibration of all monitors of this type.

The sensing head of the color analyzer is fixed over the neutral field on the monitor. One of the color analyzer memories is selected and the reference white is loaded into that memory ("taught" to the analyzer) following the manufacturer's instructions. The typical color analyzer, Figure 5.20, has three rows of LED's; one for green, one for red, and one for blue. The green scale most closely relates to the intensity (brightness) of the screen. The red and blue scales display red and blue relative to the green, that is, they provide color balance information. Once the reference white has been set, the illuminated LED's in each of the scales line up.

3. Adjust the gray scale.

   A very low intensity neutral field is next displayed (within the tracking range of the color analyzer). The low intensity (bias) controls are adjusted so the illuminated LED's line up. The full white field is again displayed and the gain readjusted until the LED's line up.

Iterate between the low intensity and full intensity fields until no additional adjustments are required. It may be necessary to allow some time for monitor phosphor stabilization before readjusting at either the full or low intensity fields. Some of the graphics monitors use "slow" phosphors with a greater color range than television phosphors but a slow decay rate. This allows the reproduction of a greater color range, however, it also results in ghosting or streaking when rapidly changing imagery is displayed. The number of iterations required between high and low intensity fields depends upon the interactivity between the bias and gain controls.

If the monitor has tracking controls, the neutral color is checked at intermediate intensities and the tracking adjusted accordingly. This can be checked with the color analyzer. The illuminated LED's should track up or down the scale and remain in line if the chromaticity of the neutral field does not change. Once again, due to the interactivity of the controls, it is necessary to iterate between low intensity, full intensity and the mid intensities until no additional adjustment is required.

4. Set the black and white levels.

   Set the black level using the brightness control and the PLUGE test pattern. The brightness is adjusted so the less than black bar and black bar are indistinguishable and the brighter than black bar is visible. If the PLUGE display is being generated by a frame buffer, turn the brightness down until the black and brighter than black bars are indistinguishable, then adjust the brightness up until the brighter than black bar becomes visible.

   Display a white field and adjust the contrast for 103 candela/meter^2 or 30 foot lamberts using the color analyzer. Recheck the black setting. There should be no interaction between black level and brightness, so the black setting should not require additional adjustment. In practice it is common to use a slightly lower intensity white point such as 28 foot lamberts to reduce burning of the monitor phosphors when high intensity imagery is displayed.

   The color analyzer readings for a white field and a low intensity field are recorded so subsequent recalibration can be performed entirely with the color analyzer to insure repeatable calibration of the monitor.

5. Adjust chroma and hue for NTSC monitors.

   Hue and chroma adjustments are made on NTSC monitors only. The NTSC composite signal is first decoded into a Y_tIQ intermediate signal which is transformed into the RGB signals which drive the monitor guns. The hue and chroma controls adjust the decoding circuitry so the correct Y_tIQ values are generated. The SMPTE split bar pattern is used to aid in adjustment. This pattern puts bars, which are different colors but have the same blue component, adjacent to each other. The monitor is set for blue display only (red and green guns are turned off). If the monitor is not equipped for blue display only, the pattern can be viewed through a Kodak Wratten 50 filter (Kane 1987) to filter out the red and green color components. Hue and chroma are adjusted until the split in the color bars is indistinguishable. The chroma control affects the outer bars the most while the hue affects the inner bars. The chroma and hue controls interact so it is again necessary to iterate between the two until no further adjustment is required.

6. Recalibrate using the color analyzer at regular intervals.
   A monitor should be recalibrated at regular intervals, perhaps once a month. The frequency of required recalibration depends upon how large the changes were when the monitor was brought into alignment. The larger the required adjustment, the more quickly the monitor will drift out of adjustment. The color analyzer is used for this recalibration assuring repeatable adjustment of the monitor. The white and black points for the monitor can be quickly recalibrated using the references established for the color analyzer during the prior steps of this procedure. Regular recalibration using the color comparator is not recommended due to the subjectivity of the adjustment. The complete calibration process using the comparator is required at long intervals such as 6 months to a year.[19]

5.5 NTSC Limitations

NTSC signal standards impose limitations on the quality of the image that can be transmitted. These limitations often reduce the quality of the image far below what can be reproduced at a typical raster workstation. Display resolution is the limiting factor for NTSC. Both result from the limited bandwidth available in transmission.

When an RGB monitor is driven directly from a frame buffer the signal bandwidth for each channel is sufficient to resolve each pixel in each of the three color components. The signal for each channel is sent to the monitor from the frame buffer separately. Because the connection is direct there are fewer signal transmission limitations than in broadcast.

An NTSC monitor or television receiver uses a 525 horizontal scanline standard. The entire screen is completely refreshed every 1/30 of a second. The odd lines (odd field) are scanned first, then the even lines (even field) for an image display rate of 60 fields per second. The

[19] Some monitors are claimed to be self calibrating. The self calibrating feature helps correct for drift once the monitor has been calibrated. Calibration and recalibration are still required. However, the frequency of recalibration should be reduced.

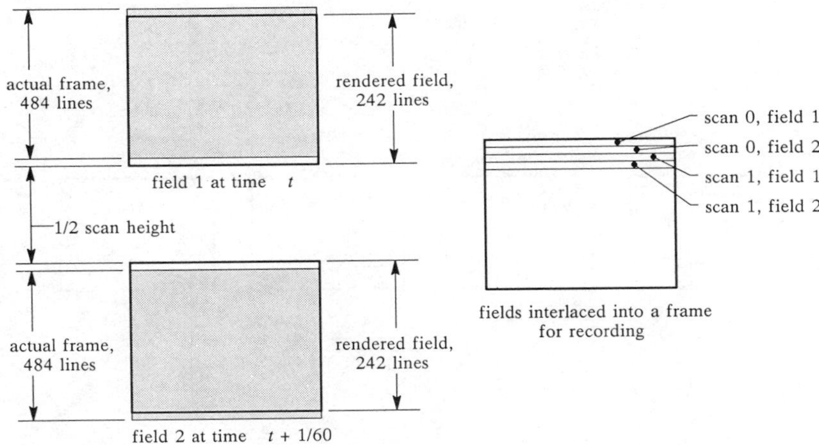

Figure 5.21: Display Methodology for field recording.

display of odd scanlines then even scanlines is called interlacing, that is, the even lines are interlaced with the odd lines. The purpose of interlacing is to minimize image flicker as phosphor glow decays between retracing. Refer to Rogers 1985 and Conrac 1980 for an in-depth discussion of NTSC display hardware.

A fortunate consequence of interlacing is that it can be used to effectively display imagery at 60 frames per second. Frames are typically computed at 1/30th of a second intervals in the animation, then displayed and recorded as complete frames (even and odd field). To take advantage of the interlacing, frames are computed at 1/60th of a second intervals in the animation. Each frame corresponds to a field. Each frame is then displayed and recorded as a single field.

Single frame recording equipment is very expensive and often difficult to locate for lease or rental. This can be overcome by combining the odd lines of the odd field image with the even lines of the even scanline field to create a single frame image that contains both field images correctly interlaced, Figure 5.21. This single frame can be displayed and recorded with standard single frame recording equipment.

Field generated imagery results in smoother motion and reduced strobing as compared to imagery generated and recorded at 30 frames per second. Note that if you display a still frame it will contain two fields that are 1/60th of a second apart, and the result may not be pleasing.

A field is displayed by an electron beam tracing the scanlines on the screen phosphors. The phosphors are excited by the beam and glow.

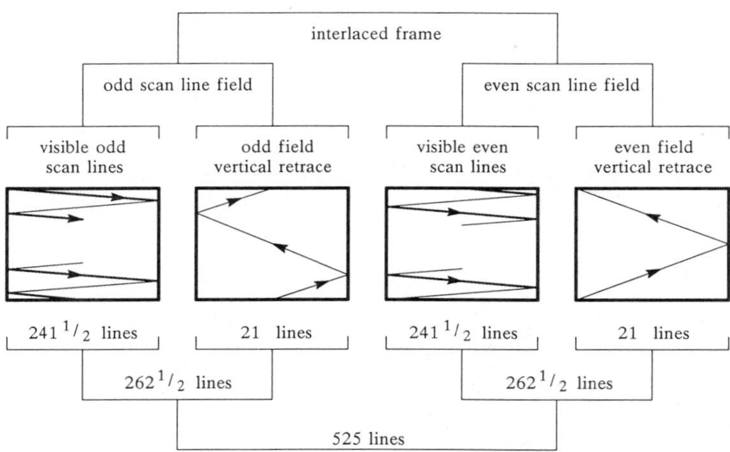

Figure 5.22: Frame display schematic for NTSC (adapted from Rogers 1985).

The brightness of the glow is determined by many factors including energy of the beam, focus of the beam, and how often the phosphor is excited by the beam. The field is traced starting at the top of the screen and writing every other scanline from left to right. When the field has been completely scanned the beam is returned to the top of the screen for the start of the next field. During the tracing there are times when the beam is being moved, but is turned off or blanked. There is a horizontal blanking period between each scan when the beam is moved from the end of the current scanline to the beginning of the next, and a vertical blanking period when the beam is moved from the bottom of the screen at the completion of one field, to the top of the screen to begin the next, Figure 5.22.

While the NTSC standard uses 525 scans, only 483 are actually seen.[20] The time for the unseen scans is taken up by the vertical blanking between fields. The time to trace a single scanline is determined by:

$$\frac{\text{1 frame}}{\text{525 scanlines}} \times \frac{\text{1 second}}{\text{30 frames}} = \frac{\text{63.5 microsecond}}{\text{scanline}} \tag{5.4}$$

A nominal horizontal blanking time of 10.9 microseconds (EIA RS-170 standard) is used resulting in an effective scanning time of 52.6 microseconds per scan.

The original NTSC specification considered only luminance, Y_t. The transmitted Y_t is proportional to the luminance. The NTSC specification

[20] While 483 scan lines are displayed, it is typical that frame buffers actually use 484 scanlines of data and that half of the first and last scanline is not displayed.

for luminance transmission (black and white pictures) uses a maximum transmission frequency of 4.2 MHz. At this bandwidth 221 cycles of image information are included in the scanning time for each scanline.

Color broadcast must be compatible with existing black and white television receivers. The Y_t signal completely determines the luminance, which is used for black and white display. The color components were selected so the axis lie in the XZ plane of the CIEXYZ color space. The NTSC color axis are called I and Q, thus, the NTSC color space is known as Y_tIQ. The I and Q information is encoded in a signal that is superimposed on the luminance signal. The bandwidth of the I and Q signals is limited to 1.3MHz and 0.5Mhz respectively. The scanning time allows for 68.3 cycles of I information and 26.3 cycles of Q information in each scanline.

During the encoding process the RGB values are transformed to Y_tIQ. The Y_tIQ signal is then low pass filtered in order to reduce the bandwidth so the composite signal can be created. This reduction in bandwidth may seriously effect image quality. Image features with sharp (high frequency) spatial properties combined with high I or Q color properties should be avoided in NTSC imagery. Figure 5.23 describes the relationship of RGB to Y_tIQ Note that colors in the blue, magenta, red range have high I and Q values coupled with low Y_t and are colors that should be handled with care.

The selection of I and Q was made to minimize the bandwidth requirements for signal transmission. Figure 5.24 provides a visual demonstration of the resolving power, and therefore the relative bandwidth requirements for the Y_tIQ primaries. Each of the wedges is identically displayed, but note that the I and Q primaries appear to merge to gray at a much lower resolution than for the Y_t primary.

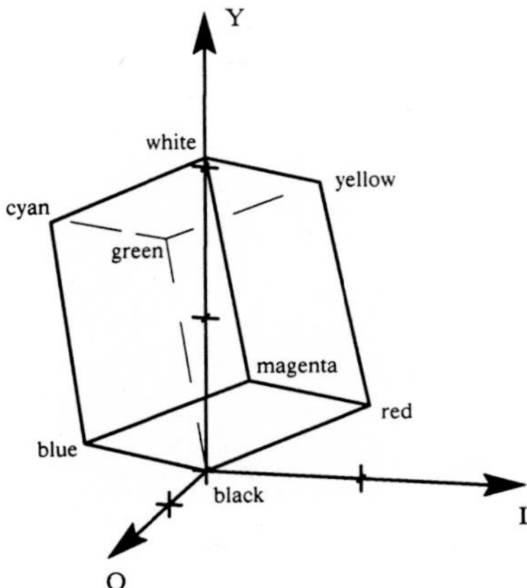

Figure 5.23: Typical monitor gamut in Y_tIQ space.

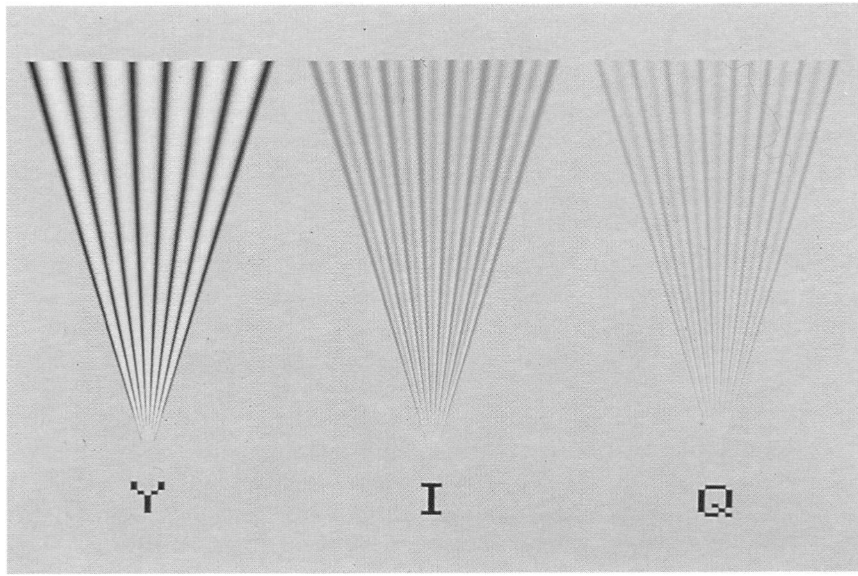

Figure 5.24: Visual demonstration of resolving power for the NTSC primaries (Courtesy G.Meyer, Program of Computer Graphics, Cornell University).

Figure 5.25: Image decomposed into the Y_tIQ color components (Courtesy G.Meyer, Program of Computer Graphics, Cornell University).

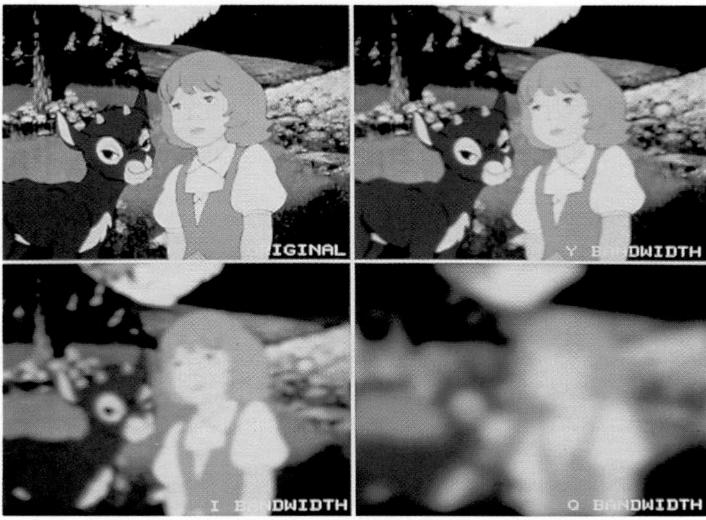

Figure 5.26: Relative bandwidth of the Y,IQ signal components (Courtesy G.Meyer, Program of Computer Graphics, Cornell University).

Figure 5.27: Comparison of original image to NTSC transmitted image (Courtesy G.Meyer, Program of Computer Graphics, Cornell University).

Figure 5.25 shows an image which has been decomposed into the Y_tIQ primaries. The primary images in this figure are displayed at the same resolution as the original image. Figure 5.26 shows the relative bandwidth at which these signals can be transmitted as part of the NTSC composite signal. The bandwidth filtering has been performed on a black and white image to simplify comparison of the results. Finally, Figure 5.27 compares the original image, upper left, with the image resulting from NTSC encoding, lower right.

Another concern in NTSC broadcast is the actual displayed image area when an image is transmitted. An image displayed on a television exhibits clipped edges due to edge curvature of the screen and is typically setup so the image more than covers the entire screen. Modern televisions have an essentially square cornered display and a greater portion of the image is seen. However, to maintain compatibility with old equipment, the limitations should be recognized. The SMPTE recommended practice RP27.3-1983, *Specifications for Safe Action and Safe Title Areas Test Pattern for Television Systems* (SMPTE 1983), provides the bounds for action and titles. All significant action should take place within the *safe action* area. All of the information that is vital to image content should be presented within the bounds of the *safe title* area. This assures visibility on the majority of home television receivers. Figure 5.28 provides a diagram of these areas.

In summary, implications of NTSC broadcast are:

- A horizontal image resolution of approximately 440 pixels is required to utilize the available NTSC transmission bandwidth. A lower pixel resolution does not use the full information bandwidth of the NTSC signal. The detail in images with pixel resolution greater than 440 is lost in the conversion to NTSC. Thus, any horizontal resolution above 440 is essentially wasted.
- High spatial frequency image elements should be avoided when they are rich in color due to the low bandwidth of the color portion of the signal. This is particularly true for colors that lie near the Q axis, such as yellow-green or blue-purple.
- Important image information should be confined to the safe areas of the image plane. The entire screen cannot be used for information presentation.

5.6 Black and White Display

Black and white video is becoming increasingly rare in many areas of the world. However, black and white technology still dominates other areas of the world. A black and white image display mode is required for evaluating imagery that may be transmitted in black and white. This mode is simply achieved by passing the RGB colors through the Y_t por-

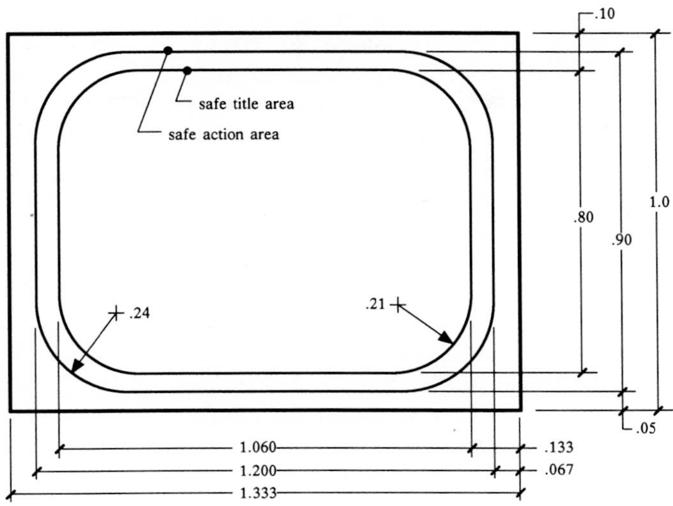

Figure 5.28: Safe action and safe title areas (adapted from SMPTE 1983).

tion of the Y_tIQ transformation. Black and white display uses the Y_t signal to drive the RGB guns together at the same intensity. Thus the $RGB_{monochrome}$ value for display is determined as:

$$RGB_{monochrome} = \begin{bmatrix} 0.299 \; 0.587 \; 0.114 \end{bmatrix} \begin{bmatrix} R \\ G \\ B \end{bmatrix} \tag{5.5}$$

The importance of viewing imagery in black and white becomes quickly evident as colors which are very different often become indiscernible when displayed in black and white. Additionally, black and white display imposes very different constraints than color when designing imagery for visual impact. An example of this is the use of chocolate syrup to portray blood in early black and white movies. The impact of an image that will be viewed both in color and in black and white can only be designed into the image if the designer can see the image both in color and in black and white.

Appendix I

Terminology

Terminology		
symbol	description	dependency
H	Required **N** for mirrior reflection	**L**,**V**,**N**
H′	Required **N** for Snell refraction	**L**,**V**,**N**,n
L	Unit light vector	
N	Unit surface normal	
R	Unit reflected vector	**N**
T	Unit transmitted vector	**N**,n
V	Unit view vector	
θ	Angular deviation from the normal	
ϕ	Radial angle	
α	angle between **N** and **H**	
β	Angle between **N** and **H** when D drops to half of D maximum	**N**,**H**,D
A	area	
ω	Solid angle	
λ	Wavelength	
$\zeta(x,y)$	Roughness function for a surface	
σ	RMS height of $\zeta(x,y)$	ζ
g	apparent surface roughness	$\sigma,\tau,\zeta,\lambda,\theta_i,\theta_r$
m	average slope of $\zeta(x,y)$, $m=2\sigma/\tau$	σ,τ,ζ
$\overline{m}$	RMS slope of $\zeta(x,y)$, $\overline{m}=\sigma\sqrt{2}/\tau$	σ,τ,ζ
τ	Correlation distance of $\zeta(x,y)$	ζ
ε	Emmissivity	
I	Intensity	
$M(\lambda)$	The spectral curve of a material	
$\xi_{s,d,a}$	Reflectivity from s to d through a	
Φ	Energy flux (energy per unit time)	
n	Index of refraction	
k	Absorption coefficient	
n/k	Absorption index	
F_r	Fresnel reflectance	**L**,**V**,**N**,n,k,λ
F_t	Fresnel transmittance	**L**,**V**,**N**,n,k,λ
r_σ	Coherent treflectance attenuation	
t_σ	Coherent transmittance attenuation	

----- continued -----

Terminology		
symbol	description	dependency
R_d, R_{dh}	Diffuse reflectance function, $M(\lambda)/\pi$	$M(\lambda)$
T_d, T_{dh}	Diffuse transmittance function	
R_{bd}	Bidirectional reflectance function	$\mathbf{L},\mathbf{V},\mathbf{N},n,k,\theta,\phi,\lambda,\zeta$
T_{bd}	Bidirectional transmittance function	$\mathbf{L},\mathbf{V},\mathbf{N},n,k,\theta,\phi,\lambda,\zeta$
K_a	Ambient reflectance	λ
K_d	Diffuse reflectance	λ
K_s	Specular reflectance	λ
N_s	Specular exponent	β
A	Attenuation within a material	
B	Magnetic field of light waves	
D	Slope distribution function	$\mathbf{N},\mathbf{H},m,\beta$
E	Electric field of light waves	
$\lvert E^2 \rvert$	Energy density	
G	Geometric attenuation	$\mathbf{N},\mathbf{L},\mathbf{V},m$
$F_{n,m}$	Form factor for m seen from n	

Appendix II

Controlling Illumination

This appendix examines the process of selecting material and lighting parameters to achieve a realistic appearance. The selection of material properties and lighting properties that result in images that "look good" is a black art. The majority of illumination models that are in use today are empirical, thus, the connection between material parameters and measurable parameters is difficult to establish. Even when models founded on sound theoretical principles are used, it is difficult to get real surface information that will provide the desired appearance.

The major aspects of appearance controlled by material parameters are the character and the surface finish of the material. The character of the material refers to representing a type of material such as metal, plastic, or painted. The surface finish refers to the microscopic geometry of the surface such as optically smooth, scratched, rough, or polished.

Surface character is controlled primarily by the relative colors used for K_a, K_d, K_s, F_r, and F_t. Guidelines for selecting these parameters can be deduced from examining the behavior of real materials. Surface finish is controlled primarily by the relative magnitudes of K_a, K_d, K_s, and β. Guidelines for selecting these can be deduced through examination of illumination models that have a theoretical basis.

II.1 Surface Character

Surface character can be broadly subdivided into that of dielectrics (insulators), conductors (metals), and composite materials. Refer to Chapter 2 for detailed descriptions of light interactions with these types of materials.

II.1.1 Dielectric Materials

The electrons in the dielectric are not free to resonate or to be excited by the light wave when the light wave strikes the surface. The result is that the light wave passes through the media interface with little modification. The reflectivity of dielectric surfaces is generally low and is uniform across the visible spectrum. This is seen in the reflectivity curves for glasses, Figure II.1.

The mechanism of light propagation through the material is complicated and is outside the scope of this discussion. There are both simple and complex results of this propagation. The simple result is the propagation of light at a reduced speed with an attenuation as a function of distance traveled through the material. The attenuation results from

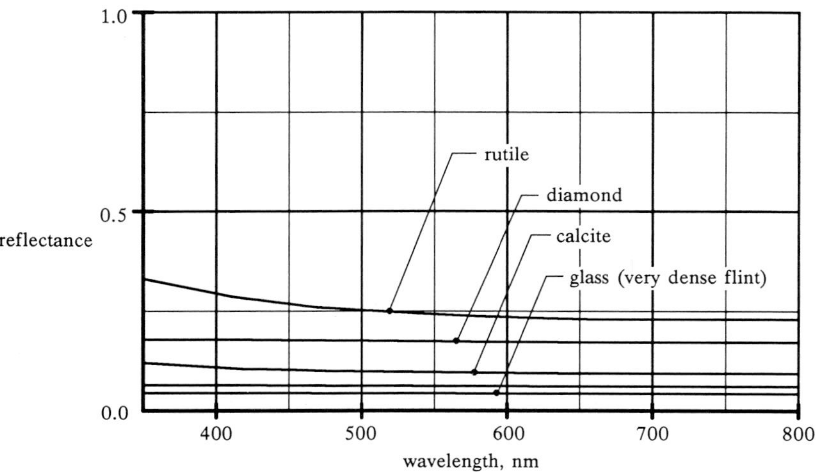

Figure II.1: Typical spectral curves for dielectric materials.

scattering, diffraction, and absorption. Computer graphics generally considers only the simple propagation with some distance attenuation.

Briefly, the behavior of dielectric materials is summarized by these observations:

- Dielectrics are not very reflective.
- Dielectrics are transparent.
- The spectral curves for ambient, diffuse, and specular color are the same.

Powders of nonconductive materials are very common, for example, salt, sugar, talc, etc. These are typically white and diffuse. The color comes from the refractions and reflections at the interfaces between air and the surfaces of the powder particles. The material itself is essentially transparent.

II.1.2 Conductive Materials

The electrons in conducting materials (metals) are free to move. This is what makes the material conductive. Light striking a conductive material causes the electrons to resonate, which in turn sets up magnetic and electric fields which reradiate the incident light.

A *perfect* conductor would have infinite conductivity. This means that the electrons would be completely free to move through the material. If light were incident upon a perfect conductor the electrons would oscillate with the wave. Since the electrons are completely free to move the oscillation would result in complete reemission (complete reflection) of the wave.

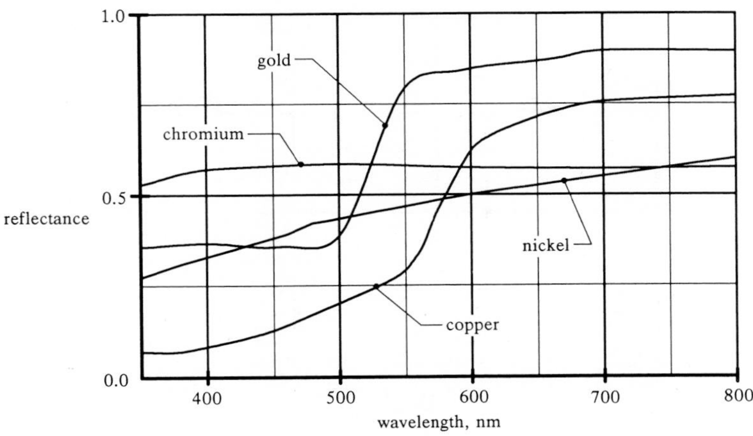

Figure II.2: Typical spectral curves for metals.

The molecular properties of the atoms which make up a metal determine the freedom of the electrons. Conductive materials have a resistance to free motion of the electrons which slows the electrons, converting the energy of movement into heat. This is the mechanism through which conductors absorb light and appear opaque.

For many metals there are sufficient free electrons to result in nearly equal reflection of all wavelengths. This results in the reflective grayish colors typical of steel, aluminum, or nickel. Reflective characteristics of other metals are affected by electrons that are bound to the atoms of the metal. This lack of freedom results in selective absorption of light at frequencies where the oscillation of the electron is damped. This results in the color of metals such as gold, copper, or bronze. This is shown in the conductive material curves in Figure II.2.

Briefly, the behavior of metals is summarized by these observations:

- Metals are very reflective.
- Metals are opaque.
- The spectral curves for ambient, diffuse, and specular color are the same.

II.1.3 Composite Materials

There are many materials that are not homogeneous which make up the world around us. These include plastics, paints, glazes, and a variety of other surface finishes. These are not nearly as simple to characterize as the homogeneous materials previously described.

These materials are generally composites consisting of a substrate or base, and a pigment. The substrate is a dielectric in which the pigment is suspended. The surface characteristics are those of the substrate. However, once the light passes into the material, the pigment reflects and absorbs resulting in the reflection of light back through the surface.

The specular character is that of the substrate. The diffuse character includes the diffuse scattering from the surface of the substrate plus the scattered reflection from the suspended pigment particles. The resultant appearance is a different color for the highlight than for the diffuse reflection. Since the substrate is a dielectric, the highlight is neutral. The diffuse color is primarily the color of the pigment.

Briefly, the behavior of composite materials is summarized by these observations:

- The specular properties are those of dielectrics.
- The diffuse properties are those of metals
- The spectral curves for ambient, diffuse, and specular color are representative of the different materials in the composite.

II.1.4 Using Published Spectral Data

There are a variety of sources for published spectral reflectivity data. A search of your local college library should produce a number of references. A source for light source curves is Judd and Wyszecki (1975). Sources for material curves are *Thermophysical Properties of High Temperature Solid Materials*, 1967, and *Thermophysical Properties of Matter*, 1970, from the Thermophysical Properties Research Center at Purdue University. Before we can use these curves, we must understand how they are generated and what they mean.

The light source data is obtained simply by splitting the light into the wavelength components and measuring the intensity of each of those components. The published data typically scales the curves to a value of 100 at a wavelength of 560nm. These curves provide the relative intensities of the light throughout the spectrum and are arbitrarily scaled as required for color computation. Relative intensities of sources is modeled by relative scaling of the spectral curves.

Material curves are created by illuminating a surface and then integrating the resulting reflection over the hemisphere above the surface. The integration is performed at several wavelengths. A curve can is fit through these points to predict the value at all wavelengths. Cook and Torrance (1982) use linear interpolation to predict the intermediate wavelengths. The incident illumination is generally from a direction very near the normal. The value of the curve is the ratio of the reflected energy at any wavelength to the incident energy at that wavelength.

Material curves are a composite of information and it is difficult to sort out the data in a meaningful way. Consider using spectral curves as the basis for approximating the index of refraction for each wavelength.

Ideally we would like the incident light to coincide with the normal, and the surface to be optically smooth so that the only attenuation is due to the Fresnel relationships for $\theta = 0$. The measurement is generally not for a smooth surface and is made by integrating light over the entire hemisphere. Thus, the curve is only an approximation of the properties required to establish material values.

In the case of composite materials such as paints or plastics the curve is a composite of both the specular and diffuse character. As a result, the curves can be very misleading. For matte composites, the curves are representative of the diffuse properties. It may not be possible to derive meaningful spectral data from curves for glossy composites.

Material curves are not scaled when used for determination of the Fresnel reflectance. The Fresnel reflectance gives the fraction of the incident energy that is reflected.

Diffuse reflection has equal intensity in all directions. Integrating the intensity over the illuminating hemisphere tells us that the reflected intensity is related to the reflected energy by a factor of $1/\pi$. If the illumination model is an energy illumination model, the material curve is divided by π. This has been specifically indicated in the discussion of these models. If the illumination model is one of the earlier empirical models, the use of the spectral curve is also empirical. This is discussed in the next section.

II.1.5 Selecting K_a, K_d, K_s, F_t, and F_r

Figure 2.1 describes the mechanisms of the surface interaction for dielectrics, conductors, and composite materials. Observe that the reflection for both dielectric and conductive materials occurs at the material interface only. The spectral character of the specular and the diffuse reflection are the same because the reflection is from the same surface. However, composite materials exhibit different spectral character in the specular and diffuse components of the reflection because the specular and diffuse components are reflected from different materials. The implications of this explain the plastic or painted appearance that was typical of computer graphics in the late 1970's, and the more realistic appearance of the images of today.

In considering the values that should be used for material properties it is helpful to cast the illumination models so that terms such as K_a, K_d, and K_s are the product of a color and a multiplier. In more recent models this separation occurs in the formulation. Some formulations do not include provisions for a spectral character of the specular reflection. Use of these models results in a plastic appearance since the specular reflection is always neutral (characteristic of dielectrics such as vinyl). A model is easily generalized to separate the spectral character from a multiplier. Additionally, spectral character is easily included in the specular computation if it is not normally supported by the model.

For example, consider the Phong model using the Blinn cosine power specular function, Eq.(4.13). This is rewritten as:

$$I(\lambda) = C_{Ka}K_a(\lambda)C_{Ia}I_a(\lambda) + C_{Kd}K_d(\lambda)\sum_{n=1}^{ls}(\mathbf{N}\bullet\mathbf{L}_n)C_{In}I_n(\lambda) \tag{II.1}$$

$$+ C_{Ks}K_s(\lambda)\sum_{n=1}^{ls}(\mathbf{N}\bullet\mathbf{H}_n)^{Ns}C_{In}I_n(\lambda)$$

Note that both the light sources and the materials are cast in terms of a spectral component, $K(\lambda)$, and a multiplier, C. Expressing the model in this form is an aid in explaining the selection of properties. In practice, the constant terms are premultiplied wherever possible before the start of rendering.

It is useful to create a database of light source curves which are normalized so that the intensity at 560nm is 1 instead of 100. A light source constant of 1 then corresponds to full intensity for display. Ambient illumination multipliers that work well are in the range $0 \le C_{Ia} \le 0.3$. Low values simulate space, or night conditions. Mid values simulate daylight on clear days when there is ambient light from the blue sky, or simulate interiors that have light colored (reflective) finishes. High values simulate overcast daylight when nearly all illumination is ambient light from the overcast sky.

When using homogeneous materials, the spectral character of the ambient, diffuse, and specular reflection are the same. Composite materials require the use of the substrate curve for the specular reflection and the pigment curve for the diffuse and ambient reflection. If the composite material has a matte finish the appearance is diffuse and there is little specular contribution. If the composite has other special properties, the specular reflection may take on the character of the pigment. This is true in the case of "metal flake" paints. The flakes are often small bits of a metal foil. These tend to orient parallel to the surface and produce a secondary specular reflection that is the color of the pigment.

When using empirical models, the spectral curves are used directly for K_a, K_d, and K_s when the illumination model is cast in terms of multipliers and spectral information. If the model uses Fresnel terms then the material curve is used as the reflectance at $\theta = 0$ and the average of the curve within the visible range is used to approximate the average index of refraction for the approximation of the Fresnel term (detailed in Appendix III.5, *Fresnel Approximation*).

II.2 Surface Finish

The appearance of the surface finish is controlled by the relative magnitude of the diffuse and specular components of reflection and by the size of the specular highlight. In empirical models, the rules of thumb are:

- The diffuse and ambient multipliers should are same, $C_{Ka} = C_{Kd}$. The brightness of ambiently lit areas is controlled by the intensity of the ambient illumination.
- The sum of the diffuse and specular multipliers should be roughly equal to one, $C_{Kd} + C_{Ks} \approx 1$. This rule is flexible because of the empirical nature of the illumination models currently used in practice.
- The spread angle of the specular function decreases as C_{Ks} gets larger.

The first rule of thumb comes from the reciprocity relationship. The ambient multiplier relates the intensity reflected in a given direction to the intensity incident from all directions. The diffuse multiplier relates the intensity reflected in all directions to the energy incident from a given direction. Note that there is a mix of energy and intensity in the diffuse statement. Since the model is empirical and is not an energy formulation, it is convenient to overlook this and use the same spectral values for both diffuse and ambient.

The second rule does not have any sound physical base, it just helps assure that the computed intensity is not outside the displayable color gamut. Analysis of the model presented by Cook and Torrance (1982) provides a guideline for the relationship of the diffuse illumination to the sharpness of the specular highlight as related to β. The graph is given in Figure II.3. When considered in the context of empirical models this graph is somewhat misleading, since it describes the division of the reflected energy, not intensity, between specular and diffuse.

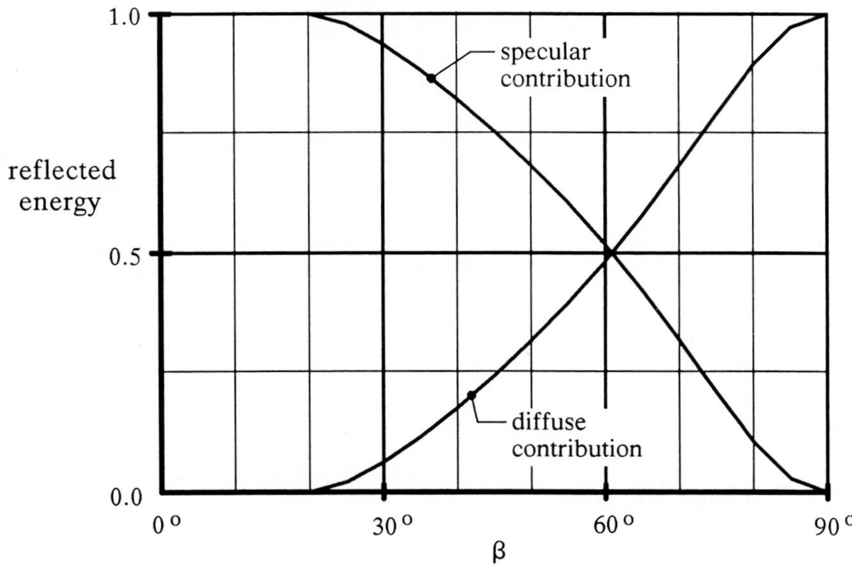

Figure II.3: Specularly and diffusely reflected energy as a function of β.

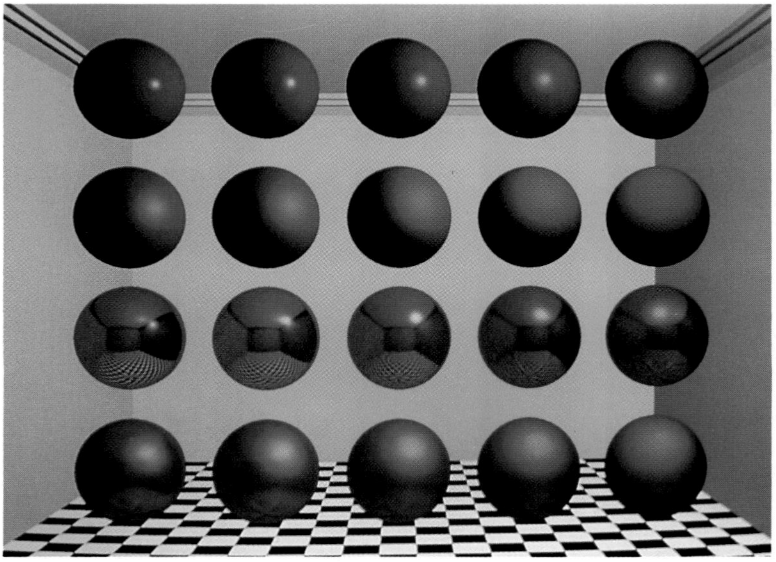

Figure II.4: Visual example of copper at different roughnesses.

	column 1	column 2	column 3	column 4	column 5
row 1 no reflection mapping	$C_{Ka} = 0.35$ $C_{Kd} = 0.35$ $C_{Ks} = 0.95$ $Ns = 330$	$C_{Ka} = 0.35$ $C_{Kd} = 0.35$ $C_{Ks} = 0.85$ $Ns = 215$	$C_{Ka} = 0.05$ $C_{Kd} = 0.05$ $C_{Ks} = 0.75$ $Ns = 135$	$C_{Ka} = 0.36$ $C_{Kd} = 0.36$ $C_{Ks} = 0.65$ $Ns = 80$	$C_{Ka} = 0.37$ $C_{Kd} = 0.37$ $C_{Ks} = 0.55$ $Ns = 45$
row 2 no reflection mapping	$C_{Ka} = 0.385$ $C_{Kd} = 0.385$ $C_{Ks} = 0.45$ $Ns = 25$	$C_{Ka} = 0.40$ $C_{Kd} = 0.40$ $C_{Ks} = 0.35$ $Ns = 15$	$C_{Ka} = 0.43$ $C_{Kd} = 0.43$ $C_{Ks} = 0.25$ $Ns = 10$	$C_{Ka} = 0.46$ $C_{Kd} = 0.46$ $C_{Ks} = 0.15$ $Ns = 7$	$C_{Ka} = 0.50$ $C_{Kd} = 0.50$ $C_{Ks} = 0.05$ $Ns = 5$
row 3 reflection mapped	$C_{Ka} = 0.025$ $C_{Kd} = 0.025$ $C_{Ks} = 0.95$ $Ns = 330$	$C_{Ka} = 0.050$ $C_{Kd} = 0.050$ $C_{Ks} = 0.90$ $Ns = 215$	$C_{Ka} = 0.075$ $C_{Kd} = 0.075$ $C_{Ks} = 0.80$ $Ns = 135$	$C_{Ka} = 0.100$ $C_{Kd} = 0.100$ $C_{Ks} = 0.70$ $Ns = 80$	$C_{Ka} = 0.125$ $C_{Kd} = 0.125$ $C_{Ks} = 0.65$ $Ns = 45$
row 4 reflection mapped	$C_{Ka} = 0.150$ $C_{Kd} = 0.150$ $C_{Ks} = 0.60$ $Ns = 25$	$C_{Ka} = 0.175$ $C_{Kd} = 0.175$ $C_{Ks} = 0.55$ $Ns = 15$	$C_{Ka} = 0.200$ $C_{Kd} = 0.200$ $C_{Ks} = 0.50$ $Ns = 10$	$C_{Ka} = 0.225$ $C_{Kd} = 0.225$ $C_{Ks} = 0.45$ $Ns = 7$	$C_{Ka} = 0.250$ $C_{Kd} = 0.250$ $C_{Ks} = 0.40$ $Ns = 5$

$K_a = K_d = K_s =$ spectral curve for copper

Figure II.5: Parameters used for Figure II.4.

In the physical world, the intensity of the specular highlight cannot exceed the intensity of the illuminating source. The intensity of the diffuse reflection cannot exceed ω/π times the intensity of the source. Thus, if the relationship of Figure II.3 is plotted as an intensity relationship, the maximum value of the diffuse curve will be much less than the maximum value of the specular curve. However, in practice the curve of Figure II.3 yields visually pleasing results. Note that the coefficients for the specular functions that correspond to β are discussed in Chapter 4 and are graphed in Figure 4.14.

Figure II.4 provides a visual example of a number of copper spheres for which the properties have been controlled as described above. Figure II.5 describes the properties used to generate these spheres. The spheres are presented both with and without reflection mapping. When reflection mapping is included, the apparently "correct" appearance is achieved with a much higher ratio of specular to diffuse reflectance. This is because the specular reflection of the reflection map adds a global illumination component that must be replaced by diffuse illumination when the reflection map is not used.

There is no substitute for experience in learning to select material parameters that will produce the desired results. This is especially true since the illumination models that are now in commercial use are empirical in nature and are not implemented in a uniform fashion.

Appendix III

Example Code

This appendix provides code examples for illumination models and the various functions used to build up the models. There is no attempt made to optimize this code. Instead, clarity of presentation is the main goal.

It is assumed that the reader has a working renderer and can easily incorporate additional illumination models. If a renderer is required, source code for a simple ray tracer is found in Whitted (1985).

The examples are written in C due to its wide acceptance in the graphics community. The examples provide both the include files and the code modules. The layout of this appendix works from basic tools to more complex functions as follows:

- Basic geometric utilities
- Numerical integrator for the illuminating hemisphere
- Geometric attenuation functions
- Microfacet distribution functions
- Fresnel approximation
- Illumination models
- Color transformations
- Spectral sampling for color computation
- RGB color clipping

The code segments are as short and concise as reasonably possible. The code presented here was used to generate the graphs throughout this text. Therefore, the examples have been tested and should be reasonably bug free.

III.1 Geometric Utilities

This is a collection of basic vector operations and reflection and/or refraction operations. A good basic reference for vector mathematics is Barnett and Fujii (1963). Other references are cited with the routines making use of the algorithms.

III.1.1 Code Summary

The following is a summary of the functions, and the figures to clarify the computations required. *Line* in this text refers to a line in space with a starting point and a direction vector. This is actually a parametric representation for a line where a point on the line is the start point plus the distance along the line multiplied by the direction vector. *Vector* in this text refers to a set of direction cosines, *i,j,k,* which give a direction relative to the x,y,z axis system in terms of the angles between the x,y,z axes and the direction vector. The *i, j,* and *k* components of the direction vector **A** are $\mathbf{A}_i$, $\mathbf{A}_j$, and $\mathbf{A}_k$. The vector is normally expressed as $[\mathbf{A}_i\ \mathbf{A}_j\ \mathbf{A}_k]$. A direction vector is always normalized in this text, i.e. $\mathbf{A}_i\mathbf{A}_i + \mathbf{A}_j\mathbf{A}_j + \mathbf{A}_k\mathbf{A}_k = 1$. The following is a summary of the routines in the code example.

Dot Product

The dot product (also referred to as scalar product or inner product) of two vectors, **A** and **B**, is given by:

$$|\mathbf{A}|\ |\mathbf{B}| \cos\theta = (\mathbf{A} \bullet \mathbf{B}) = \mathbf{A}_i\mathbf{B}_i + \mathbf{A}_j\mathbf{B}_j + \mathbf{A}_k\mathbf{B}_k \quad \text{(III.1)}$$

Where θ is the angle between the two vectors. Since **A** and **B** are unit vectors in this text, their lengths, |**A**| and |**B**|, are both equal to 1. In this case the dot product is the cosine of the angle between the two vectors. Note also that the dot product of a vector with itself is the square of the length of the vector (the cosine of the angle between a vector and itself is 1). The dot product has useful commutative, associative, and distributive properties. See Barnett and Fujii (1963) for details. The routine `geo_dot()` returns the dot product between two vectors.

Cross Product

The cross product (vector product) is a vector mutually perpendicular to two vectors. The cross product, **C**, of two vectors, **A** and **B**, is given by:

$$\mathbf{C} = \mathbf{A}\times\mathbf{B} = [(\mathbf{A}_j\mathbf{B}_k - \mathbf{A}_k\mathbf{B}_j)\ \ (\mathbf{A}_k\mathbf{B}_i - \mathbf{A}_i\mathbf{B}_k)\ \ (\mathbf{A}_i\mathbf{B}_j - \mathbf{A}_j\mathbf{B}_i)] \quad \text{(III.2)}$$

The length of the cross product is related to the two vectors by the sine of the angle between the vectors by:

$$|\mathbf{C}| = |\mathbf{A}|\ |\mathbf{B}| \sin\theta \quad \text{(III.3)}$$

The routine `geo_cross()` returns the cross product between two vectors.

Note that the cross product is a zero length vector if the two input vectors are parallel or one of them is a zero length vector. The Cross product reflects the handedness (right handed or left handed) of the coordinate system being used, thus, it is not commutative. The cross product **A**×**B** is the same magnitude but opposite direction as **B**×**A**.

Vector Normalization

Normalization is performed simply by dividing the components of a vector by the length of the vector. Note that a zero length vector cannot be normalized. The routine `geo_norm()` normalizes a vector.

Generating a Line

Lines between two points, i.e., the eye and a sample point on the viewing plane, are often required in computer graphics. In addition to the vector direction, a point on the line is required for a unique description of a line in space. The routine `geo_line()` generates the vector description of a line starting at one point and passing through another. The direction vector is normalized.

Reflected Vector

A reflection vector, $\mathbf{R}_v$, is in the plane of the incident vector, **V**, and the surface normal, **N**, with a reflected angle equal to the incident angle.

Whitted (1980) computes the reflected vector using vector algebra and similar triangles. Multiplying the normal by the dot product of the normal and incident vectors gives a vector with the length of the cosine of the incident angle:

$$\mathbf{N}' = \mathbf{N}(\mathbf{V} \bullet \mathbf{N}) \quad \text{(III.4)}$$

Subtracting the incident vector from this cosine vector gives a sine vector:

$$\mathbf{S} = \mathbf{N}' - \mathbf{V} \quad \text{(III.5)}$$

Note that the angle between the sine vector and the cosine vector is a right angle.

Using similar triangles, the sine vector is added to the cosine vector to reflect a vector, $\mathbf{R}_v$ in the same plane as the normal and

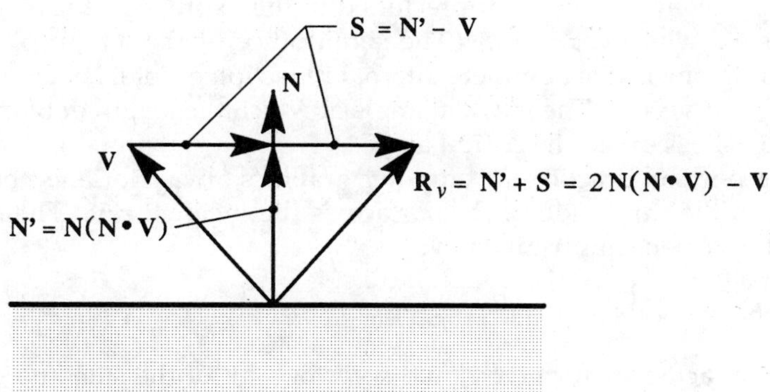

Figure III.1: Computation of the reflected vector.

incident vector such that the reflected angle is equal to the incident angle:

$$\mathbf{R}_v = \mathbf{N}' + \mathbf{S} = 2\mathbf{N}(\mathbf{V} \bullet \mathbf{N}) - \mathbf{V} \quad \text{(III.6)}$$

The routine `geo_rfr()` computes the reflected vector. A graphical representation of this computation is given in Figure III.1. Note that this formulation provides the correct reflected vector regardless of whether the incident vector is from the same side of the boundary as the surface normal.

Refracted Vector

A refracted vector, $\mathbf{T}_v$, is in the plane of the surface normal, **N**, and the incident vector, **V**, and is related to the incident vector by Snell's law of refraction (refer to Eq.2.12 and Figure 2.8). Hall (1983a) computes this vector by finding the sine vector, **S**, of the incident vector as described for reflection, Eq.(III.5); factoring it using Snell's law to get the sine vector for the refracted vector; computing a cosine vector for the refracted ray; and then adding the sine and cosine vector to give the refracted vector.

The sine vector, **S′**, for the refracted vector is related to the sine vector for the incident vector by Snell's law, Eq.(2.12). The **S′** vector is given by:

$$\mathbf{S}' = \frac{n_i}{n_t}\mathbf{S} \quad \text{(III.7)}$$

Using basic trigonometric functions the length of the cosine vector for the refracted vector is given by:

$$|\mathbf{N}''| = \sqrt{1 - |\mathbf{S}'|^2} \quad \text{(III.8)}$$

It is important to note that the length of the **S′** vector cannot exceed one. However, this is not precluded in the expression for **S′**, and is possible whenever $n_i > n_t$. The significance of the length of **S′** exceeding one is that complete internal reflection occurs, i.e. there is no refracted vector. The incident angle at which the length of **S′** first exceeds one is called the critical angle.

Common practice in computer graphics always orients the normal to the same side of the surface as the incident ray. The cosine vector is then simply given by:

$$\mathbf{N}'' = -\mathbf{N}\,|\mathbf{N}''| = -\mathbf{N}\sqrt{1 - |\mathbf{S}'|^2} \quad \text{(III.9)}$$

The refracted vector given by the vector sum of the sine and cosine vectors:

$$\mathbf{T}_v = \mathbf{N}'' + \mathbf{S}' \quad \text{(III.10)}$$

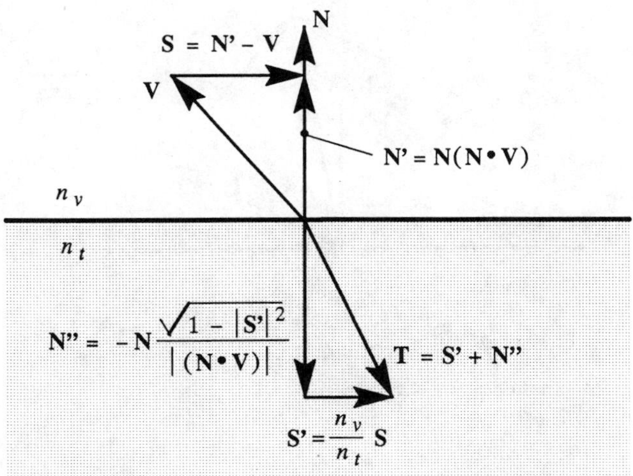

Figure III.2: Computation of the refracted vector.

In anticipation of increasingly more complex illumination modeling, the surface normal may not be on the same side of the boundary as the incident vector. This is accommodated simply by reversing the direction of the **N**″ vector if the surface normal is not on the same side as the incident vector. The routine `geo_rfr()` computes the refracted vector. A graphic representation of the computation is given in Figure III.2. The routine returns a `NULL` vector if there is complete internal reflection.

H Vector

The **H** vector is the vector bisector between two vectors. Normally it is the bisector between an incident light vector, **L**, and a outgoing vector, **R**. The **H** vector represents the orientation of the surface normal that is required for mirror reflection between the **L** and **R** vectors. Since **L** and **R** are equal length vectors (both are unit vectors), the vector their vector sum is a vector that bisects the angle between **L** and **R**. The **H** vector is found by normalizing the vector sum:

$$\mathbf{H} = \frac{\mathbf{L} + \mathbf{R}}{|\mathbf{L} + \mathbf{R}|} \qquad \text{(III.11)}$$

The routine `geo_H()` computes the **H** vector for an incident and outgoing vector. A graphic representation of the computation is given in Figure III.3. If the two input vectors are colinear and in opposite directions the **H** direction is undefined and a `NULL` vector is returned.

H′ Vector

The **H′** vector is analogous to the **H** vector except that it represents the surface normal that is required for refraction from an incident

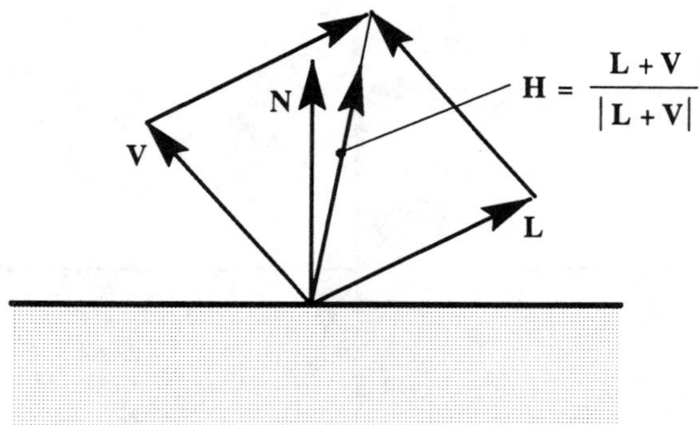

Figure III.3: Computation of the **H** vector.

vector, **L**, to a vector leaving the surface, **T**. To compute an **H′** vector in is necessary to have an incident and transmitted vector traveling through two different materials on opposite side of a surface boundary.

Consider a surface with an incident vector **L** and an outgoing vector **T** as shown in Figure III.4a. The **H′** vector is related to L and **T** by Snell's law, Eq.(2.12). The refracted geometry is projected to the same side as the **H′** vector by negating the refracted vector. The sine vectors for the incident ray and projected ray create two similar triangles, ECA and FCB. The lengths of the sine vectors is related by Snell's law. Since the triangles are similar, the sides $\overrightarrow{CB}$ and $\overrightarrow{CA}$ share the same relationship:

$$\frac{|\overrightarrow{EA}|}{|\overrightarrow{FB}|} = \frac{|\overrightarrow{CA}|}{|\overrightarrow{DB}|} = \frac{n_t}{n_i} \tag{III.12}$$

Note that $\overrightarrow{CA} = \overrightarrow{CB} + \overrightarrow{BA}$ and that $\overrightarrow{BA} = \mathbf{L} + \mathbf{T}$. Combining these, the vector $\overrightarrow{CB}$ is expressed by:

$$\overrightarrow{CB} = \frac{\overrightarrow{BA}}{\frac{n_i}{n_t} - 1} \tag{III.13}$$

A vector in the **H′** direction is given by vector addition and the **H′** vector is given by normalizing that vector:

$$\mathbf{H}' = -\frac{\mathbf{T} + \overrightarrow{CB}}{|\mathbf{T} + \overrightarrow{CB}|} \tag{III.14}$$

Note that this derivation assumes $n_i < n_t$. If $n_i > n_t$, the geometry of

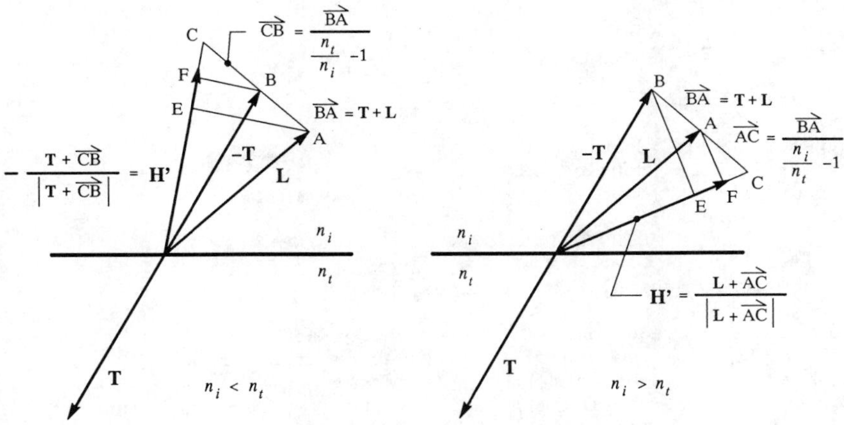

Figure III.4: Computation of the **H′** vector.

the **H′** vector is described by Figure III.4b. The **H′** vector is then given by:

$$H' = \frac{L + \overrightarrow{AC}}{|L + \overrightarrow{AC}|} ; \quad \overrightarrow{AC} = \frac{\overrightarrow{BA}}{\frac{n_i}{n_t} - 1} \tag{III.15}$$

Additionally, there are several special cases for which an **H′** vector cannot be generated. The first is when the index of refraction is the same on either side of the interface. There is no bending of the ray in this case and the input vectors must be colinear for an **H′** vector to exist. The second is when the angle between the vectors is less than the critical angle for internal reflection. The routine `geo_Ht()` computes the **H′** vector for an incident vector **L** and a refracted vector **T**. If the **H′** direction is undefined a `NULL` vector is returned.

III.1.2 Code Source

The following is the include file for the geometric utilities:

```
/* ****************************************************************
 *                           geo.h
 * ****************************************************************
 * include file for the geometric utilities
 */
#ifndef GEO_H
#define GEO_H

#ifndef TRUE
#define TRUE    1
#endif TRUE
```

```
#ifndef FALSE
#define FALSE   0
#endif FALSE

/* common geometric constructs
 */
typedef struct {double  i, j, k;}       DIR_VECT;
typedef struct {double  x, y, z;}       POINT3;
typedef struct {double  x, y, z, h;}    POINT4;
typedef struct {POINT3      start;
                DIR_VECT    dir; }      LINE;

/* geometric manipulation routines
 */
double          geo_dot();      /* vector dot product */
DIR_VECT        geo_cross();    /* vector cross product */
double          geo_norm();     /* vector normalize */
double          geo_line();     /* vector between two points */
DIR_VECT        *geo_rfl();     /* reflected vector */
DIR_VECT        *geo_rfr();     /* refracted vector */
DIR_VECT        *geo_H();       /* H vector */
DIR_VECT        *geo_Ht();      /* H' vector */

#endif GEO_H
/* ************************************************************ */
```

The following is the source module for the geometric utilities:

```
/* *************************************************************
 *                              geo.c
 * *************************************************************
 *  MODULE PURPOSE:
 *      This module contains routines that preform common
 *      geometric manipulations for image synthesis.
 *
 *  MODULE CONTENTS:
 *      geo_dot         - vector dot product
 *      geo_cross       - vector cross product
 *      geo_norm        - vector normalization
 *      geo_getv        - generate a vector
 *      geo_rfl         - compute the reflected vector
 *      geo_rfr         - compute the refracted vector
 *      geo_H           - compute H vector
 *      geo_Ht          - compute the H' vector
 */
#include <stdio.h>
#include <math.h>
#include "geo.h"

/* *************************************************************
 *  double geo_dot (v0, v1)
 *  DIR_VECT    *v0, *v1    (in) normalized direction vectors
 *
 *  Returns the dot product of two direction vectors, ref
 *   Eq.(III.1).  Note that the dot product is the cosine
 *   between the direction vectors because the direction
 *   vectors are normalized.
 */
```

```
double geo_dot (v0, v1)
DIR_VECT        *v0, *v1;
{   return (v0->i * v1->i) + (v0->j * v1->j) + (v0->k * v1->k);
}

/* ****************************************************************
 *  DIR_VECT geo_cross (v0, v1)
 *   DIR_VECT   *v0, *v1    (in)  normalized direction vectors
 *
 *  Returns the cross product of two direction vectors, refer
 *   to Eq.(III.2).
 */
DIR_VECT geo_cross (v0, v1)
DIR_VECT        *v0, *v1;
{   DIR_VECT        v2;
    v2.i = (v0->j * v1->k) - (v0->k * v1->j);
    v2.j = (v0->k * v1->i) - (v0->i * v1->k);
    v2.k = (v0->i * v1->j) - (v0->j * v1->i);
    return v2;
}

/* ****************************************************************
 *  double geo_norm (*v0)
 *   DIR_VECT   *v0           (mod) vector to be normalized
 *
 *  Returns the length of the vector before normalization.
 *   Returns zero if the vector could not be normalized.
 *   Note that the input vector is modified.
 */
double geo_norm (v0)
DIR_VECT        *v0;
{   double          len;
    if ((len = geo_dot(v0, v0)) <= 0.0) return FALSE;
    len = sqrt((double)len);
    v0->i /= len;
    v0->j /= len;
    v0->k /= len;
    return TRUE;
}

/* ****************************************************************
 *  double geo_line (*p0, *p1, *v)
 *   POINT3     *p0, *p1    (in)  from, to points
 *   LINE       *v          (out) generated line
 *
 *  Returns the distance from p0 to p1.  Returns 0.0
 *   on error (p0=p1).  The line is expressed in parametric
 *   form with a start point (p0) and a normalized direction
 *   vector. The vector direction of the line is normalized.
 */
double geo_line (p0, p1, v)
POINT3          *p0, *p1;
LINE            *v;
{   v->start = *p0;
    v->dir.i = p1->x - p0->x;
    v->dir.j = p1->y - p0->y;
    v->dir.k = p1->z - p0->z;
    return geo_norm(&v->dir);
}
```

```
/* ****************************************************************
 *  DIR_VECT *geo_rfl (V, N)
 *   DIR_VECT   *V          (in)  incident vector
 *   DIR_VECT   *N          (in)  surface normal
 *
 *  Returns the reflected direction vector.  The reflected
 *   direction is computed using the method given by Whitted
 *   (1980), refer to Eq.(III.6).
 */
DIR_VECT *geo_rfl (V, N)
DIR_VECT        *V;
DIR_VECT        *N;
{   double              N_dot_V;
    static DIR_VECT     rfl;
    N_dot_V = geo_dot (N,V);
    rfl.i = (2.0 * N_dot_V * N->i) - V->i;
    rfl.j = (2.0 * N_dot_V * N->j) - V->j;
    rfl.k = (2.0 * N_dot_V * N->k) - V->k;
    return &rfl;
}

/* ****************************************************************
 *  DIR_VECT *geo_rfr (V, N, ni, nt)
 *   DIR_VECT   *V          (in)  incident vector
 *   DIR_VECT   *N          (in)  surface normal
 *   double     ni          (in)  index of refraction for the
 *                                material on the front of the
 *                                interface (same side as N)
 *   double     nt          (in)  index of refraction for the
 *                                material on the back of the
 *                                interface (opposite size as N)
 *
 *  Returns the refracted vector, if there complete internal
 *   refracted (no refracted vector) then a NULL vector is
 *   NULL is returned.  The vector is computed using the
 *   method given by Hall (1983) with enhancements as
 *   described in Appendix III.
 */
DIR_VECT *geo_rfr (V, N, ni, nt)
DIR_VECT        *V;
DIR_VECT        *N;
double          ni;
double          nt;
{   static DIR_VECT T;       /* the refracted vector */
    DIR_VECT    sin_T;       /* sin vect of the refracted vect */
    DIR_VECT    cos_V;       /* cos vect of the incident vect */
    double      len_sin_T;   /* length of sin T squared */
    double      n_mult;      /* ni over nt */
    double      N_dot_V;
    double      N_dot_T;
    if ((N_dot_V = geo_dot(N,V)) > 0.0) n_mult = ni / nt;
    else n_mult = nt / ni;
    cos_V.i = N_dot_V * N->i;
    cos_V.j = N_dot_V * N->j;
    cos_V.k = N_dot_V * N->k;
    sin_T.i = (n_mult) * (cos_V.i - V->i);
    sin_T.j = (n_mult) * (cos_V.j - V->j);
    sin_T.k = (n_mult) * (cos_V.k - V->k);
    if ((len_sin_T = geo_dot(&sin_T, &sin_T)) >= 1.0)
        return NULL;    /* internal reflection */
```

```
    N_dot_T = sqrt(1.0 - len_sin_T);
    if (N_dot_V < 0.0) N_dot_T = -N_dot_T;
    T.i = sin_T.i - (N->i * N_dot_T);
    T.j = sin_T.j - (N->j * N_dot_T);
    T.k = sin_T.k - (N->k * N_dot_T);
    return &T;
}

/* ****************************************************************
 *  DIR_VECT *geo_H (L, V)
 *   DIR_VECT    *L           (in) incident vector
 *   DIR_VECT    *V           (in) reflected vector
 *
 *  Returns H, NULL on error (if L+H = 0).  Refer
 *   to Eq.(III.11).
 */
DIR_VECT *geo_H (L, V)
DIR_VECT        *L;
DIR_VECT        *V;
{   static DIR_VECT          H;
    H.i = L->i + V->i;
    H.j = L->j + V->j;
    H.k = L->k + V->k;
    if (!geo_norm(&H)) return NULL;
    return &H;
}

/* ****************************************************************
 *  DIR_VECT *geo_Ht(L, T, ni, nt)
 *   DIR_VECT    *L           (in) incident vector
 *   DIR_VECT    *T           (in) transmitted hector
 *   double      ni           (in) incident index
 *   double      nt           (in) transmitted index
 *
 *  Returns H' oriented to the same side of the surface
 *   as L computed using the method suggested by
 *   Hall (1983).  Returns NULL on error (if the angle
 *   between V and L is less than the critical angle).
 */
DIR_VECT *geo_Ht (L, T, ni, nt)
DIR_VECT        *L;
DIR_VECT        *T;
double          ni;
double          nt;
{
    float                    L_dot_T;
    float                    divisor;
    static DIR_VECT          Ht;

    L_dot_T = -(geo_dot(L,T));
    /* check for special cases */
    if (ni == nt) {
        if (L_dot_T == 1.0) return L;
        else return NULL;
    }
    if (ni < nt) {
        if (L_dot_T < ni/nt) return NULL;
        divisor = (nt / ni) - 1.0;
        Ht.i = -(((L->i + T->i) / divisor) + T->i);
        Ht.j = -(((L->j + T->j) / divisor) + T->j);
```

```
     Ht.k = -(((L->k + T->k) / divisor) + T->k);
    }
    else
    {   if (L_dot_T < nt/ni) return NULL;
        divisor = (ni / nt) - 1.0;
        Ht.i = ((L->i + T->i) / divisor) + L->i;
        Ht.j = ((L->j + T->j) / divisor) + L->j;
        Ht.k = ((L->k + T->k) / divisor) + L->k;
    }
    (void)geo_norm(&Ht);
    return &Ht;
}
/* ************************************************************ */
```

III.2 Hemispherical Integrator

Integration of illumination functions over the illuminating hemisphere is a basic tool in evaluating these functions. It is surprising how seldom attention is given to using numerical integration to verify models that are presented as energy equilibrium models. The integrator is provided here because of it is a basic tool for investigation and verification.

III.2.1 Code Summary

This is a simple integrator. It uses a fixed sampling size controlled by `incs`, which is the number of elevation increments (increments in θ) to be used in sampling. The number of radial sampling increments is 4 times the elevation sampling rate resulting in equal radial and elevation angle increments. The integration is a first order approximation that makes a computation of the function value at the center of each sample and assumes that value is constant over the solid angle of the sample. The full hemisphere is sampled thus allowing for integration of asymmetric functions.

The function to be integrated is passed to the integrator. The integrator calls the function passing **N** (surface normal), **V** (output sample direction), and **L** (incident light) vectors. The function is expected to return the intensity in the **V** direction. The integrator always uses a normal of [0 0 1]. Both the integrator and a short verification program are provided. The verification program integrates the energy of an identity function, i.e., a function of equal intensity in all directions. The resulting integration should be equal to π.

III.2.2 Code Source

The following is the source module for the hemispherical integrator:

```
/* ****************************************************************
 *                            integrate.c
 * ****************************************************************
 *  MODULE PURPOSE:
```

```
 *      This is a numerical integrator to integrate
 *      an intensity function over an illuminating
 *      hemisphere.
 */
#include <math.h>
#include "geo.h"

/*  double integrate (incs, theta_i, func_ptr)
 *   int      incs          (in) - number of elevation samples
 *   double   theta_i       (in) - incident angle (radians)
 *   double   (*func_ptr)() (in) - pointer to the function
 *                                 to be integrated.
 *
 *  Elevation sample rates as low as 16 can be used with
 *   relatively constant functions.  Functions with extreme
 *   variation may require rates upwards of 256.  The radial
 *   sample rate is 4*incs.
 *
 *  The function is called with pointers to N (the surface
 *   normal), L (the light vector at the incident angle given
 *   by 'theta_i'), and V (the direction for which the
 *   intensity function is being evaluated).  The intensity
 *   is assumed to be emitted or reflected from a unit
 *   surface area.
 */
double integrate (incs, theta_i, func_ptr)
int         incs;
double      theta_i;
double      (*func_ptr)();
{
    double       result = 0.0, elevation_ang = 0.0;
    double       radial_ang, angle_inc, omega, tmp;
    DIR_VECT     N, L, V;
    int          elev, radial;

    N.i = N.j = 0.0; N.k = 1.0;
    L.i = 0.0; L.j = sin(theta_i); L.k = cos(theta_i);
    angle_inc = M_PI / (2.0 * incs);
    for (elev=incs; --elev>=0; elevation_ang+=angle_inc) {
        omega = angle_inc * (cos(elevation_ang) -
            cos(elevation_ang + angle_inc));
        radial_ang = 0.0;
        V.k = cos(elevation_ang + (0.5 * angle_inc));
        tmp = sin(elevation_ang + (0.5 * angle_inc));
        for (radial=4*incs; --radial>=0; radial_ang += angle_inc) {
            V.i = tmp * sin(radial_ang + (0.5 * angle_inc));
            V.j = tmp * cos(radial_ang + (0.5 * angle_inc));
            result += omega * V.k * (*func_ptr)(&N, &L, &V);
        }
    }
    return result;
}
/* ************************************************************ */
```

The following is the source for a test of the hemispherical integrator:

```
/* **************************************************************
 *                          int_tst.c
```

```
 * ***************************************************************
 * integrator test - when run this should produce:
 *       integral is 3.142539 (32  incs)
 *       integral is 3.141829 (64  incs)
 *       integral is 3.141652 (128 incs)
 */
#include <stdio.h>
#include "geo.h"

double   ident();

main ()
{
    double      integrate();
    printf ("integral is %f (32  incs)0, integrate(32,0.0,ident));
    printf ("integral is %f (64  incs)0, integrate(64,0.0,ident));
    printf ("integral is %f (128 incs)0, integrate(128,0.0,ident));
}

double ident (N, L, V)
DIR_VECT    *N, *L, *V;
{   return 1.0;
}
/* ************************************************************** */
```

III.3 Geometric Attenuation

Geometric attenuation accounts for self shading of a rough surface due to its geometry. Geometric attenuation functions predict the degree of self shading based upon surface geometry, incident angle, and reflected angle. These are discussed in detail in Section 2.2.7, *Geometric Attenuation.*

III.3.1 Code Summary

Two expressions for the attenuation function have been explored for use in computer graphics (Blinn 1977) (Koestner 1986). To the author's knowledge, neither is used in any commercial image generation systems because of the high computational cost. The two routines in the example code have identical argument lists for ease in interchanging them.

Torrance-Sparrow Function

The routine `G_torrance()` returns the geometric attenuation using the relationship developed by Torrance and Sparrow (1967), Eq.(2.21). Refer to Section 2.2.7, *Geometric Attenuation*, for details.

Sancer Function

The routine `G_sancer()` returns the geometric attenuation using the relationship developed by Sancer (1969), Eq.(2.22). Note that the Sancer function has been cast in terms of m rather than $\overline{m}$ in this example. The Cook adaptation of the Beckmann formulation for the microfacet distribution provides a relationship between m and β (Eq.4.25). This allows the attenuation function to be easily mated to any of the specular functions whose roughness is related to m or β (see also Appendix III.4, *Microfacet Distributions*). Refer to Section 2.2.7, *Geometric Attenuation*, for details.

III.3.2 Code Source

The following is the include file for the geometric attenuation functions:

```
/* ****************************************************************
 *                           G.h
 * ****************************************************************
 * include file for the geometric attenuation functions
 */
#ifndef G_H
#define G_H
/* Microfacet distribution routines
 */
double G_torrance();
double G_sancer();
#endif G_H
/* ************************************************************* */
```

The following is the source module for the geometric attenuation functions:

```
/* ****************************************************************
 *                           G.c
 * ****************************************************************
 *  MODULE PURPOSE:
 *      This module contains geometric attenuation
 *      functions
 *
 *  MODULE CONTENTS:
 *      D_torrance       - function by Torrance and Sparrow
 *      D_Sancer         - function by Sancer
 */
#include <math.h>
#include "geo.h"

#define ROOT_PI     1.7724538509055159

/* ****************************************************************
 * double G_torrance (N, L, V)
 *  DIR_VECT    *N, *L, *V  (in) - N, L, V vectors
 *  double      dummy       (in) - just to make the
 *                                 calls identical
 *
 *  Returns geometric attenuation (Torrance and Sparrow
 *   1967), refer to Eq.(2.21).  The direction vectors
 *   N, V, and L are assumed to be oriented to the same
 *   side of the surface.
 */
double G_torrance (N, L, V, dummy)
DIR_VECT        *N, *L, *V;
double          dummy;
```

```
{
    double      N_dot_H, V_dot_H;
    double      N_dot_V, N_dot_L;
    double      g1, g2;
    DIR_VECT    *H;

    H = geo_H(V,L);
    N_dot_H = geo_dot (N,H);
    V_dot_H = geo_dot (V,H);
    N_dot_V = geo_dot (N,V);
    N_dot_L = geo_dot (N,L);

    if ((g1 = (2.0 * N_dot_H * N_dot_V) /
        V_dot_H) > 1.0) g1 = 1.0;
    if ((g2 = (2.0 * N_dot_H * N_dot_L) /
        V_dot_H) < g1) return g2;
    else return g1;
}


/* ****************************************************************
 * double G_sancer (N, L, V, m_2)
 *  DIR_VECT    *N, *L, *V  (in) - N, L, V vectors
 *  double      m_2         (in) - m squared
 *
 *  Returns geometric attenuation (Sancer 1969), refer to Eq.(4.25).
 *   The direction vectors N, V, and L are assumed to be oriented
 *   to the same side of the surface.
 *
 *  NOTE:
 *   > m can be related to beta using D_cook_init()
 *   > This implementation assumes slope relates roughness and
 *     correlation distance as described by Beckmann. This
 *     explains the missing factor of 2 with m_2 when compared
 *     to Eq.(4.25).
 */
double G_sancer (N, L, V, m_2)
DIR_VECT        *N, *L, *V;
double          m_2;
{
    double      N_dot_L, N_dot_V;
    double      c1, c2, root_c1, root_c2, ci, cr;

    if (m_2 <= 0.0) return 1.0;
    if ((N_dot_L = geo_dot(N,L)) <= 0.0) return 0.0;
    c1 = (N_dot_L * N_dot_L) / (m_2 * (1.0 - (N_dot_L * N_dot_L)));
    root_c1 = sqrt(c1);
    ci = (exp(-c1) /
        (2.0 * ROOT_PI * root_c1)) - (erfc(root_c1) / 2.0);

    if ((N_dot_V = geo_dot(N,V)) <= 0.0) return 0.0;
    c2 = (N_dot_V * N_dot_V) / (m_2 * (1.0 - (N_dot_V * N_dot_V)));
    root_c2 = sqrt(c2);
    cr = (exp(-c2) /
        (2.0 * ROOT_PI * root_c2)) - (erfc(root_c2) / 2.0);

    return 1.0/(1.0 + ci + cr);
}
/* ************************************************************** */
```

III.4 Microfacet Distributions

The microfacet distribution functions are typically used as the specular reflection functions for many illumination models. This makes presentation somewhat difficult. The distinctions between the functions and the typical use as experienced by the author is discussed in the code summary. Given that there is some disparity between what is written in the literature and what is actually implemented, coupled with empirical tuning for desired effects, it is not uncommon to run across implementations that are significantly different than those described here.

III.4.1 Code Summary

The functions included in the example code demonstrate all of the microfacet distribution functions described in Chapters 2 and 4. Since β has been used to relate these functions, routines are included to compute the specific coefficients of each function given β. The distribution functions presented use a common calling convention for ease in interchanging functions. However, the theoretical formulation from Chapter 2 required a unique calling convention because additional information is required to provide a complete surface description.

Phong specular function

The Phong (1975) function is a symmetric distribution about the reflected ray. The Phong specular function is discussed in detail in Section 4.2.3, *Specular Highlights*. Specifically, it is detailed in Eqs.(4.11) and (4.13), and plotted in Figure 4.13. The routine `D_phong()` evaluates the Phong function for a given lighting and viewing geometry. The routine `D_phong_init()` returns the specular exponent, *Ns*, given β.

Blinn microfacet distribution functions

Blinn (1977) presented a collection of microfacet distribution functions. These are detailed Section 4.3.1, *Improved Specular Reflection*. The functions are intended for combination with geometric attenuation and Fresnel attenuation as described in Eq.(4.15). In practice, the cosine power function is the specular function that is most often used for image generation. It is most often used without any additional factors (see Appendix III.6, *Illumination Models*, for details).

The cosine power function described by Blinn is the most commonly used specular function. It is given by Eq.(4.16) and appears in numerous illumination model expressions in Chapter 4. The function `D_blinn()` evaluates this cosine power distribution function for a given lighting and viewing geometry. The routine `D_blinn_init()` returns the specular exponent, *Ns*, given β as described by Eq.(4.19a).

The Gaussian distribution function used by Blinn is given by Eq.(4.17). The function `D_gaussian()` evaluates this distribution function for a given lighting and viewing geometry. The routine `D_gaussian_init()` returns the roughness coefficient, C_1, given β as described by Eq.(4.19b).

The Trowbridge and Reitz (1967) function used by Blinn is given by Eq.(4.18). The function `D_reitz()` evaluates this distribution function for a given lighting and viewing geometry. The routine `D_reitz_init()` returns the roughness coefficient, C_2^2, given β as described by Eq.(4.19c). Blinn expresses a preference for this specular function because of ease of computation.[1]

Beckmann microfacet distribution function

The microfacet distribution function developed by Beckmann (1963) appears in several forms in recent computer graphics literature. The function is given by a single series expression, Eq.(2.42b). The series is approximated by its first term for very smooth surfaces, Eq.(2.42a). Additionally, the series converges to a simple expression when the surface is very rough, Eq.(2.42c).

Cook and Torrance (1982) used the rough surface expression in the illumination model they presented (refer to Section 4.4.1, *An Energy Equilibrium Illumination Model*). The microfacet distribution was used in the formulation of the specular reflectance, R_{bd}, in combination with the Fresnel reflectance, geometric attenuation, and other factors to preserve energy equilibrium, Eqs.(2.41) and (4.23). The form of the Beckmann microfacet distribution function used by Cook and Torrance is given by Eq.(4.24). The function `D_cook()` evaluates this distribution function for a given lighting and viewing geometry. The routine `D_cook_init()` returns the average microfacet slope of the surface, m, given β as described by Eq.(4.25).

The treatment of physical process of illumination in Section 2.3, *Surface Illumination*, does not fall within the framework of illumination models that are currently in general use. However, as energy preserving rendering techniques come into practice, a theoretically correct treatment is becoming more necessary. The complexity in this treatment results from the need to have a very complete surface and illumination description. If addition to β (which was sufficient to describe the surface for all the previous models), it is necessary to know the wavelength of the incident light, λ, and either the correlation distance, τ, or the rms roughness, σ, of the surface.

The routine `D_g()` returns the apparent roughness as given by Eq.(2.36). This is used in calculating both coherent roughness attenuation and the incoherent microfacet distribution function. The

[1] While Blinn indicates this specular function to be the function of choice, the author is unaware of any commercial systems that are using this specular function.

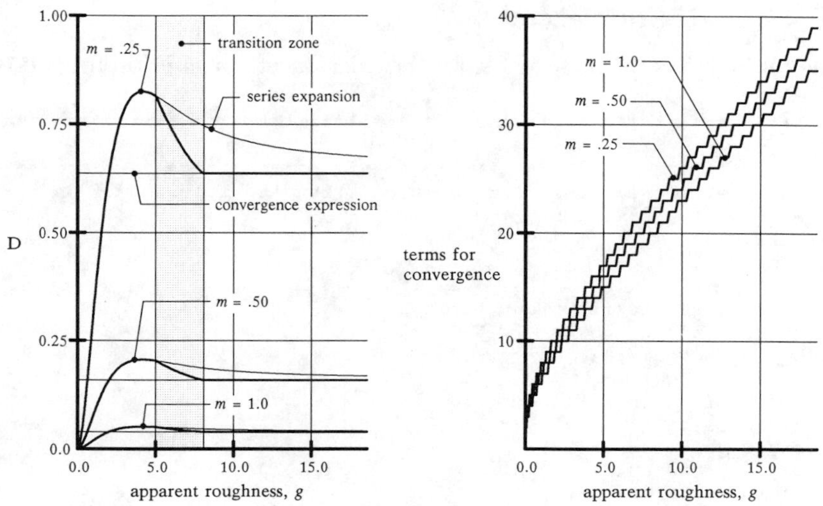

Figure III.5: Comparison of techniques for evaluating the incoherent microfacet distribution function.

routines `D_tau()`, `D_m()`, and `D_sigma()`, provide the relationships between slope, *m*, rms roughness, σ, and correlation distance τ as given by Eq.(2.19).

The coherent roughness attenuation, r_σ, is returned by `D_coherent()`. The apparent roughness is the only argument to this function. Surface finish information, illumination geometry, and illumination wavelength are all imbedded in the apparent roughness. Refer to Eqs.(2.36) and (2.37).

The interpretation for the Beckmann microfacet distribution function presented by Koestner (1986), Eqs.(2.42a), (2.42b), and (2.42c), is used as the basis for `D_incoherent()`. The application of these relationships in computing the microfacet distribution is detailed in Section 2.3.2.3, *Computing Incoherent Illumination*. Figure III.5 examines this evaluation technique for several different values of *m* as a function of *g*. the series expression; and the approximation used in `D_incoherent()`. Each value of *m* is described by three curves: the convergent expression; Note that the transition from the series to convergent expression limits the number of terms that need to be evaluated.

III.4.2 Code Source

The following is the include file for the microfacet distribution functions:

```
/* ****************************************************************
 *                              D.h
 * ****************************************************************
 * include file for the microfacet distribution functions
 */
#ifndef D_H
#define D_H

/* Microfacet distribution routines
 */
double D_phong_init();
double D_phong();
double D_blinn_init();
double D_blinn();
double D_gaussian_init();
double D_gaussian();
double D_reitz_init();
double D_reitz();
double D_cook_init();
double D_cook();
double D_g();
double D_tau();
double D_sigma();
double D_m();
double D_coherent();
double D_incoherent();
double D_Vxz();

#endif D_H
/* ************************************************************* */
```

The following is the source module for the microfacet distribution functions:

```
/* ****************************************************************
 *                              D.c
 * ****************************************************************
 *  MODULE PURPOSE:
 *    This module contains microfacet distribution routines and
 *    various support routines.  One of support functions includes
 *    computing the coefficients corresponding to beta for each
 *    function (as described in Section 4.3.1-Improved Specular
 *    Reflection).  Beta is the angle between H and N where the
 *    function is equal to half the value at N = H.  Beta is in
 *    radians.
 *
 *  MODULE CONTENTS:
 *    D_phong_init    - compute Ns given beta
 *    D_phong         - Phong cosine power function
 *    D_blinn_init    - compute Ns given beta
 *    D_blinn         - Blinn cosine power function
 *    D_gaussian_init - compute C1 given beta
 *    D_gaussian      - Gaussian distribution
```

```
 *      D_reitz_init      - compute c2 given beta
 *      D_reitz           - Trowbridge-Reitz
 *      D_cook_init       - compute m given beta
 *      D_cook            - Cook model
 *      D_g               - compute apparent roughness
 *      D_tau             - compute correlation distance
 *      D_sigma           - compute rms roughness
 *      D_m               - compute slope
 *      D_coherent        - coherent roughness attenuation
 *                             (per Beckmann)
 *      D_incoherent      - incoherent microfacet attenuation
 *                             (per Beckmann and Bahar)
 *      D_Vxy             - Vxy used in D_incoherent()
 *
 *    ASSUMPTIONS:
 *    > The following are defined in math.h
 *            HUGE          largest floating pont value
 *            M_PI          pi
 *            M_PI_2        pi/2
 *            M_PI_4        pi/4
 *            M_SQRT2       root of 2
 *
 *    > The direction vectors N, V, and L are assumed to be oriented
 *        to the same side of the surface.
 */
#include <stdio.h>
#include <math.h>
#include "geo.h"
#include "D.h"

/* ****************************************************************
 * double D_phong_init (beta)
 *   double       beta         (in) - angle between N and
 *                                    H where function = .5
 *   Returns Ns given beta for the Phong (1975) specular function,
 *     per footnote to Eq.(4.19)
 */
double D_phong_init (beta)
double          beta;
{   if (beta <= 0.0) return HUGE;
    if (beta >= M_PI_4) return 0.0;
    return -(log(2.0) / log(cos(2.0 * beta)));
}

/* ****************************************************************
 * double D_phong (N, L, V, Ns)
 *   DIR_VECT     *N, *L, *V  (in) - N, L, V vectors
 *   double       Ns           (in) - specular exponent
 *
 *   Returns the value of the Phong (1975) specular function given
 *     surface normal, incident light direction, view direction, and
 *     the specular exponent.  Refer to Eqs.(4.11) and (4.13).
 */
double D_phong (N, L, V, Ns)
DIR_VECT         *N, *L, *V;
double           Ns;
{   double       Rv_dot_L;
    if ((Rv_dot_L = geo_dot(geo_rfl(V,N),L)) < 0.0) return 0.0;
    return pow (Rv_dot_L, Ns);
}
```

```
/* ****************************************************************
 * double D_blinn_init (beta)
 *  double      beta         (in) - angle between N and
 *                                  H where function = .5
 *  Returns Ns given beta for the cosine power distribution
 *   function presented by Blinn (1977).  Refer to Eq.(4.19a)
 */
double D_blinn_init (beta)
double          beta;
{   if (beta <= 0.0) return HUGE;
    if (beta >= M_PI_2) return 0.0;
    return -(log(2.0) / log(cos(beta)));
}

/* ****************************************************************
 * double D_blinn (N, L, V, Ns)
 *  DIR_VECT     *N, *L, *V  (in) - N, L, V vectors
 *  double       Ns          (in) - specular exponent
 *
 *  Returns the cosine power distribution function presented by
 *   Blinn (1977) given surface normal, incident light direction,
 *   view direction, and the specular exponent. Refer to Eq.(4.16)
 */
double D_blinn (N, L, V, Ns)
DIR_VECT        *N, *L, *V;
double          Ns;
{   double      N_dot_H;
    if ((N_dot_H = geo_dot(N,geo_H(V,L))) < 0.0) return 0.0;
    return pow (N_dot_H, Ns);
}

/* ****************************************************************
 * double D_gaussian_init (beta)
 *  double      beta         (in) - angle between N and
 *                                  H where function = .5
 *  Returns C1 given beta for the Gaussian distribution presented
 *   by Blinn (1977).  Refer to Eq.(4.19b)
 */
double D_gaussian_init (beta)
double          beta;
{   if (beta <= 0.0) return HUGE;
    return sqrt(log(2.0)) / beta;
}

/* ****************************************************************
 * double D_gaussian (N, L, V, C1)
 *  DIR_VECT     *N, *L, *V  (in) - N, L, V vectors
 *  double       C1          (in) - shape coefficient
 *
 *  Returns the Gaussian distribution function presented by
 *   Blinn (1977) given surface normal, incident light direction,
 *   view direction, and the specular exponent. Refer to Eq.(4.17)
 */
double D_gaussian (N, L, V, C1)
DIR_VECT        *N, *L, *V;
double          C1;
{   double      tmp;
    double      N_dot_H;
    if ((N_dot_H = geo_dot(N,geo_H(V,L))) < 0.0) return 0.0;
    tmp = acos(N_dot_H) * C1;
```

```
    return exp (-(tmp * tmp));
}

/* ****************************************************************
 * double D_reitz_init (beta)
 *  double      beta         (in) - angle between N and
 *                                 H where function = .5
 *  Returns C2 squared given beta for the Trowbridge-Reitz
 *   distribution function presented by Blinn (1977). Refer to
 *   Eq.(4.19c). C2 is squared for computational efficiency later.
 */
double D_reitz_init (beta)
double          beta;
{   double      cos_beta;
    if (beta <= 0.0) return 0.0;
    cos_beta = cos(beta);
    return ((cos_beta * cos_beta) - 1.0) /
        ((cos_beta * cos_beta) - sqrt(2.0));
}

/* ****************************************************************
 * double D_reitz (N, L, V, C2_2)
 *  DIR_VECT    *N, *L, *V  (in) - N, L, V vectors
 *  double      C2_2        (in) - C2 squared
 *
 *  Returns the Trowbridge-Reitz distribution function presented
 *   by Blinn (1977) given surface normal, incident light
 *   direction, view direction, and the specular exponent. Refer
 *   to Eq.(4.18)
 */
double D_reitz (N, L, V, C2_2)
DIR_VECT        *N, *L, *V;
double          C2_2;
{   double      tmp;
    double      N_dot_H;
    if ((N_dot_H = geo_dot(N,geo_H(V,L))) < 0.0) return 0.0;
    tmp = C2_2 / ((N_dot_H * N_dot_H * (C2_2 - 1.0)) + 1.0);
    return tmp * tmp;
}

/* ****************************************************************
 * double D_cook_init (beta)
 *  double      beta         (in) - angle between N and
 *                                 H where function = .5
 *  Returns m squared corresponding to beta, refer to Eq.(4.25).
 *   m is squared for computational efficiency in later use.
 */
double D_cook_init (beta)
double          beta;
{   double      tan_beta;
    if (beta <= 0.0) return 0.0;
    if (beta >= M_PI_2) return HUGE;
    tan_beta = tan(beta);
    return -(tan_beta * tan_beta) /
        log(pow(cos(beta),4.0)/2.0);
}

/* ****************************************************************
 * double D_cook (N, L, V, m_2)
 *  DIR_VECT    *N, *L, *V  (in) - N, L, V vectors
```

```
 *  double      m_2          (in) - m squared
 *
 *  Returns microfacet distribution probability (Cook 1982) derived
 *   from (Beckmann 1963).  Refer to Eq.(4.24).
 */
double D_cook (N, L, V, m_2)
DIR_VECT         *N, *L, *V;
double           m_2;
{   double       tmp;
    double       N_dot_H;
    if ((N_dot_H = geo_dot(N,geo_H(V,L))) < 0.0) return 0.0;
    tmp = -(1.0 - (N_dot_H * N_dot_H)) / (N_dot_H * N_dot_H * m_2);
    return exp(tmp)/(4.0 * M_PI * m_2 * pow(N_dot_H,4.0));
}

/* ****************************************************************
 * double D_g (N, L, V, sigma, lambda)
 *  DIR_VECT    *N, *L, *V  (in) - N, L, V vectors
 *  double      sigma       (in) RMS roughness, nm
 *  double      lambda      (in) wavelength, nm
 *
 *  Returns the apparent roughness, g, as given by Beckmann (1963).
 *   Refer to Eq.(2.36).
 */
double D_g (N, L, V, sigma, lambda)
DIR_VECT         *N, *L, *V;
double           sigma, lambda;
{   double       tmp;
    tmp = geo_dot(N,L) + geo_dot(N,V);
    return (4.0 * M_PI * M_PI * sigma * sigma * tmp * tmp) /
        (lambda * lambda);
}

/* ****************************************************************
 * double D_tau (sigma, m)
 *  double      sigma       (in) rms roughness (nm)
 *  double      m           (in) rms slope
 *
 *  Returns tau (correlation distance) in nm.  The relationship of
 *   roughness, slope, and correlation distance given by
 *   Beckmann (1963) is assumed, refer to Eq.(2.19).
 */
double D_tau (sigma, m)
double           sigma, m;
{   return (2.0 * sigma) / m;
}

/* ****************************************************************
 * double D_sigma (m, tau)
 *  double      m           (in) rms slope
 *  double      tau         (in) correlation distance (nm)
 *
 *  Returns sigma (rms roughness). The relationship of roughness,
 *   slope, and correlation distance given by Beckmann (1963) is
 *   assumed, refer to Eq.(2.19).
 */
double D_sigma (m, tau)
double           m, tau;
{   return (m * tau)/ 2.0;
}
```

```
/* ****************************************************************
 * double D_m (sigma, tau)
 *  double      sigma       (in) rms roughness (nm)
 *  double      tau         (in) correlation distance (nm)
 *
 *  Returns m (rms slope). The relationship  of roughness, slope,
 *   and correlation distance given by Beckmann (1963) is assumed,
 *   refer to Eq.(2.19).
 */
double D_m (sigma, tau)
double          sigma, tau;
{   return (2.0 * sigma) / tau;
}

/* ****************************************************************
 * double D_coherent (g)
 *  double      g           (in) apparent roughness
 *
 *  Returns the coherent roughness attenuation given
 *  by Beckmann (1963), refer to Eq.(2.37).
 */
double D_coherent (g)
double g;
{   return exp(-g);
}

/* ****************************************************************
 * double D_incoherent (N, L, V, m, g, lambda, tau)
 *  DIR_VECT    *N, *L, *V  (in) N, L, V vectors
 *  double      m           (in) m (slope)
 *  double      g           (in) apparent roughness
 *  double      lambda      (in) wavelength (nm)
 *  double      tau         (in) correlation distance (nm)
 *
 *  Returns the microfacet distribution function given by
 *   Beckmann (1963) as interpreted by Koestner (1986), refer to
 *   Eq.(2.42).
 */
double D_incoherent (N, L, V, m, g, lambda, tau)
DIR_VECT        *N, *L, *V;
double          m, g, lambda, tau;
{   DIR_VECT    *H;
    double      D1, D2;
    double      denom;
    double      N_dot_H, N_dot_H_2;

    if (g <= 0.0) return 0.0;
    if ((H = geo_H(V,L)) == NULL) return 0.0;
    if ((N_dot_H = geo_dot(N,H)) <= 0.0) return 0.0;
    N_dot_H_2 = N_dot_H * N_dot_H;
    denom = 4.0 * M_PI * m * m * N_dot_H_2 * N_dot_H_2;

    /* if g < 8.0, evaluate the series expansion, Eq.(2.42b)
     *  terminating when a term falls below 0.00001.  For small g
     *  the evaluation terminates quickly.  For large g the series
     *  converges slowly.  If g is near 8.0 the first terms of the
     *  series will be less that the termination criteria.  This
     *  requires an additional termination criteria that the values
     *  of the terms are decreasing at the time the termination
     *  criteria is reached.
```

```
     */
    if (g < 8.0) {
        double      inc, ct, ct_factorial, g_pow;
        double      last_inc, Vxz_t_over_4;
        Vxz_t_over_4 = (tau * tau * D_Vxz(N,L,V,lambda)) / 4.0;
        D1 = 0.0;
        ct = 1.0;
        ct_factorial = 1.0;
        g_pow = g * g;
        inc = 0.0;
        do {
            last_inc = inc;
            inc = (g_pow / (ct * ct_factorial)) *
                exp(-(g + Vxz_t_over_4/ct));
            D1 += inc;
            ct += 1.0;
            ct_factorial *= ct;
            g_pow *= g;
        } while (((inc/denom) > 0.00001) || (inc > last_inc));
        D1 /= denom;

        /* if g < 5.0, only the series expansion is used.  If
         *  5.0 < g < 8.0, then we are in a transition range
         *  for interpolation between the series expansion and
         *  the convergence expression.
         */
        if (g < 5.0) return D1;
    }

    /* if g > 5.0, evaluate the convergence expression, Eq.(2.42c)
     *  (this routine would have returned earlier if G < 5.0).
     */
    {   double  tmp;
        tmp = (N_dot_H_2 - 1.0) / (N_dot_H_2 * m * m);
        D2 = exp(tmp) / denom;

        /* if g > 8.0, only the convergence expression is used,
         *  otherwise we are in a transition zone between the
         *  convergent expression and series expansion.
         */
        if (g > 8.0) return D2;
    }

    /* linear interpolation between D1 and D2 for
     *          5.0 < g < 8.0
     */
    return (((8.0 - g) * D1) + ((g - 5.0) * D2)) / 3.0;
}

/* ************************************************************
 * double D_Vxz (N, L, V, lambda)
 *  DIR_VECT     *N, *L, *V  (in) N, L, V vectors
 *  double       lambda      (in) wavelength (nm)
 *
 *  Returns the value of Vxz per Eq.(2.42d).
 */
double D_Vxz (N, L, V, lambda)
DIR_VECT         *N, *L, *V;
double           lambda;
{   double       N_dot_L, N_dot_V, cos_phi;
```

```
    DIR_VECT      sin_i, sin_r;
    double        len_2_i, len_2_r;

    /* compute the sine squared of the incident angle
     */
    N_dot_L = geo_dot(N, L);
    len_2_i = 1.0 - (N_dot_L * N_dot_L);

    /* compute the sine squared of the reflected angle
     */
    N_dot_V = geo_dot(N, V);
    len_2_r = 1.0 - (N_dot_V * N_dot_V);

    /* if the sine of either the incident or the
     *  reflected angle is zero, then the middle
     *  term is zero.
     */
    if ((len_2_i > 0.0) && (len_2_r > 0.0)) {
        /* the two sine vectors are of length equal to the sine of
         *  the angles.  The dot product is the cosine times the
         *  lengths of the vectors (sines of the angles).
         */
        sin_i.i = L->i - (N_dot_L * N->i);
        sin_i.j = L->j - (N_dot_L * N->j);
        sin_i.k = L->k - (N_dot_L * N->k);
        sin_r.i = V->i - (N_dot_V * N->i);
        sin_r.j = V->j - (N_dot_V * N->j);
        sin_r.k = V->k - (N_dot_V * N->k);
        cos_phi = geo_dot (&sin_i, &sin_r);
        return (4.0 * M_PI * M_PI * (len_2_i +
            (2.0 * cos_phi) + len_2_r)) / (lambda * lambda);
    }
    else {
        return (4.0 * M_PI * M_PI * (len_2_i + len_2_r)) /
            (lambda * lambda);
    }
}
/* ************************************************************* */
```

III.5 Fresnel Approximation

The Fresnel relationships are basic to explaining the dependence between incident angle and reflectance. They are a keystone in illumination models used for realistic representation of metals and transparent materials. Both the shift in spectral character and the magnitude of the reflection and transmission is determined by the Fresnel relationships. It is important, therefore, to represent these relationships as accurately as possible if we are attempting to simulate the real illumination processes.

While the Fresnel relationships are very well defined and easy to put into code, they are not easy to use for image generation. The barriers are the lack of sufficient material data and the computational expense. Lack of material information is by far the most severe, since it prevents use even if the computational expense is minimal. Additionally, if the materials used in an image are "invented" by the artist, then we cannot expect any realistic property information.

Approximation techniques must be brought into play if the Fresnel relationships are to be applied to illumination calculations. Cook (1981,1982) presents an approximation method that appears to produce realistic results. To the author's knowledge, there has been no testing, other than subjective observation, to verify the correctness of the result.

III.5.1 Approximation Methodology

Cook addresses two areas of concern. The first is the approximation of missing material information. The second is efficiently fitting the Fresnel relationships into the illumination model. The approximation methodology outlined here follows very closely that described by Cook.

We can classify materials according to type and available information. The types are conductors and dielectrics. The information available is generally a spectral curve (see Appendix II.1.4, *Using Published Spectral Data*) and sometimes an index of refraction, absorption index (n/k) and/or absorption coefficient (k). In some cases, wavelength dependent index of refraction information is available.

The Fresnel relationships are most easy to apply if all materials are cast in similar terms. The information used by Cook's computation method is a spectral curve, an average index of refraction, and, in the case of conductors, an average k. Spectral curves for a wide range of materials are available (Purdue 1967,1970). The spectral curve demonstrates that the index of refraction is not constant across the spectrum, but varies with wavelength. If the index of refraction is the same for all wavelengths, then the reflectivity is also the same and the spectral curve is simply a horizontal line. Although the index of refraction is not constant, rendering techniques typically assume a single representative index of refraction for a material.

The Fresnel relationships for dielectrics are established by a single material parameter, the index of refraction. For light incident from the normal direction (**L** = **N**) moving through air ($n \approx 1$) and striking a material with an index of refraction n_t, the Fresnel relationships for reflectance, Eqs.(2.13), (2.14), and (2.15), reduce to:

$$F_r = \frac{(n_t - 1)^2}{(n_t + 1)^2} \qquad \text{(III.16)}$$

This is rewritten to express n in terms of F_r by:

$$n_t = \frac{1 + \sqrt{F_r}}{1 - \sqrt{F_r}} \qquad \text{(III.17)}$$

If wavelength dependent index of refraction data is available, then a spectral curve is generated using Eq.(III.16). The average index of refraction, n_{ave} for the material is found by taking the average reflectance at normal incidence over the visible range, $F_{r,ave}(0)$, and applying Eq.(III.17).

Metals are more complex because both n and k are required to characterize the Fresnel relationships. Typically a single value of n and k for a material is found in reference literature. If either n, k, or both are not available, then an approximation must be used. Cook suggests approximating the index of refraction by assuming $k = 0$ and using the same method previously described for a dielectric. An alternate approximation is to assume that light travels at the same speed in the material as in air ($n = 1$) and solve for k. For light from normal incidence through air, the Fresnel relationships for a conductor, Eqs.(2.16) and (2.17), reduce to:

$$F_r = \frac{(n_t - 1)^2 + k^2}{(n_t + 1)^2 + k^2} \tag{III.18}$$

Setting n=1, this is rewritten to express k in terms of F_r by:

$$k = \frac{2\sqrt{F_r}}{\sqrt{1 - F_r}} \tag{III.19}$$

Figure III.6 plots the behavior of the two approximations against the correct curves for gold, silver, copper, and steel. Neither approximation is a terribly good fit once the incident angle exceeds 45°. The choice of which to use is left to the reader.

The described approximations result in a spectral curve, index of refraction, and absorption coefficient for each material. Every color computation requires repeating the illumination computation for each of the

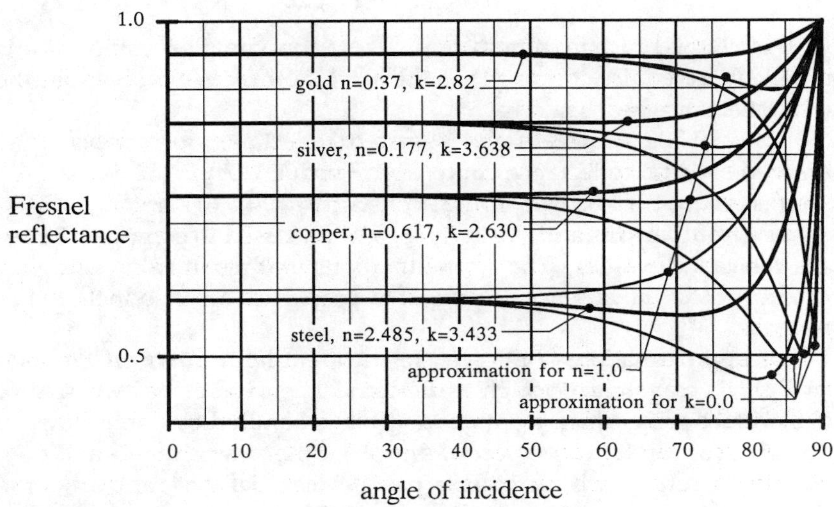

Figure III.6: Actual and approximated Fresnel reflectance for metals.

color samples. Reflectance and transmittance values are required for each of these computations. An efficient method of determining these reflectance and transmittance properties is required.

One solution is to use the spectral curve to approximate an n and k corresponding to each color sample, or use measured property information if it is available. The Fresnel relationships are then explicitly calculated for each color sample. An average n is still required for determining the direction of refraction. This approach is computationally prohibitive and is prone to error for conductors if n and k are approximated.

The approximation presented by Cook computes a single average reflectance for the material at the current incident angle, $F_{r,ave}(\theta)$, and uses this as a basis for interpolation. For dielectrics, the average reflectance for light incident at θ is computed using n_{ave}, which is computed from the average reflectance at normal incidence using the Fresnel relationships for a dielectric, Eqs.(2.13), (2.14), and (2.15). For conductors, the average reflectance is computed from n_{ave} and k_{ave} using the Fresnel relationships for a conductor, Eqs.(2.16) and (2.17). If values of n and k are available, these are used as the average values and an average reflectance at $\theta = 0$ is computed from them. If they are not available, Cook sets $k_{ave} = 0$ and uses the same approximation as that used for dielectrics. The author has found that setting $n_{ave} = 1$ and approximating k_{ave} also produces good results.

The Fresnel reflectance for spectral sample j at incident angle θ, $F_r(j,\theta)$, is interpolated from the spectral curve samples, $F_r(j,0)$, using the average reflectance at θ=0 and the computed average reflectance at the current θ as:

$$F_r(j,\theta) = F_r(j,0) + (1 - F_r(j,0))\left[\frac{F_{r,ave}(\theta) - F_{r,ave}(0)}{1 - F_{r,ave}(0)}\right] \tag{III.20}$$

$F_r(j,\theta)$ is clipped to a minimum of 0. The approximation using $k = 0$ is more likely to require clipping than the $n = 1$. approximation because the dip in reflectance near grazing.

Figure III.7 graphs the approximated reflectance for copper. The measured spectral reflectance curve from Purdue 1970, 7:162, is used for the reflectance at $\theta = 0$. The optical constants n_{ave}= 0.617 and k_{ave}= 2.630 are taken from Jenkins and White 1976, 538, and used to compute the average reflectance values. The approximations that result from assuming $k = 0$ or $n = 1$ in the absence of measured properties are also included in this figure.

This approximation works well for incident light in air. If the incident light is traveling through a dielectric, then there are two sets of $F_r(j,\theta)$ values with which to contend. This is handled by computing an index of refraction for each spectral sample of the two materials and then generating a reflectance curve for a pseudo-material that represents the interface. The approximation technique is then used with the pseudo-material.

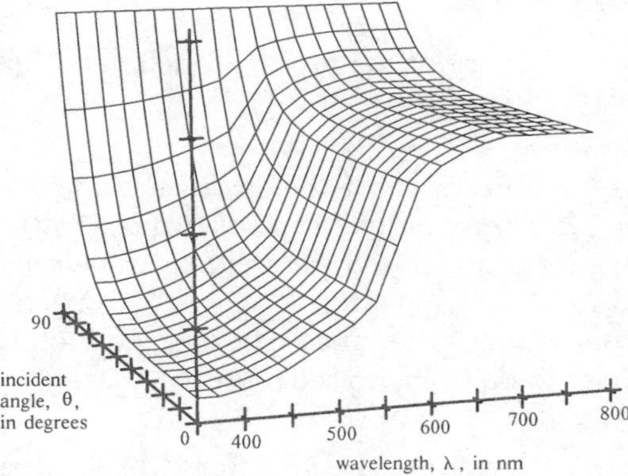

approximate Fresnel reflectance for copper using the measured properties: n = 0.617 k = 2.630

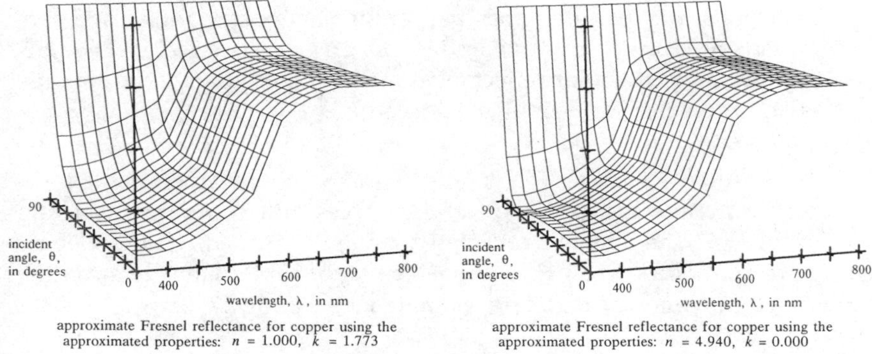

approximate Fresnel reflectance for copper using the approximated properties: n = 1.000, k = 1.773

approximate Fresnel reflectance for copper using the approximated properties: n = 4.940, k = 0.000

Figure III.7: Approximated Fresnel reflectance for copper.

While there has been no study of the error in this approximation technique, we get an intuitive feeling by examining this approximation in more detail. The spectral curve provides the index of refraction at all wavelengths for dielectrics. However, the spectral curves for dielectrics are usually nearly constant resulting in a nearly constant index of refraction across all visible wavelengths. In this case, the approximation should be close to the actual behavior. Conductors pose a different problem because of the uncertainty of material properties. The approximation techniques appear to bound the actual behavior (Figure III.6). The approximation produces the correct spectral character at normal incidence and at grazing. The error in approximated behavior between at other incident angles cannot be evaluated until there is better material information available.

III.5.2 Code Summary

The following is a summary of the Fresnel functions included in the example code:

Dielectric Reflectance

The routines for reflectance of dielectrics use the Fresnel relationships Section 2.2.5, *Reflection and Refraction*. Eqs.(2.13) and (2.14) give the reflectance for parallel and perpendicular polarization, and are implemented in `F_d_pl()` and `F_d_pp()` respectively. The parallel and perpendicular reflectances are averaged to give the average reflectance, refer to Eq.(2.15), in the routine `F_d_R()`.

Conductor Reflectance

The routines for reflectance of conductors use the assumptions that incident light is through a material with an index of refraction equal to 1, and that $n^2 + k^2 \gg 1$. This supports the using the approximation for the Fresnel relationship for conductors described in Section 2.2.5, *Reflection and Refraction*. Eqs.(2.16) and (2.17) give the reflectance for parallel and perpendicular polarization, and are implemented in `F_c_pl()` and `F_c_pp()` respectively. The parallel and perpendicular reflectances are averaged to give the average reflectance, refer to Eq.(2.15), in the routine `F_c_R()`.

Approximate n

The routine `F_approx_n()` approximates the average n for a dielectric by averaging the spectral samples and computing n using Eq.(III.17). The average reflectance is also returned. The dielectric expression of the Fresnel relationships is for $k = 0$. Thus, this routine is used for conductors to approximate n assuming $k = 0$.

Approximate k

The routine `F_approx_k()` approximates the average k for a conductor assuming $n = 1$, averaging the spectral samples, and computing k using Eq.(III.19). The average reflectance is also returned.

Approximate F_r for a Conductor

The routine `F_approx_Fr()` uses the interpolation of Eq.(III.20) to approximate the reflectance of a conductor for light at some incident angle θ. The values for n and k are required by this routine. If the measured values are available, they are used, otherwise use either the $k = 0$ or the $n = 1$ approximation as described above.

Approximate F_r for a Dielectric

The routine `F_approx_Fr_Ft()` uses the interpolation of Eq.(III.20) to approximate the reflectance and transmittance of a dielectric material for light at some incident angle θ. Note that if the material on either side of the interface is air, then the material curve used is that for the actual material. If neither material is air, then a pseudo-material for the interface is used. The pseudo material is generated by first approximating an n for each color sample of each curve (using `F_approx_n()`); then using the approximated n to compute a reflectance at each color sample at normal incidence (using `F_d_R()`).

III.5.3 Code Source

The following is the include file for the Fresnel approximation routines:

```
/* ****************************************************************
 *                              F.h
 * ****************************************************************
 * include file for the microfacet distribution functions
 */
#ifndef F_H
#define F_H

double  F_d_pl();
double  F_d_pp();
double  F_d_R();
double  F_c_pl();
double  F_c_pp();
double  F_c_R();
double  F_approx_n();
double  F_approx_k();
double  *F_approx_Fr();
double  *F_approx_Fr_Ft();

#endif F_H
/* ************************************************************** */
```

The following is the source module for the Fresnel approximation routines:

```
/* ****************************************************************
 *                              F.c
 * ****************************************************************
 *  MODULE PURPOSE:
 *      This module contains routines to for fresnel calculations.
 *
 *  MODULE CONTENTS:
 *      F_d_pl          - reflectance for a dielectric,
 *                          parallel polarized,
 *      F_d_pp          - reflectance for a dielectric,
 *                          perpendicular polarized
 *      F_d_R           - reflectance for a dielectric
 *      F_c_pl          - reflectance for a conductor,
 *                          parallel polarized,
 *      F_c_pp          - reflectance for a conductor,
 *                          perpendicular polarized
 *      F_c_R           - reflectance for a conductor
 *      F_approx_n      - approximate the average index of
 *                          refraction for a material
 *      F_approx_k      - approximate the average absoption
 *                          index for a material
```

```
 *      F_approx_Fr     - approximate conductor reflectance
 *      F_approx_Fr_Ft  - approximate dielectric reflectance
 *                           and transmittance
 *
 *
 *  ASSUMPTIONS:
 *      The following are defined in math.h
 *          HUGE    largest floating pont value
 *          M_PI_2  pi/2
 *          M_PI_4  pi/4
 */
#include <stdio.h>
#include <math.h>
#include "geo.h"
#include "F.h"

/* ****************************************************************
 *  double F_d_pl (N, L, T, ni, nt)
 *   DIR_VECT *N, *L, *T    (in) - N, L, T vectors
 *   double   ni          (in) - incident index of refraction
 *   double   nt          (in) - transmitted index of refraction
 *
 *  Returns the reflectance of a dielectric for light with
 *   polarization parallel to the plane of incidence (plane of the
 *   N and L vector), refer to Eq.(2.13). N and L are assumed to
 *   be to the same side of the surface.
 */
double F_d_pl (N, L, T, ni, nt)
DIR_VECT     *N, *L, *T;
double       ni, nt;
{   double  amplitude, N_dot_L, N_dot_T;
    N_dot_L = geo_dot(N, L);
    N_dot_T = geo_dot(N, T);
    amplitude = ((nt * N_dot_L) + (ni * N_dot_T)) /
                ((nt * N_dot_L) - (ni * N_dot_T));
    return amplitude * amplitude;
}

/* ****************************************************************
 *  double F_d_pp (N, L, T, ni, nt)
 *   DIR_VECT *N, *L, *T    (in) - N, L, T vectors
 *   double   ni          (in) - incident index of refraction
 *   double   nt          (in) - transmitted index of refraction
 *
 *  Returns the reflectance of a dielectric for light with
 *   polarization perpendicular to the plane of incidence
 *   (plane of the N and L vector), refer to Eq.(2.14). N and L
 *   are assumed to be to the same side of the surface.
 */
double F_d_pp (N, L, T, ni, nt)
DIR_VECT     *N, *L, *T;
double       ni, nt;
{   double  amplitude, N_dot_L, N_dot_T;
    N_dot_L = geo_dot(N, L);
    N_dot_T = geo_dot(N, T);
    amplitude = ((ni * N_dot_L) + (nt * N_dot_T)) /
                ((ni * N_dot_L) - (nt * N_dot_T));
    return amplitude * amplitude;
}
```

```
/* ****************************************************************
 *  double F_d_R (N, L, T, ni, nt)
 *   DIR_VECT *N, *L, *T    (in) - N, L, T vectors
 *   double   ni         (in) incident index of refraction
 *   double   nt         (in) transmitted index of refraction
 *
 *  Returns the average reflectance for a dielectric.  Refer to
 *   Eq.(2.15).  N and L are assumed to be to the same side of the
 *   surface.
 */
double F_d_R (N, L, T, ni, nt)
DIR_VECT     *N, *L, *T;
double       ni, nt;
{   return (F_d_pl (N, L, T, ni, nt) +
        F_d_pp (N, L, T, ni, nt)) / 2.0;
}

/* ****************************************************************
 *  double F_c_pl (N, L, nt, k)
 *   DIR_VECT    *N, *L  (in) - N, L vectors
 *   double      nt      (in) - index of refraction
 *   double      k       (in) - absorption coefficient
 *
 *  Returns the reflectance of a conductor for light with
 *   polarization parallel to the plane of incidence (plane of the
 *   N and L vector), refer to Eq.(2.16).  N and L are assumed to
 *   be to the same side of the surface.
 */
double F_c_pl (N, L, nt, k)
DIR_VECT     *N, *L;
double       nt, k;
{   double  tmp_f, N_dot_L;
    N_dot_L = geo_dot(N, L);
    tmp_f = ((nt * nt) + (k * k)) * N_dot_L * N_dot_L;
    return (tmp_f - (2.0 * nt * N_dot_L) + 1) /
           (tmp_f + (2.0 * nt * N_dot_L) + 1);
}

/* ****************************************************************
 *  double F_c_pp (N, L, nt, k)
 *   DIR_VECT    *N, *L  (in) - N, L vectors
 *   double      nt      (in) - index of refraction
 *   double      k       (in) - absorption coefficient
 *
 *  Returns the reflectance of a conductor for light with
 *   polarization perpendicular to the plane of incidence (plane of
 *   the N and L vector), refer to Eq.(2.17). N and L are assumed
 *   to be to the same side of the surface.
 */
double F_c_pp (N, L, nt, k)
DIR_VECT     *N, *L;
double       nt, k;
{   double  tmp_f, N_dot_L;
    N_dot_L = geo_dot(N, L);
    tmp_f = (nt * nt) + (k * k);
    return (tmp_f - (2.0 * nt * N_dot_L) + (N_dot_L * N_dot_L)) /
           (tmp_f + (2.0 * nt * N_dot_L) + (N_dot_L * N_dot_L));
}

/* ****************************************************************
```

```
 *  double F_c_R (N, L, nt, k)
 *   DIR_VECT    *N, *L  (in) - N, L vectors
 *   double      nt      (in) - index of refraction
 *   double      k       (in) - absorption coefficient
 *
 *  Returns the average reflectance for a conductor.  Refer to
 *   Eq.(2.15).  N and L are assumed to be to the same side of
 *   the surface.
 */
double F_c_R (N, L, nt, k)
DIR_VECT     *N, *L;
double       nt, k;
{   return (F_c_pl (N, L, nt, k) + F_c_pp (N, L, nt, k))/2.0;
}

/* ****************************************************************
 *  double F_approx_n (Ro, n_samp, mtl)
 *   double      *Ro      (out) - average reflectance
 *   int         n_samp   (in)  - number of material samples
 *   double      *mtl     (in)  - material spectral curve
 *
 *  Returns the approximate n, and loads Ro.  This gives the
 *   correct n for a single mtl reflectance if the material is a
 *   dielectric, and the correct n assuming k=0 for a conductor,
 *   refer to Eq.(III.17).
 */
double F_approx_n (Ro, n_samp, mtl)
double       *Ro;
int          n_samp;
double       *mtl;
{   int      ct;
    *Ro = 0.0;
    for (ct=n_samp; --ct>=0; ) *Ro += *mtl++;
    *Ro /= (double)n_samp;
    return (1.0 + sqrt(*Ro)) / (1.0 - sqrt(*Ro));
}

/* ****************************************************************
 *  double F_approx_k (Ro, n_samp, mtl)
 *   double      *Ro      (out) - average reflectance
 *   int         n_samp   (in)  - number of material samples
 *   double      *mtl     (in)  - material spectral curve
 *
 *  Returns the approximate k, and loads Ro.  This assumes n=1.0
 *   and is applicable to conductors only. Refer to Eq.(III.19).
 */
double F_approx_k (Ro, n_samp, mtl)
double       *Ro;
int          n_samp;
double       *mtl;
{   int      ct;
    *Ro = 0.0;
    for (ct=n_samp; --ct>=0; ) *Ro += *mtl++;
    *Ro /= (double)n_samp;
    return 2.0 * sqrt(*Ro / (1.0 - *Ro));
}

/* ****************************************************************
 *  double *F_approx_Fr (N, L, Ro, n, k, n_samp, mtl, Fr)
 *   DIR_VECT    *N, *L  (in) - N, L vectors
```

```
 *   double      Ro       (in) - average reflectance
 *   double      n        (in) - measured or approximate index
 *                                 of refraction
 *   double      k        (in) - measured or approximate
 *                                 absorption coefficient
 *   int         n_samp   (in)  number of material samples
 *   double      *mtl     (in)  material spectral curve
 *   double      *Fr      (out) reflectance
 *
 *  Loads the vector Fr with the approximate reflectance for each
 *   color sample point for a conductor, refer to Eq.(III.20).
 *   Returns the pointer to Fr.  The measured values for n and k
 *   should be used if they are available.  Otherwise, assume k=0
 *   and approximate n using F_approx_n(), or assume n=1 and
 *   approximate k using F_approx_k().
 */
double *F_approx_Fr (N, L, Ro, n, k, n_samp, mtl, Fr)
DIR_VECT     *N, *L;
double       Ro, n, k;
int          n_samp;
double       *mtl, *Fr;
{   double       R_theta;    /* ave R for N and L*/
    double       factor, *R_out;
    R_theta = F_c_R (N, L, n, k);
    factor = (R_theta - Ro) / (1.0 - Ro);
    for (R_out=Fr ;--n_samp>=0; Fr++, mtl++)
        if ((*Fr = *mtl + ((1.0 - *mtl) * factor)) < 0.0)
            *Fr = 0.0;
    return R_out;
}

/* ***********************************************************
 *  double *F_approx_Fr_Ft (N, L, T, Ro, ni, nt,
 *               n_samp, *mtl_p, Fr, Ft)
 *  DIR_VECT     *N, *L, *T  (in) - N, L vectors
 *   double      Ro       (in)  average reflectance
 *   double      ni       (in)  ave n for incident material
 *   double      nt       (in)  ave n for transmitted material
 *   int         n_samp   (in)  number of material samples
 *   double      *mtl_p   (in)  pseudo material curve
 *   double      *Fr      (out) reflectance
 *   double      *Tr      (out) transmittance
 *
 *  Loads the vector Fr with the approximate reflectance and Ft
 *   with the approximate transmittance for each sample point for
 *   a conductor, refer to Eq.(III.20).  Returns the pointer to Fr.
 *   The measured value for n should be used if it is available,
 *   otherwise use F_approx_n() to approximate the index of
 *   refraction.
 */
double *F_approx_Fr_Ft (N, L, T, Ro, ni, nt, n_samp, mtl_p, Fr, Ft)
DIR_VECT     *N, *L, *T;
double       Ro, ni, nt;
int          n_samp;
double       *mtl_p, *Fr, *Ft;
{   double       R_theta;    /* ave R for N and L*/
    double       factor, *R_out;

    if (T == NULL)       /* internal reflection */
        for (R_out=Fr; --n_samp>=0; *Fr++ = 1.0, *Ft++ = 0.0) ;
```

```
    else {
        R_theta = F_d_R (N, L, T, ni, nt);
        factor = (R_theta - Ro) / (1.0 - Ro);
        for (R_out=Fr; --n_samp>=0; mtl_p++) {
            if ((*Fr = *mtl_p + ((1.0 - *mtl_p) * factor)) < 0.0)
                *Fr = 0.0;
            *Ft++ = 1.0 - *Fr++;
        }
    }
    return R_out;
}
/* ************************************************************ */
```

III.6 Illumination Models

This section includes examples of code for the illumination models presented in Section 4.2, *Incremental Shading, Empirical Models,* and Section 4.3, *Ray Tracing, Transitional Models.* These illumination models are the ones found in common practice, and share a point sampling approach to illumination calculations.

Models for radiosity techniques are not presented because radiosity techniques have not yet come into common practice, because the models used thus far have been very simple. It is difficult to establish the calling conventions for radiosity models. Additionally, once the reader has mastered an understanding of the basic principles, illumination models are easily generated with the building blocks presented prior to this section.

The models generally follow the text, but have been extended to accommodate experimentation and research. The reader should keep in mind that the implementation presented is not intended to demonstrate efficient computational techniques, but is intended to demonstrate the application of previously presented concepts to the problem of computing color.

III.6.1 Illuminated Surface Description

There are three components to providing a description of the illuminated surface. The first is a description of the viewing and illumination geometry. The second is a description of the materials on either side of the boundary. The third is a description of the spectral character and intensity of the illumination sources.

The geometry is provided by describing the location and normal of the surface, the location of the viewer, and the location of the light sources. The location of the surface and normal direction are loaded into a `LINE` structure (refer to the include file `geo.h` described in Appendix III.1, *Geometric Utilities*). The viewing geometry is also described with a `LINE` structure containing the start point of the view vector and the direction of the view vector. Note that the view vector is directed **away** from the surface to follow the vector conventions used throughout this text. Light information is loaded into `ILLUM_LGT` structures defined in the include file for illumination models. Each light is loaded into a structure and a `NULL` terminated vector of pointers to the structures is passed to the illumination model. The first light is always assumed to be the ambient illumination. The remainder of the lights are used as point sources from the center specified in the structure.

The descriptions of the materials on either side of a surface are loaded into a `ILLUM_MATL` structure, also defined in the include file for illumination models. The surface is characterized as having an outside and an inside. The surface normal is always directed to the outside. In keeping with our normal perception of objects, the outside is typically air and is the side on which reflection occurs. The inside is the object material and the side on which transmission occurs. The exception to this representation is a surface between two dielectrics such as water and glass. In this case either is selected to be the outside material. Once selected, the convention must be maintained.

Materials information is maintained in the manner described in Appendix II.1.5, *Setting the Spectral Character of* K_a, K_d, K_s, F_t, *and* F_r. Each material coefficient is described by a set of spectral samples and a scale factor. The spectral samples are obtained by sampling the spectral curves for materials as described later in this appendix. The scale factor scales the contribution of the illumination component. Typically the ambient and diffuse spectral curves and scale factors are the same. If the material is homogenous, then the specular spectral curve is the same as the diffuse curve. If the material is a composite, the spectral curve is different. The relative magnitude of the diffuse and specular scale factors in combination with the surface roughness controls the surface character.

The material information also include the microfacet distribution function and the geometric attenuation function to be used. The models have been written to allow for ease in interchanging these functions.

Light sources are described by a light location (center), the sampled spectral curve, and an intensity scale. The first light is always taken to be the ambient illumination and the center is ignored.

III.6.2 Code Summary

The illumination models assemble the functions describe in the previous sections to compute colors. The early models such as those by Bouknight (1970) and Phong (1975) are straightforward. Later models such as those by Blinn (1977) and Hall and Greenberg (1983b) are rather complex due to the need to check for a variety of possible conditions influencing Fresnel relationships, geometric attenuation, and reflection and refraction. Every attempt has been made to provide adequate explanation in the code documentation.

The routines are setup without knowledge of the color representation used. Any number of sample points is used to represent colors provided all spectral values are represented with the same number of samples.

Initialization

The routine `IM_init()` initializes the illumination models for the specified number of color sample points. Additionally, a routine to be called to get colors from the reflected and/or transmitted directions is specified at this time. If a `NULL` routine pointer is specified, then recursive reflection and refraction operations are ignored. The routine `IM_exit()` completes use of the illumination models.

Bouknight Model

The routine `IM_bouknight()` implements an extensions to the model presented by Bouknight (1970). This illumination model considers diffuse reflection only. The model is described by Eq.(4.9). The model is extended for a variable number of light sources and to separate spectral curves and scale factors. Only the ambient and diffuse material properties are used.

Phong Model

The routine `IM_phong()` implements an extensions to the model presented by Phong (1975). This illumination model considers diffuse and specular reflection. The model is described by Eq.(4.11). The model is extended for a variable number of light sources and to separate spectral curves and scale factors. The spectral character of specular reflection can be specified. Additionally, the microfacet distribution function is selected from `D_phong()`, `D_blinn()`, `D_gaussian()`, `D_reitz()`, or `D_cook()`. The desired microfacet distribution function is loaded into the material along with the coefficient for the function (determined using the function initialization routine). In addition to the properties required for the Bouknight model, the specular material properties are required.

The model presented by Phong results when the identity material is selected for the specular spectral property, and the microfacet distribution `D_phong()` is used.

Blinn Model

The routine `IM_blinn()` implements an extensions to the model presented by Blinn (1977). This illumination model is similar to the Phong model with an improved description of the specular reflection. This model is described by Eq.(4.15). The model uses a variable number of lights and allows selection of the microfacet distribution function as described for the Phong model, and selection of the geometric attenuation function. The geometric attenuation function is either `G_torrance()` or `G_sancer()`. Specifying a `NULL` geometric attenuation function causes geometric attenuation to be ignored. If the `G_sancer().` function is used, then the geometric attenuation coefficient must also be specified. This is determined from β using `D_init_cook()` as described in Appendix II.3, *Geometric Attenuation*. In addition to the properties required for the Phong model, this model requires the average reflectance, the indices of refraction, the absorption coefficient, and the conductor flag.

Complexity is added to this model by the Fresnel function. Different approximations are required for dielectrics and conductors. Complete internal reflection is also a possibility. However, since this model does not allow transparency, the incident illumination is always from outside the object. Complete internal reflection can only occur if the index of refraction for the transmitted material is less than that of the material on the incident side of the interface. This cannot occur unless the object is made of a fictitious material with an index of refraction less than 1. Refer to Appendix III.5, *Fresnel Approximation*, for more detail.

The model presented by Blinn results when either `D_blinn()`, `D_gaussian()`, or `D_reitz()` is used as the microfacet distribution function, and `G_torrance()` is used as the geometric attenuation function.

Whitted Model

The routine `IM_whitted()` implements an extensions to the model presented by Whitted (1980). This illumination model is similar to the Phong model with extensions to include illumination from the reflected and transmitted directions. This model is described by Eq.(4.20). Illumination from light sources is ignored if the view vector is inside an object (traveling through a material other than air). The color from the reflected direction is factored by the specular scale and spectral coefficients. The color from the refracted direction is factored by the transmitted scale and spectral coefficients.

The model presented by Whitted results when `D_blinn()` is used as the microfacet distribution and identity material is used for both the specular and transmitted spectral samples.

Hall Model

The routine `IM_hall()` implements an extensions to the model presented by Hall and Greenberg (1983b). This illumination model is similar to the Blinn model with extensions to include illumination from the reflected and transmitted directions, filter attenuation in materials, and specular transmission of light. This model is described by Eq.(4.21). The model uses the same material properties as the Blinn model with the addition of the filter attenuation spectral information.

The filter attenuation is the fraction of light transmitted through a unit thickness of the material. For example, if a material attenuation was 0.6, then 60% of the light would pass through the first unit thickness of material, 60% of that, or 36% would pass through two unit thicknesses of the material.

The Fresnel reflectance and transmittance are derived from the specular spectral data as described in Appendix III.5, *Fresnel Approximation*. The transmitted scale and spectral data are ignored.

The model presented by Hall results when `D_blinn()` is used as the microfacet distribution and `NULL` is specified for geometric attenuation.

III.6.3 Code Source

The following is the include file for the illumination models:

```
/* ****************************************************************
 *                        illum_mod.h
 * ****************************************************************
 * include file for the illumination models
 */
#ifndef ILLUM_H
#define ILLUM_H
#include "geo.h"

/* The material structure maintains the description of a material
 *  interface.  An interface between a conductor or dielectric and
 *  air is characterized by loading the properties of the material
 *  and an index of refraction of 1 for the outside material.  An
 *  interface between two materials is characterized by generating
 *  a pseudo-material as described in appendix III.5.1, Approxima-
 *  tion Methodology.
 *
 * In filling the material structure, the reflected direction is
 *  the 'outside' of the material.  That is, for an interface
 *  between air and glass, for example, the the reflected direction
 *  or 'outside' is air (Ar_spectral = NULL, nr=1.0), and the
 *  transmitted direction is glass (nt=1.5, etc.)
 *
 * Individual spectral components of the material are characterized
 *  by the sampled spectral values and a multiplier to scale these
 *  values (as discussed in appendix II.1.5, Selecting Ka, Ka, Ks,
 *  Ft and Fr)
 */

typedef struct {
    double  Ka_scale;       /* ambient multiplier */
    double  *Ka_spectral;   /* sampled ambient spectral curve */
    double  Kd_scale;       /* diffuse multiplier */
    double  *Kd_spectral;   /* sampled diffuse spectral curve */
    double  Ks_scale;       /* specular multiplier */
    double  *Ks_spectral;   /* sampled specular spectral curve */
    double  Kt_scale;       /* transmitted multiplier           */
    double  *Kt_spectral;   /* sampled specular transmitted     */
                            /*  curve.  The Kt_ properties are  */
                            /* used for the Whitted model only  */
    double  *Ar_spectral;   /* sampled filter spectral curve.   */
    double  *At_spectral;   /* sampled filter spectral curve    */
                            /*  These are used in the Hall model */
```

```
                    /*  only.  Filter attenuation is     */
                            /*  ignored is a NULL pointer is     */
                            /*  specified.                       */
    double  beta;           /* roughness indicator */
    double  (*D)();         /* microfacet distribution */
    double  D_coeff;        /* the coefficient for the           */
                            /*  microfacet distribution function */
                            /*  computed from by microfacet      */
                            /*  distribution init function       */
    double  (*G)();         /* geometric attenuation function */
    double  G_coeff;        /* the coefficient for the geometric */
                            /*  attenuation function (m_2 for    */
                            /*  the Sancer function, unused for  */
                            /*  the Torrance-Sparrow function)   */
    double  Ro;             /* average reflectance */
    double  nr;             /* index of refraction (incident) */
    double  nt;             /* index of refraction (transmitted) */
    double  k;              /* absorption coefficient */
    int     conductor;      /* flags the specular material as a  */
                            /*  conductor */
    int     transparent;    /* flags whether the material is     */
                            /*  transparent --- note, composite  */
                            /*  materials have a dielectric      */
                            /*  specular component but may not   */
                            /*  be transparent                   */
    int     r_is_air;       /* flags that the 'outside' or       */
                            /*  reflect side of the interface is */
                            /*  air                              */
} ILLUM_MATL;

typedef struct {
    double  I_scale;        /* illumination multiplier */
    double  *I_spectral;    /* sampled source spectral curve */
    POINT3  center;         /* center of the light source */
} ILLUM_LGT;

int     IM_init();
double  *IM_bouknight();
double  *IM_phong();
double  *IM_blinn();
double  *IM_whitted();
double  *IM_hall();
int     IM_exit();

#endif CLR_H
/* ************************************************************ */
```

The following is the source module for the illumination models:

```
/* **************************************************************
 *                          illum_mod.c
 * **************************************************************
 *  MODULE PURPOSE:
 *      This module contains the source code for the illumination
 *      models discussed for in Section 4.2, Incremental Shading,
 *      Empirical Models, and in Section 4.3, Ray Tracing,
 *      Transitional Models.
 *
```

```
 *  MODULE CONTENTS:
 *      IM_init         - initialize the illumination models
 *      IM_bouknight    - Bouknight (1970) illumination model
 *      IM_phong        - Phong (1975) illumination model
 *      IM_blinn        - Blinn (1976) illumination model
 *      IM_whitted      - Whitted (1980) illumination model
 *      IM_hall         - Hall (1983) illumination model
 *      IM_exit         - finish with the illumination models
 *
 *  NOTES:
 *      > The illumination model is called once a surface has
 *          point on a surface has been identified and the list
 *          of illuminating light sources has been generated.
 *
 *      > There exists a routine that the illumination models can
 *          call to get a color from any direction.  Specifically
 *          this is used for inquiring about the reflected or
 *          transmitted directions in the ray tracing models.
 *          This routine is passed the view vector for which the
 *          color is required.
 *
 *      > a common calling convention is used for ease in
 *          interchanging the illumination model routines.  Each
 *          routine is passed the location and orientation of the
 *          surface, a view vector, an interface material, a
 *          description of the lighting, and an array to receive
 *          the computed color.
 *
 *          The orientation of the surface is given by the surface
 *          normal which is ALWAYS directed to the 'outside' or
 *          reflected side of the material.
 *
 *          The view vector is specified by start position and
 *          direction vector.  During visibility computations the
 *          view vector is typically directed towards the surface.
 *          The direction cosines MUST be negated prior to calling
 *          the illumination model for consistency with the vector
 *          conventions used.
 *
 *          See 'illum_mod.h' for material details.
 *
 *          The light vector is a list of pointers to ILLUM_LGT
 *          structures terminated by a NULL pointer.  The first
 *          entry is taken as the ambient illumination.  Only
 *          light that is incident from the air side of a material
 *          can provide illumination.
 *
 *      > These models assume that the material structure is
 *          correctly loaded and that the surface is facing the
 *          viewer (N.V > 0) for illumination models that do not
 *          consider transparency.
 */
#include <stdio.h>
#include <math.h>
#include "illum_mod.h"
#include "F.h"

static int      num_samples = 0;
static int      (*get_color)() = NULL;
static double   *Fr_buffer = NULL;
```

```
static double   *Ft_buffer = NULL;

/* ****************************************************************
 * int IM_init (num_clr_samples, get_clr_routine)
 *  int      num_clr_samples          (in) - number of color samples
 *  int      (*get_clr_routine)()     (in) - routine to call to get
 *                                      the color from some direction
 *
 * Initializes the illumination model routine set, returns TRUE
 *  if successful and FALSE upon failure.
 */
IM_init (num_clr_samples, get_clr_routine)
int      num_clr_samples, (*get_clr_routine)();
{   char     *malloc();
    if (((num_samples = num_clr_samples) <= 0) ||
          ((Fr_buffer = (double *)malloc((unsigned)(num_samples *
            sizeof(double)))) == NULL) ||
          ((Ft_buffer = (double *)malloc((unsigned)(num_samples *
            sizeof(double)))) == NULL)) {
        (void)IM_exit();
        return FALSE;
    }
    get_color = get_clr_routine;
    return TRUE;
}

/* ****************************************************************
 * double *IM_bouknight (surface, V, matl, lgts, color)
 *  LINE         *surface    (in)  - surface for color computation
 *  LINE         *V          (in)  - view vector
 *  ILLUM_MATL   *matl       (in)  - material properties
 *  ILLUM_LGT    **lgts      (in)  - illuminating sources
 *  double       *color      (mod) - array to receive the color
 *
 * Evaluates the color using the Bouknight (1970) illumination
 *  model as described in Eq.(4.9).  Returns 'color' upon
 *  success and NULL upon failure.
 */
double *IM_bouknight (surface, V, matl, lgts, color)
LINE        *surface, *V;
ILLUM_MATL  *matl;
ILLUM_LGT   **lgts;
double      *color;
{   int         ct;
    double      N_dot_L;
    LINE        L;

    /* load the ambient illumination */
    for (ct=0; ct<num_samples; ct++) {
      color[ct] = matl->Ka_scale * matl->Ka_spectral[ct] *
        (*lgts)->I_scale * (*lgts)->I_spectral[ct];
    }
    lgts++;

    /* load the diffuse component of the illumination.  Loop
     *  through the lights and compute (N.L).  If it is positive
     *  then the surface is illuminated.
     */
    while (*lgts != NULL) {
      if ((geo_line(&(surface->start),&((*lgts)->center),&L) > 0)
```

```
      && ((N_dot_L=geo_dot(&(surface->dir),&(L.dir))) > 0)) {

        /* The surface is illuminated by this light.  Loop through
         *  the color samples and sum the diffuse contribution for
         *  this light to the the color.
         */
        for (ct=0; ct<num_samples; ct++) {
          color[ct] += matl->Kd_scale * matl->Kd_spectral[ct]
            * N_dot_L * (*lgts)->I_scale * (*lgts)->I_spectral[ct];
        }
      }
      lgts++;
    }

    return color;
}

/* ****************************************************************
 * double *IM_phong (surface, V, matl, lgts, color)
 *  LINE         *surface     (in)  - surface for color computation
 *  LINE         *V           (in)  - view vector
 *  ILLUM_MATL   *matl        (in)  - material properties
 *  ILLUM_LGT    **lgts       (in)  - illuminating sources
 *  double       *color       (mod) - array to receive the color
 *
 * Evaluates the color using the Phong (1975) illumination
 *  model as described in Eq.(4.11).  Returns 'color' upon
 *  success and NULL upon failure.
 *
 * The actual Phong model results when the microfacet distribution
 *  D_phong() is used, and matl->Ks_spectral is the identity
 *  material.
 *
 * Using the microfacet distribution D_blinn() gives Blinn's
 *  interpretation of the Phong model per Eq.(4.13).
 */
double *IM_phong (surface, V, matl, lgts, color)
LINE        *surface, *V;
ILLUM_MATL  *matl;
ILLUM_LGT   **lgts;
double      *color;
{   int          ct;
    double       N_dot_L, D;
    LINE         L;

    /* load the ambient illumination */
    for (ct=0; ct<num_samples; ct++) {
      color[ct] = matl->Ka_scale * matl->Ka_spectral[ct] *
        (*lgts)->I_scale * (*lgts)->I_spectral[ct];
    }
    lgts++;

    /* load the diffuse and specular illumination components.
     *  Loop through the lights and compute (N.L).  If it is
     *  positive then the surface is illuminated.
     */
    while (*lgts != NULL) {
      if ((geo_line(&(surface->start),&((*lgts)->center),&L) > 0)
          && ((N_dot_L=geo_dot(&(surface->dir),&(L.dir))) > 0)) {
```

```
    /* The surface is illuminated.  Compute the microfacet
        *  distribution function.
        */
       D = (*(matl->D))(&(surface->dir), &(L.dir), &(V->dir),
         matl->D_coeff);

       /* Loop through the color samples and sum the diffuse
        *  and specular contribution for this light to the the
        *  color.
        */
       for (ct=0; ct<num_samples; ct++) {
         color[ct] +=
           ((N_dot_L * matl->Kd_scale * matl->Kd_spectral[ct])
           + (D * matl->Ks_scale * matl->Ks_spectral[ct]))
           * (*lgts)->I_scale * (*lgts)->I_spectral[ct];
       }
     }
     lgts++;
   }

   return color;
}

/* ****************************************************************
 * double *IM_blinn (surface, V, matl, lgts, color)
 *  LINE         *surface    (in)  - surface for color computation
 *  LINE         *V          (in)  - view vector
 *  ILLUM_MATL   *matl       (in)  - material properties
 *  ILLUM_LGT    **lgts      (in)  - illuminating sources
 *  double       *color      (mod) - array to receive the color
 *
 * Evaluates the color using the Blinn (1977) illumination
 *  model as described in Eq.(4.15).  Returns 'color' upon
 *  success and NULL upon failure.  The microfacet distribution
 *  functions D_blinn(), D_gaussian(), and D_reitz are the three
 *  functions presented by Blinn.  The geometric attenuation
 *  function G_torrance() is the attenuation function used by Blinn.
 *  If matl->G is NULL then the geometric attenuation is omitted.
 *  The Fresnel reflectance is approximated using the Cook (1983)
 *  technique.
 */
double *IM_blinn (surface, V, matl, lgts, color)
LINE        *surface, *V;
ILLUM_MATL  *matl;
ILLUM_LGT   **lgts;
double      *color;
{   int         ct;
    double      N_dot_L, N_dot_V, D, G, *Fr;
    LINE        L;
    DIR_VECT    *T, *H;

    /* load the ambient illumination */
    for (ct=0; ct<num_samples; ct++) {
      color[ct] = matl->Ka_scale * matl->Ka_spectral[ct] *
        (*lgts)->I_scale * (*lgts)->I_spectral[ct];
    }
    lgts++;

    /* load the diffuse and specular illumination components.
     *  Loop through the lights and compute (N.L).  If it is
```

```
     *  positive then the surface is illuminated.
     */
    while (*lgts != NULL) {
      if ((geo_line(&(surface->start),&((*lgts)->center),&L) > 0)
          && ((N_dot_L=geo_dot(&(surface->dir),&(L.dir))) > 0)) {

        /* The surface is illuminated.  Compute the microfacet
         *  distribution, geometric attenuation, Fresnel
         *  reflectance and (N.V) for the specular function.
         */
        D = (*(matl->D))(&(surface->dir), &(L.dir), &(V->dir),
          matl->D_coeff);
        if (matl->G == NULL)
          G = 1.0;
        else
          G = (*(matl->G))(&(surface->dir), &(L.dir),
            &(V->dir), matl->G_coeff);
        H = geo_H(&(L.dir), &(V->dir));
        if (matl->conductor) {
          Fr = F_approx_Fr(H, &(L.dir), matl->Ro, matl->nt,
           matl->k, num_samples, matl->Ks_spectral, Fr_buffer);
        }
        else {
          T = geo_rfr(&(V->dir),H, matl->nr, matl->nt);
          Fr = F_approx_Fr_Ft(H, &(L.dir), T,
            matl->Ro, matl->nr, matl->nt, num_samples,
            matl->Ks_spectral, Fr_buffer, Ft_buffer);
        }

        /* Loop through the color samples and sum the diffuse
         *  and specular contribution for this light to the the
         *  color. Note the threshold on N_dot_V to prevent
         *  divide by zero at grazing.
         */
        if ((N_dot_V=geo_dot(&(surface->dir),&(V->dir))) > 0.0001){
            for (ct=0; ct<num_samples; ct++) {
              color[ct] +=
                ((N_dot_L * matl->Kd_scale * matl->Kd_spectral[ct])
                + ((D * G * matl->Ks_scale * Fr[ct]) / N_dot_V))
                * (*lgts)->I_scale * (*lgts)->I_spectral[ct];
            }
        }
      }
      lgts++;
    }

    return color;
}

/* ****************************************************************
 * double *IM_whitted (surface, V, matl, lgts, color)
 *  LINE        *surface    (in)  - surface for color computation
 *  LINE        *V          (in)  - view vector
 *  ILLUM_MATL  *matl       (in)  - material properties
 *  ILLUM_LGT   *lgts       (in)  - illuminating sources
 *  double      *color      (mod) - array to receive the color
 *
 * Evaluates the color using the Whitted (1980) illumination
 *  model as described in Eq.(4.20).  Returns 'color' upon
 *  success and NULL upon failure.
```

```
 *
 * The actual Whitted model results when the microfacet
 *  distribution D_blinn() is used, and when both matl->Ks_spectral
 *  and matl->Kt_spectral are the identity material.
 *
 * The matl->Kt_scale and matl->Kt_spectral are required for this
 *  illumination model only.
 */
double *IM_whitted (surface, V, matl, lgts, color)
LINE        *surface, *V;
ILLUM_MATL  *matl;
ILLUM_LGT   **lgts;
double      *color;
{   int         inside = FALSE;
    int         ct;
    double      N_dot_L, D;
    LINE        L;

    /* figure out whether we are on the reflected or transmitted
     *  side of the material interface (outside or inside).  If
     *  we are inside a material, then there is no illumination
     *  from lights and such - skip directly to reflection and
     *  refraction contribution.
     */
    if ((geo_dot(&(surface->dir),&(V->dir)) < 0) ||
        (!matl->r_is_air)) {
        for (ct=0; ct<num_samples; ct++) color[ct] = 0.0;
        inside = TRUE;
        goto rfl_rfr;
    }

    /* If we are at interface between materials, neither of which
     *  is air, then skip directly to reflection and refraction
     */
    if (!matl->r_is_air) goto rfl_rfr;

    /* load the ambient illumination */
    for (ct=0; ct<num_samples; ct++) {
      color[ct] = matl->Ka_scale * matl->Ka_spectral[ct] *
        (*lgts)->I_scale * (*lgts)->I_spectral[ct];
    }
    lgts++;

    /* load the diffuse and specular illumination components.
     *  Loop through the lights and compute (N.L).  If it is
     *  positive then the surface is illuminated.
     */
    while (*lgts != NULL) {
      if ((geo_line(&(surface->start),&((*lgts)->center),&L) > 0)
          && ((N_dot_L=geo_dot(&(surface->dir),&(L.dir))) > 0)) {

        /* The surface is illuminated.  Compute the microfacet
         *  distribution function.
         */
        D = (*(matl->D))(&(surface->dir), &(L.dir), &(V->dir),
          matl->D_coeff);

        /* Loop through the color samples and sum the diffuse
         *  and specular contribution for this light to the the
         *  color.
```

```
        */
          for (ct=0; ct<num_samples; ct++) {
            color[ct] +=
              ((N_dot_L * matl->Kd_scale * matl->Kd_spectral[ct])
              + (D * matl->Ks_scale * matl->Ks_spectral[ct]))
              * (*lgts)->I_scale * (*lgts)->I_spectral[ct];
          }
        }
        lgts++;
      }

      /* compute the contribution from the reflection and
       *  refraction directions.  Get a buffer to hold the
       *  computed colors, then process the reflected direction
       *  and the refracted direction.
       */
rfl_rfr:
    if (get_color != NULL) {
      char        *malloc();
      double      *Ir_or_It;
      LINE        V_new;
      DIR_VECT    *T;

      if ((Ir_or_It = (double *)malloc((unsigned)(num_samples *
        sizeof(double)))) == NULL) return color;

      /* get the reflected vector then ask for the color from
       *  the reflected direction.  If there is a color, then
       *  sum it with the current color
       */
      V_new.start = surface->start;
      V_new.dir = *(geo_rfl(&(V->dir),&(surface->dir)));
      if ((*get_color)(&V_new, Ir_or_It) != NULL)
        for (ct=0; ct<num_samples; ct++) color[ct] +=
          Ir_or_It[ct] * matl->Ks_scale * matl->Ks_spectral[ct];

      /* if the material is transparent then get the refracted
       *  vector and ask for the color from the refracted
       *  direction.  If there is a color, then sum it with
       *  the current color
       */
      if (matl->transparent) {
        V_new.start = surface->start;
        if (inside)
          T = geo_rfr(&(V->dir),&(surface->dir),
            matl->nt, matl->nr);
        else
          T = geo_rfr(&(V->dir),&(surface->dir),
            matl->nr, matl->nt);
        if (T != NULL) {
          V_new.dir = *T;
          if ((*get_color)(&V_new, Ir_or_It) != NULL)
            for (ct=0; ct<num_samples; ct++) color[ct] +=
              Ir_or_It[ct] * matl->Kt_scale *
              matl->Kt_spectral[ct];
        }
      }
      (void)free((char *)Ir_or_It);
    }
```

```
    return color;
}

/* ****************************************************************
 * double *IM_hall (surface, V, matl, lgts, color)
 *  LINE        *surface     (in)  - surface for color computation
 *  LINE        *V           (in)  - view vector
 *  ILLUM_MATL  *matl        (in)  - material properties
 *  ILLUM_LGT   *lgts        (in)  - illuminating sources
 *  double      *color       (mod) - array to receive the color
 *
 * Evaluates the color using the Hall (1983) illumination
 *  model as described in Eq.(4.21).  Returns 'color' upon
 *  success and NULL upon failure.
 *
 * The actual Hall model results when the microfacet
 *  distribution D_blinn() is used, and matl->D = NULL.
 *
 * The transmittance is computed from the reflectance, so
 *  matl->Kt_scale and matl->Kt_spectral are not used in the model.
 */
double *IM_hall (surface, V, matl, lgts, color)
LINE        *surface, *V;
ILLUM_MATL  *matl;
ILLUM_LGT   **lgts;
double      *color;
{   int         inside = FALSE;
    int         ct;
    double      N_dot_L, D, G, *Fr;
    LINE        L;
    DIR_VECT    *T, *H, *Ht, pseudo_V;

    /* figure out whether we are on the reflected or transmitted
     *  side of the material interface (outside or inside).  If
     *  we are inside a material, then there may be illumination
     *  from outside.
     */
    if (geo_dot(&(surface->dir),&(V->dir)) < 0) {
        for (ct=0; ct<num_samples; ct++) color[ct] = 0.0;
        inside = TRUE;
    }

    /* If we are at interface between materials, neither of which
     *  is air, then skip directly to reflection and refraction
     */
    if (!matl->r_is_air) goto rfl_rfr;

    /* load the ambient illumination if we are not inside
     *  inside the material
     */
    if (!inside) {
      for (ct=0; ct<num_samples; ct++) {
        color[ct] = matl->Ka_scale * matl->Ka_spectral[ct] *
          (*lgts)->I_scale * (*lgts)->I_spectral[ct];
      }
    }
    lgts++;

    /* load the diffuse and specular illumination components.
     *  Loop through the lights and compute (N.L).  If it is
```

```
 *  positive then the surface is illuminated.  If it is
 *  negative, then there may be transmitted illumination.
 */
while (*lgts != NULL) {
  if ((geo_line(&(surface->start),&((*lgts)->center),&L) > 0)
      && ((N_dot_L=geo_dot(&(surface->dir),&(L.dir))) > 0)
      && !inside) {

    /* The surface is illuminated.  Compute the microfacet
     *  distribution, geometric attenuation, Fresnel
     *  reflectance and (N.V) for the specular function.
     */
    D = (*(matl->D))(&(surface->dir), &(L.dir), &(V->dir),
      matl->D_coeff);
    if (matl->G == NULL)
      G = 1.0;
    else
      G = (*(matl->G))(&(surface->dir), &(L.dir),
        &(V->dir), matl->G_coeff);
    H = geo_H(&(L.dir), &(V->dir));
    if (matl->conductor) {
      Fr = F_approx_Fr(H, &(L.dir), matl->Ro, matl->nt,
        matl->k, num_samples, matl->Ks_spectral, Fr_buffer);
    }
    else {
      T = geo_rfr(&(L.dir), H, matl->nr, matl->nt);
      Fr = F_approx_Fr_Ft(H, &(L.dir), T,
        matl->Ro, matl->nr, matl->nt, num_samples,
        matl->Ks_spectral, Fr_buffer, Ft_buffer);
    }


    /* Loop through the color samples and sum the diffuse
     *  and specular contribution for this light to the the
     *  color.
     */
    for (ct=0; ct<num_samples; ct++) {
      color[ct] +=
        ((N_dot_L * matl->Kd_scale * matl->Kd_spectral[ct])
        + (D * G * matl->Ks_scale * Fr[ct]))
        * (*lgts)->I_scale * (*lgts)->I_spectral[ct];
    }
  }
  else if ((N_dot_L > 0) && inside) {
    /* We are inside and the light is outside.  Compute
     *  the transmitted contribution from the light
     */
    if ((Ht = geo_Ht(&(L.dir),&(V->dir),matl->nr,
        matl->nt)) != NULL) {
      /* The microfacet distribution functions could
       *  only be equated when cast in terms of the primary
       *  vectors L, V, and N.  A pseudo_V vector is required
       *  so that any of the distribution functions can be
       *  applied.  Ht is the vector bisector between of the
       *  angle between L and pseudo_V, thus pseudo_V can be
       *  computed by reflecting L about Ht. Refer to the
       *  text for details.
       */
      pseudo_V = *(geo_rfl(&(L.dir), Ht));
      D = (*(matl->D))(&(surface->dir), &(L.dir),
```

```
          &pseudo_V, matl->D_coeff);
          Fr = F_approx_Fr_Ft(Ht, &(L.dir), &(V->dir),
            matl->Ro, matl->nr, matl->nt, num_samples,
            matl->Ks_spectral, Fr_buffer, Ft_buffer);
          if (matl->G == NULL)
            G = 1.0;
          else {
            /* To include the geometric attenuation, the view
             *  vector direction must be reversed so that it
             *  is to the same side of the surface as the
             *  normal, see text for details.
             */
            pseudo_V.i = -V->dir.i;
            pseudo_V.j = -V->dir.j;
            pseudo_V.k = -V->dir.k;
            G = (*(matl->G))(&(surface->dir), &(L.dir),
              &pseudo_V, matl->G_coeff);
          }
          for (ct=0; ct<num_samples; ct++) {
            color[ct] += (D * G * matl->Ks_scale * Ft_buffer[ct])
              * (*lgts)->I_scale * (*lgts)->I_spectral[ct];
          }
        }
      }
      lgts++;
    }

    /* compute the contribution from the reflection and
     *  refraction directions.  Get a buffer to hold the
     *  computed colors, then process the reflected direction
     *  and the refracted direction.
     */
rfl_rfr:
    if (get_color != NULL) {
      char       *malloc();
      double     *Ir_or_It;
      LINE       V_new;
      DIR_VECT   pseudo_N;

      if ((Ir_or_It = (double *)malloc((unsigned)(num_samples *
        sizeof(double)))) == NULL) return color;

      /* Determine the Fresnel reflectance and transmittance.
       *  If we are inside the material, then a pseudo normal
       *  is required that faces to the same side of the
       *  interface as the view vector.
       */
      if (matl->conductor) {
        Fr = F_approx_Fr(&(surface->dir), &(V->dir), matl->Ro,
          matl->nt, matl->k, num_samples, matl->Ks_spectral,
          Fr_buffer);
      }
      else if (inside) {
        T = geo_rfr(&(V->dir),&(surface->dir),
            matl->nt, matl->nr);
        pseudo_N.i = -surface->dir.i;
        pseudo_N.j = -surface->dir.j;
        pseudo_N.k = -surface->dir.k;
        Fr = F_approx_Fr_Ft(&pseudo_N, &(V->dir), T,
            matl->Ro, matl->nt, matl->nr, num_samples,
```

```
            matl->Ks_spectral, Fr_buffer, Ft_buffer);
        }
        else {
          T = geo_rfr(&(V->dir),&(surface->dir),
              matl->nr, matl->nt);
          Fr = F_approx_Fr_Ft(&(surface->dir), &(V->dir),
              T, matl->Ro, matl->nr, matl->nt, num_samples,
              matl->Ks_spectral, Fr_buffer, Ft_buffer);
        }

        /* get the reflected vector then ask for the color from
         *  the reflected direction.  If there is a color, then
         *  sum it with the current color
         */
        V_new.start = surface->start;
        V_new.dir = *(geo_rfl(&(V->dir),&(surface->dir)));
        if ((*get_color)(&V_new, Ir_or_It) != NULL) {
          for (ct=0; ct<num_samples; ct++) color[ct] +=
            Ir_or_It[ct] * matl->Ks_scale * Fr[ct];
        }

        /* if the material is transparent then get the refracted
         *  vector and ask for the color from the refracted
         *  direction.  If there is a color, then sum it with
         *  the current color
         */
        if (matl->transparent && (T != NULL)) {
          V_new.start = surface->start;
          V_new.dir = *T;
          if ((*get_color)(&V_new, Ir_or_It) != NULL)
            for (ct=0; ct<num_samples; ct++) color[ct] +=
              Ir_or_It[ct] * matl->Kt_scale * Ft_buffer[ct];
        }
        (void)free((char *)Ir_or_It);
      }

      /* If we are inside a material that has a filter attenuation
       *  then apply the attenuation to the color.
       */
      if ( ((!inside) && ((Fr = matl->Ar_spectral) != NULL)) ||
           ((inside) && ((Fr = matl->At_spectral) != NULL)) ) {
          double      dist;
          dist = sqrt ( ((surface->start.x - V->start.x) *
                         (surface->start.x - V->start.x)) +
                        ((surface->start.y - V->start.y) *
                         (surface->start.y - V->start.y)) +
                        ((surface->start.z - V->start.z) *
                         (surface->start.z - V->start.z)) );
          for (ct=0; ct<num_samples; ct++)
              color[ct] *= pow (Fr[ct], dist);
      }

      return color;
}

/* ****************************************************************
 * int IM_exit ()
 *
 * Finishes use of the illumination models routines.
 */
```

```
IM_exit()
{
    if (Fr_buffer != NULL) {
        (void)free((char *)Fr_buffer); Fr_buffer = NULL;
    }
    if (Ft_buffer != NULL) {
        (void)free((char *)Ft_buffer); Ft_buffer = NULL;
    }
    num_samples = 0;
    get_color = NULL;
    return TRUE;
}
/* ************************************************************ */
```

III.7 Color Transformation

There are three major areas of concern when dealing with color in image synthesis. The first is transformation between display color spaces and sampling spectral curves into display color spaces. The second is sampling spectral curves for computation and subsequent transformation from the computational samples to display color spaces. The third is bringing colors that are outside the displayable range into the displayable range through compression and/or clipping.

This section treats transformations between display color spaces and sampling from spectral curves into display color spaces. The next section addresses spectral sampling for computation, followed by a section addressing color compression and clipping. The color routines presented in these sections are part of a common library and share the same include file, and the same initialization and exit routines.

The initialization routine is called with wavelength bounds for operations involving spectral curves, and with the chromaticities and white point of the RGB color space being used. If the RGB color space is changed, the color routines must be exited and reinitialized for the new RGB color space definition.

The typical wavelength range for initialization is 380nm to 780nm. This is the visible spectrum used for most image generation applications and for which RGB, XYZ, Y_tIQ, $L^*a^*b^*$, and $L^*u^*v^*$ color spaces are meaningful. The range can be extended to other areas of the spectrum for special applications. All operators for spectral curves are insensitive to the wavelength bounds. However, note that spectral curves are saved as values at 1nm increments and that it may be necessary to change this for special applications that are outside the visible region.

Specification of a reference RGB color space is critical to all RGB, $L^*a^*b^*$, and $L^*u^*v^*$ transformation, and to color clipping. If a reference white is not specified, then the NTSC primaries with a D_{6500} white point as given in Section 5.1.1, *Color Correction for Display*, are used as the default.

III.7.1 Material Data

Material data is read from material files. The material file includes descriptive text, index of refraction, absorption coefficient, material conductivity information, and spectral curve data.

The material files are ASCII files. Descriptive text and/or comment lines begin with "#". The index of refraction is specified by a line beginning with "n " followed by the index of refraction. The absorption coefficient is specified by a line beginning with "k " followed by the absorption coefficient. A conductor is specified by the line "conductor" and a dielectric is specified by the line "dielectric". All other lines are assumed to contain spectral data. Each line of spectral data contains a wavelength in nm (integer value) followed by a reflectance value (real number). Spectral data must be in ascending wavelength order. The following is an example of a material file for the dielectric borosilicate crown glass:

```
#
#   Material:         Glass - Borosilicate Crown - 3
#   Type              511/634
#   Source:
#     reflectance:    Computed from index of refraction
#     n,k:            Fundamentals of Optics, Jenkins and White (1976)
#                         Table 23B - Refractive Indices and
#                         Dispersions for Several Common Types of
#                         Optical Glass
#   Conditions:       polished
#   Temperature:
#   Incident angle: normal
#   Solid angle:
#
dielectric
#   index of refraction at 589.2nm
n 1.51124
399 0.043291
434 0.042757
482 0.042178
509 0.041975
533 0.041784
589 0.041445
644 0.041178
656 0.041134
```

The following is an example of a material file for the conductor copper:

```
#
#   Material:         Copper
#   Source:
#     reflectance:    Thermophysical Properties of Matter (1970)
#                         v.7, p.162, curve #4 (from Cook's thesis)
#     n,k:            Fundamentals of Optics, Jenkins and White (1976)
#                         table 25A, p538 (original source R.S.Minor)
#                         measured at 589nm
#   Conditions:       as received
```

```
#    Temperature:     298 K
#    Incident angle: 9
#    Solid angle:     2pi
#
conductor
n 0.617
k 2.630
380 0.070
420 0.095
460 0.140
500 0.205
540 0.265
560 0.335
580 0.490
600 0.615
620 0.670
660 0.725
700 0.755
```

This format is also used for spectral curves of light sources. For light sources, the index of refraction, absorption coefficient, and conductivity information are not relevant. The material read routine is passed `NULL` pointers for information that is not of interest. The following is an example of a light source file for a D_{6500} light:

```
#
#    Light Source:    standard CIE illuminant D6500
#    Source:
#        Judd and Wyszecki
#        Color in Business, Science, and Industry
#        table 2.1 pg.108-109
#    Notes:
#        normalized to 1.00 at 560nm
#
300 0.0003
310 0.0330
320 0.2020
330 0.3710
340 0.3990
350 0.4490

    ---- etc. ----
```

III.7.2 Code Summary

This module of the color routine set manipulates color space transformations and spectral curves. Color transformations are always 3x3 matrices of double precision values. They are ordered as presented in Section 3.3, *Colorimetry and the RGB Monitor*, so that a transformation from a color space such as XYZ to another color space such as RGB using the matrix `xyz_rgb` is performed with a code segment as follows:

```
rgb.r = (xyz_rgb_mat[0][0] * xyz.x) +
    (xyz_rgb_mat[0][1] * xyz.y) + (xyz_rgb[0][2] * xyz.z);
rgb.g = (xyz_rgb_mat[1][0] * xyz.x) +
```

```
    (xyz_rgb_mat[1][1] * xyz.y) + (xyz_rgb[1][2] * xyz.z);
rgb.b = (xyz_rgb_mat[2][0] * xyz.x) +
    (xyz_rgb_mat[2][1] * xyz.y) + (xyz_rgb[2][2] * xyz.z);
```

Spectral curves are loaded into arrays supplied by the calling program. The length of the array is always assumed to be (*max*−min+1) where max and min are the maximum and minimum wavelengths specified at initialization.

Initialize and exit

The routine `CLR_init()` performs the initialization, establishing the wavelength bounds and reference RGB color space. The routine `CLR_exit()` completes use of the color routine set.

Querying for initialization information

The routines `CLR_get_rgb()`, `CLR_get_min_wl()`, and `CLR_get_max_wl()` return the RGB color space, minimum wavelength, and maximum wavelength specified at initialization.

Reading material curves

The routine `CLR_read_matl()` reads a material file and returns the spectral curve, n, k, and a flag indicating whether the material is a conductor. The format of the material files is given in the previous section. Linear interpolation is used to build the continuous spectral curve between data points.

Manipulating spectral curves

The routines `CLR_add_spect()` and `CLR_mult_spect()` respectively perform addition and multiplication of two spectral curves. The routine `CLR_area_spect()` returns the area under a spectral curve. The routine `CLR_scale_spect()` scales a spectral curve. These operations are sufficient to reproduce any procedures described in this text.

Sampling spectral curves

The routine `CLR_get_CIEXYZ()` returns the CIEXYZ tristimulus matching curves for the 1931 standard colorimetric observer for a 2-degree visual field. These curves are linearly interpolated from data points at 5nm increments as given by Judd and Wyszecki (1975) The routines `CLR_spect_to_xyz()` and `CLR_spect_to_rgb()` sample a spectral curve into either the XYZ or RGB color spaces. The sampling is simply the multiplication of the spectral curve by the CIEXYZ matching functions and then taking the area under the resulting curves as described in Section 3.2, *Colorimetry*. The resulting XYZ value is then scaled using a scaling that results in an identity curve sampling such that $Y = 1$. For RGB colors, the XYZ color is then transformed into RGB. These routines provide a good example of using both spectral curve operators and transformation matrices.

Color space transformation

The color space transformations in this section are linear with the exception of transformation into the $L^*a^*b^*$ or $L^*u^*v^*$ perceptual color spaces. For all of the linear transformations, the transformation matrix is returned. The RGB transformations are with respect to the color space defined at initialization. The transformations available are: `CLR_get_xyz_rgb()` returns the transformation matrix from XYZ to RGB; `CLR_get_rgb_xyz()` returns the transformation matrix from RGB to XYZ; `CLR_rgb_to_aux_rgb()` returns the transformations between the initialized RGB color space and an auxiliary RGB color space; `CLR_get_rgb_yiq()` returns the transformation from RGB to Y_tIQ; and `CLR_get_yiq_rgb()` returns the transformation from Y_tIQ to RGB. Note that the transformations between Y_tIQ and the RGB color space assume RGB primaries as defined by NTSC, thus, the returned matrices are always relative to the NTSC primaries to reflect encoding and decoding hardware configuration.

Transformations into perceptually uniform color spaces are nonlinear. The routines provided perform the transformation to the perceptually uniform color space. `CLR_xyz_lab()` and `CLR_xyz_luv()` transform from XYZ to $L^*a^*b^*$ and $L^*u^*v^*$ respectively (refer to Eqs.((3.4)) and ((3.5))). The transformation from these spaces back to XYZ is left as an exercise for the reader.

To facilitate generating complex transformation sequences the routine `CLR_t_concat()` is used to concatenate transformation matrices, and `CLR_t_inverse()` is used to invert a transformation matrix.

III.7.3 Code Source

The following is the include file for the color transformation routines:

```
/* ****************************************************************
 *                            clr.h
 * ****************************************************************
 * include file for the geometric utilities
 */
#ifndef CLR_H
#define CLR_H

#ifndef TRUE
#define TRUE    1
#endif TRUE
#ifndef FALSE
#define FALSE   0
#endif FALSE

#define CLR_SAMPLE_MEYER        0
#define CLR_SAMPLE_HALL         1

/* common geometric constructs
 */
typedef struct {double  r, g, b;}       CLR_RGB;
typedef struct {double  x, y, z;}       CLR_XYZ;
```

```
typedef struct {double  l, a, b;}       CLR_LAB;
typedef struct {double  l, u, v;}       CLR_LUV;

/* color routine declarations
 */
int          CLR_init();
int          CLR_read_mtl();
int          CLR_add_spect();
int          CLR_mult_spect();
int          CLR_scale_spect();
double       CLR_area_spect();
CLR_XYZ      CLR_spect_to_xyz();
CLR_RGB      CLR_spect_to_rgb();
int          CLR_get_rgb();
int          CLR_get_min_wl();
int          CLR_get_max_wl();
int          CLR_get_xyz_rgb();
int          CLR_get_rgb_xyz();
int          CLR_get_yiq_rgb();
int          CLR_get_rgb_yiq();
int          CLR_rgb_to_aux_rgb();
CLR_LAB      CLR_xyz_to_lab();
CLR_LUV      CLR_xyz_to_luv();
int          CLR_t_concat();
int          CLR_t_inverse();

CLR_RGB      CLR_clamp_rgb();
CLR_RGB      CLR_scale_rgb();
CLR_RGB      CLR_clip_rgb();

int          CLR_init_samples();
int          CLR_num_samples();
int          CLR_spect_to_sample();
int          CLR_get_sample_rgb();
int          CLR_get_sample_xyz();
int          CLR_reconstruct();
int          CLR_exit_samples();

#endif CLR_H
/* ************************************************************** */
```

The following is the source module for the color transformation routines:

```
/* ****************************************************************
 *                            clr.c
 * ****************************************************************
 *  MODULE PURPOSE:
 *      This module contains routines for color
 *      transformations, color space manipulations,
 *      and spectral sampling.
 *
 *  MODULE CONTENTS:
 *      CLR_init           - initialized the color routines
 *      CLR_read_mtl       - read a material file
 *      CLR_add_spect      - add two spectral curves
 *      CLR_mult_spect     - multiply two spectral curves
 *      CLR_scale_spect    - scale a spectral curve
 *      CLR_area_spect     - get the area under a curve
```

```
 *      CLR_spect_to_xyz    - sample a curve to xyz
 *      CLR_spect_to_rgb    - sample a curve to rgb
 *      CLR_get_CIEXYZ      - get the CIEXYZ matching functions
 *      CLR_get_rgb         - returns the color space primaries
 *      CLR_get_min_wl      - returns the max wavelength
 *      CLR_get_max_wl      - returns the min wavelength
 *      CLR_get_xyz_rgb     - returns the xyz to rgb matrix
 *      CLR_get_rgb_xyz     - returns the rgb to xyz matrix
 *      CLR_get_rgb_yiq     - returns the rgb to yiq matrix
 *      CLR_get_yiq_rgb     - returns the yiq to rgb matrix
 *      CLR_rgb_to_aux_rgb  - returns the matrix from the
 *                              current color space to an
 *                              auxiliary color space
 *      CLR_xyz_lab         - transforms from xyz to Lab
 *      CLR_xyz_luv         - transforms from xyz to Luv
 *      CLR_t_concat        - concatenate color transforms
 *      CLR_t_inverse       - return an inverse transform
 *      CLR_exit            - finish with the color routines
 *
 *  NOTES:
 *      > Spectral curve manipulations use the lower and upper
 *          bounds established at init.  Curves are at 1nm
 *          increments and are arrays of doubles, (max - min + 1)
 *          elements long.
 *      > Matrix scaling is so that an RGB of 1,1,1 transforms
 *          to an XYZ with a Y value of 1.0
 *      > The XYZ and RGB sampling from spectral curves are
 *          scaled so that that a mirror reflector (1.0 for all
 *          wavelengths) has a Y value of 1.0.
 *      > Wavelength bounds of 380nm to 780nm (the visible
 *          spectrum) are appropriate for most applications.
 */
#include <stdio.h>
#include <math.h>
#include "clr.h"

#define RED         0
#define GREEN       1
#define BLUE        2
#define WHITE       3
#define LOAD_MAT(a,b) \
{   int ii,jj; \
    for (ii=0; ii<=2; ii++) \
        for (jj=0; jj<=2; jj++) a[ii][jj] = b[ii][jj]; \
}

static int          init = FALSE;
static int          min_wl = 380;
static int          max_wl = 780;
static double       xyz_rgb_mat[3][3];
static double       rgb_xyz_mat[3][3];
static double       *X_tristim = NULL;
static double       *Y_tristim = NULL;
static double       *Z_tristim = NULL;
static double       *work_curve = NULL;
static double       xyz_scale = 1.0;
static CLR_XYZ      rgb_primary[4];
static int          clr__cspace_to_xyz ();
static CLR_XYZ      white;
static CLR_LUV      ref_luv;
```

```
/* This is the RGB to YIQ matrix and YIQ to RGB matrix as
 *  given in Sect 5.2 NTSC and RGB Video
 */
static double       rgb_yiq_mat[3][3] = {
    {0.299,      0.587,       0.144},
    {0.596,     -0.275,      -0.321},
    {0.212,     -0.528,       0.311}};

static double       yiq_rgb_mat[3][3] = {
    {1.0000,     0.9557,      0.6199},
    {1.0000,    -0.2716,     -0.6469},
    {1.0000,    -1.1082,      1.7051}};

/* This is the NTSC primaries with D6500 white point for use as
 *  the default initialization as given in sect 5.1.1 Color
 *  Correction for Display.
 */
static CLR_XYZ      rgb_NTSC[4] = {
    {0.670,      0.330,       0.000},      /* red */
    {0.210,      0.710,       0.080},      /* green */
    {0.140,      0.080,       0.780},      /* blue */
    {0.313,      0.329,       0.358}};     /* white */

/* This is the data for the CIEXYZ curves take from Judd and
 *  Wyszecki (1975), table 2.6, these are for the 1931 standard
 *  observer with a 2-degree visual field.
 */
static double       CIEXYZ[81][4] = {
    {380, 0.0014, 0.0000, 0.0065}, {385, 0.0022, 0.0001, 0.0105},
    {390, 0.0042, 0.0001, 0.0201}, {395, 0.0076, 0.0002, 0.0362},
    {400, 0.0143, 0.0004, 0.0679}, {405, 0.0232, 0.0006, 0.1102},
    {410, 0.0435, 0.0012, 0.2074}, {415, 0.0776, 0.0022, 0.3713},
    {420, 0.1344, 0.0040, 0.6456}, {425, 0.2148, 0.0073, 1.0391},
    {430, 0.2839, 0.0116, 1.3856}, {435, 0.3285, 0.0168, 1.6230},
    {440, 0.3483, 0.0230, 1.7471}, {445, 0.3481, 0.0298, 1.7826},
    {450, 0.3362, 0.0380, 1.7721}, {455, 0.3187, 0.0480, 1.7441},
    {460, 0.2908, 0.0600, 1.6692}, {465, 0.2511, 0.0739, 1.5281},
    {470, 0.1954, 0.0910, 1.2876}, {475, 0.1421, 0.1126, 1.0419},
    {480, 0.0956, 0.1390, 0.8310}, {485, 0.0580, 0.1693, 0.6162},
    {490, 0.0320, 0.2080, 0.4652}, {495, 0.0147, 0.2586, 0.3533},
    {500, 0.0049, 0.3230, 0.2720}, {505, 0.0024, 0.4073, 0.2123},
    {510, 0.0093, 0.5030, 0.1582}, {515, 0.0291, 0.6082, 0.1117},
    {520, 0.0633, 0.7100, 0.0782}, {525, 0.1096, 0.7932, 0.0573},
    {530, 0.1655, 0.8620, 0.0422}, {535, 0.2257, 0.9149, 0.0298},
    {540, 0.2904, 0.9540, 0.0203}, {545, 0.3597, 0.9803, 0.0134},
    {550, 0.4334, 0.9950, 0.0087}, {555, 0.5121, 1.0000, 0.0057},
    {560, 0.5945, 0.9950, 0.0039}, {565, 0.6784, 0.9786, 0.0027},
    {570, 0.7621, 0.9520, 0.0021}, {575, 0.8425, 0.9154, 0.0018},
    {580, 0.9163, 0.8700, 0.0017}, {585, 0.9786, 0.8163, 0.0014},
    {590, 1.0263, 0.7570, 0.0011}, {595, 1.0567, 0.6949, 0.0010},
    {600, 1.0622, 0.6310, 0.0008}, {605, 1.0456, 0.5668, 0.0006},
    {610, 1.0026, 0.5030, 0.0003}, {615, 0.9384, 0.4412, 0.0002},
    {620, 0.8544, 0.3810, 0.0002}, {625, 0.7514, 0.3210, 0.0001},
    {630, 0.6424, 0.2650, 0.0000}, {635, 0.5419, 0.2170, 0.0000},
    {640, 0.4479, 0.1750, 0.0000}, {645, 0.3608, 0.1382, 0.0000},
    {650, 0.2835, 0.1070, 0.0000}, {655, 0.2187, 0.0816, 0.0000},
    {660, 0.1649, 0.0610, 0.0000}, {665, 0.1212, 0.0446, 0.0000},
    {670, 0.0874, 0.0320, 0.0000}, {675, 0.0636, 0.0232, 0.0000},
    {680, 0.0468, 0.0170, 0.0000}, {685, 0.0329, 0.0119, 0.0000},
    {690, 0.0227, 0.0082, 0.0000}, {695, 0.0158, 0.0057, 0.0000},
```

```
    {700, 0.0114, 0.0041, 0.0000}, {705, 0.0081, 0.0029, 0.0000},
    {710, 0.0058, 0.0021, 0.0000}, {715, 0.0041, 0.0015, 0.0000},
    {720, 0.0029, 0.0010, 0.0000}, {725, 0.0020, 0.0007, 0.0000},
    {730, 0.0014, 0.0005, 0.0000}, {735, 0.0010, 0.0004, 0.0000},
    {740, 0.0007, 0.0002, 0.0000}, {745, 0.0005, 0.0002, 0.0000},
    {750, 0.0003, 0.0001, 0.0000}, {755, 0.0002, 0.0001, 0.0000},
    {760, 0.0002, 0.0001, 0.0000}, {765, 0.0001, 0.0000, 0.0000},
    {770, 0.0001, 0.0000, 0.0000}, {775, 0.0001, 0.0000, 0.0000},
    {780, 0.0000, 0.0000, 0.0000} };


/* ****************************************************************
 * CLR_init (min, max, rgb)
 *  int          min, max     (in) wavelength bounds (nm)
 *  CLR_XYZ      rgb[4]       (in) the primaries.  If NULL,
 *                                 then the NTSC primaries with
 *                                 a D6500 white point are used.
 *
 * Initializes the color routines for a spectral range from
 *  'min'nm to 'max'nm and an RGB color space given by 'rgb'
 *  Returns TRUE if successful and FALSE on error.
 */
int CLR_init (min, max, rgb)
int         min;
int         max;
CLR_XYZ     rgb[4];
{   int     color, ct;
    double  len;
    char    *malloc();

    if (init) return FALSE;
    init = TRUE;
    min_wl = min;
    max_wl = max;

    /* load primaries and build transformations, use the
     * defaults is rgb==NULL
     */
    for (color=RED; color<=WHITE; color++) {
        if (rgb == NULL) rgb_primary[color] = rgb_NTSC[color];
        else rgb_primary[color] = rgb[color];
        rgb_primary[color].z = 1.0 -
            rgb_primary[color].x - rgb_primary[color].y;
    }
    if (!clr__cspace_to_xyz(rgb_primary, rgb_xyz_mat)) goto error;
    if (!CLR_t_inverse(rgb_xyz_mat, xyz_rgb_mat)) goto error;

    /* build reference info for L*a*b*, L*u*v* transforms */
    white.x =
        (100.0 * rgb_primary[WHITE].x) / rgb_primary[WHITE].y;
    white.y = 100.0;
    white.z =
        (100.0 * rgb_primary[WHITE].z) / rgb_primary[WHITE].y;
    ref_luv.u = (4.0 * white.x) /
        (white.x + (15.0 * white.y) + (3.0 * white.z));
    ref_luv.v = (9.0 * white.y) /
        (white.x + (15.0 * white.y) + (3.0 * white.z));

    /* build the XYZ sampling curves - allocate space for the
```

```
     *  curves and interpolate the CIEXYZ table into continuous
     *  curves at 1nm increments.
     */
    {   int     ii, nm;
        double  *x, *y, *z;
        double  x_cur, y_cur, z_cur;
        double  x_inc, y_inc, z_inc;
        if ((work_curve = (double *)malloc((unsigned)
            (sizeof(double) * (max_wl-min_wl+1))))
            == NULL) goto error;
        if ((x = X_tristim = (double *)malloc((unsigned)
            (sizeof(double) * (max_wl-min_wl+1))))
            == NULL) goto error;
        if ((y = Y_tristim = (double *)malloc((unsigned)
            (sizeof(double) * (max_wl-min_wl+1))))
            == NULL) goto error;
        if ((z = Z_tristim = (double *)malloc((unsigned)
            (sizeof(double) * (max_wl-min_wl+1))))
            == NULL) goto error;
        for (nm=min_wl; nm<380; nm++) *x++ = *y++ = *z++ = 0.0;
        for (ct=0; ct<80; ct++) {
            x_cur = CIEXYZ[ct][1];
            y_cur = CIEXYZ[ct][2];
            z_cur = CIEXYZ[ct][3];
            x_inc = (CIEXYZ[ct+1][1] - x_cur) / 5.0;
            y_inc = (CIEXYZ[ct+1][2] - y_cur) / 5.0;
            z_inc = (CIEXYZ[ct+1][3] - z_cur) / 5.0;
            for (ii=0; ii<5; ii++, nm++) {
                if (nm > max_wl) goto XYZ_done;
                if (nm >= min_wl) {
                    *x++ = x_cur; *y++ = y_cur; *z++ = z_cur;
                }
                x_cur += x_inc; y_cur += y_inc; z_cur += z_inc;
            }
        }
        if (nm <= max_wl) {
            *x++ = x_cur; *y++ = y_cur; *z++ = z_cur; nm++;
        }
        for ( ;nm<=max_wl; nm++) *x++ = *y++ = *z++ = 0.0;
    }
XYZ_done:
    /* determine the scaling factor to be used in sampling spectral
     *  curves to bring Y os a sampled identity curve to 1.
     */
    xyz_scale = 1.0 / CLR_area_spect (Y_tristim);

    return TRUE;

error:
    CLR_exit();
    return FALSE;
}

/* ****************************************************************
 * CLR_read_mtl (file, conduct, n, k, curve)
 *  char          *file         (in) material file name
 *  int           *conduct      (out) conductor - set to FALSE if not
 *                                  specified in the material file
 *  double        *n, *k        (out) n and k, - set to 0.0 if not
 *                                  specified in the material file
```

```
 *  double      *curve      (out) curve array
 *
 * Returns TRUE if the material was read, FALSE if the material
 *  could not be found or an error was detected in the material
 *  file.  NULL pointers can be given as arguments for 'conduct',
 *  'n', 'k', and/or 'curve' if the properties are not of interest.
 *
 * The material file must be in the format given in Sect III.7.1
 *  Material Data.
 */
int CLR_read_mtl (file, conduct, n, k, curve)
char        *file;
int         *conduct;
double      *n, *k;
double      *curve;
{   FILE        *fp, *fopen();
    char        in_str[200];
    int         flag = 1;
    int         cur_wl, last_wl, ind_wl;
    double      cur_val, last_val, inc_val;

    if (!init) return FALSE;
    if ((fp=fopen(file,"r")) == NULL) return FALSE;
    if (n != NULL) *n = 0.0;
    if (k != NULL) *k = 0.0;
    if (conduct != NULL) *conduct = FALSE;
    if (curve == NULL) flag = -1;
    ind_wl = min_wl;
    while (fgets(in_str,200,fp)) {
        switch (in_str[0]) {
            case '#':           /* comment */
                break;
            case 'k':           /* absorption coefficient */
                if (k != NULL) (void)sscanf (in_str, "k %lf", k);
                break;
            case 'n':           /* index of refraction */
                if (n != NULL) (void)sscanf (in_str, "n %lf", n);
                break;
            case 'c':           /* conductor */
                if (conduct != NULL) *conduct = TRUE;
                break;
            case 'd':           /* dielectric */
                if (conduct != NULL) *conduct = FALSE;
                break;
            default:            /* spectral data */
                if ((flag != -1) && (sscanf(in_str,
                    "%d %lf", &cur_wl, &cur_val) == 2)) {
                    if (flag == 1) {
                        flag = 0;
                        while (ind_wl <= cur_wl) {
                            *curve++ = cur_val;
                            if (++ind_wl > max_wl) {
                                flag == -1;
                                break;
                            }
                        }
                    }
                    else {
                        if (cur_wl < last_wl) {
                            (void)fclose(fp);
```

```
                        return FALSE;
                    }
                    inc_val = (cur_val - last_val) /
                        (cur_wl - last_wl);
                    while (last_wl < ind_wl) {
                        last_val += inc_val;
                        last_wl++;
                    }
                    while (ind_wl <= cur_wl) {
                        *curve++ = last_val;
                        last_val += inc_val;
                        if (++ind_wl > max_wl) {
                            flag = -1;
                            break;
                        }
                    }
                }
                last_wl = cur_wl;
                last_val = cur_val;
            }
        }
    }
    while (ind_wl <= max_wl) {
        *curve++ = last_val;
        ind_wl++;
    }
    (void)fclose(fp);
    return TRUE;
}

/* ****************************************************************
 * CLR_add_spect (c1, c2, c3)
 *  double  *c1, *c2    (in)  - input curves
 *  double  *c3         (out) - output curve
 *
 * Add spectral curve 'c1' to spectral curve 'c2' to get spectral
 *  curve 'c3'.  Returns TRUE if successful, FALSE if the CLR_
 *  routines are not initialized.
 */
CLR_add_spect (c1,c2,c3)
double  *c1, *c2, *c3;
{   int     ct;
    if (!init) return FALSE;
    for (ct=max_wl-min_wl+1; --ct>=0; ) *c3++ = *c1++ + *c2++;
    return TRUE;
}

/* ****************************************************************
 * CLR_mult_spect (c1, c2, c3)
 *  double  *c1, *c2    (in)  - input curves
 *  double  *c3         (out) - output curve
 *
 * Multiply spectral curve 'c1' by spectral curve 'c2' to get
 *  spectral curve 'c3'.  Returns TRUE if successful, FALSE if
 *  the CLR_ routines are not initialized.
 */
CLR_mult_spect (c1,c2,c3)
double  *c1, *c2, *c3;
{   int     ct;
    if (!init) return FALSE;
```

```
    for (ct=max_wl-min_wl+1; --ct>=0; ) *c3++ = *c1++ * *c2++;
    return TRUE;
}

/* ****************************************************************
 * CLR_scale_spect (c1, scale, c3)
 *  double  *c1          (in)  - input curve
 *  double  scale        (in)  - scale
 *  double  *c3          (out) - output curve
 *
 * Multiply spectral curve 'c1' by 'scale' to get spectral curve
 *  'c3'.  Returns TRUE if successful, FALSE if the CLR_ routines
 *  are not initialized.
 */
CLR_scale_spect (c1,scale,c3)
double  *c1, scale, *c3;
{   int     ct;
    if (!init) return FALSE;
    for (ct=max_wl-min_wl+1; --ct>=0; ) *c3++ = *c1++ * scale;
    return TRUE;
}

/* ****************************************************************
 * double CLR_area_spect (c1)
 *  double  *c1          (in)  - input curve
 *
 * Returns the are under the spectral curve 'c1'.  Returns 0 if
 *  the CLR_ routines are not initialized.
 */
double CLR_area_spect (c1)
double  *c1;
{   int     ct;
    double  area = 0.0;
    if (!init) return FALSE;
    for (ct=max_wl-min_wl+1; --ct>=0; ) area += *c1++;
    return area;
}

/* ****************************************************************
 * CLR_XYZ CLR_spect_to_xyz(spectral)
 *  double  *spectral   (in) - the spectral curve
 *
 * Returns the sample values if successful, and a sample value
 *  of (0,0,0) if the CLR_ routines are not initialized.
 *
 * Multiplies the spectral curve by each of the sampling curves
 *  then integrates the resulting curves.  The XYZ values are then
 *  normalized such that an identity material has Y=1.
 */
CLR_XYZ CLR_spect_to_xyz (spectral)
double       *spectral;
{   CLR_XYZ     xyz;
    if (!init) {xyz.x = xyz.y = xyz.z = 0.0; return xyz;}
    (void)CLR_mult_spect(spectral, X_tristim, work_curve);
    xyz.x = xyz_scale * CLR_area_spect(work_curve);
    (void)CLR_mult_spect(spectral, Y_tristim, work_curve);
    xyz.y = xyz_scale * CLR_area_spect(work_curve);
    (void)CLR_mult_spect(spectral, Z_tristim, work_curve);
    xyz.z = xyz_scale * CLR_area_spect(work_curve);
    return xyz;
```

```
}

/* ****************************************************************
 * CLR_RGB CLR_spect_to_rgb (spectral)
 *  double  *spectral   (in) - the spectral curve
 *
 * Returns the sample values if successful, and a sample value of
 *  (0,0,0) if the CLR_ routines are not initialized.
 *
 * The curve is first sampled to XYZ then transformed to RGB
 */
CLR_RGB CLR_spect_to_rgb (spectral)
double      *spectral;
{   CLR_XYZ     xyz;
    CLR_RGB     rgb;
    if (!init) {rgb.r = rgb.g = rgb.b = 0.0; return rgb;}
    xyz = CLR_spect_to_xyz (spectral);
    rgb.r = (xyz_rgb_mat[0][0] * xyz.x) +
        (xyz_rgb_mat[0][1] * xyz.y) + (xyz_rgb_mat[0][2] * xyz.z);
    rgb.g = (xyz_rgb_mat[1][0] * xyz.x) +
        (xyz_rgb_mat[1][1] * xyz.y) + (xyz_rgb_mat[1][2] * xyz.z);
    rgb.b = (xyz_rgb_mat[2][0] * xyz.x) +
        (xyz_rgb_mat[2][1] * xyz.y) + (xyz_rgb_mat[2][2] * xyz.z);
    return rgb;
}

/* ****************************************************************
 * CLR_get_CIEXYZ (X,Y,Z)
 *  double  *X,*Y,*Z    (mod) arrays to hold the curves
 *
 * Copies the XYZ sampling curves into the user supplied buffers.
 *  Returns TRUE is successful and FALSE if the CLR_ routines are
 *  not initialized.
 */
CLR_get_CIEXYZ(X,Y,Z)
double      *X,*Y,*Z;
{   int     ct;
    double  *x,*y,*z;
    if (!init) return FALSE;
    x = X_tristim; y = Y_tristim; z = Z_tristim;
    for (ct=max_wl-min_wl+1; --ct>=0; ) {
        *X++ = *x++; *Y++ = *y++; *Z++ = *z++;
    }
    return TRUE;
}

/* ****************************************************************
 * CLR_get_rgb (rgb)
 *  CLR_XYZ     rgb[4]  (mod) the primaries
 *
 * Fills 'rgb' with the primaries the CLR_ routines are initialized
 *  to.  Returns TRUE if successful and FALSE if the CLR_ routines
 *  are not initialized.
 */
CLR_get_rgb (rgb)
CLR_XYZ     *rgb;
{   int     ct;
    if (!init) return FALSE;
    for (ct=0; ct<=3; ct++) rgb[ct] = rgb_primary[ct];
    return TRUE;
```

```
}

/* ****************************************************************
 * CLR_get_min_wl ()
 *
 * Returns the minimum wavelength bound for which the CLR_ routines
 *  are initialized, returns -1 if the CLR_ routines are not
 *  initialized.
 */
CLR_get_min_wl()
{   if (!init) return -1;
    return min_wl;
}

/* ****************************************************************
 * CLR_get_max_wl ()
 *
 * Returns the minimum wavelength bound for which the CLR_ routines
 *  are initialized, returns -1 if the CLR_ routines are not
 *  initialized.
 */
CLR_get_max_wl()
{   if (!init) return -1;
    return max_wl;
}

/* ****************************************************************
 * CLR_get_xyz_rgb (mat)
 *  double        mat[3][3]      (mod) - matrix to be loaded
 *
 *  Copies the CIEXYZ to RGB transformation into the user supplied
 *   matrix.  Returns TRUE if successful and FALSE if the CLR_
 *   routines are not initialized.
 */
int CLR_get_xyz_rgb(mat)
double mat[][3];
{   if (!init) return FALSE;
    LOAD_MAT(mat, xyz_rgb_mat);
    return TRUE;
}

/* ****************************************************************
 * CLR_get_rgb_xyz (mat)
 *  double        mat[3][3]      (mod) - matrix to be loaded
 *
 *  Copies the RGB to CIEXYZ transformation into the user supplied
 *   matrix.  Returns TRUE if successful and FALSE if the CLR_
 *   routines are not initialized.
 */
int CLR_get_rgb_xyz(mat)
double  mat[][3];
{   if (!init) return FALSE;
    LOAD_MAT(mat, rgb_xyz_mat);
    return TRUE;
}

/* ****************************************************************
 * CLR_get_yiq_rgb (mat)
 *  double        mat[3][3]      (mod) - matrix to be loaded
 *
```

```
 *  Copies the YIQ to RGB transformation into the user supplied
 *   matrix.  Returns TRUE if successful and FALSE if the CLR_
 *   routines are not initialized.
 */
int CLR_get_yiq_rgb(mat)
double mat[][3];
{   if (!init) return FALSE;
    LOAD_MAT(mat, yiq_rgb_mat);
    return TRUE;
}

/* ****************************************************************
 * CLR_get_rgb_yiq (mat)
 *  double          mat[3][3]     (mod) - matrix to be loaded
 *
 *  Copies the RGB to YIQ transformation into the user supplied
 *   matrix.  Returns TRUE if successful and FALSE if the CLR_
 *   routines are not initialized.
 */
int CLR_get_rgb_yiq(mat)
double  mat[][3];
{   if (!init) return FALSE;
    LOAD_MAT(mat, rgb_yiq_mat);
    return TRUE;
}

/* ****************************************************************
 * CLR_rgb_to_aux_rgb (to, from, rgb_aux)
 *  double          to[3][3]      (mod) - matrix to aux rgb
 *  double          from[3][3]    (mod) - matrix from aux rgb
 *  CLR_XYZ         rgb_aux[4]    (in)  - the color space definition,
 *                                        3 primaries and white
 *
 * Creates the transformations between RGB color space the CLR_
 *  routines are initialized for and another RGB color space as
 *  specified in 'aux_rgb'.  The 'to' and 'from' matrices are
 *  filled with the resulting transformations.  TRUE is returned
 *  if successful, FALSE is returned if the CLR_ routines are not
 *  initialized or if there is a singularity detected when the
 *  transformation is being generated.
 *
 * The technique used is described in Sect 3.2, Colorimetry and
 *  the RGB Monitor.
 */
int CLR_rgb_to_aux_rgb(to,from,rgb_aux)
double  to[][3], from[][3];
CLR_XYZ rgb_aux[];
{   CLR_XYZ     rgb_tmp[4];
    double      rgb_xyz_aux[3][3], xyz_rgb_aux[3][3];
    int         color;
    if (!init) return FALSE;
    /* normalize the chromaticities of the auxiliary primaries
     *  and white point.
     */
    for (color=RED; color<=WHITE; color++) {
        rgb_tmp[color] = rgb_aux[color];
        rgb_tmp[color].z = 1.0 - rgb_aux[color].x - rgb_aux[color].y;
    }
    /* get the transform between XYZ and the auxiliary RGB */
    if (!clr__cspace_to_xyz(rgb_tmp, rgb_xyz_aux)) return FALSE;
```

```
    if (!CLR_t_inverse(rgb_xyz_aux,xyz_rgb_aux)) return FALSE;
    /* concatenate with the transforms for the RGB color space
     *  that the CLR_ routine set is initialized to
     */
    (void)CLR_t_concat(xyz_rgb_aux, rgb_xyz_mat, to);
    (void)CLR_t_concat(xyz_rgb_mat, rgb_xyz_aux, from);
    return TRUE;
}

/* ****************************************************************
 * CLR_LAB CLR_xyz_to_lab (xyz)
 *  CLR_XYZ     xyz      (in) - xyz color (.01<=Y<=1)
 *
 * Returns L*a*b* given XYZ.  Returns (0,0,0) if the CLR_ routines
 *  are not initialized.  This transformation is described in
 *  Section 3.3, Alternate Color Representations, Eq.((3.4)),
 *  and is taken from Judd and Wyszecki (1975) pg.320.  The
 *  transformation is scaled for (.01 < Y < 1) for consistency
 *  within the CLR_ routine set.
 */
CLR_LAB CLR_xyz_to_lab(xyz)
CLR_XYZ     xyz;
{   CLR_LAB     lab;
    if (!init) {lab.l = lab.a = lab.b = 0.0; return lab;}
    xyz.x *= 100.0;
    xyz.y *= 100.0;
    xyz.z *= 100.0;
    lab.l = 25.0 * pow(((100.0*xyz.y)/white.y),.33333) - 16.0;
    lab.a = 500.0 *
        (pow(xyz.x/white.x,.33333) - pow(xyz.y/white.y,.33333));
    lab.b = 200.0 *
        (pow(xyz.y/white.y,.33333) - pow(xyz.z/white.z,.33333));
    return lab;
}

/* ****************************************************************
 * CLR_LUV CLR_xyz_to_luv (xyz)
 *  CLR_XYZ     xyz      (in) - xyz color (.01<=Y<=1)
 *
 * Returns L*u*v* given XYZ.  Returns (0,0,0) if the CLR_ routines
 *  are not initialized.  This transformation is described in
 *  Section 3.3, Alternate Color Representations, Eq.((3.5)),
 *  and is taken from Judd and Wyszecki (1975) pg.328.  The
 *  transformation is scaled for (.01 < Y < 1) for consistency
 *  within the CLR_ routine set.
 */
CLR_LUV CLR_xyz_to_luv(xyz)
CLR_XYZ     xyz;
{   CLR_LUV     luv;
    double      u, v;
    if (!init) {luv.l = luv.u = luv.v = 0.0; return luv;}
    xyz.x *= 100.0;
    xyz.y *= 100.0;
    xyz.z *= 100.0;
    luv.l = 25.0 * pow(((100.0*xyz.y)/white.y),.33333) - 16.0;
    u = (4.0 * xyz.x) / (xyz.x + (15.0 * xyz.y) + (3.0 * xyz.z));
    v = (9.0 * xyz.y) / (xyz.x + (15.0 * xyz.y) + (3.0 * xyz.z));
    luv.u = 13.0 * luv.l * (u - ref_luv.u);
    luv.v = 13.0 * luv.l * (v - ref_luv.v);
    return luv;
```

```
}

/* ****************************************************************
 * CLR_t_concat (m1, m2, m3)
 *  double          m1[3][3]       (in)  - matrix
 *  double          m2[3][3]       (in)  - matrix to concat
 *  double          m3[3][3]       (in)  - concatenated matrix
 *
 * Concatenate 'm1' to 'm2' resulting in 'm3'. In use, suppose you
 *  have an XYZ to RGB and an RGB to YIQ matrix.  Concatenate the
 *  RGB to YIQ matrix to the XYZ to RGB matrix to get an XYZ to
 *  YIQ matrix.  Returns TRUE.
 */
int CLR_t_concat(m1,m2,m3)
double  m1[][3], m2[][3], m3[][3];
{   double  t1[3][3], t2[3][3];
    LOAD_MAT(t1,m1);
    LOAD_MAT(t2,m2);
    {   int ii,jj;
        for (ii=0; ii<=2; ii++)
            for (jj=0; jj<=2; jj++)
                m3[ii][jj] = (t1[ii][0] * t2[0][jj]) +
                             (t1[ii][1] * t2[1][jj]) +
                             (t1[ii][2] * t2[2][jj]);
    }
    return TRUE;
}

/* ****************************************************************
 * CLR_t_inverse (mat, inv_mat)
 *  double          mat[3][3]      (in)  - matrix to be inverted
 *  double          inv_mat[3][3]  (mod) - inverted matrix
 *
 * Inverts 'mat' using Gaussian elimination.  Returns TRUE if
 *  successful and FALSE if there is a singularity.
 */
int CLR_t_inverse (mat, inv_mat)
double  mat[][3];
double  inv_mat[][3];
{   int     ii, jj, kk;
    double  tmp_mat[3][3], tmp_d;

    for (ii=0; ii<=2; ii++)
        for (jj=0; jj<=2; jj++) {
            tmp_mat[ii][jj] = mat[ii][jj];
            inv_mat[ii][jj] = (ii==jj ? 1.0 : 0.0);
        }

    for (ii=0; ii<=2; ii++) {
        for (jj=ii+1, kk=ii; jj<=2; jj++)
            if (fabs(tmp_mat[jj][ii]) > fabs(tmp_mat[kk][ii]))
                kk = jj;

        /* check for singularity */
        if (tmp_mat[kk][ii] == 0.0) return FALSE;

        /* pivot - switch rows kk and ii */
        if (kk != ii)
            for (jj=0; jj<=2; jj++) {
                tmp_d = tmp_mat[ii][jj];
```

```
        tmp_mat[ii][jj] = tmp_mat[kk][jj];
                tmp_mat[kk][jj] = tmp_d;
                tmp_d = inv_mat[ii][jj];
                inv_mat[ii][jj] = inv_mat[kk][jj];
                inv_mat[kk][jj] = tmp_d;
            }

        /* normalize the row - make the diagonal 1 */
        for (tmp_d = 1.0 / tmp_mat[ii][ii], jj=0; jj<=2; jj++) {
            tmp_mat[ii][jj] *= tmp_d;
            inv_mat[ii][jj] *= tmp_d;
        }

        /* zero the non-diagonal terms in this column */
        for (jj=0; jj<=2; jj++)
            if (jj != ii)
                for (tmp_d = -tmp_mat[jj][ii], kk=0; kk<=2; kk++) {
                    tmp_mat[jj][kk] += tmp_mat[ii][kk] * tmp_d;
                    inv_mat[jj][kk] += inv_mat[ii][kk] * tmp_d;
                }
    }

    return TRUE;
}

/* ****************************************************************
 * clr__cspace_to_xyz (cspace, t_mat)
 *  CLR_XYZ       cspace[4]    (in)  - the color space definition,
 *                                      3 primaries and white
 *  double        t_mat[3][3] (mod) - the color transformation
 *
 * Builds the transformation from a set of primaries to the CIEXYZ
 *  color space.  This is the basis for the generation of the color
 *  transformations in the CLR_ routine set.  The method used is
 *  that detailed in Sect 3.2 Colorimetry and the RGB monitor.
 *  Returns FALSE if there is a singularity.
 */
static int clr__cspace_to_xyz (cspace, t_mat)
CLR_XYZ     cspace[];
double      t_mat[][3];
{   int     ii, jj, kk, tmp_i, ind[3];
    double  mult, white[3], scale[3];

    /* normalize the white point to Y=1 */
    if (cspace[WHITE].y <= 0.0) return FALSE;
    white[0] = cspace[WHITE].x / cspace[WHITE].y;
    white[1] = 1.0;
    white[2] = cspace[WHITE].z / cspace[WHITE].y;

    for (ii=0; ii<=2; ii++) {
        t_mat[0][ii] = cspace[ii].x;
        t_mat[1][ii] = cspace[ii].y;
        t_mat[2][ii] = cspace[ii].z;
        ind[ii] = ii;
    }

    /* gaussian elimination  with partial pivoting */
    for (ii=0; ii<2; ii++) {
        for (jj=ii+1; jj<=2; jj++)
            if (fabs(t_mat[ind[jj]][ii]) >
```

```
            fabs(t_mat[ind[ii]][ii])) {
                tmp_i=ind[jj]; ind[jj]=ind[ii]; ind[ii]=tmp_i;
            }
        if (t_mat[ind[ii]][ii] == 0.0) return FALSE;

        for (jj=ii+1; jj<=2; jj++) {
            mult = t_mat[ind[jj]][ii] / t_mat[ind[ii]][ii];
            for (kk=ii+1; kk<=2; kk++)
                t_mat[ind[jj]][kk] -= t_mat[ind[ii]][kk] * mult;
            white[ind[jj]] -= white[ind[ii]] * mult;
        }
    }
    if (t_mat[ind[2]][2] == 0.0) return FALSE;

    /* back substitution to solve for scale */
    scale[ind[2]] = white[ind[2]] / t_mat[ind[2]][2];
    scale[ind[1]] = (white[ind[1]] - (t_mat[ind[1]][2] *
        scale[ind[2]])) / t_mat[ind[1]][1];
    scale[ind[0]] = (white[ind[0]] - (t_mat[ind[0]][1] *
        scale[ind[1]]) - (t_mat[ind[0]][2] * scale[ind[2]])) /
        t_mat[ind[0]][0];

    /* build matrix */
    for (ii=0; ii<=2; ii++) {
        t_mat[0][ii] = cspace[ii].x * scale[ii];
        t_mat[1][ii] = cspace[ii].y * scale[ii];
        t_mat[2][ii] = cspace[ii].z * scale[ii];
    }

    return TRUE;
}

/* ****************************************************************
 * CLR_exit()
 *
 * Completes use of the CLR_ routine set and frees any
 *   allocated space
 */
CLR_exit()
{
    if (!init) return TRUE;
    (void)CLR_exit_samples();
    if (X_tristim != NULL) free((char *)X_tristim);
    if (Y_tristim != NULL) free((char *)Y_tristim);
    if (Z_tristim != NULL) free((char *)Z_tristim);
    if (work_curve != NULL) free((char *)work_curve);
    X_tristim = Y_tristim = Z_tristim = work_curve = NULL;
    init = FALSE;
    return TRUE;
}
/* ************************************************************** */
```

III.8 Spectral Sampling

Spectral sampling in the context of this discussion means reducing a spectral curve to a set of sample values for subsequent color computations. Spectral sampling is differentiated from sampling into a perceptual color space by applicability of spectral sampling techniques to any region of the spectrum independent of the perceptual mechanism of the eye. Thus, in addition to generating realistic imagery, this technique could be used to compute infrared or ultraviolet illumination and pseudocolor used to display the resulting image information.

We intuitively expect that the interactions between light and matter to be independent of whether a human observer is present. This section demonstrates a simple approach to sampling spectral curves into a color space for computation and then subsequently transforming from the computational color space to a display color space.

There is very little discussion in the computer graphics literature regarding the mechanics of manipulating spectral data with the minimum introduction of error. The technique presented here is a simple attempt to address the problem presented by Hall (1983a,1983b,1987). It should not be construed to be a proven sampling methodology, but, should be taken as an example of an approach to addressing an issue that is typically ignored.

While illumination is independent of the viewer, we would expect that in image generation applications, the perceptual constraints dictate which portions of the spectrum should be sampled to maintain the most relevant color information. Meyer (1988) presents a technique that takes advantage of the observation that most spectral curves can be approximated by low order polynomials, coupled with an specially defined color space and Gaussian quadrature, to determine the appropriate sampling. In this technique point samples are used at selected wavelengths. The Gaussian quadrature techniques numerically integrate the low order polynomials that pass through the computed sample points resulting in the color coordinates of the reconstructed spectral curve. The color coordinates are then transformed from the specially defined color space into the display color space.

III.8.1 Code Summary

There are three basic operations performed in spectral sampling for color computation. The first is defining the sampling to be used. The second is sampling the continuous spectral curves into sample values for color computation. The third is to reconstruct spectral curves from the samples after computation so that the curve can be sampled into a display color space. In practice, the process of reconstruction and sampling into a display color space are combined into a matrix transformation from the computational color space to the display color space.

Defining the sampling

Both the sampling methodology presented by Hall (1983a,1983b) and that presented by Meyer (1988) are supported. The Hall sampling uses non-overlapping box sampling functions as described in Section 3.5.2, *Spectral Sampling Approaches*. The number of and position of samples is specified to `CLR_init_samples()` at initialization.

The Meyer sampling uses 4 samples at the prescribed locations of 456.4nm, 490.9nm, 557.7nm, and 631.4nm. The number of samples and sample bounds are ignored when this sampling is requested.

The routines `CLR_exit_samples()` completes use of the sampling routines. The routine `CLR_num_samples()` returns the number of color samples being used.

Sampling spectral curves

The routine `CLR_spect_to_sample()` samples a spectral curve and fills a sample array. These samples are used for subsequent color computations. The sampling types specified at initialization is used.

Reconstruction

The routine `CLR_reconstruct()` reconstructs a spectral curve from a set of spectral samples after color computation. Reconstruction can only be performed for the Hall sampling methodology.

The routines `CLR_get_sample_xyz()` and `CLR_get_sample_rgb()` load the transformations to go from spectral samples directly to XYZ and RGB respectively. For the Hall methodology the transformations are generated by sampling the reconstruction curve for each color sample into the display color space. For the Meyer methodology, the transformations are a concatenation of the matrix from the sampled space to AC_1C_2 and the matrix from AC_1C_2 to the display space. In addition, a scale factor is included for consistency with the other color routines so that sampling an identity curve results in a Y value of 1.

The transformation is returned as an array of doubles 3 times the number of color samples in length. The array is ordered so that transformation from spectral samples to a display color space such as RGB using the transformation `to_rgb` takes the form:

```
rgb.r = rgb.g = rgb.b = 0.0;
for (ii=0; ii<num_clr_samp; ct++) {
    rgb.r += clr_samp[ct] * to_rgb[ct];
    rgb.g += clr_samp[ct] * to_rgb[ct+num_clr_samp];
    rgb.b += clr_samp[ct] * to_rgb[ct+(2*num_clr_samp];
}
```

III.8.2 Code Source

The following is the source module for the spectral sampling and reconstruction routines:

```
/* ****************************************************************
 *                        clr_sample.c
 * ****************************************************************
 *  MODULE PURPOSE:
 *      This module contains the routines for spectral sampling.
 *      The operations include defining the sampling space,
```

```
 *      sampling spectral curves, and transformations from spectral
 *      sample space to RGB or XYZ.
 *
 *  MODULE CONTENTS:
 *      CLR_init_samples     - initialize spectral sampling
 *      CLR_num_samples      - returns the number of samples
 *      CLR_spect_to_sample  - sample a spectral curve
 *      CLR_get_sample_rgb   - get the sample to RGB matrix
 *      CLR_get_sample_xyz   - get the sample to XYZ matrix
 *      CLR_reconstruct      - reconstruct a spectral curve
 *      CLR_exit_samples     - finish with spectral sampling
 *
 *  NOTES:
 *      > The CLR_ routines must be initialized (CLR_init()) before
 *          using any of the sampling routines.
 *
 *      > When the CLR_SAMPLE_HALL method is selected, sampling
 *          uses abutting, non-overlapping, box sample and
 *          reconstruction functions are described in Section
 *          3.5.2 Spectral Sampling Approaches, and in Hall (1983).
 *          This provides continuous sampling between the low bound
 *          of the first sample and the high bound of the last
 *          sample.  For applications requiring discrete isolated
 *          samples, user modification of these routines
 *          is required.
 *
 *      > When the CLR_SAMPLE_MEYER method is used, 4 samples are
 *          used as described in Meyer (1988).
 */
#include <stdio.h>
#include "clr.h"

static int      sample_type = -1;
static int      samples = 0;
static int      *bounds = NULL;
static double   XYZ_to_ACC[3][3] = {{-0.0177,   1.0090, 0.0073},
                                    {-1.5370,   1.0821, 0.3209},
                                    { 0.1946,  -0.2045, 0.5264}};
static double   ACC_to_XYZ[3][3];
static double   samp_to_ACC[3][4] =
                  {{0.00000,  0.18892,    0.67493,    0.19253},
                   {0.00000,  0.00000,    0.31824,   -0.46008},
                   {0.54640,  0.00000,    0.00000,    0.00000}};

extern char     *malloc();

/* ****************************************************************
 * CLR_init_samples (method, num_samples, sample_bounds)
 *  int     method           (in) - sampling method:
 *                                  CLR_SAMPLE_MEYER    Meyer (1988)
 *                                  CLR_SAMPLE_HALL     Hall (1983)
 *  int     num_samples      (in) - number of sample functions
 *  int     sample_bounds[]  (in) - boundaries of the sampling
 *                                  functions.  There must be
 *                                  num_samples+1 bounds arranged in
 *                                  ascending order in this array.
 *
 * For the CLR_SAMPLE_HALL method the bound wavelength is included
 *  in the sampling function.  For example, using 3 samples with
 *  bounds at (411, 491, 571, 651), the actual samples are 411-490,
```

```
 *  491-570, and 571-650.
 *
 * The CLR_SAMPLE_MEYER method uses a prescribed sampling with 4
 *  samples.  The num_samples and sample_bounds arguments are
 *  ignored.
 *
 * Returns TRUE if successful, FALSE if sample bounds are not valid
 *  or sampling is previously initialized to some other value.
 */
CLR_init_samples (method, num_samples, sample_bounds)
int     method;
int     num_samples;
int     *sample_bounds;
{   int     ct;

    if (method == CLR_SAMPLE_MEYER) {
        samples = 4;
        sample_type = method;
        CLR_t_inverse (XYZ_to_ACC, ACC_to_XYZ);
    }
    else if (method == CLR_SAMPLE_HALL) {
        /* There are two ways to do this, one is to save a
         *  complete sampling curve for each sample.  The
         *  other is to do the computation on the fly.  Here
         *  it's done on the fly.  Only the bounds are saved.
         */
        if (num_samples <= 0) return FALSE;
        if ((bounds = (int *)malloc((unsigned)(sizeof(int) *
            (num_samples + 1)))) == NULL) goto error;

        bounds[0] = sample_bounds[0];
        for (ct=0; ct<num_samples; ct++) {
            if (sample_bounds[ct+1] <= sample_bounds[ct])
                goto error;
            bounds[ct+1] = sample_bounds[ct+1];
        }

        samples = num_samples;
        sample_type = method;
    }
    else {
        goto error;
    }
    return TRUE;

error:
    samples = 0;
    if (bounds != NULL) free((char *)bounds);
    return FALSE;
}

/* ******************************************************************
 * CLR_num_samples()
 *
 * Returns the number of samples for which sampling is initialized.
 *  Returns 0 if sampling is not initialized.
 */
CLR_num_samples()
{   return samples;
}
```

```
/* ****************************************************************
 * CLR_spect_to_sample (spectral, sample)
 *  double  *spectral    (in)  - spectral curve to be sampled
 *  double  *sample      (mod) - array to receive the sampled
 *                              values.
 * Samples 'spectral' and loads the sample values into 'sample'.
 *  Returns TRUE if successful and FALSE if CLR_ or the sampling
 *  has not been initialized
 */
CLR_spect_to_sample (spectral, sample)
double      *spectral;
double      *sample;
{   int     cur_wl, ct, max_wl, cur_samp;
    double  cur_sum;

    if (samples <= 0) return FALSE;
    if ((cur_wl = CLR_get_min_wl()) < 0) return FALSE;
    max_wl = CLR_get_max_wl();

    if (sample_type == CLR_SAMPLE_MEYER) {
        /* sample at 456.4nm, 490.9nm, 557.7nm, and 631.4nm
         */
        if ((cur_wl > 456) || (max_wl < 457)) *sample++ = 0.0;
        else *sample++ = spectral[456-cur_wl] + (0.4 *
                (spectral[457-cur_wl] - spectral[456-cur_wl]));

        if ((cur_wl > 490) || (max_wl < 491)) *sample++ = 0.0;
        else *sample++ = spectral[490-cur_wl] + (0.9 *
                (spectral[491-cur_wl] - spectral[490-cur_wl]));

        if ((cur_wl > 557) || (max_wl < 558)) *sample++ = 0.0;
        else *sample++ = spectral[557-cur_wl] + (0.7 *
                (spectral[558-cur_wl] - spectral[557-cur_wl]));

        if ((cur_wl > 631) || (max_wl < 632)) *sample++ = 0.0;
        else *sample++ = spectral[631-cur_wl] + (0.4 *
                (spectral[632-cur_wl] - spectral[631-cur_wl]));
    }
    else {
        for ( ;cur_wl<bounds[0]; cur_wl++, spectral++) ;

        for (cur_samp=1, cur_sum=0.0, ct=0; cur_wl<=max_wl;
                cur_wl++) {
            while (cur_wl>=bounds[cur_samp]) {
                if (ct == 0) *sample++ = 0.0;
                else *sample++ = cur_sum / ct;
                if (++cur_samp > samples) return TRUE;
                cur_sum = 0.0;
                ct = 0;
            }
            cur_sum += *spectral++;
            ct++;
        }
        *sample = cur_sum / ct;
    }
    return TRUE;
}

/* ****************************************************************
 * CLR_get_sample_rgb (matrix)
```

```
 *  double  *matrix     (mod) - matrix to be filled.
 *
 * Returns the matrix for conversion from the sampled space to the
 *  RGB the CLR_ routines have been initialized for.  The matrix
 *  is a 3 x num_samples matrix.
 */
CLR_get_sample_rgb(matrix)
double      *matrix;
{
    double      *xyz = NULL;
    double      xyz_rgb[3][3];
    int         ct;

    /* get the XYZ matrix, then transform it into RGB
     */
    if ((xyz = (double *)malloc((unsigned)(3 *
        sizeof(double) * samples))) == NULL) goto error;
    if (!CLR_get_sample_xyz(xyz)) goto error;
    if (!CLR_get_xyz_rgb(xyz_rgb)) goto error;

    for (ct=0; ct<samples; ct++, matrix++, xyz++) {
        matrix[0] = (xyz_rgb[0][0] * xyz[0]) +
                    (xyz_rgb[0][1] * xyz[samples]) +
                    (xyz_rgb[0][2] * xyz[2*samples]);
        matrix[samples] = (xyz_rgb[1][0] * xyz[0]) +
                    (xyz_rgb[1][1] * xyz[samples]) +
                    (xyz_rgb[1][2] * xyz[2*samples]);
        matrix[2*samples] = (xyz_rgb[2][0] * xyz[0]) +
                    (xyz_rgb[2][1] * xyz[samples]) +
                    (xyz_rgb[2][2] * xyz[2*samples]);
    }

    free((char *)xyz);
    return TRUE;

error:
    if (xyz != NULL) free((char *)xyz);
    return FALSE;
}

/* ****************************************************************
 * CLR_get_sample_xyz (matrix)
 *  double  *matrix     (mod) - matrix to be filled.
 *
 * Returns the matrix for conversion from the sampled space to
 *  CIEXYZ. The matrix is a 3 x num_samples matrix.
 */
CLR_get_sample_xyz(matrix)
double      *matrix;
{
    int     min_wl, max_wl, cur_wl, cur_samp;
    double  *reconst, *cur_r, fill, *samp_mat;
    CLR_XYZ xyz;

    if (samples <= 0) return FALSE;
    if (sample_type == CLR_SAMPLE_MEYER) {
        /* concatenate the sample to ACC matrix with the ACC_to_XYZ
         *  matrix.  The divide by 1.057863 is a normalization so
         *  than an identity curve has a Y value of 1.0 following
         *  the conventions used in the CLR_routines.
```

```
     */
        samp_mat = samp_to_ACC[0];
        for (cur_samp=0; cur_samp<samples; cur_samp++,
                matrix++, samp_mat++) {
            matrix[0] = ((ACC_to_XYZ[0][0] * samp_mat[0]) +
                (ACC_to_XYZ[0][1] * samp_mat[samples]) +
                (ACC_to_XYZ[0][2] * samp_mat[2*samples])) /
                1.057863;
            matrix[samples] = ((ACC_to_XYZ[1][0] * samp_mat[0]) +
                (ACC_to_XYZ[1][1] * samp_mat[samples]) +
                (ACC_to_XYZ[1][2] * samp_mat[2*samples])) /
                1.057863;
            matrix[2*samples] = ((ACC_to_XYZ[2][0] * samp_mat[0]) +
                (ACC_to_XYZ[2][1] * samp_mat[samples]) +
                (ACC_to_XYZ[2][2] * samp_mat[2*samples])) /
                1.057863;
        }
    }
    else {
        min_wl = CLR_get_min_wl();
        max_wl = CLR_get_max_wl();
        /* allocate space for the reconstruction function
         */
        if ((reconst = (double *)malloc(
             (unsigned)(sizeof(double) *
             (max_wl - min_wl + 1)))) == NULL) goto error;

        /* Build each reconstruction function and sample it into xyz.
         *  Load the values into the matrix
         */
        for (cur_samp=0; cur_samp<samples; cur_samp++, matrix++) {
            cur_r = reconst;

            if (cur_samp == 0) fill = 1.0;
            else fill = 0.0;

            for (cur_wl=min_wl ;(cur_wl<bounds[cur_samp]) &&
                (cur_wl<max_wl); cur_wl++) *cur_r++ = fill;
            for ( ;(cur_wl<bounds[cur_samp+1]) &&
                (cur_wl<=max_wl); cur_wl++) *cur_r++ = 1.0;
            if (cur_samp == (samples-1)) fill = 1.0;
            else fill = 0.0;
            for ( ;cur_wl<=max_wl; cur_wl++) *cur_r++ = fill;
            xyz = CLR_spect_to_xyz (reconst);
            matrix[0] = xyz.x;
            matrix[samples] = xyz.y;
            matrix[2*samples] = xyz.z;
        }
    }

    free((char *)reconst);
    return TRUE;

error:
    if (reconst != NULL) free((char *)reconst);
    return FALSE;
}

/* ****************************************************************
 * CLR_reconstruct (sample, spectral)
```

```
 *   double   *sample     (in)   - the sample values
 *   double   *spectral   (mod)  - the reconstructed spectral curve
 *
 * Reconstructs a spectral curve from the sample values.  The
 *   reconstruction functions are box functions resulting a a step
 *   function as the reconstructed curve.
 */
CLR_reconstruct (sample, spectral)
double       *sample, *spectral;
{   int      cur_wl, max_wl, cur_sample;
    if (samples <= 0) return FALSE;
    if (sample_type == CLR_SAMPLE_MEYER) {
        return FALSE;
    }
    else if (sample_type == CLR_SAMPLE_HALL) {
        cur_wl = CLR_get_min_wl();
        max_wl = CLR_get_max_wl();
        cur_sample = 1;

        while (cur_wl<=max_wl) {
            if (cur_wl < bounds[cur_sample])
                *spectral++ = *sample;
            else if (cur_sample >= samples)
                *spectral++ = *sample;
            else {
                cur_sample++;
                sample++;
                *spectral++ = *sample;
            }
            cur_wl++;
        }
    }
    return TRUE;
}

/* ****************************************************************
 * CLR_exit_samples()
 *
 * Complete use of spectral sampling, free any allocated space.
 */
CLR_exit_samples ()
{   sample_type = -1;
    samples = 0;
    if (bounds != NULL) {
        free((char *)bounds);
        bounds = NULL;
    }
    return TRUE;
}
/* ************************************************************** */
```

III.9 RGB Color Clipping

Clipping RGB colors that are outside the RGB gamut of the monitor so that they can be displayed is described in Section 5.1.3, *Color Clipping and Compressing for Display*. This section gives the clipping routines used for the generation of visual clipping comparison image.

III.9.1 Code Summary

This module is used with the color transformations described in the last section. The `CLR_init()` routine (described in Appendix III.7, *Color Transformation*, initializes information for clipping so that the Y value of the color is preserved. Each routine takes an RGB color as input and returns a clipped RGB value. The following clipping routines are included:

Color clamping

The routine `CLR_clamp_rgb()` takes an RGB color and clamps values less than 0 to 0, and greater than 1 to 1. This clipping method maintains neither hue, saturation, nor value.

Intensity scaling

The routine `CLR_scale_rgb()` takes an RGB color and first clamps values less than 0 to 0. If any values are greater than 1, the color is scaled so the maximum value is 1. If the chromaticity of the color is outside the displayable color gamut (values less than 0) this clipping method maintains neither hue, saturation, nor value. If the chromaticity is inside the displayable gamut, but the intensity is outside (values greater than 1), this clipping method maintains hue and saturation, but clips intensity.

Constant intensity clipping

The routine `CLR_clip_rgb()` attempts to maintain the intensity of the color when it is clipped. `CLR_clip_rgb()` uses the interpretation that planes perpendicular to the neutral axis of the RGB gamut are equal intensity planes.

This clipping algorithm is more complex than the other methods. The first step is to determine the location of the intersection of the plane containing the color with the neutral axis. The equation of a plane in the RGB color space is: $\mathrm{A}r + \mathrm{B}g + \mathrm{C}b + \mathrm{D} = 0$. For color clipping we are interested in colors that are between the plane than passes through the block point and the plane that passes through the white point. Setting $\mathrm{D} = 0$ and $\mathrm{A} = \mathrm{B} = \mathrm{C} = 0.333$ gives the equation of a plane that passes through the black point and is perpendicular to the neutral axis.

Substituting any color into this plane equation gives a perpendicular distance from the plane such that the white point is at a distance of 1. If the distance is greater than 1, the color is clipped to white; if less than 0, the color is assigned black (less than 0 is a color that is outside the visible color gamut and indicates a computational problem elsewhere). If the distance is between 0 and 1, then setting $\mathrm{r} = \mathrm{g} = \mathrm{b} = \text{distance}$, gives the location of the intersection with the neutral axis. The line from this point on the neutral axis to the color is a line of *constant* intensity and hue, and varying saturation. Constant is highlighted because its interpretation is rather loose in this context. The color is interpolated along this line to the point of intersection with the displayable color gamut.

III.9.2 Code Source

The following is the source module for the color compression and clipping routines:

```
/* ****************************************************************
 *                          clr_clip.c
 * ****************************************************************
 *  MODULE PURPOSE:
 *      This module contains routines for bringing colors outside
 *      the displayable gamut into the displayable gamut.
 *
 *  MODULE CONTENTS:
 *      CLR_clamp_rgb   - clamps rgb values to 0.0-1.0 range
 *      CLR_scale_rgb   - scales rgb values to 0.0-1.0 range
 *      CLR_clip_rgb    - clips rgb values to 0.0-1.0 range
 */
#include <stdio.h>
#include <math.h>
#include "clr.h"

/* define the max and min scaling values for equal intensity
 *  clipping.  These are defined to be slightly inside of the
 *  0 to 1 range to avoid numerical problems that occur when
 *  colors are on or very close to the clipping boundary.
 */
#define MAX_CLIP    0.9999  /* 1 - MAX_CLIP > 1 res step */
#define MIN_CLIP    0.0001  /* less than 1 res step */

/* ****************************************************************
 * CLR_clamp_rgb (rgb)
 *  CLR_RGB     rgb     (in)  - the input rgb
 *
 * Returns clamped color.  Values greater than 1 are  clamped to 1,
 *  values less than 0 are clamped to 0.
 */
CLR_RGB CLR_clamp_rgb(in_rgb)
CLR_RGB     in_rgb;
{   CLR_RGB     rgb;
    rgb = in_rgb;
    if (rgb.r < 0.0) rgb.r = 0.0;
    else if (rgb.r > 1.0) rgb.r = 1.0;
    if (rgb.g < 0.0) rgb.g = 0.0;
    else if (rgb.g > 1.0) rgb.g = 1.0;
    if (rgb.b < 0.0) rgb.b = 0.0;
    else if (rgb.b > 1.0) rgb.b = 1.0;
    return rgb;
}

/* ****************************************************************
 * CLR_scale_rgb (rgb)
 *  CLR_RGB     rgb     (in)  - the input rgb
 *
 * Returns scaled color.  Values less than 0 are clamped to zero.
 *  If any values are greater than 1, all color components are
 *  scaled so the offending value is equal to 1.
 */
```

```
CLR_RGB CLR_scale_rgb(in_rgb)
CLR_RGB      in_rgb;
{   double        scale=1.0;
    double        tmp_scale;
    CLR_RGB       rgb;
    rgb = in_rgb;
    if (rgb.r < 0.0) rgb.r = 0.0;
    else if ((rgb.r > 1.0) && ((tmp_scale = (1.0 / rgb.r))
        < scale)) scale = tmp_scale;
    if (rgb.g < 0.0) rgb.g = 0.0;
    else if ((rgb.g > 1.0) && ((tmp_scale = (1.0 / rgb.g))
        < scale)) scale = tmp_scale;
    if (rgb.b < 0.0) rgb.b = 0.0;
    else if ((rgb.b > 1.0) && ((tmp_scale = (1.0 / rgb.b))
        < scale)) scale = tmp_scale;
    if (scale < 1.0) {
        rgb.r *= scale;
        rgb.g *= scale;
        rgb.b *= scale;
    }
    return rgb;
}

/* ****************************************************************
 * CLR_RGB CLR_clip_rgb(in_rgb)
 *  CLR_RGB     in_rgb  (in) - the input rgb
 *
 * Returns the clipped color - clipping is by desaturating the
 *  color by shifting it towards the neutral axis in a plane
 *  perpendicular to the neutral axis.  The neutral axis is taken
 *  as the vector from the monitor black to the monitor white.
 */
CLR_RGB CLR_clip_rgb(in_rgb)
CLR_RGB      in_rgb;
{   CLR_RGB      diff, out_rgb;
    double       axis_rgb, diff_mult, tmp_mult;

    /* check to see if clipping is required
     */
    if ((in_rgb.r < 0.0) || (in_rgb.r > 1.0) ||
        (in_rgb.g < 0.0) || (in_rgb.g > 1.0) ||
        (in_rgb.b < 0.0) || (in_rgb.b > 1.0)) {
        /* clipping is required, determine the distance from
         *  the origin to the equal intensity plane containing
         *  the color.  The distance is normalized the origin
         *  at color (0,0,0) and a distance of 1 at (1,1,1)
         */
        axis_rgb = (in_rgb.r + in_rgb.g + in_rgb.b) * .333333;
        /* check for the intensity plane of the color being
         *  outside the displayable range -- if it is, set
         *  color to either black or white.
         */
        if (axis_rgb <= MIN_CLIP)
            /* this is not a visible color -- it should not
             *  have been computed
             */
            out_rgb.r = out_rgb.g = out_rgb.b = 0.0;
        else if (axis_rgb >= MAX_CLIP)
            /* This is way beyond white in intensity, set it
             *  to the white point.
```

```
            */
            out_rgb.r = out_rgb.g = out_rgb.b = 1.0;
        else {
            /* the intensity plane is within the displayable
             *  range.  Compute the vector from the neutral
             *  axis to the color on it's intensity plane.
             *  The intersection of the neutral axis and the
             *  intensity plane is at r=g=b=axis_rgb.
             */
            diff.r = in_rgb.r - axis_rgb;
            diff.g = in_rgb.g - axis_rgb;
            diff.b = in_rgb.b - axis_rgb;
            /* determine the relative length of the vector
             *  to the edge of the displayable color gamut.
             */
            diff_mult = 1.0;
            if (in_rgb.r > 1.0) {
                if ((tmp_mult = (MAX_CLIP - axis_rgb) / diff.r)
                    < diff_mult) diff_mult = tmp_mult;
            } else if (in_rgb.r < 0.0) {
                if ((tmp_mult = (MIN_CLIP - axis_rgb) / diff.r)
                    < diff_mult) diff_mult = tmp_mult;
            }

            if (in_rgb.g > 1.0) {
                if ((tmp_mult = (MAX_CLIP - axis_rgb) / diff.g)
                    < diff_mult) diff_mult = tmp_mult;
            } else if (in_rgb.g < 0.0) {
                if ((tmp_mult = (MIN_CLIP - axis_rgb) / diff.g)
                    < diff_mult) diff_mult = tmp_mult;
            }

            if (in_rgb.b > 1.0) {
                if ((tmp_mult = (MAX_CLIP - axis_rgb) / diff.b)
                    < diff_mult) diff_mult = tmp_mult;
            } else if (in_rgb.b < 0.0) {
                if ((tmp_mult = (MIN_CLIP - axis_rgb) / diff.b)
                    < diff_mult) diff_mult = tmp_mult;
            }

            /* determine the location of the color at the
             *  edge of the displayable color gamut.
             */
            out_rgb.r = axis_rgb + (diff.r * diff_mult);
            out_rgb.g = axis_rgb + (diff.g * diff_mult);
            out_rgb.b = axis_rgb + (diff.b * diff_mult);
        }
        return out_rgb;
    }
    else
        return in_rgb;
}
/* *************************************************************** */
```

Appendix IV

Radiosity Algorithms

This appendix contains pseudocode describing some of the radiosity concepts and algorithms introduced in Chapter 4, *Illumination Models*. Because the technique is rather encompassing, there is no simple way to break the task down into simple code segments as was done in the previous appendix.

For example, in the computation of hemi-cube form factors, a visible surface algorithm must be executed for each face of the cube before the form factor algorithm can be executed. After the form factors have been built, some sort of matrix solution technique must be applied to solve the resulting equation set. Presenting the hemi-cube form factor determination in code form would be difficult because of the need to quantify its relationships to other significant, but very flexible, algorithmic elements. However, the presentation in pseudocode provides a concise blueprint of functionality without belaboring the implementation issues.

This appendix is organized to first present a definition of the pseudocode, followed by the algorithms for form factor determination using the hemi-cube (Cohen 1985a), for extending the radiosity method to include specular effects (Immel 1986a), and for computing the form factors for the hybrid rendering technique (Wallace 1987) using the hemi-cube.

IV.1 Pseudocode Definition

The examples in this section are cast in a simple pseudocode. For consistency with the code examples presented in the previous appendix, there is a similarity between this pseudocode and the C language. A short summary of the conventions follows.

Keywords:

Pseudocode keywords are set in bold. For example, **SUBROUTINE**, **IF**, **END IF**, and **RETURN** are keywords.

Comments:

Comments are set in italic. They are the only italic elements in the pseudocode, so there is no need for comment delimiters.

Constants:

Constants are either integers such as `1`, `357`, `23`, or real numbers such as `2.0`, and `27.584`.

Variables:

Variables are used to store values. They are typed to indicate what kind of value is being stored. They are declared and typed before any statements in the block; the only exception is loop variables which are undeclared and always integers. Variable names may be any length. The first character of the name is always capitalized and the remainder of the characters are lower case. The underscore, is a valid character in a variable name.

Variables types are: **INTEGER** representing an integer value; **REAL** representing a real number; **VECTOR** representing a direction vector of three real numbers; and **STRUCTURE** representing some structured collection of variables. Structures are not explicitly defined because the contents are implementation specific. Instead, the functional requirements are indicated by the associated comments. The type is prefixed by the keyword **GLOBAL** if the variable is known to algorithmic elements outside of the pseudocode segment.

Array variables:

An array is a 0 based, indexed collection of values. Array variables follow the same conventions as variables. An entire array is referenced by name alone. Individual elements are referenced by subscript enclosed in brackets, i.e. `Visible_poly[2,4]`.

Statement:

Statements are terminated by new line characters. A back slash, \, is used to continue a statement onto the next line. Control statements may cover many lines and are terminated by an end keyword.

Assignment

Assignment sets a variable equal to the value of an expression an equal sign, =. The variable is on the left and the expression is on the right side of the equal sign.

Arithmetic expressions:

Arithmetic operations are +, -, *, and / indicating addition, subtraction, multiplication, and division respectively. Operator precedence is multiplication and division from left to right followed by addition and subtraction from left to right. Parenthesis are used to specify precedence if required.

The operators +, −, ×, and • are defined for **VECTOR**s as vector addition, subtraction, cross product, and dot product. Vector operators take precedence over arithmetic operators.

Logical and relational operators:

The logical **and** and **or** operators are set in lower case bold. The relational operators =, ≠, >, ≥, <, ≤ represent equal to, not equal to, greater than, greater than or equal to, less than, and less than or equal to respectively. These operators are used in conditional expressions for testing. The result of the test is true if the condition is met and false if the condition is not met. The true and false values **true** and **false** are defined.

WHILE-DO-END DO statement:

The block of statements between the **DO** and the **END DO** is repeated while the condition is true. The condition is tested before each execution of the block of statements. The general form is:

```
WHILE (condition) DO
    block of statements to execute
END DO
```

FOR-DO-END DO statement:

The block of statements between the **DO** and the **END DO** is repeated for the set of conditions described after the **FOR** keyword. To simplify the presentation the syntax construct is (**each** *element* **in** *set*) where *set* is a set of things and *element* is an element within that set. This means that the block of statements is executed once and only once for each of the elements within the set. The general form is:

```
FOR (each element in set) DO
    block of statements to execute
END DO
```

IF-THEN-ELSE-END IF statement:

This statement selects to execute or skip the block of statements after the **THEN** keyword and before the **ELSE** or **END IF** keyword based on whether the condition is true or false. The **ELSE** keyword is optional. If used, the block of statements between the **ELSE** and **END IF** is executed if the condition is false. The general form is:

```
IF (condition) DO
    block of statements to execute
ELSE
    block of statements to execute
END IF
```

Subroutine convections:

A subroutine is a group of statements that may be executed at any time by calling for their execution. The **SUBROUTINE** statement begins a subroutine and the **END SUB** statement signifies the end of the subroutine. A **CALL** statement calls for the execution of a subroutine. A **RETURN** statement within the routine returns execution to the statement after the **CALL** statement that branched execution to the subroutine.

A subroutine is named. The naming conventions follow those for variables. The name is followed by subroutine arguments in the form (*input arguments*; *output arguments*). The general form is:

```
CALL name(input arguments; output arguments)
SUBROUTINE name(input arguments; output arguments)
    block of statements to execute
    RETURN
END SUB
```

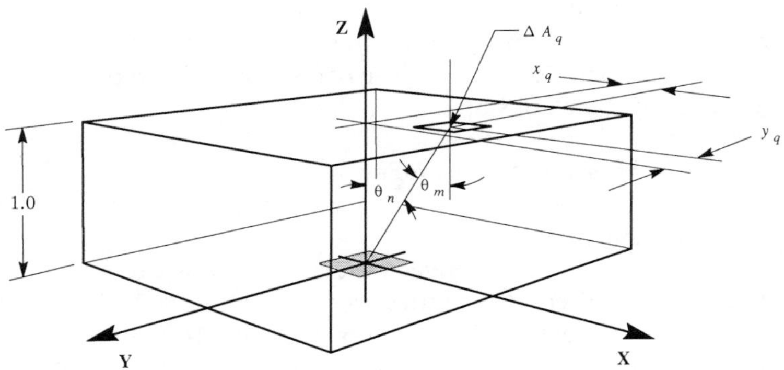

Figure IV.1: Computation of hemi-cube form factor for the top face (adapted from Cohen 1985a).

IV.2 Hemi-cube Form Factors

The procedure to generate the form factor matrix for the environment is straight forward. During the initialization of the radiosity processing, a buffer of form factors for the sample points in a hemi-cube are computed. Due to symmetry, form factors need be computed for only one eighth of the top face and one half of a single side face.

The form factor is computed using the relationship given in Eq.(4.21). A sample point on the hemi-cube represents an area that is small relative to the distance from the sample point to the target point surrounded by the hemi-cube. The cosines that appear in Eq.(4.21) are approximated as constants and the equation reduces to:

$$F_{m,n} = \frac{\cos\theta_n \cos\theta_m dA_m}{r^2_{m,n}} \tag{IV.1}$$

Consider a unit hemi-cube where the position of a sample, q, on the cube is given by $q=(x_q, y_q, z_q)$, and the area on the hemi-cube represented by the sample point is ΔA_q. For the top face of the cube $z_q=1$, see Figure IV.1. The distance between the target point and the hemi-cube sample point is given by:

$$r = \sqrt{x_q^2 + y_q^2 + 1} \tag{IV.2}$$

and the cosines are given by:

$$\cos\theta_n = \cos\theta_m = \frac{1}{\sqrt{x_q^2 + y_q^2 + 1}} \tag{IV.3}$$

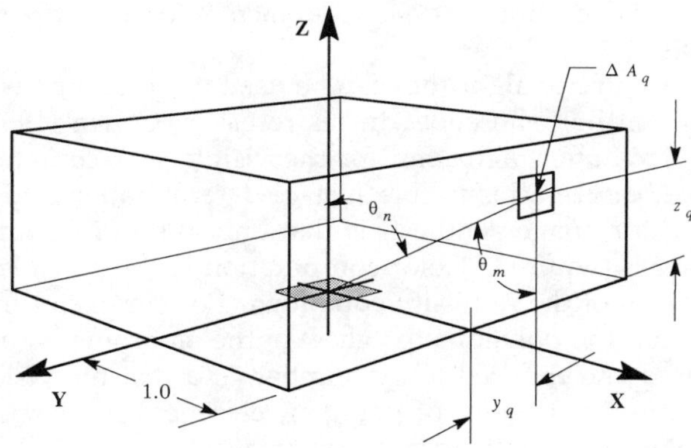

Figure IV.2: Computation of hemi-cube form factor for the side face (adapted from Cohen 1985a).

Substituting Eqs.(IV.2) and (IV.3) into Eq.(IV.1) the delta form factor for samples on the top face of the hemi-cube is given by:

$$\Delta F_q = \frac{1}{(x_q^2 + y_q^2 + 1)^2} \Delta A_q \tag{IV.4}$$

Consider the side face on which x_q=1 , see Figure IV.2. The distance between the target point and the hemi-cube sample point is given by:

$$r = \sqrt{1 + y_q^2 + z_q^2} \tag{IV.5}$$

and the cosines are given by:

$$\cos\theta_n = \frac{z_q}{\sqrt{1 + y_q^2 + z_q^2}} \tag{IV.6a}$$

$$\cos\theta_m = \frac{1}{\sqrt{1 + y_q^2 + z_q^2}} \tag{IV.6b}$$

Substituting Eqs.(IV.5), (IV.6a), and (IV.6a) into Eq.(IV.1) the delta form factor for samples on the side face of the hemi-cube is given by:

$$\Delta F_q = \frac{z_q}{(1 + y_q^2 + z_q^2)^2} \Delta A_q \tag{IV.7}$$

The difficulty in detailing an algorithm for building the form factor matrix stems from the assumptions relating to hemi-cube form factor precomputation and storage, to the visible surface algorithm and solution format, and to the form factor matrix format. For simplicity in this presentation, assume that there is a 1 dimensional array that is loaded with the delta form factors for the entire top face of the hemi-cube and another array loaded with the delta form factors for an entire side face of the hemi-cube.

Any visible surface algorithm can be used to determine what is visible for a face on the hemi-cube. In his research, Cohen (1985b) used a variation on a Z-buffer algorithm for the visible surface determination. The difference between this visible surface determination and typical algorithms used for image synthesis is that only the visible surface reference or pointer is required. Color computation at the patch level results from the solution of the radiosity equations. For simplicity in presentation, assume that the polygons (patches) in the environment are sequentially numbered and referred to by number, and that the visible surface computation returns a buffer of polygon references that are indexed in the same fashion as the delta form factor arrays.

The size of the form factor array is n^2 coefficients where n is the number of patches in the environment. In a complex environment, the size of this array becomes overwhelming. Cohen points out that this array generally has a large percentage of zero coefficients because of orientation and shadowing that makes patches invisible to each other, and that this presents opportunities for compression. Compression schemes are omitted in the description of the algorithm presented here.

The algorithm for computation of the form factor array is expressed as a subroutine in pseudocode as follows:

```
The environment contains 'N_patches' patches.  A hemi-
cube of resolution 'Hemi_res' is used.  The delta fac-
tors for the top face of the cube are precomputed and
loaded in the array 'Delta_top', and for a side face of
the cube are loaded in the array 'Delta_side'.  The ar-
ray 'Visible' is filled with the indices of the visible
patches by the routine 'Vis_surf'.  The subroutine uses
the patch information to transform the frustum for cor-
rect orientation relative to the patch and then performs
the visible surface determination.  The array of struc-
tures 'Frustums' contains the frustums and resolutions
associated with each of the faces of the hemi-cube.  El-
ement 0 in the 'Frustums' array is the top face of the
hemi-cube.

GLOBAL INTEGER      Hemi_res
GLOBAL REAL         Delta_top[Hemi_res*Hemi_res]
GLOBAL REAL         Delta_side[Hemi_res*Hemi_res/2]
GLOBAL STRUCTURE    Frustums[5]
GLOBAL INTEGER      N_patches
GLOBAL REAL         Form_factor[N_patches][N_patches]
SUBROUTINE Compute_form_factor ()
   Initialize the form factor matrix by setting all ele-
   ments equal to zero.
   FOR (each P in N_patches) DO
      FOR (each Q in N_patches) DO
         Form_factor[P][Q] = 0.0
```

```
        END DO
    END DO
    Loop through the patches and compute the form factors
    for each patch (row 'P' of the form factor matrix
    contains the form factors for patch 'P').
    FOR (each P in N_patches) DO
        Loop through the sides of the hemi-cube for the
        current patch.  Compute the visibility buffer,
        'Visible', for each face the sum the delta form
        factors for the face.
        FOR (each F in Frustums)
         DO
            REAL        Deltas[]
            INTEGER     Samples
            INTEGER     Visible[Hemi_res*Hemi_res]
            CALL Vis_surf (P, Frustums[F]; Visible)
            IF (F = 0) THEN
                Deltas = Delta_top
                Samples = Hemi_res*Hemi_res
            ELSE
                Deltas = Delta_side
                Samples = Hemi_res*Hemi_res/2
            END IF
            FOR (each S in Samples) DO
                Form_factor[P][Visible[S]] = \
                    Form_factor[P][Visible[S]] + Deltas[S]
            END DO
        END DO
    END DO
    RETURN
END SUB
```

IV.3 Specular Radiosity

The specular radiosity solution presented by Immel (1986a,1986b) includes both diffuse and specular illumination components in creating a complete solution for an for any viewer position. An illumination function for each patch that gives the intensity in any direction is computed. The technique is tremendously demanding both in computation and in data storage. While this this technique has been supplanted by hybrid techniques, it is important as a transitional step between the diffuse radiosity and hybrid techniques.

The solution process for a patch uses a temporary outgoing intensity buffer. This buffer is first set to the emissivity of the patch. Each cell of the visibility buffer is examined. If a patch is visible, the outgoing intensity buffer for that patch is queried to determine the incoming intensity for the cell. The form factor for the cell is calculated, and subsequently, the incoming energy is determined. The illumination model is evaluated for each cell of the temporary outgoing intensity buffer, and the resultant reflected intensity summed into each cell. The temporary buffer is compared with the current outgoing intensity buffer to test for convergence. The outgoing intensity buffer is then replaced by the temporary buffer. In pseudocode, the procedure is as follows (adapted from Immel 1986a):

```
The environment contains 'N_patches' patches. The glob-
al cube resolution is given by 'G_res'. The array
'Emissivity' defines the emissivity of each patch in all
directions. The array 'Out_intens' contains the inten-
sity from each patch in all directions and is updated at
each solution iteration. The array 'Visible' gives the
visible patch for each sample in the global cube of a
patch. The array ω gives the solid angle and the array
'V' gives the direction of each global cube sample. The
array 'N' gives the normal of each patch.

GLOBAL INTEGER   G_res
GLOBAL INTEGER   N_patches
GLOBAL INTEGER   Convergence = false
GLOBAL VECTOR    V[G_res*G_res*6]
GLOBAL REAL      ω[G_res*G_res*6]
GLOBAL VECTOR    N[N_patches]
GLOBAL REAL      Emissivity[N_patches][G_res*G_res*6]
GLOBAL REAL      Out_intens[N_patches][G_res*G_res*6]
GLOBAL INTEGER   Visible[N_patches][G_res*G_res*6]
REAL             New_intens[G_res*G_res*6]
REAL             Energy_in

Initialize the 'Out_intens' for the environment by set-
ting it equal to the emissivity.
FOR (each P in N_patches) DO
   FOR (each S in (G_res*G_res*6)) DO
      Out_intens[P][S] = Emissivity[P][S]
   END DO
END DO

Iterate through solution steps until convergence is
achieved. The subroutine 'Init_converge' resets the
convergence test for each iteration step. The subrou-
tine 'Sum_converge' sums convergence information for the
current patch into the step convergence. The subroutine
'Test_converge' returns 'true' if the convergence crite-
ria was met and 'false' otherwise. The function
'Inverse(S;I)' returns the sample index, 'I', for the
sample in the inverse direction of 'S'. The function
'Get_Rbd' returns the bidirectional reflectance between
an incedent and reflected ray for a patch.
WHILE (Convergence = false) DO
   CALL Init_converge( ; )
   FOR (each P in N_patches) DO
      Initialize the new intensity for the current patch
      to its emissivity.
      FOR (each S in (G_res*G_res*6)) DO
         New_intens[S] = Emissivity[P][S]
      END DO
```

```
        Take the energy from each incoming direction and
        distribute it by applying an illumination model
        and summing the reflected intensities to the out-
        going intensity.
        FOR (each In in (G_res*G_res*6)) DO
            CALL Inverse(In; In_inv)
            Energy_in = \
                Out_intens[Visible[P][In]][In_inv] * \
                (N[P] • V[In]) * ω[In]
            FOR (each Out in (G_res*G_res*6)) DO
                CALL Get_Rbd(P,In,Out; Rbd)
                New_intens[Out] = New_intens[Out] + \
                    (Rbd * Energy_in)
            END DO
        END DO
        Sum the convergence info from this patch for this
        iteration.
        CALL Sum_converge(Out_intens[P],New_intens; )
        Replace the 'Out_intens' values for this patch
        with the newly computed intensity values.
        FOR (each S in (G_res*G_res*6)) DO
            Out_intens[P][S] = New_intens[S]
        END DO
    END DO
    The iteration is complete for all the patches. Test
    the convergence criteria before starting the next it-
    eration.
    CALL Test_converge( ; Convergence)
END DO
```

The rendering technique is similar to that previously described with the exception that there is now a buffer of outgoing intensities for a patch rather than a single intensity for the patch. The direction of the view vector for a vertex is used to index into the outgoing intensity array to get the vertex color used for the subsequent rendering of the environment.

Immel presents a very complete discussion of this technique with suggestions for optimization.

IV.4 Hybrid Form Factors

The hybrid radiosity technique presented by Wallace (1987) adds terms that account for specular effects into the traditional form factor matrix. In his account of the procedure the environment is reflected about the plane of each reflective surface and the surface used as a window into the reflected environment during visibility calculations. Transparent materials were considered to be very thin membranes, and the approximation made that the ray through the transparent material without being refracted (the refraction as the ray enters the material is canceled by the refraction as the ray leaves the material).

Each row in the form factor matrix describes the contributions of other patches in the environment to the current patch. Specifically, the form factor describes energy that reaches the current patch as a function of the intensities of the other patches. Typically a single form factor matrix is generated and the diffuse reflectance for each patch for each of the color samples is factored into the matrix during the solution of the radiosity equations. The hybrid form factors include terms that describe energy that is specularly transported through the visible patches for the current patch. This is accomplished by reflecting and/or transmitting a ray for a hemi-cube sample in which a reflective and/or transparent patch is visible, and then determining the patch that is visible to that ray. The energy from that patch is reduced by the specular reflectance and/or transmittance of the patch at the hemi-cube sample. The specular reflectance and transmittance are generally wavelength dependent, thus, a form factor matrix for each color sample is required if the wavelength dependency of reflection is included.

It should be recognized that specular reflection and transmission for surfaces that are not optically smooth requires consideration of more than a point sample in the reflected and transmitted directions. Methodologies discussed in Section 4.3.4, *Distributed Ray Tracing*, can be applied for sampling the specular information. Wallace used a single ray to sample the reflected and transmitted information.

This presentation of hybrid form factor determination is intended to clarify the understanding of the process. Several simplifying assumptions are made in the interest of clarity in the presentation. These assumptions are:

- The specular reflectance (bidirectional reflectance) and the specular transmittance (bidirectional transmittance) are represented by constants that are not dependent on wavelength, incident angle, or geometric attenuation. This means that the specular reflectance and specular transmittance can be described by single material coefficients. The coefficients K_s and K_t are used to designate specular reflectance and specular transmittance.
- The specular reflectance and specular transmittance can be characterized by considering only the reflected and transmitted direction. This means that there is only a reflected and/or transmitted ray spawned at each visible patch.
- A ray tracing procedure is called to return the identity of the patch that is visible in either the reflected or transmitted direction (as suggested by Wallace (1988)).

The process of building the hybrid form factor matrix is described in pseudocode as follows:

```
The environment contains 'N_patches' patches.  A hemi-
cube of resolution 'Hemi_res' is used.  The delta fac-
tors for the top face of the cube are precomputed and
loaded in the array 'Delta_top', and for a side face of
the cube are loaded in the array 'Delta_side'.  The ar-
ray 'Vis' is filled with the indices of the visible
patches by the routine 'Vis_surf'.  The subroutine uses
the patch information to transform the frustum for cor-
rect orientation relative to the patch and then performs
the visible surface determination.  The structure
'Frustums' contains the frustums and resolutions associ-
ated with each of the faces of the hemi-cube. The form
factor matrix, 'FF', is a matrix of structures consist-
ing of a real 'Form_factor' field and an integer
'Reflect_flag' field describing whether the form factor
element results from reflection or refraction.  Element
0 in the 'Frustums' array is the top face of the hemi-
cube.  The structure for patches includes 'Ks' and 'Kt'
fields describing the specular reflectance and transmit-
tance of the patch. 'Termination' is the level of con-
tribution at which specular contribution is terminated.
GLOBAL INTEGER        Hemi_res
GLOBAL REAL           Delta_top[Hemi_res*Hemi_res]
GLOBAL REAL           Delta_side[Hemi_res*Hemi_res/2]
GLOBAL STRUCTURE      Frustums[5]
GLOBAL INTEGER        N_patches
GLOBAL STRUCTURE      Patches[N_patches]
GLOBAL STRUCTURE      Form_factor[N_patches][N_patches]
SUBROUTINE Compute_form_factor ()
   Initialize the form factor matrix by setting all ele-
   ments equal to zero.
   FOR (each P in N_patches) DO
      FOR (each Q in N_patches) DO
         FF[P][Q].Form_factor = 0.0
         FF[P][Q].Reflect_flag = true
      END DO
   END DO

   Loop through the patches and compute the form factors
   for each patch (row 'P' of the form factor matrix
   contains the form factors for patch 'P').
   FOR (each P in N_patches) DO
      Loop through the sides of the hemi-cube for the
      reflection side of the current patch.  Compute the
      visibility buffer, 'Vis', for each face the sum
      the delta form factors for the face.
      REAL       Deltas[]
      INTEGER    Samples
      INTEGER    Vis[Hemi_res*Hemi_res]
      VECTOR     V
      FOR (each F in Frustums)  DO
         CALL Vis_surf (P, Frustums[F]; Vis)
         IF (F = 0) THEN
            Deltas = Delta_top
```

```
                Samples = Hemi_res*Hemi_res
            ELSE
                Deltas = Delta_side
                Samples = Hemi_res*Hemi_res/2
            END IF
            FOR (each S in Samples) DO
                Sum in the delta form factor for the visi-
                ble patch.  This accounts for diffuse illu-
                mination from the visible patch.  The rou-
                tine Illum_dir gets the direction of illu-
                mination for the hemi-cube sample.  The
                routine Sum_spec sums the specular illumi-
                nation contribution from the currently vis-
                ible patch.
                FF[P][Vis[S]].Form_factor = \
                   FF[P][Vis[S]].Form_factor + Deltas[S]
                CALL Illum_dir(P,F,S; V)
                CALL Sum_spec(P,Vis[S],V,Deltas[S],true; )
            END DO
        END DO

        IF (Patch[P].Kt > 0.0) THEN
            The current patch is transparent. Build a
            hemi-cube on the back surface of the patch and
            sum the form factors that contribute to trans-
            parent diffuse illumination of the current
            patch. Repeat the steps in building the hemi-
            cube on the reflection side of the patch.
            FOR (each F in Frustums)  DO
                CALL Vis_surf (-P, Frustum[F]; Vis)
                IF (F = 0) THEN
                    Deltas = Delta_top
                    Samples = Hemi_res*Hemi_res
                ELSE
                    Deltas = Delta_side
                    Samples = Hemi_res*Hemi_res/2
                END IF
                FOR (each S in Samples) DO
                    FF[P][Vis[S]].Form_factor = \
                       FF[P][Vis[S]].Form_factor +
                       Deltas[S]
                    FF[P][Vis[S]].Reflect_flag = false
                    CALL Illum_dir(P,F,S; V)
                    CALL Sum_spec(P,Vis[S],V,Deltas[S], \
                       false; )
                END DO
            END DO
        END IF
    END DO
    RETURN
END SUB
```

This is the procedure to sum in the specular illumination contribution to the form factor for the current patch. The patch that is the vehicle for the specular

```
reflection or transmission is 'Last_P'.  The current
patch is passed in as 'P'. The view vector is passed in
as 'Last_V'. The current contribution is passed in as
'Last_FF'. 'R_flag' describes whether the illumination
is contributing to reflected or transmitted diffuse il-
lumination of the current patch.  This routine is recur-
sively called until the contribution falls below the
specified threshold 'Termination'.

SUBROUTINE Sum_spec(P,Last_P,Last_V,Last_FF,R_flag; )
   VECTOR     Next_V
   INTEGER    Next_P
   REAL       Next_FF

   IF (Patch[Last_P].Ks > 0.0) THEN
      The patch is reflective. The routine 'Rfl_vect'
      returns the reflected vector. The routine
      'Get_visible' returns the visible patch. The last
      form factor is factored by the specular reflec-
      tance of the last patch to determine the contribu-
      tion of the visible patch. This is summed into the
      form factor matrix.
      CALL Rfl_vect(Last_P,Last_V; Next_V)
      CALL Get_visible(Next_V; Next_P)
      Next_FF = Last_FF * Patch[Last_P].Ks
      FF[P][Next_P].Form_factor = \
         FF[P][Next_P].Form_factor + Next_FF
      FF[P][Next_P].Reflect_flag = R_flag
      IF (Next_FF > Termination) THEN
         CALL Sum_spec(P,Next_P,Next_V,Next_FF,
            R_flag; )
      END IF
   END IF

   IF (Patch[Last_P].Kt > 0.0) THEN
      The patch is transparent. The routine 'Trans_vect'
      returns the transmitted vector. Refer to notes de-
      scribing reflection for remaining details.
      CALL Trans_vect(Last_P,Last_V; Next_V)
      CALL Get_visible(Next_V; Next_P)
      Next_FF = Last_FF * Patch[Last_P].Kt
      FF[P][Next_P].Form_factor = \
         FF[P][Next_P].Form_factor + Next_FF
      FF[P][Next_P].Reflect_flag = R_flag
      IF (Next_FF > Termination) THEN
         CALL Sum_spec(P,Next_P,Next_V,Next_FF,
            R_flag; )
      END IF
   END IF
END SUB
```

Appendix V

Equipment Sources

Trade shows are one of the best sources for current information on the equipment available, for immediate access to the equipment for demonstration, and for an environment that allows comparison of equipment. Among the trade shows that display equipment of interest to the computer graphics professional are NAB, NCGA, and SIGGRAPH.

The National Association of Broadcasters (NAB) hosts an annual trade show in Las Vegas, Nevada every spring. As the name implies, this is directed primarily towards the broadcast market and is a source of information for video related products and services. The address for the NAB is:

National Association of Broadcasters
1771 N. St., N.W.
Washington, D.C. 20036

The National Computer Graphics Association (NCGA) hosts an annual trade show each spring. The NCGA favors Anaheim, California as the location. This is primarily an equipment show. However, the strength of the technical program, i.e. tutorials, panels, etc., has been growing in recent years. The address for the NCGA is:

National Computer Graphics Association
2722 Merrilee Drive
Suite 200
Fairfax, Virginia 22031

The Association For Computing Machinery (ACM) Special Interest Group on Computer Graphics (SIGGRAPH) has an annual mid summer conference. A different city hosts the conference each year. Past and planned sites include Boston, Detroit, Anaheim, Atlanta, San Francisco, Dallas, and Minneapolis. This conference began primarily as a forum for technical presentation and exchange. The technical program is the focus of the conference, however, the equipment exhibition has grown to rival that of NCGA. The address for the ACM is:

The Association for Computing Machinery, Inc.
11 West 42nd Street
New York, New York 10036

The following is a partial listing of sources for equipment referenced in the text. It is not a recommendation or endorsement list. The complexion of the hardware environment is constantly changing and the reader must investigate thoroughly before making any equipment decisions. This list merely provides a place to start.

Standards organizations:

Electronic Industries Association
2001 Eue Street, N.W.
Washington, D.C. 20006

Society of Motion Picture and Television Engineers
862 Scarsdale Avenue
Scarsdale, New York 10583

Color analyzers:

Minolta Corporation
Meter Division
101 Williams Drive
Ramsey, New Jersey 07446

Philips Test & Measuring Instruments, Inc.
85 McKee Drive
Mahwah, New Jersey 07430

Color comparators:

IRT Color Comparator
distributed by:
Bourbon Street Associates
P.O.Box 393
South Salem, New York 10590

Philips Test & Measuring Instruments, Inc.
85 McKee Drive
Mahwah, New Jersey 07430

Video equipment for distribution, test and monitoring, sync generation, recording, and encoding and decoding:

Ampex Corporation
401 Broadway
Redwood City, California 94063

The Grass Valley Group, Inc.
P.O.Box 1114
Grass Valley, California 95945

Lenco Electronics
300 N. Maryland Street, P.O.Box 348
Jackson, Missouri 63755

Sony Communications Products Company
Broadcast Products Division
1600 Queen Anne Rd.
Teaneck, New Jersey 07666

Tektronix, Inc.
P.O.Box 500
Beaverton, Oregon 97077

Color monitors:

Barco Electronics, Inc.
1500 Wilson Way
Smyrna, Georgia 30080

Conrac Corporation
Display Products Group
600 N. Rimsdale Avenue
Covina, California 91772

Ikegami Electronics, Inc.
37 Brook Avenue
Maywood, New Jersey 07607

Sony Communications Products Company
Broadcast Products Division
1600 Queen Anne Rd.
Teaneck, New Jersey 07666

Frame buffers and digital frame stores:

Abekas Video Systems, Inc.
101 Galveston Drive
Redwood City, California 94063

Adage, Inc
One Fortune Drive
Billerica, Massachusetts 01821

Raster Technologies, Inc.
Two Robbins Road
Westford, Massachusetts 01886

References

Amanatides, John (1984), "Ray Tracing with Cones," ACM Computer Graphics (SIGGRAPH 84), vol. 18, no. 3, pp. 129-135.

Bahar, Ezekial (1980), "Full-Wave Solutions for the Scattered Radiation Fields from Rough Surfaces with Arbitrary Slope and Frequency," IEEE Transactions on Antennas and Propagation, vol. AP-28, no. 1, pp. 11-21.

Barnett, Raymond A. and John M. Fujii (1963), *Vectors,* John Wiley and Sons, New York.

Baum, Daniel R., John R. Wallace, Michael F. Cohen, Donald P. Greenberg (1986), The Back-Buffer: An Extension of the Radiosity Method to Dynamic Environments," The Visual Computer, vol. 2, no. 5, pp. 298-306.

Bayer, B. E. (1973), "An Optimum Method for Two-Level Rendition of Continuous Tone Pictures," Conference Record, IEEE International Conference on Communications, vol. 1, IEEE, New York, pp. 26:11-15.

Beckmann, Petr and Andre Spizzichino (1963), *The Scattering of Electromagnetic Waves from Rough Surfaces,* Pergamon Press, Oxford, England, pp. 1-33, 70-98.

Bennett, H. E. and J. O.Porteus (1961), "Relation Between Surface Roughness and Specular Reflectance at Normal Incidence," Journal of the Optical Society of America, vol. 51, pp. 123-129.

Benson, K. Blair (1986), *Television Engineering Handbook,* McGraw-Hill, New York.

Bishop, Gary and David Weimer (1986), "Fast Phong Shading," ACM Computer Graphics (SIGGRAPH 86), vol. 20, no. 4, pp. 103-106.

Blinn, J. F. and M. E. Newell (1976), "Texture and Reflection in Computer Generated Images," Communications of the ACM, vol. 19, no. 10, pp. 542-547.

Blinn, James F. (1977), "Models of Light Reflection for Computer Synthesized Pictures," ACM Computer Graphics (SIGGRAPH 77), vol. 11, no. 2, pp. 192-198.

Blinn, James F. (1978), "Computer Display of Curved Surfaces," PhD Dissertation, University of Utah, Salt Lake City.

Blinn, James F. (1979), "Raster Graphics," from *Tutorial: Computer Graphics,* edited by John C. Beatty and Kellogg S. Booth, IEEE Computer Society Press, New York, pp. 207-213.

Blinn, James F.(1985), "The Ancient Chinese Art of Chi-Ting," SIGGRAPH 85 tutorial notes for Image Rendering Tricks.

Bouknight, W. J. (1970), "A Procedure for Generation of Three-dimensional Half-toned Computer Graphics Presentations," Communications of the ACM, vol. 13, no. 9, pp. 527-536.

Catmull, E. E. (1975), "Computer display of Curved Surfaces," Proceedings IEEE Conference on Computer Graphics, Pattern Recognition and Data Structures, May 1975, pp. 11-17.

Cohen, Michael F and Donald P. Greenberg (1985a), "The Hemi-Cube, A Radiosity Solution for Complex Environments," ACM Computer Graphics (SIGGRAPH 85), vol. 19, no. 3, pp. 31-40.

Cohen, Michael F. (1985b), "A Radiosity Method for the Realistic Image Synthesis of Complex Diffuse Environments," Masters Thesis, Cornell University, Ithaca, NY.

Cohen, Michael F., D. P. Greenberg, D. S. Immel, and P. J. Brock (1986), "An Efficient Radiosity Approach for Realistic Image Synthesis," IEEE Computer Graphics and Applications, vol. 6, no. 3, pp. 26-35.

Conrac (1980), *Raster Graphics Handbook,* Conrac Corporation, Covina, Ca.

Cook, Robert L. (1981), "A Reflection Model for Realistic Image Synthesis," Masters Thesis, Cornell University, Ithaca, NY.

Cook, Robert L. and Kenneth E. Torrance (1982), "A Reflection Model for Computer Graphics," ACM Transactions on Graphics, vol. 1, no. 1, pp. 7-24.

Cook, Robert L., Thomas Porter, and Loren Carpenter (1984), "Distributed Ray Tracing," ACM Computer Graphics (SIGGRAPH 84), vol. 18, no. 3, pp. 137-145.

Cook, Robert L. (1986), "Stochastic Sampling in Computer Graphics," ACM Transactions on Graphics, vol. 5, no. 1, pp. 51-72.

Cornsweet, T. N. (1970), *Visual Perception,* Academic Press, New York.

Crow, Franklin (1984), "Summed-Area Tables for Texture Mapping," ACM Computer Graphics (SIGGRAPH 84), vol. 18, no. 3, pp. 207-212.

Dippé, Mark A. and Erling H. Wold (1985), "Antialiasing through Stochastic Sampling," ACM Computer Graphics (SIGGRAPH 85), vol. 19, no. 3, pp. 69-78.

Ditchburn, R. W. (1976), *Light,* Academic Press, London, vols.1 & 2.

Duff, Tom (1979), "Smoothly Shaded Renderings of Polygonal Objects on Raster Displays," ACM Computer Graphics (SIGGRAPH 79), vol. 13, no. 2, pp. 270-275.

EIA (1976), "Encoded Color Bar Signal," RS-189-A, July 1976.

Floyd, R. W. and L. Steinberg (1975), "An Adaptive Algorithm for Spatial Grey Scale," *SID 75 Digest,* Society for Information Display, pp. 36-37.

Foley, J. D. and A. Van Dam (1984), *Fundamentals of Interactive Computer Graphics,* Addison-Wesley Publishing Company, Reading, PA.

Goral, Cindy M, K. E. Torrance, D. P. Greenberg, and B. Battaile (1984), "Modeling the Interaction of Light Between Diffuse Surfaces," ACM Computer Graphics (SIGGRAPH 84), vol. 18, no. 3, pp. 213-222.

Gouraud, Henri (1971), "Continuous Shading of Curved Surfaces," IEEE Transactions on Computers, June 1971, pp. 623-629.

Greenberg, Donald P., Michael F. Cohen, Kenneth E. Torrance (1986), "Radiosity: A Method for Computing Global Illumination," The Visual Computer, vol. 2, no. 5, pp. 291-297.

Greenberg, Donald P. (1988), "Coons Award Lecture," Communications of the ACM (originally presented at SIGGRAPH 87), vol. 31, no. 2, pp. 123-129.

Guralnik (1978), *Webster's New World Dictionary,* William Collins Publishers, Inc., Cleveland, Ohio.

Hall, Roy A. (1983a), "A Methodology for Realistic Image Synthesis," Masters Thesis, Cornell University, Ithaca, NY.

Hall, Roy A, and Donald P. Greenberg (1983b), "A Testbed for Realistic Image Synthesis," IEEE Computer Graphics and Applications, vol. 3, no. 8, pp. 10-20.

Hall, Roy (1986), "A Characterization of Illumination Models and Shading Techniques," The Visual Computer, vol. 2, no. 5, pp. 268-277.

Hall, Roy (1987), "Color Reproduction and Illumination Models," from *Techniques for Computer Graphics,* edited by D. F. Rogers and R. A. Earnshaw, pp. 194-238.

Hecht, Eugene and Alfred Zajac (1987), *Optics,* 2nd edition, Addison-Wesley, Reading, PA.

Hunt, R. W. G. (1975), *The Reproduction of Color,* Third Edition, John Wiley and Sons, New York.

Hunt, R. W. G. (1977), "The Specification of Colour Appearance. I. Concepts and Terms," Color Research and Applications, vol. 2, no. 2, pp. 55-68.

Hunt, R. W. G (1978), "Colour Terminology," Color Research and Application, vol. 3, no. 2, pp. 79-87.

Immel, David S., M. F. Cohen, and D. P. Greenberg (1986a), "A Radiosity Method for Non-Diffuse Environments," ACM Computer Graphics (SIGGRAPH 86), vol. 20, no. 4, pp. 133-142.

Immel, David S. (1986b), "A Radiosity Method for Non-Diffuse Surfaces," Masters Thesis, Cornell University, Ithaca, NY.

Jarvis, J. F., C. N. Judice, and W. H. Ninke (1976), "A Survey of Techniques for the Display of Continuous Tone Pictures on Bilevel Displays," Computer Graphics and Image Processing, vol. 4, pp. 13-40.

Jenkins, Francis A. and Harvey E. White (1976), *Fundamentals of Optics,* McGraw-Hill, New York.

Joblove, George H., and Donald P. Greenberg (1978) "Color Spaces for Computer Graphics," ACM Computer Graphics (SIGGRAPH 78), vol. 12, no. 3, pp. 20-25.

Judd, D. B. and G. Wyszecki (1975), *Color in Business, Science, and Industry,* John Wiley and Sons, New York.

Kane, Joseph J. Jr. (1987), private communication and Philips sales publication "Philips PM5539 Color Analyser and Monitor Calibration."

Kajiya, James T. (1985), "Anisotropic Reflection Models," ACM Computer Graphics (SIGGRAPH 85), vol. 19, no. 3, pp. 15-21.

Kajiya, James T. (1986), "The Rendering Equation," ACM Computer Graphics (SIGGRAPH 86), vol. 20, no. 4, pp. 143-150.

Kay, D. S. and D. P. Greenberg (1979), "Transparency for Computer Synthesized Images," ACM Computer Graphics (SIGGRAPH 79), vol. 13, no. 2, pp. 158-164.

Knuth, Donald E. (1987), "Digital Halftones by Dot Diffusion," ACM Transactions on Graphics, vol. 6, no. 4, pp. 245-273.

Koestner, Kevin J. (1986), "A Wave Based Reflection Model for Realistic Image Synthesis," Masters Thesis, Cornell University, Ithaca, NY.

Lee, Mark E., Richard A. Redner, and Samuel P. Uselton (1985), "Statistically Optimized Sampling for Distributed Ray Tracing," ACM Computer Graphics (SIGGRAPH 85), vol. 19, no. 3, pp. 61-67.

Limb, J. O. (1969), "Design of Wave Forms for Quantized Visual Signals," Bell System Technical Journal, vol. 48, pp. 2555-2582.

Max, Nelson (1986), "Atmospheric Illumination and Shadows," ACM Computer Graphics (SIGGRAPH 86), vol. 20, no. 4, pp. 117-124.

McCamy, C. S., H. Marcus, and J. G. Davidson (1976), "A Color Rendition Chart," Journal of Applied Photographic Engineering, vol. 11, no. 3, pp. 95-99.

Meyer, Gary W. (1983), "Colorimetry and Computer Graphics," Program of Computer Graphics, Report no. 83-1, Cornell University, Ithaca, NY.

Meyer, Gary W., Holly E. Rushmeier, Michael F. Cohen, and Donald P. Greenberg (1986a), "An Experimental Evaluation of Computer Graphics Imagery," ACM Transactions on Graphics, vol. 5, no. 1, pp. 30-50.

Meyer, Gary W. (1986b), "Tutorial on Color Science," The Visual Computer, vol. 2, no. 5, pp. 278-290.

Meyer, Gary W. (1988), "Wavelength Selection for Synthetic Image Generation," Computer Vision, Graphics, and Image Processing, vol. 41, pp. 57-79.

Mills, Michael I. (1985), "Image Synthesis, Optical Identity or Pictorial Communication," *Computer Generated Images, The State of the Art,* edited by Nadia Magnenat-Thalmann and Daniel Thalmann, Springer-Verlag, New York, pp. 3-10.

Newell, M., R. Newell, and T. Sancha (1972), "A Solution to the Hidden Surface Problem," Proceedings ACM National Conference, pp. 443-450.

Newman, W.M. and R.F.Sproull (1979), *Principles of Interactive Computer Graphics*, Second Edition, McGraw-Hill, New York.

Nishita, Tomoyuki and Eihachiro Nakamae (1985), "Continuous Tone Representations of Three Dimensional Objects Taking Account of Shadows and Interreflection," ACM Computer Graphics (SIGGRAPH 85), vol. 19, no. 3, pp. 23-30.

Nishita, Tomoyuki and Eihachiro Nakamae (1987), "A Shading Model for Atmospheric Scattering Considering the Luminous Intensity Distribution of Light Sources," ACM Computer Graphics, vol. 21, no. 4, pp. 303-308.

Norton, Alan, Alyn P. Rockwood, and Phillip T. Skolmoski (1982), "Clamping: A Method of Antialiasing Textured Surfaces by Bandwidth Limiting in Object Space," ACM Computer Graphics (SIGGRAPH 82), vol. 16, no. 3, pp. 1-8.

Perlin, Ken (1985), "An Image Synthesizer," ACM Computer Graphics (SIGGRAPH 85), vol. 19, no. 3, pp. 287-296.

Phong, Bui Toung (1975), "Illumination for Computer Generated Pictures," Communications of the ACM, vol. 18, no. 8, pp. 311-317.

Purdue University (1967), *Thermophysical Properties of High Temperature Solid Materials*, Thermophysical Properties Research Center.

Purdue University (1970), *Thermophysical Properties of Matter*, Thermophysical Properties Research Center.

Rogers, David F. and J. Alan Adams (1976), *Mathematical Elements for Computer Graphics*, McGraw Hill, New York.

Rogers, David F. (1985), *Procedural Elements for Computer Graphics*, McGraw Hill, New York.

Romney, Gordon W. (1969), "Computer Assisted Assembly and Rendering of Solids," PhD Dissertation, Department of Electrical Engineering, University of Utah, Salt Lake City, Utah.

Rushmeier, Holly E. (1986), "Extending the Radiosity Method to Transmitting and Specularly Reflecting Surfaces," Masters Thesis, Cornell University, Ithaca, NY.

Rushmeier, Holly E., and Kenneth E. Torrance (1987), "The Zonal Method for Calculating Light Intensities in the Presence of a Participating Medium," ACM Computer Graphics (SIGGRAPH 87), vol. 21, no. 4, pp. 293-302.

Sancer, Maurice I. (1969), "Shadow-Corrected Electromagnetic Scattering from a Randomly Rough Surface," vol. AP-17, no. 5, pp. 577-585.

SMPTE (1969), "Color Temperature for Color Television Studio Monitors," Recommended Practice RP37-1969.

SMPTE (1977), "Setting Chromaticity and Luminance of White for Color Television Monitors Using Shadow-Mask Picture Tubes," Recommended Practice RP71-1977.

SMPTE (1978), "Alignment Color Bar Test Signal for Television Picture Monitors," Engineering Committee Recommendation ECR1-1978, reaffirmed 1983.

SMPTE (1987), Proposed only, not yet approved, "Color Monitor Colorimetry," Recommended Practice RP 145.

SMPTE (1983), "Specifications for Safe Action and Safe Title Areas Test Patterns for Television Systems," Recommended Practice RP27.3-1983.

Smith, Alvy Ray (1978), "Color Gamut Transformation Pairs," ACM Computer Graphics (SIGGRAPH 78), vol. 12, no. 3, pp. 12-19.

Smith, B. G. (1967), "Geometrical Shadowing of a Random Rough Surface," IEEE Transactions on Antennas and Propagation, vol. AP-15, pp. 668-671.

Sparrow, E. M., and R. D. Cess (1978), *Radiation Heat Transfer,* Hemisphere Publishing Corporation.

Sutherland, I. E., R. F. Sproull and R. A. Schumacker (1974), "A Characterization of Ten Hidden-Surface Algorithms," Computing Surveys, vol. 6, no. 1, pp. 1-55.

Torrance, K. E. and E. M. Sparrow (1966), "Polarization, Directional Distribution, and Off-Specular Peak Phenomena in Light Reflected from Roughened Surfaces," Journal of the Optical Society of America, vol. 56, no. 7, pp. 916-925.

Torrance, K. E. and E. M. Sparrow (1967), "Theory for Off-Specular Reflection from Roughened Surfaces," Journal of the Optical Society of America, vol. 57, no. 9, pp. 1105-1114.

Trowbridge, T. S. and K. P. Reitz (1967), "Average Irregularity Representation of a Roughened Surface for Ray Reflection," Journal of the Optical Society of America, vol. 65, no. 5.

Verbeck, Channing P. and Donald P. Greenberg (1984), "A Comprehensive Light-Source Description for Computer Graphics," IEEE Computer Graphics and Applications, vol. 4, no. 7, pp. 66-75.

Wallace, Bruce A. (1981), "Merging and Transformation of Raster Images for Cartoon Animation," ACM Computer Graphics (SIGGRAPH 81), vol. 15, no. 3, pp. 253-262.

Wallace, John R., M. F. Cohen, and D. P. Greenberg (1987), "A Two-Pass Solution to the Rendering Equation: A Synthesis of Ray Tracing and Radiosity Techniques," ACM Computer Graphics (SIGGRAPH 87), vol. 21, no. 4, pp. 311-328.

Wallace, John R. (1988), "A Two-Pass Solution to the Rendering Equation: A Synthesis of Ray Tracing and Radiosity Methods," Masters Thesis, Cornell University, Ithaca, NY.

Watkins, Gary S. (1970), "A real-time visible surface algorithm," University of Utah, Salt Lake City, Report UTECH-CSc-70-101.

Warnock, John E. (1969), "A Hidden Surface Algorithm for Halftone Picture Representation," PhD Dissertation, Department of Computer Science, University of Utah, Salt Lake City.

Whitted, Turner (1980), "An Improved Illumination Model for Shaded Display," Communications of the ACM, vol. 23, no. 6, pp. 343-349.

Whitted, Turner (1982), "Processing Requirements for Hidden Surface Elimination and Realistic Shading," Digest of Papers, COMPCON, spring 1982.

Whitted, Turner (1985), "Simple Ray Tracing," Couse Notes for Image Rendering Tricks, SIGGRAPH 85.

Williams, Lance (1983), "Pyramidal Parametrics," ACM Computer Graphics (SIGGRAPH 83), vol. 17, no. 3, pp. 1-11.

Index